the Union

Diaries, Memoirs and Letters of the Civil War

We have attempted to reproduce this collection of letters, diaries and memoirs as closely to the original presentation as possible. In their own words, these men and women told of their experiences in the midst of or shortly after the Civil War. We have not corrected any grammatical or spelling errors and, with the exception of editing for length of inclusion and replacing derogatory terms with spaces, we have endeavored to preserve their accounts as originally written.

ISBN 978-1-882077-27-4

Editing by Amy Gary
Book Research by Michele Gay
Jacket and text design by TaylorDesign

Printed in China

Contents

The Twenty-Fifth Regiment Connecticut Volunteers In The War Of The Rebellion

History, Reminiscences, Description of Battle of Irish Bend, Carrying of Pay Roll

Brief History of the Twenty-fifth Regiment, Connecticut Volunteers, from the pen of Colonel George P. Bissell

Experiences and Reminiscences of Samuel K. Ellis of Rockville, who went out as a Private in Company G, Twenty-fifth Regiment

A Complete Account of the Battle of Irish Bend, Given by Major Thomas McManus

How the Pay of a Regiment Was Carried to New Orleans, by First Lieutenant Henry Hill Goodell

Winter quarters of Capt. Bissell, Army of the Potomac

Brief History Of The Twenty-Fifth Regiment, C. V.
by Colonel George P. Bissell

The Twenty-fifth Regiment, Connecticut Volunteers, (George P. Bissell, Colonel), was recruited in Hartford and Tolland Counties, in the fall of 1862. The regiment was composed of the very best material, being almost exclusively young men impelled by patriotic motives, and from the first they took a high stand for efficiency and good discipline.

Later in its history, when the regiment had been tried in marches and battles, it was thus described by Adjutant-General Morse in his report to the Legislature for 1864: "This is one of the best of our nine months' regiments and bore a conspicuous part in the advance upon, and the campaign preceding, the fall of Port Hudson. By the bravery always displayed on the field of battle, and the patience and endurance manifested on many long and arduous marches, it has won for itself a high and lasting reputation."

The Twenty-fifth was mustered into the United States service November 11, 1862, and on the 14th sailed from Hartford for Centerville, L.I., to join at that rendezvous the Banks Expedition. The muster-roll showed 811 men thoroughly drilled and well appointed, except that they were without rifles which were later served to them on the ship after their arrival on the Mississippi River. The regiment embarked November 29, 1862, in two divisions;—one division of five companies under command of Colonel Bissell on the Steamer Mary Boardman; and the remainder under command of Lieutenant-Colonel Stevens on the Steamer Empire City. The destination of the expedition was unknown when the vessels sailed as the sealed orders were not to be opened until we had sailed twenty-four hours to the southward and eastward. The orders, when opened, were found to be simply to report at Ship Island, off the mouth of the Mississippi River, allowing a stop at Dry Tortugas for coal if necessary. The ships duly arrived at Ship Island and proceeded at once up the river to New Orleans where they arrived on the 14th of December, 1862. On the 16th, the Mary Boardman, with several of the other ships proceeded to Baton Rouge, where they arrived the next day. The Empire City landed the left wing of the regiment at Camp Parapet, just above New Orleans. The forces landed at Baton Rouge after a brief bombardment of the city and the Twenty-fifth (five companies), went into camp first on the United States Arsenal ground in the city and later near the cemetery, back of the city, where after some delay the left wing joined the colonel's command and the regiment was once more united and in fighting trim. The regiment was first brigaded under General Albert E. Payne of Wisconsin, a noble and brave officer, afterwards with the Thirteenth Connecticut. The Twenty-sixth Maine and One-Hundred and Fifty-ninth New York, under Colonel H. W. Birge, of the Thirteenth Connecticut, as Brigade Commander, an officer of rare ability and bravery and a disciplinarian of the best stamp. Under his command the Twenty-fifth served during its entire term of service. He led them in many battles and marches and while he was strictness personified, he was so magnanimous, brave, reasonable and such a thorough soldier, that the men worshiped him and would follow him into the face of any fire. Now that he is gone they revere his memory.

The first work of the regiment was on the advance on Port Hudson, March 10, 1863, when Colonel Bissell, in command of his own regiment, two detachments of cavalry and a regular army battery, occupied Bayou Montesano, constructed earthworks and built a bridge across Bayou Sara. This bridge was designed by Sergeant William Webster of Company I, after a West Point engineer had despaired of the job. The regiment was seven miles in advance of the rest of the army and in a very exposed and dangerous position. This position they held under a frequently severe fire till the remainder of the army came up when they joined the column and went on to Port Hudson. They were in the front of the land forces when Farragut sailed by the forts in the Flagship Hartford. From the banks of the river the Twenty-fifth witnessed this grand bombardment and the burning of the frigate Mississippi in the night.

When the object of the expedition had been accomplished (to use the words of General Banks' order), the regiment returned to Baton Rouge, passing a wet and dreary night in Camp Misery, a night which will never be forgotten, nor will any one ever forget the noble act of Quartermaster John S. Ives, who rode his tired horse several miles to Baton

Rouge and brought out to the men coffee, which they managed to prepare over small fires and which no doubt saved many a man's life. After a short stay at Baton Rouge, the army made another advance on the west bank of the Mississippi, starting March 28th, 1863, marching with frequent skirmishes, sailing up the Atchafalaya bayou and landing at Irish Bend, where the regiment engaged in its first real battle, April 14th, 1863. The severity of this battle may be judged of as we read in the Adjutant-general's report: "Our loss, as you will see from the accompanying returns of the casualties has been very severe, being in all, ninety-six killed and wounded out of 350 with which the regiment went into action."

From this point the regiment marched up to within six miles of the Red River and of this march the regimental report speaks thus: "What with our loss in battle, details for special service and the number who have given out on our very long and severe marches, this regiment is much reduced and has today only 299 men present of whom but 248 are fit for duty. You will thus see, though this campaign has been eminently successful, driving the enemy before us through the entire valley of the Teche, from its mouth to its source, it has been very trying upon the troops. Four engagements and 300 miles march in twenty days call for proportionate suffering which cannot be avoided."

During May and June the regiment was actively engaged in the siege of Port Hudson, and was almost constantly under fire in the trenches and in the various assaults on that stronghold, leading the advance on the 23rd of May when a junction was formed with General Auger's column which completed the investment of the place. During all the siege the regiment was constantly in the front and finally participated in the glories of the surrender of the fortress on the 8th of July, having been in almost constant, arduous duty, marching and fighting since early in March.

After the surrender of Port Hudson, the regiment returned to Donaldsonville, where it encamped till the expiration of term of service. Colonel Bissell sent to General Banks and offered himself and his command to remain longer in the department if our services were needed; but he replied that there would probably be no more fighting, and thanking us for our offer, he issued an order returning us to our homes. The regiment was finally mustered out at Hartford, August 26, 1863.

In closing this brief sketch of the history of the gallant Twenty-fifth Regiment, a few words may be permitted in praise of the good and true men of which it was composed. With very few and unimportant exceptions, they were of the best sort of men, who were ever banded together for the defense of their country. They submitted to rigorous discipline cheerfully, they marched promptly and they fought bravely. A review of official records shows that the regiment was complimented a great many times by General Grover A. Birge for the promptness with which it always moved and for its bravery as shown time and again in battle and under severe fire.

Ever ready and always pushed to the front in time of danger of an attack, the Twenty-fifth was an organization of which the state need not be ashamed. When it was in the field it was an honor to the army and to the volunteer service of our country, and now that fifty years have rolled by the heart of many a survivor swells with just pride as he says to his children and grandchildren: "I was a member of the Twenty-fifth Connecticut."

In closing this brief sketch of the Twenty-fifth Regiment, of which Colonel Bissell is the author, you will see that he was very proud of the men under his command and if you could have seen him drilling his regiment at that time, as I still see him in memory, you would know that he fairly worshiped them. I am sure the men would have followed him into any fire against overwhelming odds. And now he is gone, the men that are left cherish his memory.

Interesting Reminiscences And Experiences
By Samuel K. Ellis.

In opening the subject of my experiences as a private in the War of the Rebellion, I hardly know how to begin as this is the first time I have attempted to write at length upon this subject. I earnestly hope that all those who read this little book will excuse all grammatical errors.

Fifty years have come and gone and as my life has been spared to see the fiftieth anniversary of my army life, and as I kept a diary during my term of service in the War of the Rebellion, I thought it no more than right and just to myself and descendants that I leave in book form some of the many experiences I saw and passed through during that time. It seemed to me that it was a grand opportunity on this the fiftieth anniversary to do it, if I ever did. Hoping that this account of my army life may be highly appreciated and prized by my children and grandchildren and any others that may be interested, I will endeavor to give a complete account as I saw and recorded events.

I was a Vernon Center boy but was working in the town of Glastonbury, when the war broke out, with Hubbard and Broadhead at teaming and farm work. At this time the gloom was deep but the people were not discouraged. At the request of the governors of eighteen loyal states, President Lincoln, on July 2nd, 1862, called out three hundred thousand men for three years' service, and on August 4, ordered a call for three hundred thousand men for nine months. At this time it was hard to tell what one's duty was, but I had made up my mind to go and of course I have never been sorry, as I look back and say with just pride that I was one who went out to help save our Republic from dissolution and preserve civilization itself on this Western Hemisphere from destruction.

I fear I have been wandering from my subject already but I could not help giving expression to the thoughts that were burning within me. Yes, I was a Vernon Center boy, my father moving there when I was sixteen years old. I enlisted September 2nd, 1862, in Company G, Twenty-fifth Regiment, C.V. Our company met in Hartford, near the old State House (what is now City Hall), on the morning of September 8th. We marched down to camp before noon on that day, but instead of finding tents to sleep in we found a string of barracks long enough for a thousand men. I want to tell you how they looked as I remember them. They resembled the cattle sheds that we see nowadays at our fairs, except that they were built with three tiers, instead of one. The bunks were made for two men, one above the other, about four feet wide. Of course we had to have a little straw to lay over the "soft side" of the boards. This building I believe we named "The Palace Hotel" because of its "great beauty and comfort." I wonder if you can imagine how tempting those bunks looked after leaving the good beds that we had been accustomed to. I think there were some pretty homesick boys that first night in our new quarters, if I remember correctly. But the food! Well, I don't think I had better say much about that, for I had been a farmer boy and I think I had the advantage over some of the boys, as I knew what it was to rough it and go without my dinner in the winter time when the days were short and I would be out in the woods all day chopping, or drawing logs with an ox team.

We left our old camp ground on November 18, 1862, with flying colors, to the tune of "Dixie" and "The Star Spangled Banner," and other patriotic airs. But all this did not occur without many tearful eyes, for the streets were crowded with friends and loved ones that were to be left behind. We pulled out of the dock at the foot of State street on the steamer City of Hartford about four o'clock in the afternoon. We arrived at Williamsburg, L.I., early the next morning, and the good people of that city treated us with all the sandwiches and coffee that we wanted. We marched about ten miles, with a portable bureau or what you might call a knapsack on our backs, before one o'clock that day, to the Centerville race course. We pitched our tents and made things as comfortable as we could for the night as you must know it was quite cold weather, it being the last of November. There is no place that reveals the real character of a man so quickly and so clearly as a shelter tent in an army on the field. All there is in him, be it noble or base, strong or weak, is brought to the front by the peculiar experiences of the soldier. The life of a soldier in camp is tedious and wearisome, but when a regiment starts for the field under a government not prepared for war (ours was not), the real trials of the soldier begin. When our regiment arrived at the camp at Centerville, after a march of ten miles, we found that no provision had been made for us,—and it now being the last of November. In the small hours of the morning Colonel Bissell drilled the regiment on a double quick movement on the race course to warm us up. The regiment was ordered to embark on November 29. The Twenty-fifth regiment was to have started on Saturday when lo! just as we were drawn up in line preparatory to a start, General Banks' orderly gallops up, bringing an order for Companies C, D, F, and G to remain behind and go with the Twenty-sixth Connecticut. Here was a pretty fix, for tents, baggage, and everything had already gone. To add to our troubles up came one of the hardest rainstorms, such as only Long Island can produce. As there was no other place, we were compelled to quarter in the old barn which was later turned into a guard house, where we slept on bare boards. Not a wisp of straw had we to lie on, for it was so rainy we could not gather any.

On the evening of the fourth of December, we received marching orders, and at about 8 o'clock, we were very glad to get away from this forsaken place, which we did in a hurry. We arrived in Brooklyn about 12 o'clock that night and I assure you it was no easy matter to find a place to stay till morning. It was a long cold December night. The men got places wherever they could find them. I and several other comrades stayed with a Doctor Green. We were up early in the morning and the doctor wanted us all to stay and have breakfast with him, an invitation which we accepted with thanks. I wrote a letter to my mother while there.

On the morning of the fifth of December we embarked on the steamer Empire City with the Twenty-sixth Connecticut Regiment. The men of the Twenty-sixth were in the hold of the vessel while the Twenty-fifth men took a deck passage which we didn't appreciate especially at this season of the year, December 6th. We left the Atlantic Dock, Brooklyn, at six o'clock that morning. We hadn't been out long before the water became quite rough and the steamer plunged and rolled dreadfully which made the soldiers very sea-sick.

December 7th was dark and boisterous and the good old ship creaked and swayed on the mighty deep. By the way, I hadn't been sea-sick since we left the Atlantic dock, but I could not help laughing, the first day we were out, to see the guards of the vessel from stem to stern lined up with anxious sea-gazers, their knees knocking together, their countenances ashen and a very intimate connection evidently existing between the stomach and the mouth. Even my risibiles were aroused though myself not entirely insensible to the attractions of Neptune.

December 8th. It was Sunday and when daylight came it brought with it a calmer sea and a more jolly set of soldiers, although the water was several inches deep on deck. That day was spent, as all others, without any religious exercises so we had nothing to do but watch the porpoises, of which there had been a great many in sight all day.

We had been out of sight of land since the previous day at noon. Well, we had found out where our expedition was going. It was going to sea. One thing was certain, we were going pretty far south.

December 9th. The weather had become quite fine. The boys had, most of them, gotten over being sea-sick. As the Twenty-sixth boys began to feel as though they had rather be on deck than down in that dirty hole, we were in pretty close quarters, for I think there were as many as twelve hundred men on this old unseaworthy ship which had been used as a transport in the California trade for a great many years. So I was told by Harlan Skinner, who went out as Sutler's clerk of the Twenty-fifth Regiment. (He was a brother of Town Clerk Francis B. Skinner of Rockville and went to California on board of her in 1849.)

December 10th. We were still out of sight of land. Some of us might be imagined reading the Bible or some other interesting book and others were lying asleep on deck, while the rest were watching and wondering where we were going to land, I suppose.

December 11th. It was much warmer, and very pleasant. We were still out of sight of land. Spying an English vessel, we ran up the Stars and Stripes and they ran up their flag to let us know that all was right. Some of the boys sang out, just for a little fun, that the old Rebel gunboat Alabama was in sight.

December 12th we came in sight of the coast of Florida. We had seen the trees and the snow white beach about all day. We also saw several lighthouses. The porpoises and flying fish attracted a great deal of attention and when a school came in sight, all eyes were turned upon them.

December 13th. It has been very pleasant and there has been a smooth sea, consequently we have had a very pleasant day's sail, with a cool breeze. We have been out of sight of land all day, and we long to be on shore once more. As we are so dove-tailed in, when we try to lie down at night, we get very little sleep.

December 14th, Sunday. We were now in the Gulf of Mexico and there had not been a living thing in sight all day. We had a sermon preached on deck. The text was, "Thou shall not take the name of the Lord, thy God, in vain."

December 16th. We arrived at the mouth of the Mississippi River. A pilot came aboard and took us over the bar in the river in compliance with the rules of navigation. We had a very pleasant day's sail coming up the old Mississippi. We saw many half clad slaves on the banks who seemed much pleased to think that Massa Lincoln's soldiers were coming to set them free. We arrived in New Orleans, La., on the 17th of December and got our fill of oranges and victuals before the peddlers were stopped from supplying us.

I want to tell you here what a beautiful sight a sunrise and sunset is at sea. There is something very fascinating about it.

We arrived at Carrollton, just above New Orleans, and went ashore at Camp Parapet, on the morning of December 18. We pitched our tents in the afternoon and were very glad to be on land once more and have room to lie down at night.

This completes my narrative of our sea voyage which I certainly have never forgotten, after having such an experience as I had on a vessel crowded to its utmost capacity and a deck passage at that.

December 19th. We have cleaned up, washed our clothing and are drying it upon our backs, thereby saving the trouble of hanging it on the bushes to dry.

December 20th. We received our rifles and now I suppose we shall have to put on our accoutrements and get right down to drilling in the manual of arms.

December 21st. I was on guard for the first time at Camp Parapet. I am beginning to find out that camp life in Hartford, Connecticut, was quite different from camp life of instruction at Camp Parapet, La.

From this date I shall omit many of the dates and unimportant events of camp life, as one day we drill the next have inspection, so every day brings us many troubles.

Christmas Day. We don't expect a very elaborate dinner. No doubt we shall be thinking of the good things our friends and loved ones are having at home. Such was a soldier's life fifty years ago.

December 30th. Wrote a letter to mother and put some small magnolia leaves, a magnolia bud, a live oak, a cypress and several other varieties into it which I have in my possession to this day. I had an exquisitely fine sympathy with vegetable life in all its forms and especially with trees.

I wrote at that time: "The country charms me with its magnificent lemon and orange groves. The trees are perfectly bowed down with their weight of fruit. Upon my word, I am in love with the Sunny South. I think when this cruel war is over and I can find my affinity, I shall settle down in this beautiful country for life. But I am not thinking much about that just now, for the girls are not much in love with the Union soldiers. The ladies here wear secesh cockades in their bonnets and it is really amusing to see the curl of the lip and the contempt of countenance with which they sweep by us. Of course it is no wonder, when we take into consideration the way they have always lived, and thought that they were fighting for a just cause."

The object of our expedition was to cooperate with General Grant in the reduction of Vicksburg, but General Banks did not know until he arrived at New Orleans that Port Hudson was fortified and manned by almost as large a force as he could bring against it, or that fifty miles west of New Orleans was a force of five or six thousand men ready to move on the city and cut his lines of communication the moment he moved up the river. In addition to this he was furnished with transportation for only one division of his army and instructions from General Grant. There was only one thing that could be done and that was to destroy the Confederate Army west of the Mississippi; before he could, with safety, leave New Orleans in the rear, and advance on Port Hudson. Therefore, concentrating his army at Donaldsonville, we marched across the country to Burwick's Bay and followed up the Bayou Teche to Alexandra, on the Red River, to the Mississippi. We advanced upon Port Hudson from the north.

On the 15th of January, 1863, our regiments at New Orleans were sent up the river. We went on board a little steamer, called the Laurel Hill at about eight o'clock in the evening. We arrived in Baton Rouge about one o'clock on the sixteenth of January and had our tents pitched before night. We were brigaded with the Thirteenth Connecticut, the Twenty-sixth Maine and the One Hundred and Fifty-ninth New York, under Colonel H. W. Birge as brigade commander. These regiments formed the Third Brigade of the Fourth Division of the Nineteenth Army Corps, General Grover division commander.

January 25th. We were now in the presence of the enemy and the position assigned to the Twenty-fifth was on the extreme left in advance and we were getting our first taste of active service.

January 26th. Our camp was about half a mile from the town, just on the edge of a dense forest and cypress swamp. Last night I went out on picket duty for the first time in Baton Rouge. General Payne warned us that we must look out for the enemy. In the afternoon the officer of the day came running his horse out where we were on picket and ordered us to stand by our arms for there was danger of an attack. Toward night we had a man badly wounded and he was sent to the hospital. During the night there was a great deal of firing upon the out-posts. We certainly thought there was going to be an attack and half the camp was up all night.

January 27th. I came in from picket in the morning. We were relieved by the Twenty-sixth Maine. We fired off our rifles at a target and started for camp. We thought sometimes that Louisiana was a very "quare country," as the Irish man said when he got lost in the woods, and ran up against an owl in a tree, and thought it was a man calling to him. The woods were plentifully stocked with game and we could hear most every sound from the hooting of the owls, growling of wild hogs, to the snarl of the wild-cat and cry of the opossum. It was also a strange sight to see the limbs festooned from tree to tree.

Some of them were gigantic. The trees were covered with moss or vines that encircled them. Strange as it may seem, we gathered this moss for bedding. I wonder it didn't kill the whole lot of us, but I think the country agreed with me, for I could sleep right on the ground under the magnolia trees with nothing but a log for a pillow, while some of our sentry kept watch.

[January 28, 1913. It is with great sorrow that I sit down to resume this narrative of my army life, for since my last writing I have lost a dear son by death. He died on the morning of January 7th, after a long and painful illness of seventeen weeks, and was laid to rest in Grove Hill cemetery on the afternoon of January 9th. Strange that this affliction should come on the fiftieth anniversary of my hardships in the Civil War, but I thought that I couldn't proceed until I had made mention of this sad trial.]

And now I must resume my story as best I can. For some weeks we had been very busy doing picket and guard duty, and acquiring the use of fire-arms. Everything seemed peaceful and quiet, but it was fearfully cold. It was very singular weather. Following every rainstorm it cleared intensely cold for several days; then it became very hot again; next we had another storm to subdue the intense heat. I don't think these sudden changes agreed with the men for we had a large number on the sick list. Our ranks were very much reduced by sickness. Some of the companies dwindled down to about half their original number. The result was we had to work very hard; every day we had to have a large number for picket and guard duty. It was a comical sight to see the men going out on picket. First we had our overcoats and fixings, then our cartridge box and belt, then in a sling a good sized blanket and a rubber blanket, then the haversack with a day's rations and lastly the coffee cup and canteen. The boys got up some fine dishes, although we hardly knew how to name some of them, but they were fine. I managed to get hold of some fish and made a delicious fry. Soaked it over night with some hard tack and the next morning threw the pieces into a frying pan (that our company had confiscated) along with a little salt pork; to this I added a little concentrated milk that I happened to have; next toasted some bread and poured the whole over it; why it was a dish fit for anybody. We were glad to be able to get some soft bread; at first we couldn't get anything but hard tack and very little of that. Fresh meat we hadn't tasted since we landed till one day, when out on picket, one of our boys caught a pig and we forthwith skinned and roasted it. You can imagine that that pig tasted pretty good after going without meat for over a month. The next day when we were out on picket, a contraband brought us some fresh eggs and sweet potatoes, but such instances were not very common. Why I became a nine-days' wonder on returning to camp and relating my experience. We managed to get some fun out of camp life, and my health was good (about this time I was flourishing like the owl of the desert and the pelican of the wilderness). One thing we missed was books. The only books we had were our Testaments which I enjoyed reading very much, for I meant to read some of it every day. The Testament I had was presented to me, about the time we left Hartford for the seat of war, by a Vernon lady, and I have it in my possession yet. I prize it still as a great treasure.

February 22d, Sunday, Washington's Birthday. Had inspection in the forenoon and in afternoon we had a sermon preached to us by our chaplain, Mr. Oviate, whom some might remember when he preached in Somers, Connecticut.

February 23rd. I was detailed to go on guard duty this morning for 24 hours. The day was celebrated as Washington's Birthday and the boys had a ball game. At sunset we had a dress parade and brigade review. Most of the boys were getting pretty short of money, and if we sent any letters home we had to have them franked as soldiers' letters. This means that soldiers' letters can be sent without a stamp.

February 24th. Came off guard this morning; had the forenoon to myself; in the afternoon we had a brigade drill under General Birge in the unpleasant duty of reversed arms and rest, a duty which we were called upon to perform quite often those days.

February 25th. I went to the hospital with Sergeant Sam Harding of our company. It was a sickening sight to go over the hospital and see the thin and wasted sufferers, many of them stretched on the floor with only a blanket and scarce a comfort, let alone a luxury of any kind; many of them stricken down in their strength by swamp fever; and one by one they dropped off. They had not even seen the enemy. Poor fellows!

February 26th. It was a very rainy day and we stayed in our tents and cleaned our muskets. Mortar and gunboats are daily arriving at this port. We have six of the former and four or five of the latter. The Confederate gunboats are continually making reconnoissance up the river and occasionally give Port Hudson a taste of their shells. But most of them give her a wide berth and I think they had better. By the way I want to tell you how hard it was for us poor boys to get reading matter. When the New York papers arrived they commanded 25 and 30 cents apiece. You can see that we fellows had to go without, for we had not received a cent of pay since arriving here. You can't imagine what it is to be cut off from all communication from the outer world for a week or ten days at a time as we were and during that interval hear nothing but discouraging rumors and false reports circulated by the Rebels.

February 27th. Came off guard in a soaking rain, in a very cross state of mind, but being neither sugar nor salt didn't melt away; but I felt that I could stand it awhile longer if our hard-tack and salt horse held out as well as it had and I felt it would, for I noticed that it stood by pretty well.

Having a prisoner consigned to my tender mercy to be fed on the bread of affliction and waters of repentance until further orders, this same prisoner did at dead hour of night break from the guard-house and abscond to his quarters, did there fare sumptuously on hard-tack and salt-horse. This coming to the ears of the colonel he did get angry with the officer of the guard and sending this same officer of the guard a pair of hand-cuffs, did order to arrest this delinquent and confine him in close quarters and in this performance a spirited encounter did thereupon take place in which the offender did get upset in one corner and the officer very nearly in the other; this criminal being finally secured did create such a row he was forced to be gagged and bound hand and foot.

That the weather hath proved very unpleasant for some time raining hard most of the time when your humble servant did hope to go round and view the pretty maidens of Baton Rouge and now that our three commissioned officers not knowing better than to all fall sick at once and go to the hospital, it bringeth us many cares when we had to have Lieutenant Goodell of Company F detailed to take command of our company and that the paymaster, (that much desired individual), hath again disappointed us and we are here as usual without a cent to buy anything for our comfort or luxury of any kind.

March 7th. However, this camp life was not to last. Admiral Farragut wished to run his fleet past the batteries of Port Hudson so that we might intercept the Red River traffic and cooperate with General Grant at Vicksburg. Therefore he asked General Banks to make a demonstration behind the fortress. This movement was intended to divert the attention of the enemy. General Banks at once put his army in motion, and our army, with a squadron of cavalry and a battery of regular artillery men, commenced the advance.

March 9th. Had marching orders this morning and struck our tents about seven o'clock. And we have been here all day waiting for orders to start.

March 10th. We had marching orders this morning and left camp about five o'clock; when we got outside the picket lines, our regiment was detailed to do skirmish duty and we immediately deployed on both sides of the road and into the woods, when we came to the remnants of a bridge that had been destroyed by the Confederates. We halted here and our regiment was sent out on picket duty for the night.

March 11th. This morning we had a sharp skirmish with the enemy. One man was killed in Company I. His name was Rockwell.

March 12th. Last night one-half of our regiment stood by our arms for fear of an attack. Sergeant Benjamin Turner and myself were up together on the same post. Our army at this time was within cannon shot of the Confederate works, but they could not get their guns up in time to be of any service. We were witnesses of a terrible scene, at 1:20 A.M. Two rockets burst into the air and in an instant all the guns of the fortress lit up the darkness with the flash of their firing. The fleet replied and until half past one, the roar of one hundred and fifty guns was incessant. To add terror to the awful scene, the U.S. Frigate Mississippi, which had grounded, was set on fire to save her from capture. She was soon wrapped in flames and lighted up the sky for miles around. This good old gunboat which had been in so many battles went up with a terrific explosion. This desperate enterprise consisted of four ships, and three gunboats, the latter being lashed to the port side of the ships. But only the Hartford, which flew the Admiral's dauntless blue, and her consort, the little Albatross, succeeded in running past the batteries. The other ships were disabled by the enemy's fire and dropped down stream. The Mississippi, which had no consort, grounded and to save the lives of her men was abandoned and fired.

March 15th. We started at two o'clock on our return march for Baton Rouge. When we had been on our way a short time, a hard thunder shower came up, and it rained hard until we halted for camp about eight miles from Baton Rouge. It was a wet, muddy place, and we named it Camp Misery. It was very dark and it continued to rain at times during all that long dreary night. Our quartermaster, John Ives, furnished us with coffee which he brought from Baton Rouge. I think that we must have had it about every hour during the night.

I cannot refrain from speaking right here of our first surgeon, Dr. Alden Skinner, who went out with the Twenty-fifth Regiment. For it was at Camp Misery that Dr. Alden Skinner, father of Town Clerk Francis B. Skinner, contracted a cold that developed into pneumonia and resulted in his death a short time later. Dr. Skinner, after whom the Rockville Sons of Veterans named their camp, was a highly respected Rockville physician, who went with us down into that Rebel stronghold in 1862, as many in town will remember. He was a man of many noble qualities. I knew him personally, for I had lived with him one winter when I attended school in Rockville. I felt it a great personal loss, as well as a loss to the regiment when he died. I desire to express myself at some length relative to this good man who gave his life for our country's cause fifty years ago about March 30th, 1863. He was very kind to me when we were encamped at Baton Rouge and especially when that thunder shower came up, as we were marching back from our first advance on Port Hudson. This experience was on Sunday, March 15, 1863. Dr. Skinner was on horseback and I can see him now in memory, as he was in that drenching rain, wet to the skin, as all were. That was the last time I ever saw Dr. Skinner, for he died a few days after in the hospital at Baton Rouge. He was brought home and was laid to rest in our beautiful Grove Hill Cemetery.

March 16th. It cleared off very pleasant this morning. Had breakfast of hard-tack and coffee. We had orders to march, about three o'clock in the afternoon. We marched about ten miles and went into camp on the bank of the Mississippi River. We managed to get some fence rails, build a fire and dry off, I was so drenched it took me nearly all day to get thoroughly dry. I felt much happier upon this old cotton plantation, for it was about as pleasant a place as I had seen in Louisiana. We were situated on a high bluff overlooking the Mississippi River, which spread out before us like a broad lake. The banks were lined with live-oak, and back of us were dense forests. Hardly had we arrived when I was detailed to go on guard duty. Pretty rough on a fellow who hadn't slept any for about forty-eight hours, but most of us were in the same predicament. We were a pretty sleepy set to go on guard but we had to stand it, two hours on and four off, until morning, when our cavalry were driven back upon us without loss. At three o'clock, I was relieved and lying down on the ground I slept like a stone till eight o'clock when the new guard came on. Here let me say, that the thunder storm we had on a Sunday afternoon was very likely the means of saving many lives, as the Confederates, when they found that we were retreating, turned out infantry, cavalry and artillery and pressed hard upon us but the rain Providentially deterred them. The Thirteenth and Twenty-fifth Connecticut Regiments covered the retreating column.

March 17th found us still in Camp Alden, for so we had named our new camp ground. In the afternoon a half dozen of us went out on a foraging expedition. We spotted a cow, which a bullet soon laid low. When we got her dressed, we started for a sugar plantation, a short distance away. We found it entirely deserted but lots of sugar and molasses, as this had not been confiscated by the United States government. We helped ourselves and managed to get a small quantity of the sweetening ingredient up to camp, where we received a warm reception. We were all out of sugar for our coffee and also meat for soup. That was about all the old cow was fit for. We held dress parade at sunset in marching costume. I was quite ragged by this time, having torn the legs nearly off my trousers, and my blouse had been badly torn while skirmishing through the woods and cane brakes.

March 18th. Spent most of the forenoon mending the holes in my breeches. In the afternoon visited the Twelfth Connecticut regiment for the first time in Louisiana. Saw some of the Hartford boys and had a good time generally. After dress-parade went out on a foraging expedition, with several others, after fence rails, as we had to have a fire to keep warm, also to make coffee and soup. I am sure the Rebs had good reason to bring "railing accusations" against us, for I am quite certain there wasn't a rail left within several miles of Baton Rouge.

March 19th. There was an order for inspection of arms this morning. While waiting I, with several others, was detailed to go out foraging after corn. Went out a short distance and got all that we could bring into camp. We received marching orders at nine o'clock in the evening.

March 20th. We were up early and on our way at four o'clock this morning. After a weary, hot march we reached our old camp-ground at Baton Rouge at seven o'clock. As we marched past General Banks' headquarters he came out and saluted, while the bands of the different regiments played and we marched past at shoulder arms. That night we lay on the ground again for it was too late and the men were too tired to pitch the tents.

March 21st. In the morning we pitched our tents, cleaned up and put our old Camp Grover in order once more.

March 22nd, Sunday. We were ordered to be ready for inspection but there was none on account of some of the rifles being loaded. Toward night we were ordered to be ready for marching, and have such things as we could get along without, packed in boxes. It was raining as we were getting ready for another start. Horace Newbury of our company died last night and we laid him to rest this morning under a beautiful magnolia tree.

March 24th. In the forenoon we worked on our guns and in the afternoon we had inspection and dress-parade.

March 25th. I was detailed to go on picket duty this morning. Lieutenant Gorman was officer of the picket. The night was cool and clear and everything was quiet all along the lines.

March 26th. A beautiful morning with the birds singing merrily. I got into camp about eleven o'clock. We had orders about nine o'clock in the evening to be ready for marching. It was very rainy weather and there was very little done in camp.

March 27th. We had orders to march and all was packing and confusion. I was ordered to help put our tents and baggage aboard the boat, the St. Mary. We had all our things aboard this little craft about five o'clock in the afternoon. At last, after being over a week packing up, waiting for orders, we were on the move. We left Baton Rouge at five o'clock and reached this place at nine, (as luck would have it) in a rain-storm. Lay on the ground under the trees all night.

March 28th. We just received marching orders again. Where we were going to nobody seemed to know. I supposed our destination was Brashear City and Burwick Bay, but beyond that nothing was known. Rumor said, Texas and Red River. We took tents and all our baggage and did not expect again to see Baton Rouge.

Sunday morning, March 29th. Arrived in Donaldsonville about nine o'clock last evening. Slept on the ground all night. In the morning had some hard-tack and coffee. We received a mail. I got several letters, one was from mother. I went to a Catholic meeting. Donaldsonville is an exceedingly pretty place, very old-fashioned, shingled-roofed town. A bayou extends through the center, some three hundred yards wide; it runs to the gulf and is so deep that a frigate lies in it about a mile from where it sets in from the Mississippi. The catalpa and China-bell trees were in full blossom and the pecans were leafing out. There was a Catholic church here that looked like a barn outside but quite pretty inside, as I saw for myself, and thither the people who were mostly French and Spanish, were flocking. We here enjoyed the luxury of seeing ladies, in clean white petticoats, walking the streets. And really we had to laugh, for actually those petticoats were the most home-like things we had seen for some months. "Billy" Wilson's Zouaves, who were in our division, were placed under arrest and had their arms taken from them. They got very drunk coming down on the boat and mutinied.

March 30th. You can't imagine how beautiful the flowers were looking. Cherokee roses, jessamines, jonquils, and a great variety of flowers were in blossom. We lived out under the trees with the rain pattering upon us. We were greatly bothered with vermin, which it is almost impossible to pick off. Campaigning evidently agreed with me, for I had gained several pounds since leaving New York.

April 1st. We were on the march very early. Our brigade went ahead as skirmishers. We went through a very pleasant country. We started about seven o'clock on the morning of April 2nd. Our company was guard of the baggage train. We went through a place called Thibodeaux, a very pretty village. We stopped "a right smart way," from Thibodeaux, as the contrabands used to tell us when we inquired the distance of them. We were there only a short time, when we were crowded on to some freight cars like cattle and transported to Bayou Boeuf, arriving at ten o'clock at night, pretty well fagged out.

We had some awfully hot and fatiguing marches and the boys were very foot-sore. I held out wonderfully; did not so much as raise a sign of a blister, though carrying a rubber blanket, a heavy overcoat, canteen full of water, haversack, with two days' rations in it,—by no means a small load as I found after a few miles' march. My nose and cheeks underwent a skinning operation on our Port Hudson expedition and I felt quite badly when I found that they were again peeling.

April 3rd. We have fixed up our shelter tents, and I helped unload our baggage. The day was pleasant but Bayou Boeuf was a very unpleasant place. A comrade came into our camp from the Twelfth Regiment, C.V. His name was Wells Hubbard of Glastonbury, Conn.

April 5th, Sunday. On camp guard I was stationed in front of General Grover's headquarters for the night. During the day we crossed over the Bayou Lefourche to the main part of the town and spent some time in exploring it. It must have been an exceedingly beautiful place before the bombardment a short time before. Many of the houses were lying in ruins. Then there was a very pretty cemetery embowered in red and white roses which hung in clusters over the monuments. I saw on some of the graves fresh wreaths of roses and pinks and on many pictures were hanging showing the weeping survivors beneath a weeping willow. Blue pinks seemed to be a favorite flower and were planted around a great many of the graves. There were some old tombstones at that place. On one was the following inscription:

> "Affliction sore, long time I bore;
>
> Physicians were in vain,
>
> Till God did please, that death should come,
>
> And ease me of my pain."

Again we were all packed up and on the move at about 8 A.M. The road, in fact all the way to Thibodeaux, lay along the Bayou Lefourche, a clear and cool stream, on which our steamers were passing bearing the sick and baggage. As we wound along under the catalpa and China-ball trees, the people were out on the piazzas watching us; this seemed to be their occupation almost everywhere. Such a slovenly set you never saw,—the women with frizzled hair and slipshod shoes. They were evidently very poor. But, oh, the fine clover fields we passed. The heart of a cow would have leaped with joy at the sight; and it was just so all the way to Thibodeaux. It must have been a splendid farming country. Sugar cane and cotton fields were also looking fine. After marching about twelve miles we encamped at Paincourtville, pretty well tired out. There were plenty of chickens, pigs, and sheep running loose of which we were not slow to avail ourselves. About the last thing I saw when I had lain down for the night was a porker squealing for all he was worth and charging blindly among the camp-fires over bunks and slumbering soldiers pursued by a band of shouting men discharging all kinds of deadly missiles at him.

April 7th. We were off at 7 A.M. Still among clover fields. On our march we passed some beautiful plantations; one was especially so. It was perfectly embowered in trees, had a smooth-cut lawn. There was a fountain and some swans swimming in the pond in front of the house. On the veranda there were two ladies working and some little children were playing. It was the prettiest sight I had seen in Louisiana. It fairly stilled the boys, seeing those children, and I heard more than one tough fellow sing out "God bless them." At another little white cottage we saw a lady whose husband had fallen in the army. She sent her slaves out where we were with pails of cool water. It was a simple act but we could not help blessing her for it.

And then we resumed our dusty way. The heat and dust were very intense; not a breath of air was stirring. We marched fourteen miles to Labadieville, and camped for the night on a sugar plantation, where we just had sugar and molasses to our hearts' content. Early the next morning we started in a flood of moonlight that silvered the grass with dewdrops. There is something very fascinating in camping-out; the camp-fires far and wide, the hum and bustle everywhere. It makes one forget his troubles.

April 9th. We had marching orders this morning. We marched as far as Brashear City, and camped for the night. It was the hardest day's march of all. The men staggered over the road from fatigue and sore feet. We felt better when we passed from the road into the clover field to lie down. At 6 P.M. came the order to fall in and we were ordered on board the little steamer, St. Mary. We stayed there all night,—expecting to start every minute.

April 11th. Although it was a small boat, the Fifty-second Massachusetts, the Twenty-fourth and Twenty-fifth Connecticut, and a battery with horses, were just packed on board. Just imagine how we must have been crowded together.

April 12th. We steamed out of the bay at 9 o'clock, the Clifton flagship ahead, then the Calhoun, Arizona, Laurel Hill, and St. Mary, also several tugs. We were now under convoy of these gunboats; they were to pilot us up through the chain of lakes from Burwick Bay into Grand Lake, where we arrived about 12 o'clock. It was an extremely hot day for so many to be crowded together, and we slept but little.

Mississippi River Fleet, U.S. gunboat "Brown"

April 13th. We went ashore at one o'clock. There was some firing on our picket line at night. I was detailed to go back to the lake and help bring up some rations where our forces were stationed. There was a heavy thunder shower and we slept but little all night.

I want to say here that we landed our forces, after sending out a party to reconnoitre under cover of the Calhoun, which shelled the woods while we came ashore. Our object was to cut off the retreat of the Confederates while Emory's and Sherman's division crossed Burwick Bay to attack them.

April 14th. On this date came the hard-fought battle of Irish Bend. We started out at daylight as skirmishers without any breakfast. When we had gone about a mile, brisk firing commenced on both sides. We advanced very fast, loading and firing as we went. When we had advanced very near the Rebel batteries and supposed that everything was going well, we were flanked by the enemy. We were immediately ordered to fall back a short distance. The Thirteenth Connecticut took our places soon in solid column, when the tune changed and the Confederates retreated into the woods, whence they came. When our brigade got together and formed in line of battle, we were again ordered to the front, where the Rebels sent shells into our ranks from their gunboat Diana. They burned her about two o'clock and retreated.

April 15th. This morning I thought I must write a little in my diary. I think it was through the mercy of God that my life was spared through the previous day's fight. It seemed a miracle that one came out alive. I felt very thankful that I was able to come out of the Battle of Irish Bend without a scratch, after hearing the horrible results. Our regiment suffered severely. For about two hours we were under a hot fire entirely unsupported. We went into the fight with 380 men and lost 83 killed and wounded and 14 missing. Our third brigade was about the only one engaged and we lost in that short space of time over 300 men killed, wounded and missing. Colonel Birge had his horse shot from under him. We had two officers killed and four wounded. It seems almost a miracle, when I think of it at this time, that so many escaped without a mark. We started on the march on the morning of April 15, about nine o'clock pursuing the Rebels very closely through the day. It was a fine rich country that we passed through; the cane and cotton fields were looking finely. We went into camp at night near a sugar mill that had a quantity of sugar in it, to which we helped ourselves. There was considerable firing through the day.

April 16th. We started at seven o'clock, marching quite slowly through the day. We were on the way to Newton or New Iberia, distance about 35 miles from Irish Bend,— where the battle took place. It was very hot and dusty and the men were getting very foot sore; a good many had to fall out by the road-side to rest. We had formed a junction with Emory's division and Weitzel's brigade and were at this time in close pursuit of the enemy, seven miles from New Iberia. We had taken a large number of prisoners, three pieces of artillery and several caissons and the Confederates fearful of the gunboats Diana and the Queen of the West falling into our hands burned them. In addition to this the Arizona engaged and blew up a Rebel gunboat. We were in hot pursuit of the Rebels, our advance skirmishing with Rebel General Moulton's rear guard.

April 17th. We were up at three o'clock, and started soon after getting some hard-tack and coffee. Our division was alone, Emory's division having taken a different route. We made a hard march of twenty miles. A great many men fell out, but we pushed the Rebels hard. At 5 P.M. they made a stand and an artillery duel ensued in which we lost a few men. The Confederates then retired, burning the bridge over the bayou. We then halted for the night, supposing that our next move would be Alexandra, via Opelousas, which since the capture of Baton Rouge had been the capital of the state of Louisiana.

April 19th, Sunday. This morning we had a hard thunder shower, arousing us from our bunks and soaking us thoroughly. We started on the march at eight o'clock. It was very muddy and we had to march very slow on that account. We went into camp at night pretty well fagged out. About midnight I was called up to go out quite a distance to an out-post on picket. We had a very hard time of it, for we had to be up until morning and stand by our arms.

April 20th. We marched rather slow on account of it being so excessively hot. We forded quite a bayou where the Rebels had burned another bridge. We went into camp at night at Opelousas, where we expected to have a fight but on our approach, we found the Rebels had retreated from the town, which was pretty good news for us.

Opelousas, April 21st. I will endeavor to give a few of my experiences at this place. Here General Banks gave his worn and tired army a rest. The Twenty-fifth Connecticut took position about seven miles east of headquarters, at Barre's Landing. While we privates were enjoying a suspension of active operations, the officers were unusually busy, as their numbers were greatly reduced by resignation, sickness and death. We were still wondering why that long looked for paymaster had not blessed us with his appearance and we were still in despair about it. Since the battle of Irish Bend we pressed the Confederates hard all the way to Opelousas, fighting their rear guard and taking prisoners every day. Our cavalry made a fierce charge at New Iberia. With sabers drawn they charged into the Texicans, scattering them in every direction. We were then at the port of Opelousas and shipping cotton at a great rate. We had shipped some two thousand bales; there was still a large quantity at the landing and more coming in hourly. We had to all take hold and help load it on the boat. While we were out on picket one day we had the good luck to come across one hundred and thirty bales. Opelousas was a very pleasant little city of several thousand inhabitants. There were some splendid mansions with grounds laid out in fine style. There was a small foundry in the place and two magazines; one of its three churches was stored with powder and ammunition, abandoned by the Confederates in their flight. The people were more Union than any we had previously seen and were of a better class. Provisions were sold at fabulous prices; eggs fifty cents a dozen, coffee five dollars a pound, and flour fifty dollars a barrel, and scarcely any at that. We learned from some of our Rebel prisoners how their soldiers lived. They had only one commissary wagon drawn by three yoke of oxen for an army of five thousand men. They lived principally upon the plantations as they passed along, as we had done.

The slaves appeared to me, all the way through this long march, to be contented and happy with their families in their cabins. I think they lived principally on corn which they ground by hand power and made into corn bread and hoe cake, with plenty of sweet potatoes which grew abundantly in Louisiana. I think they must have gotten along pretty well. At many plantations where the Union soldiers would stop at nightfall for chickens, the slaves would come out of their cabins and plead with us to let them be. This, our boys were very loath to do, and I don't know as anyone could blame them, for a good chicken was a great temptation after a long hard day's march.

May 5th. We started on our return march this morning very early. We came through a little village by the name of Washington. We marched twenty miles and went into camp for the night very tired and some very foot-sore. I was sick all day but managed to keep up with the regiment. It was very hot and dry.

May 7th. This morning I was sick and got a pass from Doctor Wood, our army surgeon, to go on to the ambulance wagon. But found on investigation that there was no room for me, as the wagons were full of sick men unable to sit up. Therefore I was obliged to ride on a baggage wagon all day. Went into camp at night feeling some better. Went out with other comrades and bought some chickens of the darkies. About this time the paymaster arrived. It was a time of great interest to the men, as we had not been paid for more than four months. A great many wanted to send money to their families and friends who, in some cases were in great need. But we were about two hundred miles from New Orleans, the nearest point from which money could be sent with safety. There were no Confederates in arms between us and New Orleans but the country was full of men who had broken all laws and who held any human life very cheap, when money was at stake. How to send home the money the soldiers could spare was a very important question. In a chapter printed elsewhere in this book, entitled "How the Pay of the Regiment was Carried to New Orleans by Lieutenant Henry Hill Goodell," it will be told how it was accomplished.

On May 21st we received marching orders and about noon we embarked on board the little steamer Empire Parish along with the One Hundred and Fifty-ninth New York and the Thirteenth Connecticut. I wonder if anyone can imagine how crowded we were, also taking into consideration that a good many of the soldiers were inclined to be troublesome. Colonel Bissell was taken quite sick at about this time and had to find a place to lie down. Soon after 3 P.M., while the rest of the boats were being loaded we shipped from the dock and away up the Atchafalaya to the Red River where we passed the Switzerland and another little boat watching for Rebel craft. Here we slipped down the Red River to the Mississippi, where we came upon the grim old Hartford, Rear Admiral Farragut's flagship. The Thirteenth Connecticut band saluted her as we passed, with "The Star Spangled Banner" and "Yankee Doodle." At about midnight we went ashore at Bayou Sara, sixteen miles from Port Hudson. A portion of our brigade marched on and left our regiment to unload the boats. It was after 2 A.M. before we had any chance to lie down.

May 22nd, at about four o'clock, we started, breakfastless, to overtake the rest of our brigade. Colonel Bissell was left at a house with a guard. Major McManus assumed command of the regiment. We marched a short distance and found the remainder of our brigade encamped at St. Francisville, which was upon a hill the first we had seen since coming to Louisiana. Soon after eight o'clock our column was set in motion, the Third brigade in advance. As we passed through the village of St. Francisville the people thronged to the doors. Some would curse and swear, while others seemed glad to see us. One woman in a spiteful tone called out to another woman: "Come in, for God's sake, and don't stay there looking at those Yankee devils." The manners of these Southern women were astonishing. They would curse and call us vile names and call upon God to save a just cause. We had a hard march climbing up hill between magnificent hedges of jessamine in bloom, the flowers of which were very beautiful. We advanced very slowly for it was quite warm and the dust was stifling. To add to all this it was a terrible country to skirmish through. We had two men seriously wounded during that day. At about 4 o'clock we halted and our regiment was ordered to the front as advance picket for the night. We deployed into a field near a beautiful creek,—Thompson's,—where the water was knee-deep and very clear. Our forces were ordered across the creek to the edge of the adjoining woods. After a short skirmish we succeeded in accomplishing our object. It rained quite hard and we had to be upon the watch most of the night.

May 23rd. We started on the march, our men pretty well tired out by two nights' duty. But we had no mercy shown us. The Twenty-fifth regiment was ordered to take the advance as skirmishers and a hard time we had of it, forcing our way through bamboo brake, pushing over vine and bushes, wading through water, scratching and tearing ourselves with thorns and stumbling over ploughed fields. It was very hard work and many a strong man gave out with fatigue and exhaustion. At 10 o'clock A.M. we met the advance of Colonel Grierson's cavalry. Our wearied column of soldiers were called in, therefore we were very much pleased to see them. We advanced a short distance and halted near a well of delicious cool water, some two miles from Port Hudson. In a few minutes, General Augur rode up and held a conference with General Grover.

At 7 P.M. I was detailed to go on picket. Rather rough on a fellow to be two days and nights on duty. But a soldier's first duty is to obey without grumbling and so I went, but I could hardly keep from going to sleep. It was a beautiful moonlight night and I stood and watched the bombs from the mortar boats curling around in the sky and bursting in a fiery show, making a splendid sight. The night passed quietly, save for a couple of false alarms. At about 5 o'clock A.M., Jared Wells, my old tent mate, and I went out blackberrying. In a little while we had enough for a good meal for ourselves and some for the boys in camp. This was the 24th of May, under the guns of Port Hudson. We got back into camp about 9 o'clock and commenced making preparations for a Sunday advance on the fortifications. The Second Brigade was in advance and the Twenty-fourth Connecticut lost a few men; at about noon the first earthworks were taken and we deployed into the woods on our right. We lay here for two long hours while shells burst all around us, but we were mercifully preserved, though in great danger.

Soon after 4 P.M., our regiment was ordered out as picket-skirmishers and we were stationed behind trees all through the woods to keep the enemy back. On our right was the Thirteenth Connecticut and on the left was the One Hundred and Fifty-ninth New York. This was the third night that we had been on duty and we were pretty well tired out but it seems they hadn't got through with the Twenty-fifth yet.

May 25th. At about 9 A.M. we were relieved and called in. As we were being relieved by the Twelfth Maine we had to pass over a place commanded by the sharpshooters of the enemy. The bullets whizzed most unpleasantly near, killing one man of the Thirteenth Connecticut. We thought that after being relieved we should get some rest. But about as soon as we got into camp we were ordered to fall in again. We marched out of the woods, over the hill and the entrenchments taken the day before, immediately coming under a sharp fire from the Rebel sharpshooters. We were immediately ordered to fire upon them and drive them out. After a sharp skirmish of half an hour we drove them clear out of the woods and into their rifle-pits. We then occupied the woods, and we kept up such a sharp fire upon them that not one of the rascally Rebs dared lift his head above the works. We were just in time to save the Twelfth Maine from being flanked and cut to pieces.

About 3 P.M. General Weitzel's brigade attacked, and after a severe fight, drove the Rebels out of the woods. While this was going on our right, we could hear the yells, hurrahs and the crackle of musketry, roar of artillery and many other concomitants of the fight, but could see but little. Consequently we stood and fidgeted round not knowing when our turn might come.

May 26th. Our regiment remained on the reserve till 5 P.M., when the four right companies were ordered to the front. We had a splendid view of an artillery duel. The work of Nim's battery was perfect. Our artillery unlimbered two or three guns and their fire was so sharp, the Rebel gunners did not dare load their pieces.

May 27th. We were relieved at about 6 P.M., by the Twelfth Maine regiment, but we were almost immediately ordered out to the support of Nim's battery which had just been put into position. Here we lay five or six hours while the enemy's shells burst in most unpleasant proximity. Then our regiment and the One Hundred and Fifty-ninth New York were ordered out to the support of General Weitzel on our right. We marched on the double-quick down through the woods, when we were ordered by General Grover to advance to the front and carry the earthworks. We were informed that there were hardly any Rebels there. Major Burt of the One Hundred and Fifty-ninth, who was in command, was told that his regiment alone would be able to carry the works and to send back our regiment if it wasn't needed. But we found out very soon that our assistance would be necessary to carry the earthworks. We rushed on through the woods and down a hill, swept by the enemy's artillery. Here we turned to the right and emerged on to a plain. I shall never forget that sight. The valley was filled with felled trees, and heavy underbrush, while thick and black rolled the battle-smoke. There was a hill on our left, strongly entrenched and from here loomed up a big gun. Just below on a little bridge was planted a stand of the Stars and Stripes, the glorious old banner, and gathered around it stood a handful of brave men firing a stream of bullets upon that piece. For six long hours the gunners did not dare approach to load and that wicked looking gun was kept silent. It was here that we had a taste of real war in all its horrors. It was a sort of a floating panorama that passed before me, a hideous dream. There was a roaring and crashing of artillery, bursting of shells and the rattle of muskets, with hissing and whistling of minie balls and battle-smoke lowering down upon us. There were men dropping here and there and all the horrid experiences of war. Still we kept on; there was a short turn to the right and in single file we commenced ascending through a deep ravine. Wading through water, stumbling over and under fallen trees, we finally came to a pit about six feet deep; when we had gotten out of that we were on the side of the hill where we had to prepare to make a charge. It was a wicked place to charge. The nature of the ground was such it was impossible to form in battle line, so to make the attack in three columns over felled trees which were cris-crossed in every shape imaginable. We waited here for a few moments with beating hearts, waiting for the forward charge. The word came and with a terrifying yell we rose to our feet and rushed forward. It was a terrible time, when bounding over the last tree and crashing through some brush we came out within a short distance of the enemy's entrenchments, and it seemed as though a thousand rifles were cracking our doom. This fire was too deadly for men to stand against. Our brave fellows, shot down as fast as they could come up, were beaten back. Then occurred one of those heroic deeds we sometimes read about. The colors of the One Hundred and Fifty-ninth were left on the hill, their color sergeant having been killed. Corporal Buckley of our regiment calmly worked back in that terrific fire, picked up the dear old flag and brought it in, turned to pick up his gun and was killed. He was a noble fellow and much beloved in the regiment.

Resting here a short time, we made a second charge with the same deadly results. Our regiment and the One Hundred and Fifty-ninth New York lost 80 men killed and wounded. It was a terrible position we were in. Sharpshooters on the left picking us off; sharpshooters on right giving it to us and the rifle pits in front. Here we had to stay till after 10 o'clock that night when the order came to fall back, which we did, bringing off our wounded. I was so tired I fell asleep and barely woke in time to get away. We had several killed and wounded in our regiment. I will say here that our little company was not entirely dissolved at this time though reduced to less than 20 men. Our colonel we missed sadly, but earnestly hoped to welcome him back soon. Our regiment numbered 162 men and eight officers at this time.

May 28th. There was lively firing this morning on the picket lines, but the cannons were quiet. We were expecting reinforcements and we needed them if we were ever to take Port Hudson. This was the seventh day of the siege and we were pretty well fagged out. We had to fight for every foot of ground. But we had carried the first two earthworks by storm. It had been one continual fight since we started in but there was a cessation of hostilities for a short time, and the lull was a great relief, for my ears had been half-deafened by the awful roar of artillery and cracking of musketry. There were three men killed and about twenty wounded, and thirty in our regiment missing. Again in our little company we had several wounded, one fatally. So I think that I must have been in great danger several times, but I felt that a kind Providence watched over me, and brought me out safely. The regiment at this time was under the command of Major McManus, Colonel Bissell being sick with remittent fever at Bayou Sara and the lieutenant-colonel prostrated at New Orleans. The colored regiments fought bravely and made some splendid charges.

May 31st. There has been some firing by the infantry and artillery during the day. About ten o'clock last night we withdrew our forces very cautiously, bringing away all the wounded we could reach, but there were some poor unfortunates lying up under the breastworks that it was impossible to reach. Every time we tried to get to them the Rebs would fire on us. We threw them canteens of water but it was of little use. We marched back and lay upon the battlefield of the preceding day.

June 1st. We marched back into the woods and were there in support of a battery. It was very trying for us. The Rebs had a perfect range on us and several times a day they would throw those immense twelve-inch shells right into our midst. We could hear them coming for several seconds and we all stood close to the trees for protection. There must have been a large number killed that day. The next day there was a cessation of hostilities to bury the dead. At about seven o'clock the enemy made a terrible onslaught on our right but they were repulsed with heavy loss. We fell into our places expecting to be called into action but we were spared for once. We remained there until the 7th when Lieutenant-Colonel Weld came up from New Orleans and assumed command.

June 7th. We were ordered to the front to relieve the One Hundred and Fifty-ninth New York in the rifle-pits. We went out in the night as the enemy's sharpshooters rendered it very dangerous to go in the daytime. We had rifle pits dug about two hundred yards from the rifle-pits of the Rebs, and we had loop-holes made from which to fire. About one hundred yards back of us was planted one of our batteries and as they fired over our heads anyone might imagine what a deafening report rang in our ears. We boys got the range of the rifle-pits of "Mr. Secesh" opposite, perfectly, consequently they didn't dare show their heads. Though from their hiding place they annoyed us all day. After dark we usually held some conversation with the Rebs across the ravine. We would ask them if they wanted any soft bread. If they did we would put some in a mortar and send it over. They said they didn't care to have any sent that way and as we didn't have much to spare we didn't send any. Our bean soup and coffee and such other food as might be handy was sent out before daylight in the morning and after dark at night. We were here in this trench or pit for three long days and nights and one can imagine how we suffered from heat and thirst. We were relieved on the tenth by the One Hundred and Fifty-ninth New York. We returned to our old camp-ground June 11th between 12 and 1 A.M. A general assault was planned but owing to some misunderstanding the plan failed.

June 14th, Sunday. The day was an eventful one in the siege of Port Hudson, of which the Twenty-fifth Connecticut was engaged. We were under way at an early hour, for we formed the reserve in the attacking column. Colonel Birge was in command of the reserve. We were up at 3 A.M., had a little hard-tack and coffee and started under command of Captain Naughton at 4. Suddenly we heard a terrifying yell and the crash and roar of artillery and musketry. Soon the dead and wounded began to be brought in. All kinds of conflicting stories were circulated as to the success of our brave fellows. Very soon General Payne was wounded, and Colonel H. W. Birge assumed command, we forming the reserve. Soon we were ordered forward. On through the scene of our first day's fight, then down through a ravine, where a road had been cut. Here we halted at the foot of the hill where we formed in battle line and made another charge right up over the hill, exposed to a raking fire, as we went over the crest and down through the ravine before we could reach the breastworks. There we lost two lieutenants. A large number of men were killed or wounded. We arrived at the other side of the hill in great confusion. I shall never forget that horrible scene. There were parts of several regiments all mixed up together, entangled among fallen trees. But after getting straightened out, and the line once more formed, the order to charge was countermanded and we had to lay up there in that fearful hot sun all day. I was taken sick and had to rest for awhile but I soon got better and joined the regiment. At about 10 P.M. we were ordered down into the outer ditch of the breastworks. We were there but a short time, when we were ordered to the right to our old position in the rifle-pits, which we reached at midnight.

General Payne had been wounded in the leg in the forenoon, but we could not get up where he was to give him any aid, consequently he had to lay there in the burning sun till night, when he was brought away in safety. It was a scorching hot day and a number were sunstruck, some cases proving fatal. I was exhausted and had to lie down in the shade.

It was a miserable Sunday scrape and ended like all the rest that had been started on a Sunday, disastrously. The loss of life was very great.

We were relieved at night by the Twenty-eighth Connecticut and returned once more to our old camp-ground, where, after the whizzing of the bullets and the cracking of firearms had died away, all was still but the groans that could be heard upon the bloody battlefield.

June 15th. The day after the second assault on Port Hudson, General Banks issued a call for volunteers "for a storming column of a thousand men to vindicate the Flag of the Union, and the memory of its defenders who had fallen. Let them come forward, every officer and soldier who shares its perils and its glory shall receive a medal fit to commemorate the first grand success of the campaign of 1863 for the freedom of the Mississippi River. His name will be placed upon the roll of honor." The next day, June 16, the order was promulgated and two days later, June 18, these "stormers," as they were called, were gathered into a camp by themselves and put into training calculated to promote physical strength and endurance. By every conceivable way they prepared themselves for the work that they were expected to do. These brave men knew that all the arrangements for their support had been made but the expected order did not come. They had had three or four dreadful experiences in charging earthworks and yet these men were willing to assault those same earthworks again.

June 26th. There has been considerable bombarding on account of the Rebels opening some big guns but I think they are doing very little damage. We heard today that the enemy had driven our army across the Potomac and that there was great excitement throughout the North. We hoped that the report was false. Last night I was detailed to go on picket being sent out to an outpost about a mile from the reserve. We stood by our arms most of the time during the night. There was brisk firing on our left most of the time.

June 27th. Came in from picket. Today we have been reviewed by Major-General Banks. He made a temperance speech to us. I think he must have thought that we were getting to be a pretty tough set of fellows. I don't see how he could have thought that, when we couldn't get very much that was intoxicating, only what quinine and whiskey Uncle Sam issued to us when we came off picket duty.

July 1st. There has been a reason for my not writing in my diary for a few days. We had been told that no soldiers' letters could be sent North and I put off writing in the hope that I could record the fall of Port Hudson, that Rebel stronghold. But still the siege drags slowly along. Our days were divided between rifle-pits and making assaults. The Rebs hold their rifle-pits and we advance ours or remain stationary.

Yesterday, the colored brigade carried a hill by storm and have held it, notwithstanding the great effort made by the Rebels to regain it.

Sunday, July 3rd. We attacked Port Hudson at two points, but were beaten back with great loss. The battle still rages and omnipotence still holds the scales in equal balance. This is the 25th day of the siege and we are still stuck outside the fortification. Last Sunday we made a general assault. We got inside three times but for want of support were driven back. Men were mowed down on our right and left. It was a wonder how I was preserved. I have been in four direct assaults on the breastworks, several skirmishes and yet not a scratch have I received.

Port Hudson, July 4th, (Independence Day). As will be seen, we had no idea of what was going on more than two hundred miles up the river at Vicksburg, or fifteen hundred miles at Gettysburg. At Vicksburg, General Grant was quietly smoking a cigar when he wrote a dispatch to be sent to Cairo to be telegraphed to the General-in-Chief at Washington: "The enemy surrendered this morning. The only terms allowed is their parole as prisoners of war." The same dispatch was sent to General Banks at Port Hudson. At Gettysburg the army of the Potomac had inflicted a terrible defeat on the army of Northern Virginia. I really believe this is the quietest Fourth of July I have ever spent. Verily, I don't believe there has been as much powder burnt here as in New York or Boston. I wouldn't wonder if Hartford, with its swarm of boys, could outstrip us. Every little while there's a bang, a boom and the bursting of a shell, for we must keep the besieged from falling asleep and stir them up occasionally. Now, the music is becoming lively, the gunboats and the batteries are pitching in and altogether we are giving them Hail Columbia to the tune of Yankee Doodle.

For the last few days we have been in a very enviable frame of mind, expecting every day to be ordered to participate in another assault. Yet the orders have not come and each night we have drawn a long breath and exclaimed one more day of grace. Well, so it is, but while we are getting uneasy for another fight we have a strong desire to avoid charging on the breastworks again. We've been in three, and some of us four, assaults on the Rebel fortifications and each time we have been driven back. The first of July, General Banks made us a great speech promising us that within three days we would be inside Port Hudson. But the three days have passed and those rascally Rebs still persist in keeping us outside. Although the fortifications could probably be stormed any day, yet why waste life when a few days will bring them to terms, as they are now reduced to mule-meat and a little corn. Deserters are coming in fast. One day as many as one hundred and fifty came in saying they couldn't stand mule-meat any longer. Now I am feeling sure that within a few days I shall be able to record the fall of Port Hudson. The Rebel cavalry are harassing our rear ranks continually. They made a dash day before yesterday from Clinton and Jackson, striking here and there and picked up some stragglers and foraging parties. A few days ago they dashed into Springfield Landing whence we draw our stores and ammunition, but our cavalry went after them so quick they found pressing business in other quarters.

On the other side of the Mississippi quite a force came down. They attacked Donaldsonville a few days ago demanding the surrender of the town. But the provost-marshal gathered his forces together, amounting to about two hundred, got inside his fortifications, and waited for them to come up. The contest was kept up from midnight till daylight, when the sudden appearance of a gunboat caused the Rebels to skedaddle, leaving about one hundred dead on the field, several hundred wounded and one hundred and twenty prisoners.

Now comes the great surprise of all. The confounded Rebs have got into Bayou Boeuf and destroyed or captured the whole of our division property stored there. Tents, baggage, knapsacks, company and regimental books are all gone. At this time we were all as poor as Job's turkey. Except for the rags that cover us, we haven't a thing. Were I where I could, I should like to write a letter to the Soldiers' Aid Society for some handkerchiefs, being reduced to the last shift, i. e., the flap of an old shirt picked up in a deserted mansion. Word comes from Colonel Bissell that he is slowly improving. We are hoping that we shall see him with us again soon. But I really believe his sickness saved his life, for it is doubtful if he would have come out alive from the charge the regiment made on the 27th of May. We are having some very hot weather. We are spending most of our time on picket duty and trying to keep cool. You would have laughed if you could have seen us at our meals wearing only shirt and drawers, while our comical colored boy, Adam, squatted down on the ground in front of us keeping the flies off. This Adam was a corker. Speaking of Mobile one day, he said: "Reckon you couldn't fool dis n___a much in dat town. Specks he was born and raised dar. Yah! yah! yah! Reckon he knows ebry hole dar from de liquor-shops to de meeting houses."

July 8th. The dispatch from General Grant, previously referred to, was received. The booming of big guns, the cheers and shouts of the Union soldiers and the strains of patriotic music informed the besieged that something had happened. They were not slow to find out the cause of the rejoicing. General Gardner sent a flag of truce to General Banks to know if the report that Vicksburg had surrendered was true and received in reply a copy of General Grant's dispatch. The garrison had done their duty with brave fortitude. The Union lines were already in some places up to their breastworks. Starvation was staring them in the face and taking everything into consideration about the only thing for General Gardner to do was to surrender. Should the expected charge have been made by the "stormers" it would have been a waste of life for they could not expect to hold their position.

The 8th was spent in arranging terms for the surrender of the fortress and on the 9th, the storming column led the advance as the victorious army marched into Port Hudson to put the Stars and Stripes in the place of the stars and bars.

President Lincoln's long-desired hope was realized and he could now say: "The Father of Waters again goes unmolested to the sea." The time of the nine-months' men was soon to expire and the Twenty-fifth Connecticut left very soon for New Orleans, but was detained at Donaldsonville for a few days.

About fifty years ago the people in the North were probably in a frenzy of excitement. We soldiers in the South had learned to take things cool. Vicksburg, the stumbling block, had fallen; Port Hudson had caved in; Lee and his army had gone to one eternal smash; Port Hudson had scarcely surrendered when we were called upon again to take the field. Those confounded Rebels didn't know how to stay whipped, and General Taylor, reinforced by General Magruder's Texicans, had again taken the field. They attacked us at Donaldsonville with a much larger force in proportion to ours but got soundly thrashed; we being strongly reinforced, came out to meet them and got whipped, and so the matter rested. The commanding officer of the brigade was flanked through carelessness and they had to fall back with a loss of two cannon. Our brigade was on the reserve. We fell in and rushed to the rescue but too late, for they were in full retreat. A new line was formed, the

Twenty-fifth deployed as skirmishers and sent forward. After advancing quite a distance through the corn we were ordered back and our whole force fell back about half a mile, where we were still holding a strong position. The Rebels meanwhile had left and fortified at Labordieville, some twenty miles distant. The Twenty-fifth Connecticut regiment, after one of the most trying campaigns of the war, was about to take another sea voyage.

Here are a few verses which I have written on the siege of Port Hudson:

PORT HUDSON.

Well do I remember, how fifty years ago,

Down on the banks of the Mississippi,

We met the Southern foe,

And faced a storm of shot and shell;

That many a life was sacrificed

Mid battle hell of smoke and flame

On the field of Port Hudson.

Well do I remember, how those days,

The gallant Third Brigade went

Marching down into the woods

Like men on dress parade;

Though from the wood in front

The foe their deadly missiles sent.

Thinning our ranks

Those days at Bloody Port Hudson.

How on the left the Connecticut Thirteenth engaged in desperate fight

And left in front the Twenty-fifth was marshaled on the right;

Side by side, New York and Maine for honors did contend,

When Rebel yell and Yankee cheer was heard at Port Hudson.

And though we drove away the foe

How dear was victory won,

For when the din of battle ceased,

The burning sun shone down upon the bloody field

And shone on foe and friend,

Who bravely met a soldier's fate,

That day on the field of Port Hudson.

Now fifty years have gone,

How soon they pass away,

Since we did wear the army blue;

And now we wear the gray,

For time has turned our hair to gray,

To show us near the end,

And soon will none be left to

Tell the tale of Port Hudson.

Were I to pledge those bygone days

Oh this would be my toast:

"Here's to the dear old Stars and Stripes,

Our country's pride and boast;

Here's to the Union Volunteers,

Who did the flag defend,

And here's to my old comrades

Who fought at Port Hudson."

August 8th. It was a beautiful morning and we were in camp waiting for orders to start. We had orders to be ready to go on board the Steamer Thomas Scott at twelve o'clock. At two o'clock we were gliding down the old Mississippi. We stopped at New Orleans, took some horses aboard and started again at about six o'clock. Arrived at the mouth of the Mississippi at midnight. Here we waited for a pilot, took him on board and was off again.

August 9th, Sunday. At 6:30 o'clock we passed the bar, left the pilot and in a short time were out of sight of land. The captain of the boat said he would land us in New York by Saturday night, if all went well.

August 10th. It was a fine morning and we were enjoying ourselves with a deck passage at that.

August 11th. This morning we passed several lighthouses; one was upon Tortugas Island.

August 12th. The old steamer was making good speed. Comrade Chadwick died last night; this morning he was buried at sea. He was a member of our regiment and enlisted from Andover, this state.

August 13th. This morning was very fine, but the ship rolled and pitched considerable, owing to being in the Gulf Stream.

August 14th. The old ship was making good speed and we were hoping to get into New York harbor by Saturday night, as it was getting pretty tiresome on the old filthy vessel, with the vermin almost unbearable.

August 15th. This was a beautiful day and the old steamer continued making good time.

August 16th. The day was fine and we expected to get into port at night and our expectations were realized, about seven o'clock after being in this dirty place for a whole week.

August 17th. We arrived in port last night but had to stay upon the ship another night. I managed to get a small loaf of bread and if I remember correctly, I wasn't long devouring it, for we had had nothing but hard-tack and raw salt pork to eat and condensed water to drink since we went aboard the ship at New Orleans. This (Sunday) morning we were allowed to go ashore and were kept penned up till about night when we went aboard the good-looking old boat, City of Hartford. We arrived in Hartford, if my memory serves me correctly, at about 10 o'clock Monday morning, August 18th, 1863, and I guess we were about as tough a looking set of fellows as ever came off the boat. Yes, I must admit, we were a pretty hard looking set, what there was left of us, for we had dwindled down to less than one-third the number which left Hartford about a year previous. What a change had come over us. Why, some of our friends didn't know us, we had changed so. One comrade in particular I will mention, Wm. Goodrich. He went from Glastonbury in my company. He was a big fine looking man, weighing two hundred and fifty pounds when we went away, and when he came home he hardly weighed one hundred and fifty. Was it any wonder that our friends couldn't recognize us with the beards we had grown on our faces, and the soiled clothing we were wearing? Well, I finally reached home and you can imagine how glad I was. I think that I felt much as the Prodigal Son did when he returned home. To get my clothes off and get into a good bed, (which I had not done for about a year) and to be cared for by a kind and loving mother, I never felt more like singing, "Home, Sweet Home."

In closing this sketch of the gallant Twenty-fifth Regiment, I would say that war, as far as my experience goes, is not the thing it's cracked up to be. Though anyone can get used to all kinds of horrid sights, in a measure, I could tell some things that I don't think one would care to hear. But I will omit all description as it is best learned by experience. I think scant justice has been done to the Nineteenth Army Corps and General Banks, inasmuch as the field of action while in Louisiana was far away and until the fall of Port Hudson, was cut off from the North except by the sea. The public attention was taken up in the States along the border and even our great victory at Port Hudson was eclipsed and looked upon as a consequence of the fall at Vicksburg. But they did a great deal of hard fighting and made hundreds of miles of hard marchings in a climate to which the men were not accustomed.

An Interesting Incident.

It was in the Spring of 1863, and General Banks had inaugurated the campaign which ended in the capture of the last stronghold. We had marched to the very outworks of Port Hudson, and engaged the Confederate forces, on that historic night, when lashed to the maintop, high above the boiling surges, stout-hearted, Farragut, drove his vessels through the storm of shot and shell, that was hurled upon him from the heights above, and cut the Rebel communications between Port Hudson and Vicksburg. These two fortified places were the only ones left on the Mississippi River, not in our hands. Grant, was already hammering at Vicksburg, but before Port Hudson could be invested, it was necessary to dispose of Confederate General Taylor and his forces, who from their position in the South, could fall upon our unprotected rear or make a dash for New Orleans. Returning then, to our camp at Baton Rouge, after a few days' rest, we were suddenly divided into two forces, one marching down through the country, to engage the enemy at New Iberia, and the rest of us sent around by water and up through the Atchafalaya to intercept and cut them to pieces. It was only a partial success. Driven from their position in Fort Bisland, they fell upon us before we were fairly in position, and held us in check while the whole army slipped by. Then commenced a long pursuit, enlivened by daily skirmish and fighting which lasted from the shores of the Gulf to Shreveport, in the extreme northwestern corner of the state where they were driven across the border into Texas.

It was on this march that the incident occurred which I am about to narrate. We had been marching all day, in fact, from before the dawn, trying to reach the Bayou Vermillion, before the enemy could destroy the bridge. Men fell out by the scores, but still we hurried on with all the speed our wearied limbs could support. Just as it was growing too dark to see, a battery opened upon us, and there was a sharp charge of cavalry. We were hastily thrown into position to receive them, but in an instant, wheeling, they dashed across the bridge, destroying it in our very faces before it could be prevented.

The next day was Sunday and while we camped there waiting for the construction of a new bridge, about half the advance division took the opportunity to strip and go in bathing. Suddenly, without an instant's warning, a troupe of cavalry dashed down the opposite bank, and opened fire upon us. Such a spectacle never before was seen. The long roll was sounding and naked men, in every direction were making a dash for their guns, trying to dress as they ran. Some with their trousers on hind side before, didn't know whether they were advancing or retreating, and some ran the wrong way, others, with simply a shirt and cap, were trying to adjust their belts. Officers were swearing and mounted aids were dashing about, trying to make order out of confusion.

The next day we were ordered to Barry's Landing, to act as guard for a steamer coming up through the bayous with supplies, and here my story properly begins. It was April 22, 1863, and the regiment, exhausted by the conflict of the 14th, and the rapid march ensuing, following hard upon the track of Taylor's flying forces, from Franklin to Opelousas, was resting at Barry's Landing, when suddenly the whole camp was thrown into a ferment of excitement by the news that the paymaster had arrived, and would be at headquarters at 12 o'clock. Oh, welcome news to men who had been without pay for six months. How the eye glistened, and the mouth watered for the leeks and flesh-pots of Louisiana!

What visions of Sutler's delicacies opened up once more to those whom long-tick had gradually restricted to a Spartan diet of hard-tack and salt pork. What thoughts of home and the money that could be sent to loved ones far away, suffering, perhaps for lack of that very money—but how to do it,—there was the question. Here we were in the very heart of the Rebel country, two hundred miles at least from New Orleans, in the midst of an active campaign. No opportunity to send letters except such as chance threw in the way, and no certainty that such letters would ever reach their destination. Added to this, came the order to be ready to march at four o'clock. Whither we knew not, but the foe was ahead, and our late experience had taught us that life was but an uncertain element and that a Rebel bullet had a very careless way of seeking out and finding its victim. In the midst of all the bustle and confusion, the sergeant-major, William E. Simonds came tearing along through the camp excitedly inquiring for Lieut. Goodell. That estimable officer, I am sorry to say, having received no pay, owing to some informality in his papers when mustered in from second to first lieutenant, had retired into the shade of a neighboring magnolia tree, and was there meditating on the cussedness of paymasters, mustering officers, the army in general. In fact, everything looked uncommonly black and never before had he so strongly believed in universal damnation. To him, then, thus communing came Sergeant-major Simonds, and said: "You will report for duty at once to headquarters; you are directed to receive the pay of the regiment and proceed forthwith to New Orleans, there to express same home, returning to the regiment as soon thereafter as practicable."

A more detailed account of the Battle of Irish Bend is here given by Major Thomas McManus of the Twenty-fifth.

The Battle Of Irish Bend
by *General Thomas McManus*

Interesting Reminiscences of Terrible Conflict Between States

Horrors of War Graphically Told by General Thomas McManus, Who Was Major of the Twenty-fifth Regiment, Connecticut Volunteers

By request of Major Thomas McManus I will give a brief account of the country of lower Louisiana and the battle of Irish Bend, as given by him in an address at St. Patrick's Church, Collinsville, April 23, 1893, and published in the Hartford Post of the date of April 14, 1913, being fifty years to a day after that terrible conflict:

Lower Louisiana is a marshy, swampy level stretch of country with an imperceptible coast line. No one can tell where the solid ground ends or where the sea begins. Approaching from the Gulf of Mexico, you find your ship in muddy waters, and by and by you see here and there a speck of mud itself, emerging above the surface, and barely large enough to be noticed, and after a while these small islands grow together and you begin to realize that there are distinctly defined banks each side of the broad muddy channel through which you are sailing, intersected here and there by other channels extending in every direction. Twenty miles perhaps from the place where you first perceived indications of real mud, the land will be firm enough to sustain a few piles supporting a fisherman's cabin or pilot's hut. Ten miles further on and you may see signs of life and cultivation. The river banks have risen to a height of two or three feet above the level of the water. The whole southwestern part of the state is a network of bayous or natural canals, usually narrow and always deep. In summer they are mere channels of drainage, but in spring they are full to the top and often overflowing thus making a system of natural waterways that reach within a mile or two of every plantation with currents strong enough to carry the flat boats laden with sugar, cotton and corn to New Orleans, Brashear or the ports on the coast. Here and there the yet unfilled depressions in the soil form large but shallow lakes, that in the dry season are mere marshes.

This was the region where it was fated that the Twenty-fifth Connecticut regiment should make its spring campaign in 1863. Early in December we had taken possession of Baton Rouge on the Mississippi and had employed our time in practically learning the art of war, and we prided ourselves on our proficiency in drill and discipline. The winter had been, to us who were accustomed to our rigorous climate here, very mild, but we had begun to feel as early as the end of March, a foretaste of that terrible enervation that the coming summer was to bring to our men habituated to our bracing air of Connecticut. We were somewhat hardened to the little outdoor inconveniences of Louisiana. We didn't mind the mosquitoes, although they were ten times as big—a hundred times as hungry and a thousand times as vicious as those we raise here. We didn't mind the wood-ticks, and although we preferred not to have moccasin snakes in our tents, they would come sometimes. We had made a movement on Port Hudson early in March and the Twenty-fifth was in the lead, seven miles in advance of the main army. We had built a bridge over the Bayou Montecino, and had lain on our arms all night awaiting orders to attack Port Hudson, when Farragut's fleet attempted to pass the batteries. Only two of his ships, the Hartford and Albatross, succeeded, while the Richmond was disabled and the Mississippi was destroyed. We had engaged in a night skirmish with the enemy at Montecino, and had lost one man in that affair. We had retired from Port Hudson as rear guard to the column. Ours was the post of danger every time, and we had encountered the worst storm and waded through the deepest mud to be found on the continent and had bivouacked in a field almost as dry as the bottom of Lake Ontario.

With these experiences we felt like veterans, but we didn't then know how much we had to learn. On March 31, our regiment was transported to Donaldsonville, fifty miles below Baton Rouge, from there we marched beside Bayou Lefourche to Thibodeaux and then took the cars for Bayou Boeuf, and after a few days' halt, marched over to Brashear. We knew that something was going to be done, but didn't know what. We knew that somebody was going to be hurt, but didn't know who. We knew that some folks were going to get badly whipped, but it wasn't us. We were certain of that. Our superior officer and officers couldn't tell us anything or wouldn't tell us anything, and I have since come to the conclusion that they were very much like some of the wire pulling politicians of the present day. They didn't know themselves. It may be wisdom sometimes in war and in politics, not to let your followers know just what you intend to make them do, but it's mighty poor policy to let your enemy know it first.

On Saturday, April 11, 1863, the Twenty-fifth Connecticut, less than 500 strong, embarked on the steamer St. Mary, a New York and Galveston liner built to carry 500 passengers at a pinch, but loaded on this occasion with 2,500.

We were crowded. We were just packed as close as the squares of hardtack in the bread barrels, closer than sardines in a box. So close that we didn't have room to sweat. We had to hold our haversacks that contained three days' rations of sheet iron biscuit and salt pork, on our heads. The decks were covered with a solid mass of humanity. We cast off the lines and our ship slowly steamed up the Atchafalaya, now and then rubbing the banks so closely that we could grasp the branches of the magnolia and cypress that formed one green, unbroken fringe on either side.

General Emory's division of Banks' army had already moved up the west bank of the Bayou Teche, fighting its way against the fresh active troops of Dick Taylor. We were in General Cuvier Grover's division, and were expected to sail up Grand Lake and disembark at Hutchins Landing, where the Teche, by a sharp bend, comes within two miles of the lake; and on this narrow strip was the only road (as we supposed) over which an army and especially artillery and baggage wagons could pass. During Saturday night, Sunday, and Sunday night we were crammed, stifled and suffocated on the steamer's deck, as she slowly felt her way up through the muddy and shallow water of Grand Lake. To have run aground would have been disastrous failure to the whole expedition. Towing astern were large flat bottomed scows, loaded with artillery and artillery men. These were indispensable when on Monday morning we found that it was impossible for our ship to approach within half a mile of the shore, and the men were ferried from the steamer to the bank, where a lively little skirmish was going on between some Confederate scouts and Col. Dick Holcomb's First Louisiana. General Grover was ahead of us, smoking as usual, and in his excitement he had lighted a second cigar and was vigorously puffing and pulling at both corners of his mouth. He grasped Colonel Bissell by the hands in welcome, as the colonel leaped from the boat. No delay now, forward! A few hundred yards brought us to the woods. Our skirmishers went through and we soon had orders to follow. We halted at the open clearing on the other side and awaited to hear from General Grover, who had gone ahead to reconnoitre. Off to the southwest we could hear the artillery firing that told us that Emory's forces were having a fierce fight with Taylor's, only a few miles away. Another half mile advance, another halt and again forward. Just as the sun was going down we crossed the Teche over a drawbridge and filed into the main road and skirted the fertile plantation of Madame Porter. This stately, handsome lady, surrounded by scores of fat, happy looking and well clad slaves, stood in front of her elegant home and sadly watched us as we passed. No farm in Connecticut, however carefully supervised, could show better evidences of wise management than this. The houses, fences, granaries, fields, slave quarters and everything, were in perfect order—all were clean, whole, and systematically arranged. The fertile soil seemed to proclaim audibly to our farmer boys its readiness to give back a hundred and fifty fold for its seed and care. The shades of night were falling fast when we filed into an open ploughed field and moved by the right of companies to the rear into columns. We halted, stacked arms, ate hardtack and raw pork, and rested. The ground was soft alluvial; mist came with sundown and rain came with the darkness, and the surface of the earth was soon transformed into soft, deep mud. There was no noise, no music, no laughter. Every man knew instinctively that the morrow's sun would shine upon many a corpse. Our generals had believed, and we had hoped, that as soon as Taylor would find this large force of ours suddenly occupying the road in his rear, he would submit to the inevitable and surrender, but he had not surrendered and would not surrender, and that meant a fierce engagement for us. As soon as darkness had set in, General Grover sent up rockets to apprise General Banks of our position. Sleep was impossible. Colonel Bissell and I sat on a bread box, back to back, our feet in the soft mud and our clothing gradually absorbing the rain that fell steadily upon us. The hours dragged slowly along, and before daybreak our men were aroused, made a hasty breakfast, and in the grey of the morning we set out in advance of our brigade that consisted of the Thirteenth and Twenty-fifth Connecticut, Twenty-sixth Maine and One Hundred and Fifty-ninth New York, Colonel Birge in command. We were all on foot, officers and men alike. Our horses, baggage, and impediments had been left at Brashear to follow the column of General Emory.

For a mile below Madame Porter's plantation the Bayou Teche runs to the southeast and then turns sharply to the southwest towards Franklin, a very pretty village, some five miles below. The road following the sinuosities of the stream runs parallel to it, with a strip of a few rods in width between. We enter an immense cane field, its furrows in line with the road. On the west the field was bounded by a rail fence, beyond which arose a dense wood of magnolias, cotton wood and semi-tropical trees looking like a long green wall. Far in front arose a transverse wall like to the first, and making at its intersection a right angle. At this angle, the road entered the wood, near to the ground this forest was absolutely impenetrable to the sight, by reason of the suffocating growth of briars, vines, palmettos and underbrush. We ought to have occupied these woods the night before, and have hemmed the enemy in the open beyond. We now knew that the foe was in our immediate front. We marched down the field, the right wing deployed as skirmishers, the left wing in close battalion front following a few rods in its rear. By and by a puff of smoke from the green wall in front of us and a second or two afterwards the crack of a rifle. The fight had begun; another puff, another crack then more and more, multiplying as we approached. The bend in the road is now disclosed, the enemy's skirmishers disappeared from our front to reappear in greater numbers on our right. Our skirmishers were called in and we changed front forward on first company, moved down towards the wood on the right, and halting about 150 yards from the fence, we poured a volley into the enemy's ranks. The One Hundred and Fifty-ninth New York came down into line on our left, the Twenty-sixth Maine formed in our rear, the Thirteenth Connecticut took position on our extreme left occupying both sides of the road. The canes of the previous year's sugar crop stood in the field and their volley firing didn't get our range, and our lines were parallel with the furrows. The enemy's shot rattled through the dry stalks, crackling like hail against the windows. The enemy were armed with the smooth bores, every cartridge charged with a bullet and three buck shot, while our regiment was armed with Enfield rifles and so the Rebels, man for man were giving us four shots to our one in return.

The enemy had an immense advantage in position and the conviction was stealing over us that they had the advantage in numbers also. Our men had warmed up to their work; every soldier had long before drained the last drop from his canteen; the sun was rising high and hot and we learned then that there is no thirst so burning and terrible as that which seizes upon the soldier in battle. Every command given by the Confederate officers was as distinctly heard by us as if given in our own companies. Their lines already extended far beyond our flank and their oft-repeated cheers told us how rapidly their ranks were being increased by new arrivals. Suddenly a loud cheer from the Rebels; then the thundering war of a field piece, and in an instant from overhead came a crack, with a rain of iron fragments as a shell exploded right over our line; another roar, a crack, and iron shower and we see to our dismay two brazen guns admirably served, trained directly upon us pouring shell grape and cannister into our ranks, while their musketry fire grew hotter and fiercer than ever. Our men were nearing the end of their supply of ammunition. If the Confederates had charged upon us at this time they would have annihilated our brigade!

Wounded men were crawling to the rear, where Dr. Wood, with McGill and his assistants, stood under their yellow hospital flag. Col. Bissell's voice rang clear and cheerful as ever, but his face was anxious. Down into the field came Bradley's battery at a gallop and very soon their guns were answering the enemy's. Up went Bissell's sword, with a joyful cheer, as he shouted to Lieutenant Dewey "There's music in the air!" Our re-enforcements of artillery gave us renewed spirits but it was in vain to hope for victory against a better posted and overwhelming force.

Hurrah! At last, here comes Dwight's brigade. But suddenly, as if evoked by magic, arose a long gray line of armed men. They had crawled unperceived through the thick high canes and our first intimation of their presence was a murderous volley raking our lines from right to left. Bradley's battery was retreating to the rear, with nine of his men dead or disabled on the ground. "Fall back!" shouted the Colonel. Our right wing was in confusion and disorder. The left wing fell back steadily but only for a few rods, the advancing brigade opened ranks to let us pass and we halted and we formed in its rear and sank exhausted on the ground anxiously watching the fate of our gallant supporters. Ninety-five of our brave boys were dead or wounded, nine-tenths of them by that terrible flank fire. In our last five minutes on the field lay the lifeless bodies of Captain Hayden and young Lieutenant Dewey. Arnold and Wilson lay dead. Lieutenant Oliver had been carried from the field with a bullet in his head, to linger for six weeks before death came to his relief. Lieutenant Waterman stood resolute at the head of his company with his arm bandaged and bleeding. Lieutenant Harkness limped painfully along disabled by a spent bullet. John H. Hunt of Coventry had his side torn open by an explosion, and his sufferings were intense. It was strange that he didn't die instantly, yet he lingered for seven days. John Martin fell dead at the final volley from the Rebels. Old Button was carried off the field, his shoulder mangled, the bone splintered in the socket and with but a few days more of life before him. Graham lay dead. Brooks, the tall young sapling whose extraordinary height made him a conspicuous mark, had fallen pierced by a dozen bullets. Sergeant Taft, with a shattered arm, was carried off the field by his lieutenant. Brennan, Gray, Prindle, Lawton, Holden and Carlos Bissell lay dead. Cook lay mortally wounded. Lieutenant Banning was crippled for life. John Thompson of Ellington had a bullet hole through his jaws, incapacitating him for further service. Goodwin, Lincoln, and Avery Brown were also seriously injured in this battle, as were also many others whom I cannot name.

How the Pay of a Regiment Was Carried to New Orleans
by Lieutenant Henry Hill Goodell

"Gone at once were my sulks, vanished in an instant my ill-humor, black demons and everything. Though I could not help wondering how in all creation I was going to perform a journey of several hundred miles that would occupy a week at least without a cent of money in my pocket, a clerk was detailed to assist me, and for the next hour I counted money over a hard-tack box, jamming it away instantly into my haversack while he entered in a little book the amount received from each person, the sums given to pay for its expressage, and the addresses to which it was to be sent. No time to make change. Even sums were given, counted, and tucked away with rapidity. At the landing was a little stern-wheel steamer, captured from the Rebels, which was to leave from Brashear City in an hour or two. The sick and wounded were hastily transferred to it, and as the regiment marched off, I stepped on board with my precious haversack, now swollen out to unwonted proportions. Not a state-room, not a berth was to be had. There was no safe in which I could deposit valuables. Too many knew what I was carrying, and I dared not for an instant lift the weight from my shoulder or to remove my sword and pistol. Like Mary's lamb, where'er I went, the haversack was sure to go.

"Never shall I forget the beauty of that sail, and but for the feeling of distrust and suspicion that made me look upon every man that approached me, as a personal enemy, I should have thoroughly enjoyed it. We were dropping down one of those little bayous that intersect the state in every direction. The spring freshets had swollen the stream and set its waters far back into the forests that lined its banks on either side. Festoons of Spanish moss, drooped like a mourning veil from bough to bough. Running vines with bright colored sprays of flowers twined in and out among the branches of the trees. The purple passion flowers flung out its starry blossoms to the world, the sign and symbol of the suffering Saviour. While the air was heavy with the scent of magnolias and yellow jassamine. Crested herons, snowy white, rose from the water, and stretching their long necks and legs out into a straight line with their bodies winged their flight above the tree-tops. Pelicans displayed their ungainly forms, as they snapped at the passing fish and neatly laid them away for future reference in their pouches. Strange birds of gaudy plumage flew from side to side, harshly screaming as they hid themselves in the dense foliage. Huge alligators sunned themselves along the shore, or showed their savage muzzles, as they slowly swam across our path. Frequently at some sharp bend, it seemed as if we must certainly run ashore, but the engine being reversed, the current would swing the bow around and by dint of hard pushing with poles, we would escape the threatened danger, and start again in our new direction. Sunset faded into twilight, and twilight deepened into the darkness, and silence of a Southern night, and then the entire loneliness and responsibility of my position suddenly overwhelmed me. I had no place to lie down, and hardly dared sit for fear of falling asleep. It seemed as though I could hear whispers behind me, and every now and then I would catch myself nodding, and wake with a cold chill running up and down the small of my back, as I felt sure that some unlawful hand was tampering with my burden. With the coming of the dawn, I breathed more freely, and the day seemed interminable, and it became a very burden to live. Twice we broke down and tying up to a friendly tree repaired the damage. Night came again and found us still miles away from our destination. It was horrible. I walked the deck, drank coffee, pinched myself. 'Oh, if I can only keep awake!' I kept repeating to myself. But at 2 o'clock in the morning we broke down again, with the prospect of being detained some hours. I knew that if I did not reach Brashear City by 7 o'clock I should be another dreary day on the way, and lose my connections with the single train for New Orleans. Time was an element of importance, for I should lose the mail steamer for New York and be delayed in my return to the regiment which I had left in the heart of Louisiana marching onward—I knew not where, but with faces set toward the North.

"Finding that we were distant from eight to twelve miles across country according to the different estimates, I determined to make the attempt to reach it on foot. Any danger, anything seemed preferable to staying on the boat. With the first breaking of the dawn, when I could get my bearings, I slung myself ashore. A private in my regiment discharged for disability, begged to accompany me. With weapons ready for instant use, we pushed along, afraid of our own shadows, looking for a lurking foe behind every bush, and when some startled bird suddenly broke from its cover, the heart of one at least stood still for a moment and then throbbed away like a steam engine. If a man was seen, however distant, we dropped to cover and watched him out of sight before we dared move. For the first mile our progress was very slow—now wading through water, now sinking in the mud, floundering about as best we could, while the mosquitoes and gnats settled down on us in swarms, uttering a triumphant buzzing as though they recognized the fact that they had fresher blood to feed on than that offered by the fever-stricken victims of the South and were determined to make the most of their opportunity. But the open country once reached we lengthened out our steps and struck into a six-mile gait. Soon my companion began to falter and fall behind. But I could not afford to wait, telling him I presumed he was all right, but I could not run any risks, I stood him up by a tree and taking his gun, marched off a couple hundred yards, then laying it down I shouted to him to come on, and, setting off at the top of my speed, saw him no more. Whether he ever reached his destination or whether wandering helplessly along—he was swooped down upon by some gorilla, and led away to starve and die in a Southern prison, I did not learn for many years. At the last reunion I attended, I was called upon to respond to the toast 'The Postal Service of the Regiment, and What You Know About It,' and at the conclusion of my remarks, a stout grizzled veteran grasped my hand and said: 'Look, I'm glad to see you. I thought it pretty cruel to leave me alone in Dixie, but you had warned me beforehand and I guess you were right.'

"Avoiding the houses and striking across the fields, I made the last part of my way at full run, and drew up panting and exhausted at Berwick Bay shortly after six. Not a moment was to be lost. I could hear the engine puffing across the waters. Shouting to a darkey, who seemed to rise up preternaturally out of the ground, I ordered him to row me over; and a more astonished man I think I never saw than he was. When on reaching the opposite shore, with but ten minutes to spare, I bolted from the boat without a word, and started on the run for headquarters. The general was asleep, but an aid carried in my pass, signed by General Banks, brought it back countersigned, and in five minutes more I was aboard the train moving on to New Orleans.

"Of this part of my journey I have a very indistinct remembrance. My impression is that I dozed whenever I sat down, and I was so tired I could hardly stand. I had had nothing to eat since the night before and was faint and exhausted with hunger, and my exertions. Nothing but the special training my class had taken in gymnasium during the previous year, for just such an emergency, pulled me through the long run and long fast following it. It was only a run of 100 miles but I think we must have stopped to wood and water at every cotton-wood grove and swamp along the way; and I remember at one of these periodical stops, going out on the platform, and falling into an altercation with a little red-headed doctor, who, whether he had scented my secret or not, with that divine intuition for discovering the hidden, peculiar to the craft, had made himself officially offensive to me, and now, wanted to borrow my revolver to shoot a copper-head that lay coiled up by the side of the track. Refused in that, he next wanted to examine my sword, and when under some trifling pretext, I abruptly left him and going inside the car, sat down as near as possible to a bluff-looking lieutenant, whose honest face seemed a true indication of character, his wrath knew no bounds and was quite outspoken. 'Peace to your injured spirit, oh fiery-headed son of Esculapius, if you are still in the land of the living! I here tender you my humble apologies. Doubtless you intended nothing more than to compare the efficiency of my leaden balls with one of your own deadly Bolouses or to see how my cleaver compared in sharpness with one of your own little scalpels.' But at that particular time I should have been suspicious of my own brother had he desired to inspect or use my arms.

"It was late Saturday afternoon when, tired and faint, I landed in the city. Pushing straight to the office of the Adams Express Company, I told them I had the pay of a regiment to express home and wanted five or six hundred money order blanks and envelopes. I shall never forget the look of incredulity with which the clerk looked at me. I was dirty and ragged, just in from the front, with no shoulder-straps, for we had been ordered to remove them and diminish the chances of being picked off by the sharpshooters but had sword and pistol and an innocent looking haversack hanging at my side. However, he said not a word, but passed over the papers.

"My next adventure was in a saloon where on calling for a drink of whiskey, I was informed that they were not allowed to sell to privates. On my throwing down my pass signed by Gen. Banks, the courteous keeper acknowledged his mistake, and invited me to take something at his expense. Immediately after supper to which—it is hardly necessary to say—I was accompanied by that confounded haversack, I fairly loathed it by this time—I retired to my room, locked the door and went to work. Excitement kept me up and by 2 o'clock everything was done. The money counted and placed in the envelopes, and the blanks filled out, and the footing correctly made. Then, only did I know how much I had carried with me and how precious were the contents of my haversack. Barricading my door, with the table, and wedging a chair in between it and the bed, I thrust the haversack between the sheets, slid in after it, laid my revolver by the pillow, and in an instant was sound asleep. The next morning on going down to breakfast I innocently inquired of the clerk in the office if he would give me a receipt for valuables. 'Certainly,' was his smiling rejoinder. 'For how much?' 'Twenty-four thousand three hundred and forty-six dollars,' I replied and half opening my haversack, showed him the bundles of express envelopes, explaining that it was the pay of a regiment. 'Where did you keep this last night?' was the next question. 'In my room.' 'You d—— fool, it might have been stolen.' 'True, but I thought it would be safe enough and besides I did not know how much I had.'

"Breakfast over I repaired at once to the office of the express company and by noon, with my receipts in my pocket, I stepped forth, feeling as if a gigantic load had rolled from my shoulders.

"Of my journey back there is no need to speak; suffice it to say that two or three weeks thereafter, one night as the sun was setting, I stood with beating heart on the levee, outside of Simsport on the Red River, waiting for the coming of the regiment on its march down from Alexandria. Column after column passed and still I waited. But suddenly I caught the roll of drums and there came a dimness over my eyes, for I recognized familiar forms. The colonel riding at the head, the little drum major, the colors and each well known face. As they came up I saluted, someone recognized me, and called my name. Instantly the cry, 'Lieutenant Goodell has come!' swept down the line, and with one mighty shout, the boys welcomed back the bearer of their pay. That night I went from camp-fire to camp-fire and gave to each orderly sergeant the receipts for his company. Of all that money, only one envelope went astray, and the express company made good the loss."

Hospital Sketches
By Louisa May Alcott

THE LATE LOUISA MAY ALCOTT.—From a Photograph.—[See Page 187.]

Chapter I Obtaining Supplies

"I want something to do."

This remark being addressed to the world in general, no one in particular felt it their duty to reply; so I repeated it to the smaller world about me, received the following suggestions, and settled the matter by answering my own inquiry, as people are apt to do when very much in earnest.

"Write a book," quoth the author of my being.

"Don't know enough, sir. First live, then write."

"Try teaching again," suggested my mother.

"No thank you, ma'am, ten years of that is enough."

"Take a husband like my Darby, and fulfill your mission," said sister Joan, home on a visit.

"Can't afford expensive luxuries, Mrs. Coobiddy."

"Turn actress, and immortalize your name," said sister Vashti, striking an attitude.

"I won't."

"Go nurse the soldiers," said my young brother, Tom, panting for "the tented field."

"I will!"

So far, very good. Here was the will—now for the way. At first sight not a foot of it appeared, but that didn't matter, for the Periwinkles are a hopeful race; their crest is an anchor, with three cock-a-doodles crowing atop. They all wear rose-colored spectacles, and are lineal descendants of the inventor of aerial architecture. An hour's conversation on the subject set the whole family in a blaze of enthusiasm. A model hospital was erected, and each member had accepted an honorable post therein. The paternal P. was chaplain, the maternal P. was matron, and all the youthful P.s filled the pod of futurity with achievements whose brilliancy eclipsed the glories of the present and the past. Arriving at this satisfactory conclusion, the meeting adjourned, and the fact that Miss Tribulation was available as army nurse went abroad on the wings of the wind.

In a few days a townswoman heard of my desire, approved of it, and brought about an interview with one of the sisterhood which I wished to join, who was at home on a furlough, and able and willing to satisfy all inquiries. A morning chat with Miss General S.—we hear no end of Mrs. Generals, why not a Miss?—produced three results: I felt that I could do the work, was offered a place, and accepted it, promising not to desert, but stand ready to march on Washington at an hour's notice.

A few days were necessary for the letter containing my request and recommendation to reach headquarters, and another, containing my commission, to return; therefore no time was to be lost; and heartily thanking my pair of friends, I tore home through the December slush as if the rebels were after me, and like many another recruit, burst in upon my family with the announcement—

"I've enlisted!"

An impressive silence followed. Tom, the irrepressible, broke it with a slap on the shoulder and the graceful compliment—

"Old Trib, you're a trump!"

"Thank you; then I'll take something:" which I did, in the shape of dinner, reeling off my news at the rate of three dozen words to a mouthful; and as every one else talked equally fast, and all together, the scene was most inspiring.

As boys going to sea immediately become nautical in speech, walk as if they already had their "sea legs" on, and shiver their timbers on all possible occasions, so I turned military at once, called my dinner my rations, saluted all new comers, and ordered a dress parade that very afternoon. Having reviewed every rag I possessed, I detailed some for picket duty while airing over the fence; some to the sanitary influences of the wash-tub; others to mount guard in the trunk; while the weak and wounded went to the Workbasket Hospital, to be made ready for active service again. To this squad I devoted myself for a week; but all was done, and I had time to get powerfully impatient before the letter came. It did arrive however, and brought a disappointment along with its good will and friendliness, for it told me that the place in the Armory Hospital that I supposed I was to take, was already filled, and a much less desirable one at Hurly-burly House was offered instead.

"That's just your luck, Trib. I'll tote your trunk up garret for you again; for of course you won't go," Tom remarked, with the disdainful pity which small boys affect when they get into their teens. I was wavering in my secret soul, but that settled the matter, and I crushed him on the spot with martial brevity—

"It is now one; I shall march at six."

I have a confused recollection of spending the afternoon in pervading the house like an executive whirlwind, with my family swarming after me, all working, talking, prophesying and lamenting, while I packed my "go-abroady" possessions, tumbled the rest into two big boxes, danced on the lids till they shut, and gave them in charge, with the direction,—

"If I never come back, make a bonfire of them."

Then I choked down a cup of tea, generously salted instead of sugared, by some agitated relative, shouldered my knapsack—it was only a traveling bag, but do let me preserve the unities—hugged my family three times all round without a vestige of unmanly emotion, till a certain dear old lady broke down upon my neck, with a despairing sort of wail—

"Oh, my dear, my dear, how can I let you go?"

"I'll stay if you say so, mother."

"But I don't; go, and the Lord will take care of you."

Much of the Roman matron's courage had gone into the Yankee matron's composition, and, in spite of her tears, she would have sent ten sons to the war, had she possessed them, as freely as she sent one daughter, smiling and flapping on the door-step till I vanished, though the eyes that followed me were very dim, and the handkerchief she waved was very wet.

My transit from The Gables to the village depot was a funny mixture of good wishes and good byes, mud-puddles and shopping. A December twilight is not the most cheering time to enter upon a somewhat perilous enterprise, and, but for the presence of Vashti and neighbor Thorn, I fear that I might have added a drop of the briny to the native moisture of—

"The town I left behind me;"

though I'd no thought of giving out: oh, bless you, no! When the engine screeched "Here we are," I clutched my escort in a fervent embrace, and skipped into the car with as blithe a farewell as if going on a bridal tour—though I believe brides don't usually wear cavernous black bonnets and fuzzy brown coats, with a hair-brush, a pair of rubbers, two books, and a bag of ginger-bread distorting the pockets of the same. If I thought that any one would believe it, I'd boldly state that I slept from C. to B., which would simplify matters immensely; but as I know they wouldn't, I'll confess that the head under the funereal coal-hod fermented with all manner of high thoughts and heroic purposes "to do or die,"—perhaps both; and the heart under the fuzzy brown coat felt very tender with the memory of the dear old lady, probably sobbing over her army socks and the loss of her topsy-turvy Trib. At this juncture I took the veil, and what I did behind it is nobody's business; but I maintain that the soldier who cries when his mother says "Good bye," is the boy to fight best, and die bravest, when the time comes, or go back to her better than he went.

Till nine o'clock I trotted about the city streets, doing those last errands which no woman would even go to heaven without attempting, if she could. Then I went to my usual refuge, and, fully intending to keep awake, as a sort of vigil appropriate to the occasion, fell fast asleep and dreamed propitious dreams till my rosy-faced cousin waked me with a kiss.

A bright day smiled upon my enterprise, and at ten I reported myself to my General, received last instructions and no end of the sympathetic encouragement which women give, in look, touch, and tone more effectually than in words. The next step was to get a free pass to Washington, for I'd no desire to waste my substance on railroad companies when "the boys" needed even a spinster's mite. A friend of mine had procured such a pass, and I was bent on doing likewise, though I had to face the president of the railroad to accomplish it. I'm a bashful individual, though I can't get any one to believe it; so it cost me a great effort to poke about the Worcester depot till the right door appeared, then walk into a room containing several gentlemen, and blunder out my request in a high state of stammer and blush. Nothing could have been more courteous than this dreaded President, but it was evident that I had made as absurd a demand as if I had asked for the nose off his respectable face. He referred me to the Governor at the State House, and I backed out, leaving him no doubt to regret that such mild maniacs were left at large. Here was a Scylla and Charybdis business: as if a President wasn't trying enough, without the Governor of Massachusetts and the hub of the hub piled on top of that. "I never can do it," thought I. "Tom will hoot at you if you don't," whispered the inconvenient little voice that is always goading people to the performance of disagreeable duties, and always appeals to the most effective agent to produce the proper result. The idea of allowing any boy that ever wore a felt basin and a shoddy jacket with a microscopic tail, to crow over me, was preposterous, so giving myself a mental slap for such faint-heartedness, I streamed away across the Common, wondering if I ought to say "your Honor," or simply "Sir," and decided upon the latter, fortifying myself with recollections of an evening in a charming green library, where I beheld the Governor placidly consuming oysters, and laughing as if Massachusetts was a myth, and he had no heavier burden on his shoulders than his host's handsome hands.

Like an energetic fly in a very large cobweb, I struggled through the State House, getting into all the wrong rooms and none of the right, till I turned desperate, and went into one, resolving not to come out till I'd made somebody hear and answer me. I suspect that of all the wrong places I had blundered into, this was the most so. But I didn't care; and, though the apartment was full of soldiers, surgeons, starers, and spittoons, I cornered a perfectly incapable person, and proceeded to pump for information with the following result:

"Was the Governor anywhere about?"

No, he wasn't.

"Could he tell me where to look?"

No, he couldn't.

"Did he know anything about free passes?"

No, he didn't.

"Was there any one there of whom I could inquire?"

Not a person.

"Did he know of any place where information could be obtained?"

Not a place.

"Could he throw the smallest gleam of light upon the matter, in any way?"

Not a ray.

I am naturally irascible, and if I could have shaken this negative gentleman vigorously, the relief would have been immense. The prejudices of society forbidding this mode of redress, I merely glowered at him; and, before my wrath found vent in words, my General appeared, having seen me from an opposite window, and come to know what I was about. At her command the languid gentleman woke up, and troubled himself to remember that Major or Sergeant or something Mc K. knew all about the tickets, and his office was in Milk Street. I perked up instanter, and then, as if the exertion was too much for him, what did this animated wet blanket do but add—

"I think Mc K. may have left Milk Street, now, and I don't know where he has gone."

"Never mind; the new comers will know where he has moved to, my dear, so don't be discouraged; and if you don't succeed, come to me, and we will see what to do next," said my General.

I blessed her in a fervent manner and a cool hall, fluttered round the corner, and bore down upon Milk Street, bent on discovering Mc K. if such a being was to be found. He wasn't, and the ignorance of the neighborhood was really pitiable. Nobody knew anything, and after tumbling over bundles of leather, bumping against big boxes, being nearly annihilated by descending bales, and sworn at by aggravated truckmen, I finally elicited the advice to look for Mc K. in Haymarket Square. Who my informant was I've really forgotten; for, having hailed several busy gentlemen, some one of them fabricated this delusive quietus for the perturbed spirit, who instantly departed to the sequestered locality he named. If I had been in search of the Koh-i-noor diamond I should have been as likely to find it there as any vestige of Mc K. I stared at signs, inquired in shops, invaded an eating house, visited the recruiting tent in the middle of the Square, made myself a nuisance generally, and accumulated mud enough to retard another Nile. All in vain: and I mournfully turned my face toward the General's, feeling that I should be forced to enrich the railroad company after all; when, suddenly, I beheld that admirable young man, brother-in-law Darby Coobiddy, Esq. I arrested him with a burst of news, and wants, and woes, which caused his manly countenance to lose its usual repose.

"Oh, my dear boy, I'm going to Washington at five, and I can't find the free ticket man, and there won't be time to see Joan, and I'm so tired and cross I don't know what to do; and will you help me, like a cherub as you are?"

"Oh, yes, of course. I know a fellow who will set us right," responded Darby, mildly excited, and darting into some kind of an office, held counsel with an invisible angel, who sent him out radiant. "All serene. I've got him. I'll see you through the business, and then get Joan from the Dove Cote in time to see you off."

I'm a woman's rights woman, and if any man had offered help in the morning, I should have condescendingly refused it, sure that I could do everything as well, if not better, myself. My strong-mindedness had rather abated since then, and I was now quite ready to be a "timid trembler," if necessary.

Dear me! how easily Darby did it all: he just asked one question, received an answer, tucked me under his arm, and in ten minutes I stood in the presence of Mc K., the Desired.

"Now my troubles are over," thought I, and as usual was direfully mistaken.

"You will have to get a pass from Dr. H., in Temple Place, before I can give you a pass, madam," answered Mc K., as blandly as if he wasn't carrying desolation to my soul. Oh, indeed! why didn't he send me to Dorchester Heights, India Wharf, or Bunker Hill Monument, and done with it? Here I was, after a morning's tramp, down in some place about Dock Square, and was told to step to Temple Place. Nor was that all; he might as well have asked me to catch a hummingbird, toast a salamander, or call on the man in the moon, as find a Doctor at home at the busiest hour of the day. It was a blow; but weariness had extinguished enthusiasm, and resignation clothed me as a garment. I sent Darby for Joan, and doggedly paddled off, feeling that mud was my native element, and quite sure that the evening papers would announce the appearance of the Wandering Jew, in feminine habiliments.

"Is Dr. H. in?"

"No, mum, he aint."

Of course he wasn't; I knew that before I asked: and, considering it all in the light of a hollow mockery, added:

"When will he probably return?"

If the damsel had said, "ten to-night," I should have felt a grim satisfaction, in the fulfillment of my own dark prophecy; but she said, "At two, mum;" and I felt it a personal insult.

"I'll call, then. Tell him my business is important:" with which mysteriously delivered message I departed, hoping that I left her consumed with curiosity; for mud rendered me an object of interest.

By way of resting myself, I crossed the Common, for the third time, bespoke the carriage, got some lunch, packed my purchases, smoothed my plumage, and was back again, as the clock struck two. The Doctor hadn't come yet; and I was morally certain that he would not, till, having waited till the last minute, I was driven to buy a ticket, and, five minutes after the irrevocable deed was done, he would be at my service, with all manner of helpful documents and directions. Everything goes by contraries with me; so, having made up my mind to be disappointed, of course I wasn't; for, presently, in walked Dr. H., and no sooner had he heard my errand, and glanced at my credentials, than he said, with the most engaging readiness:

"I will give you the order, with pleasure, madam."

Words cannot express how soothing and delightful it was to find, at last, somebody who could do what I wanted, without sending me from Dan to Beersheba, for a dozen other to do something else first. Peace descended, like oil, upon the ruffled waters of my being, as I sat listening to the busy scratch of his pen; and, when he turned about, giving me not only the order, but a paper of directions wherewith to smooth away all difficulties between Boston and Washington, I felt as did poor Christian when the Evangelist gave him the scroll, on the safe side of the Slough of Despond. I've no doubt many dismal nurses have inflicted themselves upon the worthy gentleman since then; but I am sure none have been more kindly helped, or are more grateful, than T. P.; for that short interview added another to the many pleasant associations that already surround his name.

Feeling myself no longer a "Martha Struggles," but a comfortable young woman, with plain sailing before her, and the worst of the voyage well over, I once more presented myself to the valuable Mc K. The order was read, and certain printed papers, necessary to be filled out, were given a young gentleman—no, I prefer to say Boy, with a scornful emphasis upon the word, as the only means of revenge now left me. This Boy, instead of doing his duty with the diligence so charming in the young, loitered and lounged, in a manner which proved his education to have been sadly neglected in the—

"How doth the little busy bee,"

direction. He stared at me, gaped out of the window, ate peanuts, and gossiped with his neighbors—Boys, like himself, and all penned in a row, like colts at a Cattle Show. I don't imagine he knew the anguish he was inflicting; for it was nearly three, the train left at five, and I had my ticket to get, my dinner to eat, my blessed sister to see, and the depot to reach, if I didn't die of apoplexy. Meanwhile, Patience certainly had her perfect work that day, and I hope she enjoyed the job more than I did.

Having waited some twenty minutes, it pleased this reprehensible Boy to make various marks and blots on my documents, toss them to a venerable creature of sixteen, who delivered them to me with such paternal directions, that it only needed a pat on the head and an encouraging—"Now run home to your Ma, little girl, and mind the crossings, my dear," to make the illusion quite perfect.

Why I was sent to a steamboat office for car tickets, is not for me to say, though I went as meekly as I should have gone to the Probate Court, if sent. A fat, easy gentleman gave me several bits of paper, with coupons attached, with a warning not to separate them, which instantly inspired me with a yearning to pluck them apart, and see what came of it. But, remembering through what fear and tribulation I had obtained them, I curbed Satan's promptings, and, clutching my prize, as if it were my pass to the Elysian Fields, I hurried home. Dinner was rapidly consumed; Joan enlightened, comforted, and kissed;

the dearest of apple-faced cousins hugged; the kindest of apple-faced cousins' fathers subjected to the same process; and I mounted the ambulance, baggage-wagon, or anything you please but hack, and drove away, too tired to feel excited, sorry, or glad.

Chapter II A Forward Movement.

As travellers like to give their own impressions of a journey, though every inch of the way may have been described a half a dozen times before, I add some of the notes made by the way, hoping that they will amuse the reader, and convince the skeptical that such a being as Nurse Periwinkle does exist, that she really did go to Washington, and that these Sketches are not romance.

New York Train—Seven P.M.—Spinning along to take the boat at New London. Very comfortable; much gingerbread, and Mrs. C.'s fine pear, which deserves honorable mention, because my first loneliness was comforted by it, and pleasant recollections of both kindly sender and bearer. Look much at Dr. H.'s paper of directions—put my tickets in every conceivable place, that they may be get-at-able, and finish by losing them entirely. Suffer agonies till a compassionate neighbor pokes them out of a crack with his pen-knife. Put them in the inmost corner of my purse, that in the deepest recesses of my pocket, pile a collection of miscellaneous articles atop, and pin up the whole. Just get composed, feeling that I've done my best to keep them safely, when the Conductor appears, and I'm forced to rout them all out again, exposing my precautions, and getting into a flutter at keeping the man waiting. Finally, fasten them on the seat before me, and keep one eye steadily upon the yellow torments, till I forget all about them, in chat with the gentleman who shares my seat. Having heard complaints of the absurd way in which American women become images of petrified propriety, if addressed by strangers, when traveling alone, the inborn perversity of my nature causes me to assume an entirely opposite style of deportment; and, finding my companion hails from Little Athens, is acquainted with several of my three hundred and sixty-five cousins, and in every way a respectable and respectful member of society, I put my bashfulness in my pocket, and plunge into a long conversation on the war, the weather, music, Carlyle, skating, genius, hoops, and the immortality of the soul.

Ten P.M.—Very sleepy. Nothing to be seen outside, but darkness made visible; nothing inside but every variety of bunch into which the human form can be twisted, rolled, or "massed," as Miss Prescott says of her jewels. Every man's legs sprawl drowsily, every woman's head (but mine,) nods, till it finally settles on somebody's shoulder, a new proof of the truth of the everlasting oak and vine simile; children fret; lovers whisper; old folks snore, and somebody privately imbibes brandy, when the lamps go out. The penetrating perfume rouses the multitude, causing some to start up, like war horses at the smell of powder. When the lamps are relighted, every one laughs, sniffs, and looks inquiringly at his neighbor—every one but a stout gentleman, who, with well-gloved hands folded upon his broad-cloth rotundity, sleeps on impressively. Had he been innocent, he would have waked up; for, to slumber in that babe-like manner, with a car full of giggling, staring, sniffing humanity, was simply preposterous. Public suspicion was down upon him at once. I doubt if the appearance of a flat black bottle with a label would have settled the matter more effectually than did the over dignified and profound repose of this short-sighted being. His moral neck-cloth, virtuous boots, and pious attitude availed him nothing, and it was well he kept his eyes shut, for "Humbug!" twinkled at him from every window-pane, brass nail and human eye around him.

Eleven P.M.—In the boat "City of Boston," escorted thither by my car acquaintance, and deposited in the cabin. Trying to look as if the greater portion of my life had been passed on board boats, but painfully conscious that I don't know the first thing; so sit bolt upright, and stare about me till I hear one lady say to another—"We must secure our berths at once;" whereupon I dart at one, and, while leisurely taking off my cloak, wait to discover what the second move may be. Several ladies draw the curtains that hang in a semi-circle before each nest—instantly I whisk mine smartly together, and then peep out to see what next. Gradually, on hooks above the blue and yellow drapery, appear the coats and bonnets of my neighbors, while their boots and shoes, in every imaginable attitude, assert themselves below, as if their owners had committed suicide in a body. A violent creaking, scrambling, and fussing, causes the fact that people are going regularly to bed to dawn upon my mind. Of course they are; and so am I—but pause at the seventh pin, remembering that, as I was born to be drowned, an eligible opportunity now presents itself; and, having twice escaped a watery grave, the third immersion will certainly extinguish my vital spark. The boat is new, but if it ever intends to blow up, spring a leak, catch afire, or be run into, it will do the deed to-night, because I'm here to fulfill my destiny. With tragic calmness I resign myself, replace my pins, lash my purse and papers together, with my handkerchief, examine the saving circumference of my hoop, and look about me for any means of deliverance when the moist moment shall arrive; for I've no intention of folding my hands and bubbling to death without an energetic splashing first. Barrels, hen-coops, portable settees, and life-preservers do not adorn the cabin, as they should; and, roving wildly to and fro, my eye sees no ray of hope till it falls upon a plump old lady, devoutly reading in the cabin Bible, and a voluminous night-cap. I remember that, at the swimming school, fat girls always floated best, and in an instant my plan is laid. At the first alarm I firmly attach myself to the plump lady, and cling to her through fire and water; for I feel that my old enemy, the cramp, will seize me by the foot, if I attempt to swim; and, though I can hardly expect to reach Jersey City with myself and my baggage in as good condition as I hoped, I might manage to get picked up by holding to my fat friend; if not it will be a comfort to feel that I've made an effort and shall die in good society. Poor dear woman! how little she dreamed, as she read and rocked, with her cap in a high state of starch, and her feet comfortably cooking at the register, what fell designs were hovering about her, and how intently a small but determined eye watched her, till it suddenly closed.

Sleep got the better of fear to such an extent that my boots appeared to gape, and my bonnet nodded on its peg, before I gave in. Having piled my cloak, bag, rubbers, books and umbrella on the lower shelf, I drowsily swarmed onto the upper one, tumbling down a few times, and excoriating the knobby portions of my frame in the act. A very brief nap on the upper roost was enough to set me gasping as if a dozen feather beds and the whole boat were laid over me. Out I turned; and after a series of convulsions, which caused my neighbor to ask if I wanted the stewardess, I managed to get my luggage up and myself down. But even in the lower berth, my rest was not unbroken, for various articles kept dropping off the little shelf at the bottom of the bed, and every time I flew up, thinking my hour had come, I bumped my head severely against the little shelf at the top, evidently put there for that express purpose. At last, after listening to the swash of the waves outside, wondering if the machinery usually creaked in that way, and watching a knot-hole in the side of my berth, sure that death would creep in there as soon as I took my eye from it, I dropped asleep, and dreamed of muffins.

Five A.M.—On deck, trying to wake up and enjoy an east wind and a morning fog, and a twilight sort of view of something on the shore. Rapidly achieve my purpose, and do enjoy every moment, as we go rushing through the Sound, with steamboats passing up and down, lights dancing on the shore, mist wreaths slowly furling off, and a pale pink sky above us, as the sun comes up.

Seven A.M.—In the cars, at Jersey City. Much fuss with tickets, which one man scribbles over, another snips, and a third "makes note on." Partake of refreshment, in the gloom of a very large and dirty depot. Think that my sandwiches would be more relishing without so strong a flavor of napkin, and my gingerbread more easy of consumption if it had not been pulverized by being sat upon. People act as if early traveling didn't agree with them. Children scream and scamper; men smoke and growl; women shiver and fret; porters swear; great truck horses pace up and down with loads of baggage; and every one seems to get into the wrong car, and come tumbling out again. One man, with three children, a dog, a bird-cage, and several bundles, puts himself and his possessions into every possible place where a man, three children, dog, bird-cage and bundles could be got, and is satisfied with none of them. I follow their movements, with an interest that is really exhausting, and, as they vanish, hope for rest, but don't get it. A strong-minded woman, with a tumbler in her hand, and no cloak or shawl on, comes rushing through the car, talking loudly to a small porter, who lugs a folding bed after her, and looks as if life were a burden to him.

"You promised to have it ready. It is not ready. It must be a car with a water jar, the windows must be shut, the fire must be kept up, the blinds must be down. No, this won't do. I shall go through the whole train, and suit myself, for you promised to have it ready. It is not ready," &c., all through again, like a hand-organ. She haunted the cars, the depot, the office and baggage-room, with her bed, her tumbler, and her tongue, till the train started; and a sense of fervent gratitude filled my soul, when I found that she and her unknown invalid were not to share our car.

Philadelphia.—An old place, full of Dutch women, in "bellus top" bonnets, selling vegetables, in long, open markets. Every one seems to be scrubbing their white steps. All the houses look like tidy jails, with their outside shutters. Several have crape on the door-handles, and many have flags flying from roof or balcony. Few men appear, and the women seem to do the business, which, perhaps, accounts for its being so well done. Pass fine buildings, but don't know what they are. Would like to stop and see my native city; for, having left it at the tender age of two, my recollections are not vivid.

Baltimore.—A big, dirty, shippy, shiftless place, full of goats, geese, colored people, and coal, at least the part of it I see. Pass near the spot where the riot took place, and feel as if I should enjoy throwing a stone at somebody, hard. Find a guard at the ferry, the depot, and here and there, along the road. A camp whitens one hill-side, and a cavalry training school, or whatever it should be called, is a very interesting sight, with quantities of horses and riders galloping, marching, leaping, and skirmishing, over all manner of break-neck places. A party of English people get in—the men, with sandy hair and red whiskers, all trimmed alike, to a hair; rough grey coats, very rosy, clean faces, and a fine, full way of speaking, which is particularly agreeable, after our slip-shod American gabble. The two ladies wear funny velvet fur-trimmed hoods; are done up, like compact bundles, in tar tan shawls; and look as if bent on seeing everything thoroughly. The devotion of one elderly John Bull to his red-nosed spouse was really beautiful to behold. She was plain and cross, and fussy and stupid, but J. B., Esq., read no papers when she was awake, turned no cold shoulder when she wished to sleep, and cheerfully said, "Yes, me dear," to every wish or want the wife of his bosom expressed. I quite warmed to the excellent man, and asked a question or two, as the only means of expressing my good will. He answered very civilly, but evidently hadn't been used to being addressed by strange women in public conveyances; and Mrs. B. fixed her green eyes upon me, as if she thought me a forward hussy, or whatever is good English for a presuming young woman. The pair left their friends before we reached Washington; and the last I saw of them was a vision of a large plaid lady, stalking grimly away, on the arm of a rosy, stout gentleman, loaded with rugs, bags, and books, but still devoted, still smiling, and waving a hearty "Fare ye well! We'll meet ye at Willard's on Chusday."

Soon after their departure we had an accident; for no long journey in America would be complete without one. A coupling iron broke; and, after leaving the last car behind us, we waited for it to come up, which it did, with a crash that knocked every one forward on their faces, and caused several old ladies to screech dismally. Hats flew off, bonnets were flattened, the stove skipped, the lamps fell down, the water jar turned a somersault, and the wheel just over which I sat received some damage. Of course, it became necessary for all the men to get out, and stand about in everybody's way, while repairs were made; and for the women to wrestle their heads out of the windows, asking ninety-nine foolish questions to one sensible one. A few wise females seized this favorable moment to better their seats, well knowing that few men can face the wooden stare with which they regard the former possessors of the places they have invaded.

The country through which we passed did not seem so very unlike that which I had left, except that it was more level and less wintry. In summer time the wide fields would have shown me new sights, and the way-side hedges blossomed with new flowers; now, everything was sere and sodden, and a general air of shiftlessness prevailed, which would have caused a New England farmer much disgust, and a strong desire to "buckle to," and "right up" things. Dreary little houses, with chimneys built outside, with clay and rough sticks piled crosswise, as we used to build cob towers, stood in barren looking fields, with cow, pig, or mule lounging about the door. We often passed colored people, looking as if they had come out of a picture book, or off the stage, but not at all the sort of people I'd been accustomed to see at the North.

Wayside encampments made the fields and lanes gay with blue coats and the glitter of buttons. Military washes flapped and fluttered on the fences; pots were steaming in the open air; all sorts of tableaux seen through the openings of tents, and everywhere the boys threw up their caps and cut capers as we passed.

Washington.—It was dark when we arrived; and, but for the presence of another friendly gentleman, I should have yielded myself a helpless prey to the first overpowering hackman, who insisted that I wanted to go just where I didn't. Putting me into the conveyance I belonged in, my escort added to the obligation by pointing out the objects of interest which we passed in our long drive. Though I'd often been told that Washington was a spacious place, its visible magnitude quite took my breath away, and of course I quoted Randolph's expression, "a city of magnificent distances," as I suppose every one does when they see it. The Capitol was so like the pictures that hang opposite the staring Father of his Country, in boarding-houses and hotels, that it did not impress me, except to recall the time when I was sure that Cinderella went to housekeeping in just such a place, after she had married the inflammable Prince; though, even at that early period, I had my doubts as to the wisdom of a match whose foundation was of glass.

The White House was lighted up, and carriages were rolling in and out of the great gate. I stared hard at the famous East Room, and would have liked a peep through the crack of the door. My old gentleman was indefatigable in his attentions, and I said, "Splendid!" to everything he pointed out, though I suspect I often admired the wrong place, and missed the right. Pennsylvania Avenue, with its bustle, lights, music, and military, made me feel as if I'd crossed the water and landed somewhere in Carnival time. Coming to less noticeable parts of the city, my companion fell silent, and I meditated upon the perfection which Art had attained in America—having just passed a bronze statue of some hero, who looked like a black Methodist minister, in a cocked hat, above the waist, and a tipsy squire below; while his horse stood like an opera dancer, on one leg, in a high, but somewhat remarkable wind, which blew his mane one way and his massive tail the other.

"Hurly-burly House, ma'am!" called a voice, startling me from my reverie, as we stopped before a great pile of buildings, with a flag flying before it, sentinels at the door, and a very trying quantity of men lounging about. My heart beat rather faster than usual, and it suddenly struck me that I was very far from home; but I descended with dignity, wondering whether I should be stopped for want of a countersign, and forced to pass the night in the street. Marching boldly up the steps, I found that no form was necessary, for the men fell back, the guard touched their caps, a boy opened the door, and, as it closed behind me, I felt that I was fairly started, and Nurse Periwinkle's Mission was begun.

Chapter III A Day.

"They've come! they've come! hurry up, ladies—you're wanted."

"Who have come? the rebels?"

This sudden summons in the gray dawn was somewhat startling to a three days' nurse like myself, and, as the thundering knock came at our door, I sprang up in my bed, prepared

"To gird my woman's form,

And on the ramparts die,"

if necessary; but my room-mate took it more coolly, and, as she began a rapid toilet, answered my bewildered question,—

"Bless you, no child; it's the wounded from Fredericksburg; forty ambulances are at the door, and we shall have our hands full in fifteen minutes."

"What shall we have to do?"

"Wash, dress, feed, warm and nurse them for the next three months, I dare say. Eighty beds are ready, and we were getting impatient for the men to come. Now you will begin to see hospital life in earnest, for you won't probably find time to sit down all day, and may think yourself fortunate if you get to bed by midnight. Come to me in the ball-room when you are ready; the worst cases are always carried there, and I shall need your help."

So saying, the energetic little woman twirled her hair into a button at the back of her head, in a "cleared for action" sort of style, and vanished, wrestling her way into a feminine kind of pea-jacket as she went.

I am free to confess that I had a realizing sense of the fact that my hospital bed was not a bed of roses just then, or the prospect before me one of unmingled rapture. My three days' experiences had begun with a death, and, owing to the defalcation of another nurse, a somewhat abrupt plunge into the superintendence of a ward containing forty beds, where I spent my shining hours washing faces, serving rations, giving medicine, and sitting in a very hard chair, with pneumonia on one side, diphtheria on the other, five typhoids on the opposite, and a dozen dilapidated patriots, hopping, lying, and lounging about, all staring more or less at the new "nuss," who suffered untold agonies, but concealed them under as matronly an aspect as a spinster could assume, and blundered through her trying labors with a Spartan firmness, which I hope they appreciated, but am afraid they didn't. Having a taste for "ghastliness," I had rather longed for the wounded to arrive, for rheumatism wasn't heroic, neither was liver complaint, or measles; even fever had lost its charms since "bathing burning brows" had been used up in romances, real and ideal; but when I peeped into the dusky street lined with what I at first had innocently called market carts, now unloading their sad freight at our door, I recalled sundry reminiscences I had heard from nurses of longer standing, my ardor experienced a sudden chill, and I indulged in a most unpatriotic wish that I was safe at home again, with a quiet day before me, and no necessity for being hustled up, as if I were a hen and had only to hop off my roost, give my plumage a peck, and be ready for action. A second bang at the door

Wounded soldiers from the battles in the "Wilderness" at Fredericksburg, Va., May 20, 1864

sent this recreant desire to the right about, as a little woolly head popped in, and Joey, (a six years' old contraband,) announced—

"Miss Blank is jes' wild fer ye, and says fly round right away. They's comin' in, I tell yer, heaps on 'em—one was took out dead, and I see him,—hi! warn't he a goner!"

With which cheerful intelligence the imp scuttled away, singing like a blackbird, and I followed, feeling that Richard was not himself again, and wouldn't be for a long time to come.

The first thing I met was a regiment of the vilest odors that ever assaulted the human nose, and took it by storm. Cologne, with its seven and seventy evil savors, was a posy-bed to it; and the worst of this affliction was, every one had assured me that it was a chronic weakness of all hospitals, and I must bear it. I did, armed with lavender water, with which I so besprinkled myself and premises, that, like my friend Sairy, I was soon known among my patients as "the nurse with the bottle." Having been run over by three excited surgeons, bumped against by migratory coal-hods, water-pails, and small boys, nearly scalded by an avalanche of newly-filled tea-pots, and hopelessly entangled in a knot of colored sisters coming to wash, I progressed by slow stages up stairs and down, till the main hall was reached, and I paused to take breath and a survey. There they were! "our brave boys," as the papers justly call them, for cowards could hardly have been so riddled with shot and shell, so torn and shattered, nor have borne suffering for which we have no name, with an uncomplaining fortitude, which made one glad to cherish each as a brother. In they came, some on stretchers, some in men's arms, some feebly staggering along propped on rude crutches, and one lay stark and still with covered face, as a comrade gave his name to be recorded before they carried him away to the dead house. All was hurry and confusion; the hall was full of these wrecks of humanity, for the most exhausted could not reach a bed till duly ticketed and registered; the walls were lined with rows of such as could sit, the floor covered with the more disabled, the steps and doorways filled with helpers and lookers on; the sound of many feet and voices made that usually quiet hour as noisy as noon; and, in the midst of it all, the matron's motherly face brought more comfort to many a poor soul, than the cordial draughts she administered, or the cheery words that welcomed all, making of the hospital a home.

The sight of several stretchers, each with its legless, armless, or desperately wounded occupant, entering my ward, admonished me that I was there to work, not to wonder or weep; so I corked up my feelings, and returned to the path of duty, which was rather "a hard road to travel" just then. The house had been a hotel before hospitals were needed, and many of the doors still bore their old names; some not so inappropriate as might be imagined, for my ward was in truth a ball-room, if gun-shot wounds could christen it. Forty beds were prepared, many already tenanted by tired men who fell down anywhere, and drowsed till the smell of food roused them. Round the great stove was gathered the dreariest group I ever saw—ragged, gaunt and pale, mud to the knees, with bloody bandages untouched since put on days before; many bundled up in blankets, coats being lost or useless; and all wearing that disheartened look which proclaimed defeat, more plainly than any telegram of the Burnside blunder. I pitied them so much, I dared not speak to them, though, remembering all they had been through since the rout at Fredericksburg, I yearned to serve the dreariest of them all. Presently, Miss Blank tore me from my refuge behind piles of one-sleeved shirts, odd socks, bandages and lint; put basin, sponge, towels, and a block of brown soap into my hands, with these appalling directions:

"Come, my dear, begin to wash as fast as you can. Tell them to take off socks, coats and shirts, scrub them well, put on clean shirts, and the attendants will finish them off, and lay them in bed."

If she had requested me to shave them all, or dance a hornpipe on the stove funnel, I should have been less staggered; but to scrub some dozen lords of creation at a moment's notice, was really—really—. However, there was no time for nonsense, and, having re-solved when I came to do everything I was bid, I drowned my scruples in my wash-bowl, clutched my soap manfully, and, assuming a business-like air, made a dab at the first dirty specimen I saw, bent on performing my task vi et armis if necessary. I chanced to light on a withered old Irishman, wounded in the head, which caused that portion of his frame to be tastefully laid out like a garden, the bandages being the walks, his hair the shrubbery. He was so overpowered by the honor of having a lady wash him, as he expressed it, that he did nothing but roll up his eyes, and bless me, in an irresistible style which was too much for my sense of the ludicrous; so we laughed together, and when I knelt down to take off his shoes, he "flopped" also, and wouldn't hear of my touching "them dirty craters. May your bed above be aisy darlin', for the day's work ye ar doon!—Whoosh! there ye are, and bedad, it's hard tellin' which is the dirtiest, the fut or the shoe." It was; and if he hadn't been to the fore, I should have gone on pulling, under the impression that the "fut" was a boot, for trousers, socks, shoes and legs were a mass of mud. This comical tableau produced a general grin, at which propitious beginning I took heart and scrubbed away like any tidy parent on a Saturday night. Some of them took the performance like sleepy children, leaning their tired heads against me as I worked, others looked grimly scandalized, and several of the roughest colored like bashful girls. One wore a soiled little bag about his neck, and, as I moved it, to bathe his wounded breast, I said,

"Your talisman didn't save you, did it?"

"Well, I reckon it did, marm, for that shot would a gone a couple a inches deeper but for my old mammy's camphor bag," answered the cheerful philosopher.

Another, with a gun-shot wound through the cheek, asked for a looking-glass, and when I brought one, regarded his swollen face with a dolorous expression, as he muttered—

"I vow to gosh, that's too bad! I warn't a bad looking chap before, and now I'm done for; won't there be a thunderin' scar? and what on earth will Josephine Skinner say?"

He looked up at me with his one eye so appealingly, that I controlled my risibles, and assured him that if Josephine was a girl of sense, she would admire the honorable scar, as a lasting proof that he had faced the enemy, for all women thought a wound the best decoration a brave soldier could wear. I hope Miss Skinner verified the good opinion I so rashly expressed of her, but I shall never know.

The next scrubbee was a nice looking lad, with a curly brown mane, and a budding trace of gingerbread over the lip, which he called his beard, and defended stoutly, when the barber jocosely suggested its immolation. He lay on a bed, with one leg gone, and the right arm so shattered that it must evidently follow: yet the little Sergeant was as merry as if his afflictions were not worth lamenting over; and when a drop or two of salt water mingled with my suds at the sight of this strong young body, so marred and maimed, the boy looked up, with a brave smile, though there was a little quiver of the lips, as he said,

"Now don't you fret yourself about me, miss; I'm first rate here, for it's nuts to lie still on this bed, after knocking about in those confounded ambulances, that shake what there is left of a fellow to jelly. I never was in one of these places before, and think this cleaning up a jolly thing for us, though I'm afraid it isn't for you ladies."

"Is this your first battle, Sergeant?"

"No, miss; I've been in six scrimmages, and never got a scratch till this last one; but it's done the business pretty thoroughly for me, I should say. Lord! what a scramble there'll be for arms and legs, when we old boys come out of our graves, on the Judgment Day: wonder if we shall get our own again? If we do, my leg will have to tramp from Fredericksburg, my arm from here, I suppose, and meet my body, wherever it may be."

The fancy seemed to tickle him mightily, for he laughed blithely, and so did I; which, no doubt, caused the new nurse to be regarded as a light-minded sinner by the Chaplain, who roamed vaguely about, informing the men that they were all worms, corrupt of heart, with perishable bodies, and souls only to be saved by a diligent perusal of certain tracts, and other equally cheering bits of spiritual consolation, when spirituous ditto would have been preferred.

"I say, Mrs.!" called a voice behind me; and, turning, I saw a rough Michigander, with an arm blown off at the shoulder, and two or three bullets still in him—as he afterwards mentioned, as carelessly as if gentlemen were in the habit of carrying such trifles about with them. I went to him, and, while administering a dose of soap and water, he whispered, irefully:

"That red-headed devil, over yonder, is a reb, damn him! You'll agree to that, I'll bet? He's got shet of a foot, or he'd a cut like the rest of the lot. Don't you wash him, nor feed him, but jest let him holler till he's tired. It's a blasted shame to fetch them fellers in here, along side of us; and so I'll tell the chap that bosses this concern; cuss me if I don't."

I regret to say that I did not deliver a moral sermon upon the duty of forgiving our enemies, and the sin of profanity, then and there; but, being a red-hot Abolitionist, stared fixedly at the tall rebel, who was a copperhead, in every sense of the word, and privately resolved to put soap in his eyes, rub his nose the wrong way, and excoriate his cuticle generally, if I had the washing of him.

My amiable intentions, however, were frustrated; for, when I approached, with as Christian an expression as my principles would allow, and asked the question—"Shall I try to make you more comfortable, sir?" all I got for my pains was a gruff—

"No; I'll do it myself."

"Here's your Southern chivalry, with a witness," thought I, dumping the basin down before him, thereby quenching a strong desire to give him a summary baptism, in return for his ungraciousness; for my angry passions rose, at this rebuff, in a way that would have scandalized good Dr. Watts. He was a disappointment in all respects, (the rebel, not the blessed Doctor,) for he was neither fiendish, romantic, pathetic, or anything interesting; but a long, fat man, with a head like a burning bush, and a perfectly expressionless face: so I could dislike him without the slightest drawback, and ignored his existence from that day forth. One redeeming trait he certainly did possess, as the floor speedily testified; for his ablutions were so vigorously performed, that his bed soon stood like an isolated island, in a sea of soap-suds, and he resembled a dripping merman, suffering from the loss of a fin. If cleanliness is a near neighbor to godliness, then was the big rebel the godliest man in my ward that day.

Having done up our human wash, and laid it out to dry, the second syllable of our version of the word war-fare was enacted with much success. Great trays of bread, meat, soup and coffee appeared; and both nurses and attendants turned waiters, serving bountiful rations to all who could eat. I can call my pinafore to testify to my good will in the work, for in ten minutes it was reduced to a perambulating bill of fare, presenting samples of all the refreshments going or gone. It was a lively scene; the long room lined with rows of beds, each filled by an occupant, whom water, shears, and clean raiment, had transformed from a dismal ragamuffin into a recumbent hero, with a cropped head. To and fro rushed matrons, maids, and convalescent "boys," skirmishing with knives and forks; retreating with empty plates; marching and counter-marching, with unvaried success, while the clash of busy spoons made most inspiring music for the charge of our Light Brigade:

"Beds to the front of them,

Beds to the right of them,

Beds to the left of them,

Nobody blundered.

Beamed at by hungry souls,

Screamed at with brimming bowls,

Steamed at by army rolls,

Buttered and sundered.

With coffee not cannon plied,

Each must be satisfied,

Whether they lived or died;

All the men wondered."

Very welcome seemed the generous meal, after a week of suffering, exposure, and short commons; soon the brown faces began to smile, as food, warmth, and rest, did their pleasant work; and the grateful "Thankee's" were followed by more graphic accounts of the battle and retreat, than any paid reporter could have given us. Curious contrasts of the tragic and comic met one everywhere; and some touching as well as ludicrous episodes, might have been recorded that day. A six foot New Hampshire man, with a leg broken and perforated by a piece of shell, so large that, had I not seen the wound, I should have regarded the story as a Munchausenism, beckoned me to come and help him, as he could not sit up, and both his bed and beard were getting plentifully anointed with soup. As I fed my big nestling with corresponding mouthfuls, I asked him how he felt during the battle.

"Well, 'twas my fust, you see, so I aint ashamed to say I was a trifle flustered in the beginnin', there was such an allfired racket; for ef there's anything I do spleen agin, it's noise. But when my mate, Eph Sylvester, caved, with a bullet through his head, I got mad, and pitched in, licketty cut. Our part of the fight didn't last long; so a lot of us larked round Fredericksburg, and give some of them houses a pretty consid'able of a rummage, till we was ordered out of the mess. Some of our fellows cut like time; but I warn't a-goin' to run for nobody; and, fust thing I knew, a shell bust, right in front of us, and I keeled over, feelin' as if I was blowed higher'n a kite. I sung out, and the boys come back for me, double quick; but the way they chucked me over them fences was a caution, I tell you. Next day I was most as black as that darkey yonder, lickin' plates on the sly. This is bully coffee, ain't it? Give us another pull at it, and I'll be obleeged to you."

I did; and, as the last gulp subsided, he said, with a rub of his old handkerchief over eyes as well as mouth:

"Look a here; I've got a pair a earbobs and a handkercher pin I'm a goin' to give you, if you'll have them; for you're the very moral o' Lizy Sylvester, poor Eph's wife: that's why I signalled you to come over here. They aint much, I guess, but they'll do to memorize the rebs by."

Burrowing under his pillow, he produced a little bundle of what he called "truck," and gallantly presented me with a pair of earrings, each representing a cluster of corpulent grapes, and the pin a basket of astonishing fruit, the whole large and coppery enough for a small warming-pan. Feeling delicate about depriving him of such valuable relics, I accepted the earrings alone, and was obliged to depart, somewhat abruptly, when my friend stuck the warming-pan in the bosom of his night-gown, viewing it with much complacency, and, perhaps, some tender memory, in that rough heart of his, for the comrade he had lost.

Observing that the man next him had left his meal untouched, I offered the same service I had performed for his neighbor, but he shook his head.

"Thank you, ma'am; I don't think I'll ever eat again, for I'm shot in the stomach. But I'd like a drink of water, if you aint too busy."

Civil war surgeons

I rushed away, but the water-pails were gone to be refilled, and it was some time before they reappeared. I did not forget my patient patient, meanwhile, and, with the first mugful, hurried back to him. He seemed asleep; but something in the tired white face caused me to listen at his lips for a breath. None came. I touched his forehead; it was cold: and then I knew that, while he waited, a better nurse than I had given him a cooler draught, and healed him with a touch. I laid the sheet over the quiet sleeper, whom no noise could now disturb; and, half an hour later, the bed was empty. It seemed a poor requital for all he had sacrificed and suffered,—that hospital bed, lonely even in a crowd; for there was no familiar face for him to look his last upon; no friendly voice to say, Good bye; no hand to lead him gently down into the Valley of the Shadow; and he vanished, like a drop in that red sea upon whose shores so many women stand lamenting. For a moment I felt bitterly indignant at this seeming carelessness of the value of life, the sanctity of death; then consoled myself with the thought that, when the great muster roll was called, these nameless men might be promoted above many whose tall monuments record the barren honors they have won.

All having eaten, drank, and rested, the surgeons began their rounds; and I took my first lesson in the art of dressing wounds. It wasn't a festive scene, by any means; for Dr P., whose Aid I constituted myself, fell to work with a vigor which soon convinced me that I was a weaker vessel, though nothing would have induced me to confess it then. He had served in the Crimea, and seemed to regard a dilapidated body very much as I should have regarded a damaged garment; and, turning up his cuffs, whipped out a very unpleasant looking housewife, cutting, sawing, patching and piecing, with the enthusiasm of an accomplished surgical seamstress; explaining the process, in scientific terms, to the patient, meantime; which, of course, was immensely cheering and comfortable. There was an uncanny sort of fascination in watching him, as he peered and probed into the mechanism of those wonderful bodies, whose mysteries he understood so well. The more intricate the wound, the better he liked it. A poor private, with both legs off, and shot through the lungs, possessed more attractions for him than a dozen generals, slightly scratched in some "masterly retreat;" and had any one appeared in small pieces, requesting to be put together again, he would have considered it a special dispensation.

The amputations were reserved till the morrow, and the merciful magic of ether was not thought necessary that day, so the poor souls had to bear their pains as best they might. It is all very well to talk of the patience of woman; and far be it from me to pluck that feather from her cap, for, heaven knows, she isn't allowed to wear many; but the patient endurance of these men, under trials of the flesh, was truly wonderful. Their fortitude seemed contagious, and scarcely a cry escaped them, though I often longed to groan for them, when pride kept their white lips shut, while great drops stood upon their foreheads, and the bed shook with the irrepressible tremor of their tortured bodies. One or two Irishmen anathematized the doctors with the frankness of their nation, and ordered the Virgin to stand by them, as if she had been the wedded Biddy to whom they could administer the poker, if she didn't; but, as a general thing, the work went on in silence, broken only by some quiet request for roller, instruments, or plaster, a sigh from the patient, or a sympathizing murmur from the nurse.

It was long past noon before these repairs were even partially made; and, having got the bodies of my boys into something like order, the next task was to minister to their minds, by writing letters to the anxious souls at home; answering questions, reading papers, taking possession of money and valuables; for the eighth commandment was reduced to a very fragmentary condition, both by the blacks and whites, who ornamented our hospital with their presence. Pocket books, purses, miniatures, and watches, were sealed up, labelled, and handed over to the matron, till such times as the owners thereof were ready to depart homeward or campward again. The letters dictated to me, and revised by me, that afternoon, would have made an excellent chapter for some future history of the war; for, like that which Thackeray's "Ensign Spooney" wrote his mother just before Waterloo, they were "full of affection, pluck, and bad spelling;" nearly all giving lively accounts of the battle, and ending with a somewhat sudden plunge from patriotism to provender, desiring "Marm," "Mary Ann," or "Aunt Peters," to send along some pies, pickles, sweet stuff, and apples, "to yourn in haste," Joe, Sam, or Ned, as the case might be.

My little Sergeant insisted on trying to scribble something with his left hand, and patiently accomplished some half dozen lines of hieroglyphics, which he gave me to fold and direct, with a boyish blush, that rendered a glimpse of "My Dearest Jane," unnecessary, to assure me that the heroic lad had been more successful in the service of Commander-in-Chief Cupid than that of Gen. Mars; and a charming little romance blossomed instanter in Nurse Periwinkle's romantic fancy, though no further confidences were made that day, for Sergeant fell asleep, and, judging from his tranquil face, visited his absent sweetheart in the pleasant land of dreams.

At five o'clock a great bell rang, and the attendants flew, not to arms, but to their trays, to bring up supper, when a second uproar announced that it was ready. The new comers woke at the sound; and I presently discovered that it took a very bad wound to incapacitate the defenders of the faith for the consumption of their rations; the amount that some of them sequestered was amazing; but when I suggested the probability of a famine hereafter, to the matron, that motherly lady cried out: "Bless their hearts, why shouldn't they eat? It's their only amusement; so fill every one, and, if there's not enough ready to-night, I'll lend my share to the Lord by giving it to the boys." And, whipping up her coffee-pot and plate of toast, she gladdened the eyes and stomachs of two or three dissatisfied heroes, by serving them with a liberal hand; and I haven't the slightest doubt that, having cast her bread upon the waters, it came back buttered, as another large-hearted old lady was wont to say.

Then came the doctor's evening visit; the administration of medicines; washing feverish faces; smoothing tumbled beds; wetting wounds; singing lullabies; and preparations for the night. By eleven, the last labor of love was done; the last "good night" spoken; and, if any needed a reward for that day's work, they surely received it, in the silent eloquence of those long lines of faces, showing pale and peaceful in the shaded rooms, as we quitted them, followed by grateful glances that lighted us to bed, where rest, the sweetest, made our pillows soft, while Night and Nature took our places, filling that great house of pain with the healing miracles of Sleep, and his diviner brother, Death.

Personal Memoirs Of P. H. Sheridan
Volume Ii., Chapter I.

General Sheridan (right), General Katz (sitting) and friend

While occupying the ground between Clifton and Berryville, referred to in the last chapter of the preceding volume, I felt the need of an efficient body of scouts to collect information regarding the enemy, for the defective intelligence-establishment with which I started out from Harper's Ferry early in August had not proved satisfactory. I therefore began to organize my scouts on a system which I hoped would give better results than had the method hitherto pursued in the department, which was to employ on this service doubtful citizens and Confederate deserters. If these should turn out untrustworthy, the mischief they might do us gave me grave apprehension, and I finally concluded that those of our own soldiers who should volunteer for the delicate and hazardous duty would be the most valuable material, and decided that they should have a battalion organization and be commanded by an officer, Major H. K. Young, of the First Rhode Island Infantry. These men were disguised in Confederate uniforms whenever necessary, were paid from the Secret-Service Fund in proportion to the value of the intelligence they furnished, which often stood us in good stead in checking the forays of Gilmore, Mosby, and other irregulars. Beneficial results came from the plan in many other ways too, and particularly so when in a few days two of my scouts put me in the way of getting news conveyed from Winchester. They had learned that just outside of my lines, near Millwood, there was living an old colored man, who had a permit from the Confederate commander to go into Winchester and return three times a week, for the purpose of selling vegetables to the inhabitants. The scouts had sounded this man, and, finding him both loyal and shrewd, suggested that he might be made useful to us within the enemy's lines; and the proposal struck me as feasible, provided there could be found in Winchester some reliable person who would be willing to co-operate and correspond with me. I asked General Crook, who was acquainted with many of the Union people of Winchester, if he knew of such a person, and he recommended a Miss Rebecca Wright, a young lady whom he had met there before the battle of Kernstown, who, he said, was a member of the Society of Friends and the teacher of a small private school. He knew she was faithful and loyal to the Government, and thought she might be willing to render us assistance, but he could not be certain of this, for on account of her well known loyalty she was under constant surveillance. I hesitated at first, but finally deciding to try it, despatched the two scouts to the old negro's cabin, and they brought him to my headquarters late that night. I was soon convinced of the negro's fidelity, and asking him if he was acquainted with Miss Rebecca Wright, of Winchester, he replied that he knew her well. There upon I told him what I wished to do, and after a little persuasion he agreed to carry a letter to her on his next marketing trip. My message was prepared by writing it on tissue paper, which was then compressed into a small pellet, and protected by wrapping it in tin-foil so that it could be safely carried in the man's mouth. The probability, of his being searched when he came to the Confederate picket-line was not remote, and in such event he was to swallow the pellet. The letter appealed to Miss Wright's loyalty and patriotism, and requested her to furnish me with information regarding the strength and condition of Early's army. The night before the negro started one of the scouts placed the odd-looking communication in his hands, with renewed injunctions as to secrecy and promptitude. Early the next morning it was delivered to Miss Wright, with an intimation that a letter of importance was enclosed in the tin-foil, the negro telling her at the same time that she might expect him to call for a message in reply before his return home. At first Miss Wright began to open the pellet nervously, but when told to be careful, and to preserve the foil as a wrapping for her answer, she proceeded slowly and carefully, and when the note appeared intact the messenger retired, remarking again that in the evening he would come for an answer.

On reading my communication Miss Wright was much startled by the perils it involved, and hesitatingly consulted her mother, but her devoted loyalty soon silenced every other consideration, and the brave girl resolved to comply with my request, notwithstanding it might jeopardize her life. The evening before a convalescent Confederate officer had visited her mother's house, and in conversation about the war had disclosed the fact that Kershaw's division of infantry and Cutshaw's battalion of artillery had started to rejoin General Lee. At the time Miss Wright heard this she attached little if any importance to it, but now she perceived the value of the intelligence, and, as her first venture, determined to send it to me at once, which she did with a promise that in the future she would with great pleasure continue to transmit information by the negro messenger.

"SEPTEMBER 15, 1864.

"I learn from Major-General Crook that you are a loyal lady, and still love the old flag. Can you inform me of the position of Early's forces, the number of divisions in his army, and the strength of any or all of them, and his probable or reported intentions? Have any more troops arrived from Richmond, or are any more coming, or reported to be coming?

"You can trust the bearer."

"I am, very respectfully, your most obedient servant,
P. H. SHERIDAN, Major-General Commanding."

"SEPTEMBER 16, 1864.

"I have no communication whatever with the rebels, but will tell you what I know. The division of General Kershaw, and Cutshaw's artillery, twelve guns and men, General Anderson commanding, have been sent away, and no more are expected, as they cannot be spared from Richmond. I do not know how the troops are situated, but the force is much smaller than represented. I will take pleasure hereafter in learning all I can of their strength and position, and the bearer may call again.

"Very respectfully yours,"

....

Miss Wright's answer proved of more value to me than she anticipated, for it not only quieted the conflicting reports concerning Anderson's corps, but was most important in showing positively that Kershaw was gone, and this circumstance led, three days later, to the battle of the Opequon, or Winchester as it has been unofficially called. Word to the effect that some of Early's troops were under orders to return to Petersburg, and would start back at the first favorable opportunity, had been communicated to me already from many sources, but we had not been able to ascertain the date for their departure. Now that they had actually started, I decided to wait before offering battle until Kershaw had gone so far as to preclude his return, feeling confident that my prudence would be justified by the improved chances of victory; and then, besides, Mr. Stanton kept reminding me that positive success was necessary to counteract the political dissatisfaction existing in some of the Northern States. This course was advised and approved by General Grant, but even with his powerful backing it was difficult to resist the persistent pressure of those whose judgment, warped by their interests in the Baltimore and Ohio railroad, was often confused and misled by stories of scouts (sent out from Washington), averring that Kershaw and Fitzhugh Lee had returned to Petersburg, Breckenridge to southwestern Virginia, and at one time even maintaining that Early's whole army was east of the Blue Ridge, and its commander himself at Gordonsville.

During the inactivity prevailing in my army for the ten days preceding Miss Wright's communication the infantry was quiet, with the exception of Getty's division, which made a reconnoissance to the Opequon, and developed a heavy force of the enemy at Edwards's Corners. The cavalry, however, was employed a good deal in this interval skirmishing heavily at times to maintain a space about six miles in width between the hostile lines, for I wished to control this ground so that when I was released from the instructions of August 12, I could move my men into position for attack without the knowledge of Early. The most noteworthy of these mounted encounters was that of McIntosh's brigade, which captured the Eighth South Carolina at Abraham's Creek September 13.

It was the evening of the 16th of September that I received from Miss Wright the positive information that Kershaw was in march toward Front Royal on his way by Chester Gap to Richmond. Concluding that this was my opportunity, I at once resolved to throw my whole force into Newtown the next day, but a despatch from General Grant directing me to meet him at Charlestown, whither he was coming to consult with me, caused me to defer action until after I should see him. In our resulting interview at Charlestown, I went over the situation very thoroughly, and pointed out with so much confidence the chances of a complete victory should I throw my army across the Valley pike near Newtown that he fell in with the plan at once, authorized me to resume the offensive, and to attack Early as soon as I deemed it most propitious to do so; and although before leaving City Point he had outlined certain operations for my army, yet he neither discussed nor disclosed his plans, my knowledge of the situation striking him as being so much more accurate than his own.

["Extract from Grant's Memoirs," page 328.]

"....Before starting I had drawn up a plan of campaign for Sheridan, which I had brought with me; but seeing that he was so clear and so positive in his views, and so confident of success, I said nothing about this, and did not take it out of my pocket...."

The interview over, I returned to my army to arrange for its movement toward Newtown, but while busy with these preparations, a report came to me from General Averell which showed that Early was moving with two divisions of infantry toward Martinsburg. This considerably altered the state of affairs, and I now decided to change my plan and attack at once the two divisions remaining about Winchester and Stephenson's depot, and later, the two sent to Martinsburg; the disjointed state of the enemy giving me an opportunity to take him in detail, unless the Martinsburg column should be returned by forced marches.

While General Early was in the telegraph office at Martinsburg on the morning of the 18th, he learned of Grant's visit to me; and anticipating activity by reason of this circumstance, he promptly proceeded to withdraw so as to get the two divisions within supporting distance of Ramseur's, which lay across the Berryville pike about two miles east of Winchester, between Abraham's Creek and Red Bud Run, so by the night of the 18th Wharton's division, under Breckenridge, was at Stephenson's depot, Rodes near there, and Gordon's at Bunker Hill. At daylight of the 19th these positions of the Confederate infantry still obtained, with the cavalry of Lomax, Jackson, and Johnson on the right of

Ramseur, while to the left and rear of the enemy's general line was Fitzhugh Lee, covering from Stephenson's depot west across the Valley pike to Applepie Ridge.

My army moved at 3 o'clock that morning. The plan was for Torbert to advance with Merritt's division of cavalry from Summit Point, carry the crossings of the Opequon at Stevens's and Lock's fords, and form a junction near Stephenson's depot, with Averell, who was to move south from Darksville by the Valley pike. Meanwhile, Wilson was to strike up the Berryville pike, carry the Berryville crossing of the Opequon, charge through the gorge or canyon on the road west of the stream, and occupy the open ground at the head of this defile. Wilson's attack was to be supported by the Sixth and Nineteenth corps, which were ordered to the Berryville crossing, and as the cavalry gained the open ground beyond the gorge, the two infantry corps, under command of General Wright, were expected to press on after and occupy Wilson's ground, who was then to shift to the south bank of Abraham's Creek and cover my left; Crook's two divisions, having to march from Summit Point, were to follow the Sixth and Nineteenth corps to the Opcquon, and should they arrive before the action began, they were to be held in reserve till the proper moment came, and then, as a turning-column, be thrown over toward the Valley pike, south of Winchester.

McIntosh's brigade of Wilson's division drove the enemy's pickets away from the Berryville crossing at dawn, and Wilson following rapidly through the gorge with the rest of the division, debouched from its western extremity with such suddenness as to capture a small earthwork in front of General Ramseur's main line; and not-withstanding the Confederate infantry, on recovering from its astonishment, tried hard to dislodge them, Wilson's troopers obstinately held the work till the Sixth Corps came up. I followed Wilson to select the ground on which to form the infantry. The Sixth Corps began to arrive about 8 o'clock, and taking up the line Wilson had been holding, just beyond the head of the narrow ravine, the cavalry was transferred to the south side of Abraham's Creek.

The Confederate line lay along some elevated ground about two miles east of Winchester, and extended from Abraham's Creek north across the Berryville pike, the left being hidden in the heavy timber on Red Bud Run. Between this line and mine, especially on my right, clumps of woods and patches of underbrush occurred here and there, but the undulating ground consisted mainly of open fields, many of which were covered with standing corn that had already ripened.

Much time was lost in getting all of the Sixth and Nineteenth corps through the narrow defile, Grover's division being greatly delayed there by a train of ammunition wagons, and it was not until late in the forenoon that the troops intended for the attack could be got into line ready to advance. General Early was not slow to avail himself of the advantages thus offered him, and my chances of striking him in detail were growing less every moment, for Gordon and Rodes were hurrying their divisions from Stephenson's depot— across-country on a line that would place Gordon in the woods south of Red Bud Run, and bring Rodes into the interval between Gordon and Ramseur.

When the two corps had all got through the canyon they were formed with Getty's division of the Sixth to the left of the Berryville pike, Rickett's division to the right of the pike, and Russell's division in reserve in rear of the other two. Grover's division of the Nineteenth Corps came next on the right of Rickett's, with Dwight to its rear in reserve, while Crook was to begin massing near the Opequon crossing about the time Wright and Emory were ready to attack.

Just before noon the line of Getty, Ricketts, and Grover moved forward, and as we advanced, the Confederates, covered by some heavy woods on their right, slight underbrush and corn-fields along their Centre, and a large body of timber on their left along the Red Bud, opened fire from their whole front. We gained considerable ground at first, especially on our left but the desperate resistance which the right met with demonstrated that the time we had unavoidably lost in the morning had been of incalculable value to Early, for it was evident that he had been enabled already to so far concentrate his troops as to have the different divisions of his army in a connected line of battle, in good shape to resist.

Getty and Ricketts made some progress toward Winchester in connection with Wilson's cavalry, which was beyond the Senseny road on Getty's left, and as they were pressing back Ramseur's infantry and Lomax's cavalry Grover attacked from the right with decided effect. Grover in a few minutes broke up Evans's brigade of Gordon's division, but his pursuit of Evans destroyed the continuity of my general line, and increased an interval that had already been made by the deflection of Ricketts to the left, in obedience to instructions that had been given him to guide his division on the Berryville pike. As the line pressed forward, Ricketts observed this widening interval and endeavored to fill it with the small brigade of Colonel Keifer, but at this juncture both Gordon and Rodes struck the weak spot where the right of the Sixth Corps and the left of the Nineteenth should have been in conjunction, and succeeded in checking my advance by driving back a part of Ricketts's division, and the most of Grover's. As these troops were retiring I ordered Russell's reserve division to be put into action, and just as the flank of the enemy's troops in pursuit of Grover was presented, Upton's brigade, led in person by both Russell and Upton, struck it in a charge so vigorous as to drive the Confederates back in turn to their original ground.

The success of Russell enabled me to re-establish the right of my line some little distance in advance of the position from which it started in the morning, and behind Russell's division (now commanded by Upton) the broken regiments of Ricketts's division were rallied. Dwight's division was then brought up on the right, and Grover's men formed behind it.

The charge of Russell was most opportune, but it cost many men in killed and wounded. Among the former was the courageous Russell himself; killed by a piece of shell that passed through his heart, although he had previously been struck by a bullet in the left breast, which wound, from its nature, must have proved mortal, yet of which he had not spoken. Russell's death oppressed us all with sadness, and me particularly. In the early days of my army life he was my captain and friend, and I was deeply indebted to him, not only for sound advice and good example, but for the inestimable service he had just performed, and sealed with his life, so it may be inferred how keenly I felt his loss.

As my lines were being rearranged, it was suggested to me to put Crook into the battle, but so strongly had I set my heart on using him to take possession of the Valley pike and cut off the enemy, that I resisted this advice, hoping that the necessity for putting him in would be obviated by the attack near Stephenson's depot that Torbert's cavalry was to make, and from which I was momentarily expecting to hear. No news of Torbert's progress came, however, so, yielding at last, I directed Crook to take post on the right of the Nineteenth Corps and, when the action was renewed, to push his command forward as a turning-column in conjunction with Emory. After some delay in the annoying defile, Crook got his men up, and posting Colonel Thoburn's division on the prolongation of the Nineteenth Corps, he formed Colonel Duval's division to the right of Thoburn. Here I joined Crook, informing him that I had just got word that Torbert was driving the enemy in confusion along the Martinsburg pike toward Winchester; at the same time I directed him to attack the moment all of Duval's men were in line. Wright was instructed to advance in concert with Crook, by swinging Emory and the right of the Sixth Corps to the left together in a half-wheel. Then leaving Crook, I rode along the Sixth and Nineteenth corps, the open ground over which they were passing affording a rare opportunity to witness the precision with which the attack was taken up from right to left. Crook's success began the moment he started to turn the enemy's left; and assured by the fact that Torbert had stampeded the Confederate cavalry and thrown Breckenridge's infantry into such disorder that it could do little to prevent the envelopment of Gordon's left, Crook pressed forward without even a halt.

Both Emory and Wright took up the fight as ordered, and as they did so I sent word to Wilson, in the hope that he could partly perform the work originally laid out for Crook, to push along the Senseny road and, if possible, gain the valley pike south of Winchester. I then returned toward my right flank, and as I reached the Nineteenth Corps the enemy was contesting the ground in its front with great obstinacy; but Emory's dogged persistence was at length rewarded with success, just as Crook's command emerged from the morass of Red Bud Run, and swept around Gordon, toward the right of Breckenridge, who, with two of Wharton's brigades, was holding a line at right angles with the Valley pike for the protection of the Confederate rear. Early had ordered these two brigades back from Stephenson's depot in the morning, purposing to protect with them his right flank and line of retreat, but while they were en route to this end, he was obliged to recall them to his left to meet Crook's attack.

To confront Torbert, Patton's brigade of infantry and some of Fitzhugh Lee's cavalry had been left back by Breckenridge, but, with Averell on the west side of the Valley pike and Merritt on the east, Torbert began to drive this opposing force toward Winchester the moment he struck it near Stephenson's depot, keeping it on the go till it reached the position held by Breckenridge, where it endeavored to make a stand.

The ground which Breckenridge was holding was open, and offered an opportunity such as seldom had been presented during the war for a mounted attack, and Torbert was not slow to take advantage of it. The instant Merritt's division could be formed for the charge, it went at Breckenridge's infantry and Fitzhugh Lee's cavalry with such momentum as to break the Confederate left, just as Averell was passing around it. Merritt's brigades, led by Custer, Lowell, and Devin, met from the start with pronounced success, and with sabre or pistol in hand literally rode down a battery of five guns and took about 1,200 prisoners. Almost simultaneously with this cavalry charge, Crook struck Breckenridge's right and Gordon's left, forcing these divisions to give way, and as they retired, Wright, in a vigorous attack, quickly broke Rodes up and pressed Ramseur so hard that the whole Confederate army fell back, contracting its lines within some breastworks which had been thrown up at a former period of the war, immediately in front of Winchester.

Here Early tried hard to stem the tide, but soon Torbert's cavalry began passing around his left flank, and as Crook, Emory, and Wright attacked in front, panic took possession of the enemy, his troops, now fugitives and stragglers, seeking escape into and through Winchester.

When this second break occurred, the Sixth and Nineteenth corps were moved over toward the Millwood pike to help Wilson on the left, but the day was so far spent that they could render him no assistance, and Ramseur's division, which had maintained some organization, was in such tolerable shape as to check him. Meanwhile Torbert passed around to the west of Winchester to join Wilson, but was unable to do so till after dark. Crook's command pursued the enemy through the town to Mill Greek, I going along.

Just after entering the town, Crook and I met, in the main street, three young girls, who gave us the most hearty reception. One of these young women was a Miss Griffith, the other two Miss Jennie and Miss Susie Meredith. During the day they had been watching the battle from the roof of the Meredith residence, with tears and lamentations, they said, in the morning when misfortune appeared to have overtaken the Union troops, but with unbounded exultation when, later, the tide set in against the Confederates. Our presence was, to them, an assurance of victory, and their delight being irrepressible, they indulged in the most unguarded manifestations and expressions. When cautioned by Crook, who knew them well, and reminded that the valley had hitherto been a race-course—one day in the possession of friends, and the next of enemies—and warned of the dangers they were incurring by such demonstrations, they assured him that they had no further fears of that kind now, adding that Early's army was so demoralized by the defeat it had just sustained that it would never be in condition to enter Winchester again. As soon as we had succeeded in calming the excited girls a little I expressed a desire to find some place where I could write a telegram to General Grant informing him of the result of the battle, and General Crook conducted me to the home of Miss Wright, where I met for the first time the woman who had contributed so much to our success, and on a desk in her schoolroom wrote the despatch announcing that we had sent Early's army whirling up the valley.

My losses in the battle of the Opequon were heavy, amounting to about 4,500 killed, wounded, and missing. Among the killed was General Russell, commanding a division, and the wounded included Generals Upton, McIntosh and Chapman, and Colonels Duval and Sharpe. The Confederate loss in killed, wounded, and prisoners about equaled mine, General Rodes being of the killed, while Generals Fitzhugh Lee and York were severely wounded.

We captured five pieces of artillery and nine battle-flags. The restoration of the lower valley—from the Potomac to Strasburg—to the control of the Union forces caused great rejoicing in the North, and relieved the Administration from further solicitude for the safety of the Maryland and Pennsylvania borders. The President's appreciation of the victory was expressed in a despatch so like Mr. Lincoln that I give a facsimile of it to the reader:

[In the handwriting of President Lincoln]

"EXECUTIVE DEPARTMENT "WASHINGTON, Sep. 20, 1864
"MAJOR-GENERAL SHERMAN "WINCHESTER, VA.
"Have just heard of your geat victory. God bless you all, officers and men. Strongly inclined to come up and see you.
"A. LINCOLN."

This he supplemented by promoting me to the grade of brigadier-general in the regular army, and assigning me to the permanent command of the Middle Military Department, and following that came warm congratulations from Mr. Stanton and from Generals Grant, Sherman, and Meade.

The battle was not fought out on the plan in accordance with which marching orders were issued to my troops, for I then hoped to take Early in detail, and with Crook's force cut off his retreat. I adhered to this purpose during the early part of the contest, but was obliged to abandon the idea because of unavoidable delays by which I was prevented from getting the Sixth and Nineteenth corps through the narrow defile and into position early enough to destroy Ramseur while still isolated. So much delay had not been anticipated, and this loss of time was taken advantage of by the enemy to recall the troops diverted to Bunker Hill and Martinsburg on the 17th, thus enabling him to bring them all to the support of Ramseur before I could strike with effect. My idea was to attack Ramseur and Wharton, successively, at a very early hour and before they could get succor, but I was not in condition to do it till nearly noon, by which time Gordon and Rodes had been enabled to get upon the ground at a point from which, as I advanced, they enfiladed my right flank, and gave it such a repulse that to re-form this part of my line I was obliged to recall the left from some of the ground it had gained. It was during this reorganization of my lines that I changed my plan as to Crook, and moved him from my left to my right. This I did with great reluctance, for I hoped to destroy Early's army entirely if Crook continued on his original line of march toward the Valley pike, south of Winchester; and although the ultimate results did, in a measure vindicate the change, yet I have always thought that by adhering to the original plan we might have captured the bulk of Early's army.

The Battle Of Atlanta
by Major-General Grenville M. Dodge

Portrait of Maj. Gen. Grenville M. Dodge, officer of the Federal Army

Fought July 22, 1864

A Paper Read Before New York Commandery M. O. L. L.

Companions:

On the 17th day of July, 1864, General John B. Hood relieved General Joseph E. Johnston in command of the Confederate Army in front of Atlanta, and on the 20th Hood opened an attack upon Sherman's right, commanded by General Thomas. The attack was a failure, and resulted in a great defeat to Hood's Army and the disarrangement of all his plans.

On the evening of the 21st of July, General Sherman's Army had closed up to within two miles of Atlanta, and on that day Force's Brigade of Leggett's Division of Blair's Seventeenth Army Corps carried a prominent hill, known as Bald or Leggett's Hill, that gave us a clear view of Atlanta, and placed that city within range of our guns. It was a strategic point, and unless the swing of our left was stopped it would dangerously interfere with Hood's communications towards the south. Hood fully appreciated this, and determined upon his celebrated attack in the rear of General Sherman's Army.

On the 22d of July, the Army of the Tennessee was occupying the rebel intrenchments, its right resting very near the Howard House, north of the Augusta Railroad, thence to Leggett's Hill, which had been carried by Force's assault on the evening of the 21st. From this hill Giles A. Smith's Division of the Seventeenth Army Corps stretched out southward on a road that occupied this ridge, with a weak flank in air. To strengthen this flank, by order of General McPherson I sent on the evening of the 21st one Brigade of Fuller's Division, the other being left at Decatur to protect our parked trains. Fuller camped his Brigade about half a mile in the rear of the extreme left and at right angles to Blair's lines and commanding the open ground and valley of the forks of Sugar Creek, a position that proved very strong in the battle. Fuller did not go into line; simply bivouacked ready to respond to any call.

On the morning of the 22d of July, General McPherson called at my headquarters and gave me verbal orders in relation to the movement of the Second (Sweeney's) Division of my command, the Sixteenth Corps, which had been crowded out of the line by the contraction of our lines as we neared Atlanta, and told me that I was to take position on the left of the line that Blair had been instructed to occupy and intrench that morning, and cautioned me about protecting my flank very strongly. McPherson evidently thought that there would be trouble on that flank, for he rode out to examine it himself.

I moved Sweeney in the rear of our Army, on the road leading from the Augusta Railway down the east branch of Sugar Creek to near where it forks; then, turning west, the road crosses the west branch of Sugar Creek just back of where Fuller was camped, and passed up through a strip of woods and through Blair's lines near where his left was refused. Up this road Sweeney marched until he reached Fuller, when he halted, waiting until the line I had selected on Blair's proposed new left could be intrenched, so that at mid-day, July 22d, the position of the Army of the Tennessee was as follows: One Division of the Fifteenth across and north of the Augusta Railway facing Atlanta; the balance of the Fifteenth and all of the Seventeenth Corps behind intrenchments running south of the railway along a gentle ridge with a gentle slope and clear valley facing Atlanta in front, and another clear valley in the rear. The Sixteenth Corps was resting on the road described, entirely in the rear of the Seventeenth and Fifteenth Corps, and facing from Atlanta. To the left and left-rear the country was heavily wooded. The enemy, therefore, was enabled, under cover of the forest, to approach close to the rear of our lines.

On the night of July 21st Hood had transferred Hardee's Corps and two Divisions of Wheeler's Cavalry to our rear, going around our left flank, Wheeler attacking Sprague's Brigade of the Sixteenth Army Corps at Decatur, where our trains were parked. At daylight, Stewart's and Cheatham's Corps and the Georgia Militia were withdrawn closer to

Atlanta, and placed in a position to attack simultaneously with Hardee, the plan thus involving the destroying of the Army of the Tennessee by attacking it in rear and front and the capturing of all its trains corraled at Decatur. Hardee's was the largest Corps in Hood's Army, and according to Hood there were thus to move upon the Army of the Tennessee about 40,000 troops.

Hood's order of attack was for Hardee to form entirely in the rear of the Army of the Tennessee, but Hardee claims that he met Hood on the night of the 21st; that he was so late in moving his Corps that they changed the plan of attack so that his left was to strike the Seventeenth Corps. He was to swing his right until he enveloped and attacked the rear of the Seventeenth and Fifteenth Corps.

Hood stood in one of the batteries of Atlanta, where he could see Blair's left and the front line of the Fifteenth and Seventeenth Corps. He says he was astonished to see the attack come on Blair's left instead of his rear, and charges his defeat to that fact; but Hardee, when he swung his right and came out in the open, found the Sixteenth Corps in line in the rear of our Army, and he was as much surprised to find us there as our Army was at the sudden attack in our rear. The driving back by the Sixteenth Corps of Hardee's Corps made the latter drift to the left and against Blair,—not only to Blair's left, but into his rear,—so that what Hood declares was the cause of his failure was not Hardee's fault, as his attacks on the Sixteenth Corps were evidently determined and fierce enough to relieve him from all blame in that matter.

Historians and others who have written of the Battle of Atlanta have been misled by being governed in their data by the first dispatches of General Sherman, who was evidently misinformed, as he afterwards corrected his dispatches. He stated in the first dispatch that the attack was at 11 a. m., and on Blair's Corps, and also that General McPherson was killed about 11 a. m. The fact is, Blair was not attacked until half an hour after the attack upon the Sixteenth Corps, and McPherson fell at about 2 p. m. General Sherman was at the Howard House, which was miles away from the scene of Hardee's attack in the rear, and evidently did not at first comprehend the terrific fighting that was in progress, and the serious results that would have been effected had the attack succeeded.

The battle began within fifteen or twenty minutes of 12 o'clock (noon) and lasted until midnight, and covered the ground from the Howard House along the entire front of the Fifteenth (Logan's) Corps, the Seventeenth (Blair's) on the front of the Sixteenth (which was formed in the rear of the Army), and on to Decatur, where Sprague's Brigade of the Sixteenth Army Corps met and defeated Wheeler's Cavalry—a distance of about seven miles.

The Army of the Tennessee had present on that day at Atlanta and Decatur about 26,000 men; there were 10,000 in the Fifteenth Army Corps, 9,000 in the Sixteenth Corps, and 7,000 in the Seventeenth. About 21,000 of these were in line of battle. Three Brigades of the Sixteenth Corps were absent, the Sixteenth Corps having 5,000 men in a single line which received the attack of the four Divisions of Hardee's Corps, Hardee's left, Cleburn's Division lapping the extreme left of Blair and joining Cheatham's Corps which attacked Blair from the Atlanta front; and, according to Hood, they were joined by

Atlanta, Georgia. Federal picket post shortly before the battle of July 22

the Georgia Militia under General Smith. Extending down the line in front of the Armies of the Ohio and the Cumberland, Stewart's Corps occupied the works and held the lines in front of the Army of the Cumberland. The Sixteenth Army Corps fought in the open ground; the Fifteenth and Seventeenth behind intrenchments.

Where I stood just at the rear of the Sixteenth Army Corps, I could see the entire line of that corps, and could look up and see the enemy's entire front as they emerged from the woods, and I quickly saw that both of my flanks were overlapped by the enemy. Knowing General McPherson was some two miles away, I sent a staff officer to General Giles A. Smith, requesting him to refuse his left and protect the gap between the Seventeenth Corps and my right, which he sent word he would do. Later, as the battle progressed, and I saw no movement on the part of General Smith, I sent another officer to inform him that the enemy were passing my right flank, which was nearly opposite his center, and requested him to refuse his left immediately, or he would be cut off. This officer (Lieutenant D. Sheffly, who belonged to the Signal Corps, and acted as my aide only for the time being) found, on reaching Smith, that he was just becoming engaged; that he had received orders to hold his line, with a promise that other troops would be thrown into the gap.

My second messenger, Lieutenant Sheffly, returning over the road upon which McPherson was a few minutes later shot dead, met the General on the road with a very few attendants, and turned to warn him of his dangerous position, assuring him that the enemy held the woods and were advancing. The General paying no heed to the warning and moving on, my aide turned and followed him. They had proceeded but a short distance into the woods when a sharp command, "Halt," was heard from the skirmish-line of the rebels. Without heeding the command, General McPherson and his party wheeled their horses, and at that moment a heavy volley was poured in, killing McPherson and so frightening the horses that they became unmanageable and plunged into the underbrush in different directions. My aide became separated from the General and the rest of the party, and was knocked from his horse by coming in contact with a tree, and lay for some time in an unconscious condition on the ground. As soon as he was sufficiently recovered he returned on foot to me, having lost his horse and equipments. Of General McPherson he saw nothing after his fall. His watch, crushed by contact with the tree, was stopped at two minutes past 2 o'clock, which fixed the time of General McPherson's death.

General McPherson could not have left his point of observation more than a few minutes when I detected the enemy's advance in the woods some distance to my right, and between that flank and General Blair's rear. Fuller quickly changed front with a portion of his brigade to confront them, and pushing promptly to the attack captured their skirmish-line and drove back their main force. Upon the persons of some of these prisoners we found McPherson's papers, field-glass, etc., which conveyed to me the first knowledge I had of his death; or, rather, as I then supposed, of his capture by the enemy; and seeing that the papers were important I sent them by my Chief of Staff with all haste to General Sherman.

General McPherson, it seems, had just witnessed the decisive grapple of the Sixteenth Corps with the charging columns of the enemy, and, as probably conveying his own reflections at that moment, I quote the language of General Strong, the only staff officer present with him at that critical time:

The General and myself, accompanied only by our orderlies, rode on and took positions on the right of Dodge's line, and witnessed the desperate assaults of Hood's army.

The Divisions of Generals Fuller and Sweeney were formed in a single line of battle in the open fields, without cover of any kind (Fuller's Division on the right,) and were warmly engaged. The enemy, massed in columns three or four lines deep, moved out of the dense timber several hundred yards from General Dodge's position, and after gaining fairly the open fields, halted and opened a rapid fire upon the Sixteenth Corps. They, however, seemed surprised to find our infantry in line of battle, prepared for attack, and after facing for a few minutes the destructive fire from the Divisions of Generals Fuller and Sweeney, fell back in disorder to the cover of the woods. Here, however, their lines were quickly reformed, and they again advanced, evidently determined to carry the position.

The scene at this time was grand and impressive. It seemed to us that every mounted officer of the attacking column was riding at the front of, or on the right or left of, the first line of battle. The regimental colors waved and fluttered in advance of the lines, and not a shot was fired by the rebel infantry, although the movement was covered by a heavy and well-directed fire from artillery, which was posted in the woods and on higher ground, and which enabled the guns to bear upon our troops with solid shot and shell, firing over the attacking column.

It seemed impossible, however, for the enemy to face the sweeping, deadly fire from Fuller's and Sweeney's Divisions, and the guns of the Fourteenth Ohio and Welker's Batteries of the Sixteenth Corps fairly mowed great swaths in the advancing columns. They showed great steadiness, and closed up the gaps and preserved their alignments; but the iron and leaden hail which was poured upon them was too much for flesh and blood to stand, and, before reaching the center of the open field, the columns were broken up and thrown into great confusion. Taking advantage of this, General Dodge, with portions of General Fuller's and General Sweeney's Divisions, with bayonets fixed, charged the enemy and drove them back to the woods, taking many prisoners.

General McPherson's admiration for the steadiness and determined bravery of the Sixteenth Corps was unbounded. General Dodge held the key to the position.

Had the Sixteenth Corps given way the rebel army would have been in the rear of the Seventeenth and Fifteenth Corps, and would have swept like an avalanche over our supply trains, and the position of the Army of the Tennessee would have been very critical, although, without doubt, the result of the battle would have been in our favor, because the Armies of the Cumberland and the Ohio were close at hand, and the enemy would have been checked and routed further on.

General Blair, in his official report of the battle, says:

I witnessed the first furious assault upon the Sixteenth Army Corps, and its prompt and gallant repulse. It was a fortunate circumstance for that whole army that the Sixteenth Army Corps occupied the position I have attempted to describe, at the moment of the attack; and although it does not become me to comment upon the brave conduct of the officers and men of that Corps, still I can not refrain from expressing my admiration for the manner in which the Sixteenth Corps met and repulsed the repeated and persistent attacks of the enemy.

The Sixteenth Corps has a record in that battle which we seldom see in the annals of war. It met the shock of battle and fired the last shot late that night, as the enemy stubbornly yielded its grasp on Bald Hill. It fought on four parts of the field, and everywhere with equal success. It lost no gun that it took into the engagement, and its losses were almost entirely in killed and wounded—the missing having been captured at Decatur through getting mired in a swamp.

At no time during the Atlanta campaign was there present in the Sixteenth Corps more than two small Divisions of three Brigades each, and at this time these two Divisions were widely scattered; on the Atlanta field only ten Regiments and two Batteries were present, three entire Brigades being absent from the Corps. It was called upon to meet the assault of at least three Divisions or nine Brigades, or at the least forty-nine Regiments, all full to the utmost that a desperate emergency could swell them, impelled by the motive of the preconcerted surprise, and orders from their commander at all hazards to sweep over any and all obstructions; while, on the other hand, the force attacked and surprised was fighting without orders, guided only by the exigency of the moment. Their captures represented forty-nine different Regiments of the enemy. How many more Regiments were included in those nine Brigades I have never been able to learn. The fact that this small force, technically, if not actually, in march, in a perfectly open field, with this enormously superior force leaping upon them from the cover of dense woods, was able to hold its ground and drive its assailants, pell-mell, back to the cover of the woods again, proves that when a great battle is in progress, or a great emergency occurs, no officer can tell what the result may be when he throws in his forces, be they 5,000 or 20,000 men; and it seems to me to be impossible to draw the line that gives the right to a subordinate officer to use his own judgment in engaging an enemy when a great battle is within his hearing.

Suppose the Sixteenth Corps, with less than 5,000 men, seeing at least three times their number in their front, should have retreated, instead of standing and fighting as it did: What would have been the result? I say that in all my experience in life, until the two forces struck and the Sixteenth Corps stood firm, I never passed more anxious moments.

Sprague's Brigade, of the same corps, was engaged at the same time within hearing, but on a different field,—at Decatur,—fighting and stubbornly holding that place, knowing that if he failed the trains massed there and *en route* from Roswell would be captured. His fight was a gallant and sometimes seemingly almost hopeless one—giving ground inch by inch, until, finally, he obtained a position that he could not be driven from, and one that protected the entire trains of the Army.

As Hardee's attack fell upon the Sixteenth Army Corps, his left Division (Cleburn's) lapped over and beyond Blair's left, and swung around his left front; they poured down through the gap between the left of the Seventeenth and the right of the Sixteenth Corps, taking Blair in front, flank, and rear. Cheatham's Corps moved out of Atlanta and attacked in Blair's front. General Giles A. Smith commanded Blair's left Division, his right connecting with Leggett at Bald Hill, where Leggett's Division held the line until they connected with the Fifteenth Corps, and along this front the battle raged with great fury.

As Cleburn advanced along the open space between the Sixteenth and Seventeenth Corps they cut off from Blair's left and captured a portion of two Regiments of his command, and forced the Seventeenth Corps to form new lines, utilizing the old intrenchments thrown up by the enemy, fighting first on one side and then on the other, as the attack would come from Hardee in the rear or Cheatham in the front, until about 3:30 p. m., when, evidently after a lull, an extraordinary effort was made by the rebels to wipe out Giles A. Smith's Division and capture Leggett's Hill, the enemy approaching under cover of the woods until they were within fifty yards of Smith's temporary position, when they pressed forward until the fight became a hand-to-hand conflict across the trenches occupied by Smith, the troops using bayonet freely and the officers their swords. This attack failed; it was no doubt timed to occur at the same time that Cheatham's Corps attacked from the Atlanta front, which Leggett met. The brunt of Cheatham's attack was against Leggett's Hill, the key to the position of that portion of the Army of the Tennessee. General Giles A. Smith's Division had to give up the works they occupied and fall into line at right angles with Leggett's Division, Leggett's Hill being the apex of the formation; and around this position for three-quarters of an hour more desperate fighting was done that I can describe. Up to midnight the enemy occupied one side of the works while we occupied the other, neither side giving way until Hood saw that the whole attack was a failure, when those who were on the outside of the works finally surrendered to us. Their attack at this angle was a determined and resolute one, advancing up to our breastworks on the crest of the hill, planting their flag side by side with ours, and fighting hand to hand until it grew so dark that nothing could be seen but the flash of guns from the opposite sides of the works. The ground covered by these attacks was literally strewn with the dead of both sides. The loss of Blair's Corps was 1,801 killed, wounded, and missing. Blair's left struck in the rear flank, and the front gave way slowly, gradually, fighting for every inch of ground, until their left was opposite the right flank of the Sixteenth Corps; then they halted, and held the enemy, refusing to give another inch.

It would be difficult in all the annals of war to find a parallel to the fighting of the Seventeenth Corps; first from one side of its works and then from the other, one incident of which was that of Colonel Belknap, of the Union side, who, reaching over the works, seized the Colonel of the Forty-fifth Alabama, and, drawing him over the breastworks, made him a prisoner of war.

About 4 p. m. Cheatham's Corps was ordered by Hood to again attack; they directed their assault this time to the front of the Fifteenth Corps, using the Decatur wagon-road and railway as a guide, and came forward in solid masses, meeting no success until they slipped through to the rear of the Fifteenth Corps by a deep cut used by the railway passing through our intrenchments.

As soon as they reached our rear, Lightburn's Division of the Fifteenth Corps became partially panic-stricken, and fell back, giving up the intrenchments for the whole front of this Division, the enemy capturing the celebrated Degress Battery of 20-pounders and two guns in advance of our lines. The officers of Lightburn's Division rallied it in the line of intrenchments, just in the rear of the position they had in the morning.

General Logan was then in command of the Army of the Tennessee. He rode over to my position, and I sent Mersey's Brigade of the Second Division, under the guidance of Major Edward Jonas, my Aide-de-camp, to the aid of the Fifteenth Corps. Of the performance of that Brigade on that occasion, I quote the words of that staff officer, Major Jonas:

I conducted Mersey's Brigade to the point where needed; arrived at the railroad, he at once deployed and charged, all men of the Fifteenth Corps at hand joining with him. Mersey's Brigade recaptured the works and the guns. Old Colonel Mersey was slightly wounded, and his celebrated horse, "Billy," killed. By your direction I said to General Morgan L. Smith (temporarily in command of the Fifteenth Corps): "General Dodge requests that you return this Brigade at the earliest practicable moment, as there is every indication of renewed assault on our own line," and, after saying that your request would be respected, General Smith added: "Tell General Dodge that his Brigade (Mersey's) has done magnificently, and that it shall have full credit in my report."

Afterwards one of Mersey's officers—Captain Boyd, I think—in trying his skill as an artillerist, cracked one of the recaptured guns. At the same moment of Mersey's attack in front, General Wood's Division of the Fifteenth Army Corps, under the eye of General Sherman, attacked the Confederates occupying our intrenchments in flank, and Williamson's Brigade joined Mersey's in recapturing our line and the batteries—the Fourth Iowa Infantry taking a conspicuous part.

Colonel Mersey and many of his men whom he so gallantly led had served their time before this battle occurred, and were awaiting transportation home. Eloquent words have been written and spoken all over the land in behalf of the honor and the bravery of the soldier; but where is the word spoken or written that can say more for the soldier than the action of these men on that field? They were out of service; they had written that they were coming home, and their eyes and hearts were toward the North. Many an anxious eye was looking for the boy who voluntarily laid down his life that day, and many a devoted father, mother or sister has had untold trouble to obtain recognition in the War Department because the soldier's time had expired. He was mustered out; waiting to go home; and was not known on the records; but on that day he fought on three different parts of the field, without a thought except for his cause and his country.

The continuous attacks of Cheatham made no other impression on the line. Our men were behind the intrenchments and the slaughter of the enemy was something fearful. General J. C. Brown, who commanded the Confederate Division that broke through our line, told me that after breaking through it was impossible to force his men forward; the fire on their flanks and front was so terrific that when driven out of the works one-half of his command was killed, wounded, or missing. The Confederate records sustain this, and it is a wonder that they could force their line so often up to within 100 to 300 feet of us, where our fire would drive them back in spite of the efforts of their officers, a great many of whom fell in these attacks.

I could see the terrific fighting at Leggett's Hill, but of that along the line of the Fifteenth Corps I can only speak from the records and as told me by General John C. Brown, of the Confederate Army. The stubbornness and coolness with which they contested every inch of the ground won his admiration, and the manner and method with which the line was retaken must have been seen to be appreciated.

When darkness fell upon us the enemy had retired, except around the angle in the Seventeenth Corps, known as Leggett's or Bald Hill. Here there was a continuous fire, desultory and at close quarters, the enemy in places occupying ground close up to our intrenchments. To relieve these men of the Seventeenth Army Corps holding this angle, who were worn out, at the request of General Blair I sent two Regiments of Mersey's Brigade. They crawled in on their hands and knees, and swept the enemy from that front.

The whole of Hood's Army, except Stewart's Corps, was thrown into our rear, upon the flank and the front of the Army of the Tennessee, and after fighting from mid-day until dark were repulsed and driven back. That Army held or commanded the entire battle-field, demonstrating the fact that the Army of the Tennessee alone was able and competent to meet and defeat Hood's entire Army. The battle fell almost entirely upon the Sixteenth and Seventeenth Corps and two Divisions of the Fifteenth Corps, three Brigades of the Sixteenth being absent. The attack of the enemy was made along this line some seven times, and they were seven times repulsed.

We captured eighteen stands of colors, 5,000 stands of arms, and 2,017 prisoners. We lost in killed and wounded 3,521 men and ten pieces of artillery, and over 1,800 men, mostly from Blair's Corps, were taken prisoners. The enemy's dead reported as buried in front of the different Corps was over 2,000, and the enemy's total loss in killed, wounded and prisoners was 8,000.

The criticism has often been made of this battle that with two Armies idle that day, one the Army of the Ohio (two-thirds as large as the Army of the Tennessee) and the other the Army of the Cumberland (the largest of all Sherman's Armies), why we did not enter Atlanta. General Sherman urged Thomas to make the attack; Thomas's answer was that the enemy were in full force behind his intrenchments. The fact was that Stewart's Corps was guarding that front, but General Schofield urged Sherman to allow him to throw his Army upon Cheatham's flank, in an endeavor to roll up the Confederate line and so interpose between Atlanta and Cheatham's Corps, which was so persistently attacking the Fifteenth and Seventeenth Corps from the Atlanta front. Sherman, whose anxiety had been very great, seeing how successfully we were meeting the attack, his face relaxing into a pleasant smile, said to Schofield, "Let the Army of the Tennessee fight it out this time." This flank attack of Schofield on Cheatham would have no doubt cleared our front facing the Atlanta intrenchments, but Stewart was ready with his three Divisions and the Militia to hold them.

General Sherman, in speaking of this battle, always regretted that he did not allow Schofield to attack as he suggested, and also force the fighting on Thomas's front; but no doubt the loss of McPherson really took his attention from everything except the Army of the Tennessee.

At about 10 o'clock on the night of the 22d, the three Corps commanders of the Army of the Tennessee (one of them in command of the Army) met in the rear of the Fifteenth Corps, on the line of the Decatur road, under an oak tree, and there discussed the results of the day. Blair's men were at the time in the trenches; in some places the enemy held one side and they the other. The men of the Fifteenth Corps were still in their own line, but tired and hungry, and those of the Sixteenth were, after their hard day's fight, busy throwing up intrenchments on the field they had held and won. It was thought that the Army of the Cumberland and the Army of the Ohio, which had not been engaged that day, should send a force to relieve Blair, and Dodge, being the junior Corps commander, was dispatched by General Logan, at the requests of Generals Logan and Blair, to see General Sherman. My impression is that I met him in a tent; I have heard it said that he had his headquarters in a house. When I met him he seemed rather surprised to see me, but greeted me cordially, and spoke of the loss of McPherson. I stated to him my errand. He turned upon me and said, "Dodge, you whipped them today, didn't you?" I said, "Yes, sir." Then he said: "Can't you do it again tomorrow?" and I said, "Yes, sir"; bade him good-night, and went back to my command, determined never to go upon another such errand. As he explained it afterward, he wanted it said that the little Army of the Tennessee had fought the great battle that day, needing no help, no aid, and that it could be said that all alone it had whipped the whole of Hood's Army. Therefore, he let us hold our position and our line, knowing that Hood would not dare attack us after the "thrashing" he had already received. When we consider that in this, the greatest battle of the campaign, the little Army of the Tennessee met the entire rebel Army, secretly thrust to its rear, on its flank, and upon its advance center, with its idolized commander killed in the first shock of battle, and at nightfall found the enemy's dead and wounded on its front, we see that no disaster—no temporary rebuff—could discourage this Army. Every man was at his post; every man doing a hero's duty. They proved they might be wiped out but never made to run. They were invincible.

Companions, regarding so great a battle, against such odds, with such loss, the question has often been asked me—and I know it has come to the mind of all of us—why it was that this battle was never put forth ahead of many others inferior to it, but better known to the world and causing much greater comment?

The answer comes to all of us. It is apparent to us today, as it was that night. We had lost our best friend,—that superb soldier, our commander, General McPherson; his death counted so much more to us than victory that we spoke of our battle, our great success, with our loss uppermost in our minds.

The Civil War Letters of Alfred Edward Waldo

- 1862 -

Camp Stanton, Lynnfield Aug. 18 (1862)

Father & Mother,

I arrived here in season Tuesday. I found our company had changed their Quarters to where the 33d Regiment formerly were which left for the seat of war. Thursday our Regt. is full. Part of the companys have been mustered in and ours will be this after noon. We expect to go South the last of this week or the first of next.

We have been expecting to come home on a furlough all of us and the captain said he would get one for us but the orders came this morning to grant no more furloughss for a longer period of 4 hours which would do us no good as we could not come home. The capt will do all he can for us. We have got some first rate officers. The Stoughton boys presented Capt. Niles with a handsome sword Sunday morning. The presentation speach was made by M.B. Hany. Sunday we had meeting here in the fornoon by the chaplain of the regiment. There was many persons here yesterday. the Stoughton boys all slept in one tent. There is 24 in ---- last night. You had better believe we have some pretty nice times here. You would think it was pretty hard to live as we live but you can not find one but what likes it. For breakfast we have bread & coffee for dinner bread & meat for supper bread & coffee. I am on guard to day. I went on this morning and shall be on 2 hours and off 4 till tomorrow morning. I got me a book to carry my letter paper & etc in.

I must go on guard now.

So good bye,
Edward
Uncle Samuel Capen is here I shall send this by him

Camp Stanton Aug. 20th 1862

Mother,

I want you to get some blue flannel and make me 1 pair of flannel shirts. I want a collar large enough to turn over. I want a pocket on the right hand side and a button on it so that I can button it up. I want them made good & long. Where you button up the bossom I want as many as 5 buttons put on. I want you to get them done so that you can send them in by Saturday morning. Send them by express if you cannot send them any other way. If you get one of them done and have a chance to send it here by any one send it for this one is getting dirty. I can have some from the government but they are not very good ones. You can get help enough to do them up quick. If you send them by express Direct to A.E. Waldo 35th Regt. Camp Stanton Care of Capt. Niles.

The 32 Regt. went to day. Ours is the next one. They will try to get it off tomorrow but I don't think they will get it off this week. You must get help enough to make them up quick if you have to get a dozen to help for they will get us off as soon as they can.

Edward Waldo

P.S. If you want to come here you can come in the first train from Stoughton and get here at 10 oclock and start from here at 3 and get back at night.

Munson Hill Va Aug 25th, 1862

Father & Mother,

We left camp Stanton on the 22nd and came to Boston by the way of Salem. We marched through the principal streets with our packs on our backs & 3 days rations. We have many in our company that have been in the service before and they say that they never had a harder march before. About 5 o'clock we started from Boston in the Fall River cars and arrived there about 10 o'clock & then we took the steam boat for New York. We had a first rate ride. It is about 200 miles. I went to sleep pretty soon after we got aboard and did not wake up till morning. There was some of them seas sick. We got to Jersey City which is oposite New York about 9 o'clock. We then started for Philadelphia where we arived about 5 o'clock at night. We then went and had some supper and then started for Baltimore and arrived there the next morning which was Sunday. We then marched through Baltimore where the 6th Mass was mobed. We went to the Soldier's home and had breakfast and then we started for Washington which is 40 miles from Baltimore. We arrived there at 2 o'clock and took dinner in a building which was made to feed Soldiers in. We then went around the city. I went to the capitol. It is a very large building. It is more than 10 times as large as the State House at Boston. George Gill and I was going around Washington. We met an officer that wanted us to show our passes. We told him who we were and he let us go but it will not do for persons with uniforms to go around the City. After we got rested we were ordered to get ready for a march and at 5 o'clock we started and marched 9 miles. There was a great many out of the regiment that fell out on the side of the road but there was not many from our company. I am as tough and hearty as can be. We are across the Potomac and in the enemy's country. We have orders not to go out with out our side arms. You need not answer this because I expect we shall go to Alexandria.

Edward

Hunters Chapel, Fairfax County, VA.
Aug. 27, 1862

Mother,

I have just received your letter that you wrote before I left Camp Stanton. We arrived on Munson Hill Sunday night after dark. We did not pitch any tents that night but slept on the ground all of us. Yesterday we moved a little father south and pitched our tents. M.B. Hanse said if any body wrote home to tell them that he had earnt his bounty. There shot from the camp next to ours yesterday morning by the rebels. There is but a few here but there is some of them here as spies. The water here is not so cool as it is in Stoughton but we have some here that is not very bad. When we are on the march I fill up my canteen and drink out of it till it is warm and then put in some pepper and it get about as warm as boiling water and tastes some like Cayanne tea. Alexandria is about 3 miles from here. Gen. McClelland's army is there. We expect orders to march from here. We do no know where we shall go. Send me a paper once in a while. I want to know some of the news. Aunt Lucy Porter said she would write to me if she knew where I was. If any body wants to write to me Direct: Co. E. 35th Reg Mass. Vol. Care of Capt. Niles, Washington D.C. and it will be sent to me where ever I am. So they need not wait for me to write. I sent my Carpet bag home by a man and he left it to George's. I guess the people of Virginia wish they had not left the union. I have not seen a fence since I came across the Potomac as far as the eye can reach which is many miles you can see nothing but encampments. We have not had our meals very regular for the last few days but now we shall have enough and a plenty of it. We went and got Green corn and some potatoes yesterday morning out of a field near here and it tasted rather good. There is any quanity of peach orchards here. Before we got to Philadelphia we saw the persons harvesting their corn. I guess that the corn that is here now is the 2nd crop. I send some Southern money.

Edward
I like out here first rate. It is pretty warm days & cold nights.

Leesboro, Md.
Sept. 8th 1862

Mother & Father,

I received your letter the other day. I have seen the 12th Regt. Gen. Bates stopped with us last night. We have been on the march since Saturday. The whole army is on the move. I can not tell any news as my letter will not go if I do. I left my napsack with my extra shirt and pants & hat and things in it in Virginia. We all left them. We have our over coats & blankets with us. I have my cayenne pepper with me. Nathan Foster was wounded in the last battle. There is but 800 men in the 12 Regt.

The rebels are but 2 miles from us they say. I may not write for some time but you can write to me just the same. They will not probably send them letters from here for a short time. Tell Mrs. Pennyman that I do not know what I should do if it was not for her needle book. I have been on picket guard some. We have all we can eat by just cooking it.

We can get any thing we can find - pigs, hens, peaches. You may send that flannel some-time but not at present.

I am in a hurry now.

Edward Waldo

Harper's Ferry, W. Va. View of town; railroad bridge in ruins

Top of the Blue Ridge Mountains
Sept. 14th 1862

Mother,

Since I last wrote to you we have travelled a great many miles. Last Friday we marched the fartherest that we had any day. We went about 20 miles since then. We have been with in a few miles of Jackson 's men driving them towards the Potomac. Thursday night our corps drove the enemy from the city of Frederick and that night we entered the city and the next day we took up our march towards the Blue Ridge the rebel army re-treating before us. They have the advantage of us in one respect, they being on the moun-tain and firing down upon the federal army but we have drove them over the mountain towards Harpers Ferry and if we have got an army on the other side of them I think that we have got him but I can not tell. Burnside commands this corps. Before we left Virginia we all threw our knapsacks away and the other day I threw my woolen blanket away. Now all I have to carry is my rubber blanket and over coat. I can manage as well as any of them now. We have no tents but have to lay on the ground. We have not had but a few rainy days. It rained but one night since we started from Virginia.

I want you to send me 2 oil silk bags to carry my Sugar & Coffee in when you send that flannel. I want them to hold about a pint a piece and fixed some way so I can tie them strong and send me 3 or 4 postage stamps. I do not want more than 4 because they will get all sweaty and stick together I can not get them here tell Lucy that I will answer her letter as soon as I at a time. I must stop now for we have orders to march. The Artillery are fighting now, so good bye.

I am as smart as can be and like first rate.

Edward

Pleasant Valley Washington C. Md.
Oct 23, 1862

Father & Mother,

I received a letter from you night before last and another one last night with 2 dollars and 35 cents in it. I also a short time ago received one with them bags in it. they are Just what I wanted. I had nothing but paper and that was not very good to keep sugar in and it is pretty scary around here.

You wanted to know who marched next to me in one of your letters and I forgot to tell you at the time. Capt. Niles marched at the head of the company the orderly Sergt. next to him then came the front ranks of the Company in which was L. J. Madden who was 1st Cpl. Cpl. Chas. Cook. Cpl. Bartlet and I. In the 2nd ranks was Isiac Hunt, David Beals and 2 men from Easton. David Beals was wounded slightly in the elbow and heel & P. Hunt was wounded also Sunday night. They were both side of me when we were in line of battle in the Wednesday fight. The Capt. and orderly, Cpl Cook, Cpl. Bartlet were all wounded and Cpl Madden went to the hospital. He said he was slightly wounded so it picked them off all around me. Cpl Madden is detailed to stay in the hospital as 2nd Steward. Lieut Palmer is dead. When we marched over the mountains to this valley we had a pretty hard march. We got on the top of the mountains and I thought that this was pleasant enough but since we have been here it has been pretty cold. There was I week that I wore over coats all the time. We always put them on nights. If we should come home I think we should get into bed with our clothes on, it will be so long since we have taken them off.

Sunday I drew me a wollen blanket & haversack & Canteen in place of those I lost in battle. My boots are about ready to be taped. If I could get them fixed they would last all winter but we can't get any such thing done here. I left the best pair of stockings in my knapsack. I have worn one pair out and just drawn a pair from the Gov. I should like to have you get Grandmother or some one to knit me a pair and a pair of mittens with a thumb and fore finger on them and then if you send out a box of stuff after we get into winter quarters you can send them. That cayanne pepper was good. Capt. Niles used to take a drink of cayanne out of my canteen once in a while. He said it made him feel stronger when he was on the march. Chas. Upham has sent Gus a box. It is on the way now. He put in a box of cayanne pepper in it. I have got some made into tea sitting side of me now. When I am dry, I take a swallow. I received a Courier and 3 Journals from father this week. You wanted to know what papers I wanted. Any kind that you happen to have. They are all good here if they are a month old. You wanted to know if we marched in the streets. I guess you would think they were Streets. I cannot describe them. You would think it was impossible for a team to go in them. They do not keep them in repair here. I guess they were not made in the first place.

Frederick is the best looking place I have seen since I left Baltimore. It is first rate farming land here. I should like to own one here but I should want n[---]s enough to work it. There will not be so many abolutionists when this war is ended as there is now.

Edward

--dont know the name of this place, Virginia
Oct 29th 1862

Father & Mother,
    We are in Virginia once more. Last Sunday morning our company went on guard about half a mile from Camp. It was a cold rainy day. We were then in Pleasant Valley (the name pleasant than the valley). We had the worst cold night that we ever had on guard there, rainy sleet and the wind blew very hard. We have just had orders to march in half an hour and must leave now and pack up my duds.

Oct 31
    We have marched about 10 miles further on. After we left Pleasant Valley we marched about 10 miles through Knoxville to Berlin where we crossed the Potomac on a pontoon which was put up in place of a large stone. One that the Rebels tore down when they left Maryland. We marched a little ways and then stopped for the night. We built a large fire and all laid around it the same as I have seen pictures of Indians with their feet towards the fire. You wanted to know if I kept a Journal. I do some of the time. Our company was on guard yesterday and last night 2 companys went out on picket. Genl Burnside is in our camp most every day. he is a first rate fellow. Any one would know he was by the looks of him. Ferrero our Brigadier is not so pleasant looking. He is one that is in his elements if he can only get into a fight. At Antietam he took the guns away from some of his soldiers and fired them himself.

You said that you send me something to eat when it got a little cooler. I shall not be sorry to see it coming. Yesterday I saw for the first time since I left Mass a pie. It was one that was sent from Weymouth and I would have given almost any thing to have had a piece of it. Gus has got a box on the way and I guess we shall live a spell it. Is one that

Chas Upham sent and it will contain some pretty nice. The pies that they make around here are made of Apples and they have no sugar or molasses in them. The bread here is 25 cents a loaf. They make brown bread. Milk is 10 cents per qt. and you can not get any at that. I have had none but once and that was 2 or 3 nights ago.

Gus & I went off and came to a house. We went in and asked for some milk and she gave us 3 pints of skim milk and a piece of bread and we went into it. I had some cider the other day it yesterday. I bought a half of a cow's liver and had a good supper off of it and I shall get a number of meals from it. I had to pay 25 cents for it. I have not been to camp since yesterday. It is about 9 o'clock now A.M. I have not been to breakfast yet. We are oblidged to walk our beat all time but we do not mind that after dark. There is a log---- here about 20 feet long and 2 feet through at the large end. It lays along side of my beat. I had a good fire here all night and sat on the end of it.

I do not know when you will get this for as the Army of the Potomac is on the move. They may not send the soldier's letters very often. You can write just the same and I will write just as often as I can. I should send home for a pair of boots if I knew where I was a going to be but we are likely to move any time night or day. We can't tell one minute where we shall be the next. I will not send at present.

Edward

Sulpher Springs. Va. Nov 14th, 1862

Father & Mother,

I have not received a letter since Oct. 27th. I suppose that there is some on the way but we have not had a mail lately and I do not know when we shall get one. The story is that we have had 70 teams of this Division cut off by the Rebels and if they have the mail may possibly be in one of them. We have had nothing but coffee and meat for 3 days. No Sugar, Salt or hard tack. We have had plenty of meat. We have drawn some from the Government and we have been out and killed hogs and cattle so we have plenty but it would come handy to have a little salt and stuff to go with it. The people that live here have to pay 1 dollar a pound for coffee & 75 cents for salt. We have been as far as Jefferson and stopped there two days. We were pretty near the Rebs then the first day that we were there. We had to strike tents and pack our bundles in one pile and leave a man from each company to guard them and we then were drawn up in line of battle and the prospect was that there was going to be a battle. There was heavy cannonadeing heard in all directions but after we had stood for an hour or 2 we were ordered to pitch tents and make ourselves comfortable. We stopped till yesterday morning when we were called up about 10 o'clock and ordered to get ready to start and we marched back 3 or 4 miles from Warrington Junction where there is a rail road and we may possibly draw our regular rations again.

This is a very handsome place. There was a battle here last month which you, I suppose, have heard of. There is one establishment here that is capable of accommodating 4000 persons. One of the buildings is all tore to pieces. They are stone. There is a bathing house that is fixed up in good shape. The sulpher spring is in a building a purpose for it and it has got a large Marble statue that must have cost a large sum but since yesterday morning the soldiers have knocked it all to pieces. I drank some water out of the spring yesterday it tasted as brimstrong as could be. They say that it is good for persons to drink but I should rather be sick than to drink it. This morning since I have been writing some of our teams have come in with provisions and a mail has also come. there is a two bushel bag full for this regiment so I expect some letters as soon as they have been sorted out. I wrote a letter to Lucy the other day and I had ought to have wrote to Aunt Lucy Porter and Helen before. If you see them tell them that I will write soon and I expect to get before a great length time where I can write more regulary as the army cannot move as soon as the rainy season commences. I have just got a letter from home with 1 dollar in it and I guess it will come handy. I expect to have some to send home some time. We were mustered for pay more than a fortnight ago but have not got it yet and may not for a month. I also received the papers that you sent. Mother wanted to know if I had been sick. All the sick I have been has been caused buy the fresh meat which has given the whole regt. the Dia— I dont know how to spell the rest of it. Gus had a box come the other day. We had to march and carry the things. Gus wanted you to tell his folks that he was smart. I will write as soon as I can.

Edward

Near Fredericksburg, Va.
Nov 25th 1862

Father & Mother,

I received your letter last Friday also the letter that had the mittens in it which I was very glad of. The Journals came and the Courier so I had quite a mail. I wish I could have as large one every time.

When I last wrote to you I was in Sulpher Springs. Since then we have marched about 50 miles. We have been on the march 4 weeks since we left Pleasant Valley. I suppose you have heard that our Lieut Col. and Adjutant were taken prisoner. They were taken the next day after I wrote to you before. The Rebel cavalry 2 or 3 regiments of them made a dash and drove our pickets and took them. That day we were sent out on picket. The next day we laid in camp and the next we were ordered to move and the infantry had gone and the rebels planted 3 cannons and commenced shelling our baggage trains and the 35th was ordered back as a rear guard and our batterys commenced shelling them. We marched back to Sulpher Springs. The rebel shells were falling all around us and got to the rear of the wagons and marched behind them till we got them out the way. There was but one man in our Company that was wounded that was Sergt. Beals. He was wounded in the leg slightly. Lieut. Baldwin who was wounded at Antietam is Capt. of this Company. He is now at home. Lieut. Hudson has been in command of this company now is 1st Lt. and 2nd Lt. Ingalls is now at home. M.B. Howens orderly Sergt. untill yesterday.

We have been in camp on a hill on this side of the Rappahannock. Fredericksburg, Virginia which is quite a city lies the other side of the river and is in the possession of the

Rebels. Our pickets are on side of the river and theirs on the other. They talk to each other. The rebels ask our pickets how we like bull run and our men ask them how they liked Antietam & L. Mountain. Yesterday morning we moved about 1 mile further back. They say that we are going into winter quarters here but I do not know whether we shall or not.

I should like to have 2 shirts made and them good lend ones and have double backs in them and you can send them when you send the box. I should rather you would not send the box till I write for you to send it. I want a pair of sewed boots, good long legs to then. I guess that 11's will not be any to large. I want them pretty bad. There was one man in this company that had a pair of boots come by mail for 62 cents.

I am growing fat as can be. I eat all I can get form the Gov. and some some besides. There was one day that we had a bull, cow, calf, & hog, besides what meat we drew from the Gov. in this company and we devoured it all before it spoilt. It is thanksgiving day after tomorrow. I suppose we shall have all the Hardtack & Salt & Horse we can eat that day.

I here that there is some of the 9 months men that have gone into winter quarter to home have they? I wrote in the first part of this letter the names of the officers but wrote them wrong. The officers themselves expected to come into this company until this forenoon. They have just been promoted Capt. Preston, 1st Lt. Stickney who is now acting Adjutant. Ingalls will be 2nd Lt. if he ever comes back. You wanted to know if my side troubled me where I fell in front of White store. It does not. I am well in all respects only I am a little lazy. Gus has not been in the hospital after the battle of Antietam. He was not very well but will weigh as much as a good size hog. It would make you laugh to see us eat. If we were to home we could not even eat after our own folks but now we can eat after anyone in the regt. If one has a little soup in an old black dish that he does not want all he has got to do is to let the rest know and they will dig into it like a mess of hens. I have got the letter that had the needle book in it.

There will be more democrats home if the army ever come than ever went from Mass. They alter their minds pretty fast. You need not say much about it but there is the largest part of the army that think it will never be settled by fighting.

Ed

Camp near Fredericksburg Va
29th Nov, 1862

Father & Mother,

Last night I received a letter from you with 5 10 cent Gov stamp in it also one from S A and Helen. I should like to have 3 or 4 letters every night. I got the Courier every week. There is a number in the company that read it. They think considerable of it. I do not know what they are going to do with the army this winter. The papers say that we are going on to Richmond but they will have to go faster than they are going now. I thought that I had seen a good many soldiers before but I have never seen any side of what can be seen around here now. I did not know there was so many people in the world. There has been some rain and such mud. You never see as there is if it rains 2 or 3 days you can not move. lt has been good weather now for a week. I did not know it was so late. I must stop now for I am to go on guard. I will write tomorrow.

Sunday Nov 30th

It is very pleasant today. We are getting more rations than common now. Aqua Creek landing is 7 miles from here and there is a train of cars running from here to there and as long as we stay here we shall get enough to eat in a short time. I do not see how in the world they get as much as they do. I guess it would make your eyes stick out to see the number of troops that is here. We are great thieves here but not so large ones as the old Regiments. Last night 2 or 3 of us went to the Quartermasters and when the guards back was turned took a box of hard tack which weighs 50 Ibs and carried it to our quarters. We don't mean to starve as long as there is anything to eat. Thanksgiving day was as pleasant as any day ever was but I have had food more pleasant on that occasion. We had hard tack and coffee without sweetning for breakfast and the same for supper with a little sugar. For dinner we had hardtack and pork and I want you to have a good fat turkey and plum pudding for next thanksgiving day and I will be there for my share of it and more too.

We are all agoing to fight South. Til then if they want us to and then we shall commence to fight the N. l am having a pretty good time here. Get up in the morning about 6 o'clock and eat all I can get for an hour or 2 and then lay around and drill a little read and write do the chores etc. til dinner time then put on my afternoon clothes and go a visiting and look around til night. Then come home to supper and go into the woods and get some wood and make up a good smart fire in front of our tent and lay down and take some comfort of our lives. We always sleep down stairs in the winter but shall move up again in the spring. The 11th N.H. regt. in our brigade has not been in a single fight. lt has come out since we came and it has lost a number of men by death. lt has burried one most every day lately. I do not know of a single one that has died in our regt. unless he was wounded. The 16th Regt. Mass Vol is right side of us also the 11th. The 16th John Turner was in. He I suppose is dead now. Mark Morse is in the 11th. He was here yesterday. I did not hardly know him. He was as fat as a goose. lt was the first time that I ever saw him but what he was drunk. This is a first rate place for them that drink and use tobacco for they can not get either. Thanksgiving day Geo. Tower was here. He is in the 20th. I see some one that I know most everyday. I like them mittens first rate. They came in handy last night handeling the cold gun.

Edward

Near Fredericksburg

Dec 21th 1862

Father & Mother,

It has been rather more than a week since I wrote you much of a letter but I have been pretty busy for a short time past for a week after I last wrote to you I was on picket on the banks of the Rappahannock. We got the water that we used out of the river. On the opposite bank the Rebel picket is stationed. They were about as far off as Mr Uphams house. There is no picket firing. They are just as good friends as the Union soldiers are. After we had been there a week we were paid off up to the 31st of Oct. so they owe us most 2 months pay now. They paid us off at night and the next morning we had to pack up to go into battle. They commenced shelling the city. We started with all of our money with us in all probabily there was about $15000 with us. They shelled the city all day and we did not go across the river that day and May or Fay of Chelsea came to get the pay of the Chelsea boys and I put mine in an envelope and he said he would put it in the office at Washington. There was 20 dollars you must write if you get it. That night we went back to camp and started again the next morning and crossed the river. We remained that day on the bank of the river also that night. We got plenty of flour and molasses in the city. The Rebels threw in a few shells but did not hurt any body. There is hardly a house in the city but what has a cannon ball or more in it. The next morning the battle infantry commenced and a hard one it was too. They shoved in brigade after brigade but they were mowed down by the hundreds. This battle took place just the other side of the city. They have it very strongly fortified and their grape shot makes sad work with our men. Gus was killed. He lay up side of a board fence and a cannon ball came through the fence killing him and 2 others. It took his left leg right off up next to his body so it only hung by a piece of skin it was bound up but he lived but a few minutes. We did not drive the rebs an inch that day. The battle field had more dead and wounded than any that I have seen yet. The next day they carried our wounded across the river all day and that night. A soldier by the name of Wright and I went into one of the houses and slept. We got up in the morning and went down where we left the Regt. and it was gone and the pontoon bridges were taken up and the city had been evacuated by our forces during the night and there amongst the Rebels. We did not know what to do, whether to try to get across the river or stop and get taken prisoners but we decided to go across and get a boat and put her for our lines. Wednesday there was men detailed from all Divisions that were in the battle to go over and bury the dead under a flag of truce. I was detailed for our company. I went over & buried Augustus and marked the grave so that if there is a chance and his folk wish to they can get his body. I should like to have you send me 1 of my shirts by mail and a pair of stockings. They charge an awful price to the center. if you could find a chance to send them to Randolph you could send them for most nothing. Let them toll them up. Geo. Hawes had a shirt, Gloves, & a pair of stockings come for only 7 cents and there has 3 or 4 pairs of boots come for 64 cents a pair in the company. If you send them by express they may not get here for a month or so. I threw my shirt away and have none.

Edward

- 1863 -

Near Fredericksburg Jan. 4th [1863]

Father & Mother,

I received a letter from you Thursday and my shirt came boots came and a letter from Martha & you with a 50 cent stamp in it. I was very glad to receive them. Our regiment has been on picket a number of times lately and the last time I thought I would get an excuse and I went to the acting Col. which is Capt. Andrews and and unbuttoned by coat and showed him that I had not got any shirt and my boots were all worn out and told me to go to Surgeon Lincoln and get a shirt. I went there and and he gave me a blue one and it will be just the thing for an under shirt now I like this shirt first rate. My boots had to go around the whole company and be examined and they passed. They all said that the one that made them knew how to make boots. You have no Idea how different my feet feel now. You spoke about sending me some soap. The company have got as much as a dozen bars that they would give away if anyone wanted them and salt any quantity of it. We draw such things when we are in camp any time to speak of.

We had for dinner to day stewed beans. I have got a pint dipper that I have to eat out of. I had it full for dinner and I have got an other one that I am going to warm up for supper. We do not draw but one dipper full but I am on pretty good terms with the cook and when that was gone he slapped in an other dish full. For supper the company are going to have rice and they will get some molasses on it. When I was home I used to like rice but out here I do not eat any. I shall draw my molasses and eat it on hard tack.

I found a lead pencil in my shirt (the one I am now writing with) and a box of pepper. The pencil that I had is most used up and this one came handy and the pepper also for Gus had his in his haversac and I had rather be woth out most anything else than pepper. All my vitules that I use pepper with it and before I go to bed I very often have a good drink of cayanne tea which I was always fond of.

You wanted to know what became of Augustus things. His money he sent home at the same time that I did.

He enlisted before I did therefore he got more pay. We were all paid up to the 31st of Oct. He received I believe 24 dollars & some odd cents and I think he sent home 24 dollars to Chas. Upham. He had a 50 cent stamp left. We all sent home most all of it for we were all drawn up in line of battle in front of the city over 500 hundred guns minute firing into the city. You can not imagine the noise that they made, one continual rpar all the time and we expected every moment to be into the hot work ourselves so we got rid of the greenbacks as fast as we could for if we did not we thought the Grey Backs might get them that night. We went to our camp again and started the next morning for the city and Saturday we had a pull at the cards. Sergt. Hawes is orderly and it was his business to take charge of the property of those that are killed. He took the 50 cents and what few little things that could be got that night and I suppose will send them to his folks. You wanted to know if we had to carry off the things of them that were killed. The rebels saved us the trouble. there was not but a very few men that had a thing on their bodies. Not a thread of any kind. Gus had on all of his clothes but a shoe.

Edward

Near Fredericksburg Va Jan. 11th [1863]

Father & Mother,

I received a letter from you last friday morning I got one from William Capen yesterday. I wish I could get one from some one every morning. I have not received one from James Albert or Frank yet. Do you know what regt. James Albert is in? What regt. is Alphonso Burrell in? I have not seen him but Luther Bryant told me that he had seen him once.

We are in camp at the same place that we were before the battle. We have nothing but shelter tents yet. We have been under marching orders for over a month now. When we shall get off I know not. Gen. Sturges Commanding this Division is in command of the Department of Washington and they say that we shall go there to do guard duty. I hope we shall for if we do we shall be likely to have good comfortable quarters but we can not tell much by what we here.

The 11th N.H. regt. is in this brigade it is a new regt. The Battle of Fredericksburg was the first one that they was ever in. Robert Fisher, Ed Fisher's son, belongs to them. I don't know as I ever wrote that he was here before. He was wounded in the last battle. I saw him on the battlefield wounded through the calf of the leg.

There was a barrel of dried apples that came to the Co. from Randolph day before yesterday. I tell you we can make sauce out of them that will make the hard tack go down a little better. We drew a ration of onions yesterday. We got 5 a piece. It is the first ones that we have drawn. I had a good plate full of fried ones for breakfast. It rained pretty hard last night when I went to sleep I could feel it spatter through the tent a little.

Last Wednesday we went on picket down to Falmouth. We go about once a week. It was pretty cold that night. (I think it is to bad to have so many men stand out on picket. They might make some arrangements with the Rebels and let them stand one night and we the next and not have us both together). Gen Ferrers and Staff are now at home on a furlough (at New York). Do Augustus folks ever say anything about sending for his body? I heard that Charles Upham was coming out after it. Has James Osgood got home yet?

We have to bring all of our wood two or 3 miles and water is pretty handy now for they have dug another spring but I have been after water for the cook sometimes and have to wait two hours. I am going to get a pass someday and go and find the 12th regt. I have not seen them since the night before we went into battle. That night they stoped side of us and Gus & I went over to see them. They were all smart then and Capt. Ripley looked fat and healthy but he was wounded and I have since heard that he was dead. Lieut. Whitman stopped here one night since the battle. He had just come out to join his Regt. and was looking after it and found this one.

Edward

Near Fredericksburg
Jan 18th 1863

Father & Mother,

I received a letter from you Friday morning. As usual the courier comes every week and it gets pretty well worn before it gets through the whole company. We had orders Friday to have 3 days rations cooked and be ready to march yesterday morning but we did not march yesterday and today being Sunday I think we shall not go before tomorrow. It is very cold here today and was yesterday. The water froze in the camp kittles side of the cook fire.

You wanted to know where I tented now. I stay in the cook tent for the present. I am assistant cook. We have got a tent with the sides boarded about 2 feet high with cracker box boards and our tents put on the top of that and a fire place made of logs in one corner so it is quite comfortable and now we have got to move and leave it.

I hope we shall not move a great ways in this weather for we shall have to lay out nights. The ground being froze, we can not drive any tent pins. We drew some dried apples from the Gov. the other day and I have some apple sauce to wash down my hard-tack. I do not have any duty to do now only to help the cook and we cooks have enough to eat such as it is.

Phinney Burrell came over here to see me the other day. He looks just the same as he always did only a little darker complexion same as the rest of us. *The other day one of our company died* an he was buried with the honors due to a soldier. The brigade band and the whole regt. turned out and there was a squad of men detailed out of ther company under the charge of Cpl. Thayer to fire a volley over his grave.

The officers had a regular drunk here last night chaplain and all. They kept us awake all night. They sang till about 12 o'clock then they turned in and a fight they have not had one before since New years night. Capt. Preston the commander of this company is a very nice man. I like him full as well as I did Capt Niles and I thought that he was as good as any one could be. Lieut. Stickney is our first Lieut. He has been acting adjutant of the regt. He is a nice little fellow.

You wanted to know if Sergt. Hawes gave me any thing out of his boxes. I will tell you. Gus you know had a box come and George Hawes had all of his molasses and Sergt. Hawes had some of his things but he never gave Augustus or I any of his things or any of the rest of the company. If you know his father you can know what he is as far as money is concerned. I like him. He will do as much for me as he will for any one but he will not give any thing that costs money.

George Hawes had a box come the other day that was as large as a boot box. It cost 4 dollars to get it here there was 20 mince pies in it and some other stuff. You can keep this to yourself.

Ed

Near Fredericksburg, Va. Jan. 25, [1863]

Father & Mother,

I received your letter yesterday morning. It came one day later than usual. If it bad not been for the bad weather that we have had for the last few days you would ere this have heard of another great battle at Fredericksburg. Who could have come off victor? I do not know. It have been a tough battle and if we got whipped there again, I think that it would have done as much towards settling this war as it would if they got whipped.

The whole Army of the Potomac marched by our camp last Tuesday amongst the rest was the 12th regt. which is in Franklin's Grand Division. George Bates was eating a piece of nice cake which he had come in his box. I saw E. Clark, Isaac Burnham, Leonard Holmes. That night it rained and the next day the whole army was stuck in the mud and have been marching back ever since. The 35th did not have to move because we are near the city and could march there and there in season to fight the same day but the next day it rained all day and night and our regt. had to go on picket and they had a pretty hard time of it.

There was one man in company B was drowned in the river. It was very dark and he fell down the bank and they did not get his body till to day. The Government lost a great many horses & cannon. It takes 16 mules to draw as much as 4 would draw in good weather.

The Rebels have got stack up on the other side of the river on a large board printed in large letters, "Burnside stuck in the mud".

Arabella you said wanted to know about the money that Gus carried out with him. He did not have 2 dollars when he got to Washington and I owed him 75 cents and I paid him at Camp Whipple and he was all out of money then. He got one hundred and fifty dollars, 30 dollars of that he paid towards getting a grave stone for his mother and he went to Livingston to see that girl up there and that cost him 25 or 30 dollars and he owed some and put it all together he did not have much when he got out here and it is lucky that he spent it and had the good of it.

I think we shall remain here for the present now and if you want send out a box you can. If you do, send one I want you to put in 1 pair of stocking, 1 pair of suspenders, a little cheese & molasses & sugar tea, one cake of chocolate, some corn starch, butter and if that does not fill it up put in what you have a mind to. I don't want you to send another shirt. I have been so long with but one I should not know what to do with an extra one as I have no knapsack to carry any thing in. I have got a new pair of pants, a cap, and hand-kerchief hung up in my tent. They have been there a fortnight. I am saving them to go into battle with. If we had moved this week I should have put them on but as we did not

I shall wait til we have orders to move again. If you send a box put in a comb & towel. I never smarter in my life.

Ed

You write Lois & Everlyn on that letter and give it to them. Now I have got my new boots I don't care if the mud comes knee deep. I guess I can out of it.

Near Fredericksburg
Feb. 1st 1863

Father & Mother,

I received a letter from you Thursday night containing a 50 cent stamp. It is very pleasant today but rather muddy. It storms about 2 or 3 days a week and it keeps muddy all the time.

Last Tuesday our regt. went down on picket. It rained all day and night till about 4 o'clock the next morning. Then it began to snow and the men came in Wednesday morning most froze up being out all night. And Thursday morning the snow was six or eight inches deep and some of the men were all covered up in their little shelter tents. That little painter, John Gill, that worked for Samuel Capen is in this Company. He is a Cpl. and his father in law is in the Weymout Company which is the next Company to ours.

The first 3 or 4 days of this week I made all of my meals out of raw pork and vinegar & hardtack but yesterday and day before I have had slapjacks & sugar & potatoes & steak. I suppose old fighting Joe Hooker is in command of the army now and they will give him a good chance to get whipped then he will resign and after they have all resigned I dont know what they will do then. Gen. Sumner is in command of the right Grand Division of the army of the Potomac (the one that this Brig. is in) and Gen. Franklin is the commander of the Left Grand Division. They say have resigned and gone with Burnside but I dont know how true it is.

The Government owes this regt. just three months pay today. I do not know when they will pay us off. We were mustered for pay the 1st of Jan. and shall be again the 1st of March.

We are in camp at the same place that we have been since we evacuated the city and I don't see but we shall stop here for a long time to come but I can't tell. We have to bring our wood 2 or 3 miles. It is mostly pine. This regt. keeps 10 or 12 six mule teams carting all the time. We have got a good fire place in this tent it being the cook's tent. We have all the wood we want to keep warm. There is an old man that lives close to this camp that owns the land around here. He owns 700 acres. It was all fenced with rails (there is no stone here to make fences of) and well wooded. (He) had a good drove of cattle mules & horses and a lot of slaves and a good house and all he has got left now is his house and 1 cow and his land. There is not a stick of wood on it or a fence or nothing to make one of.

That is only one case. It is so over the whole of Virginia. The people will have to wait a good many years before they can go to farming here again.

I am going to have some hard tack and molasses for supper and I wish I had some of those mince pies that you wrote of to top off with. If you get this before you send the box put in something to make bread rise.

Edward Waldo

Camp Near Fredericksburg Va.
Feb 8th 1863

Father & Mother,

I received a letter stating that you had sent a box and last Friday. I received one with a twenty five cent stamp in it the same day I received one from James Albert & James Osgood and Saturday one from Grandmother. James Albert is about 20 miles from Memphis. He has been in the service about 16 months.

James Osgood is in the hospital at Chester, Penn. The surgeon has found the ball but does not dare to remove it. It is in so bad a place. He says he had suffered a great sight with his wound. He said sometimes he would rather have died than not. The Dr says he will get his discharge.

I suppose before you get this we shall be on the move way down south in the land of cotton. Thursday night we had orders to pack up and be ready to march but it began to rain and they were afraid that they would get stuck in the mud so we are waiting for it to dry up a little. The men will not have to march far this time. The depot is but 1 mile from here that is where we shall take the cars for Aqua Creek and there is transports there waiting to take us to Fortress Monroe and from there we shall have a ride to Newbern North Carolina or New Orleans or some of them places I don't care where they go with us. Any where to see some of the world. They have took us all over Vairginia 2 or 3 times all ready. That part of it that the Rebs would let them.

The order came the other day that 2 men out of every hundred men fit for duty could have a furlough and go home. There was 7 going out of this Regt. and we all drew lots and it fell on our cook and he got all ready to go and I was to be head cook while he was gone but as we had orders to move the order was countermanded in this brigade, but in all probability there will be some of the Stoughton boys home from the 12th or some other regt.

Last Thursday Lieut. Ingalls, our great Lieut. as we used to call him came back. He is promoted to 1st Lieut in Company. P. He is the largest man we have in the regt. and Lieut Palmer (who died at Antietam) was very small. That is why we used call Lieut. Ingalls our great Lieut. and Lieut. Palmer our Little Lieut. Sergt. Wales also came back. They found it rather hard to stop in our quarters after being to home 4 or 5 months. It rained very hard at the time that they came. Friday we drew a loaf of soft bread a piece weighting 22 oz. I eat mine for supper with some molasses and some coffee and could have eat a good slice out of another one if I could have got it. We had got a brigade bake house a building out of logs and the oven had come and in a few days we expected to have soft bread instead of hard but yesterday we tore it down and burnt it to cook with as we are going off. I suppose Old Burnside is going to command this corps. It is his old one. They call this the fighting corps.

Edward

Direct your letters as before till I write to direct different.

Newport News, Va

Feb 14th 1863

Father & Mother,

I have had quite a little ride since I last wrote to you last. Monday morning we started from Falmouth Station in the cars from Aqua Creek. The regt. went early in the morning and I went 2 or 3 hours later with the baggage. When we got to the creek, the regt. had gone aboard the steamer Lousina and had gone out in the stream. We were taken out to her with the baggage about dark. She was pretty well crowded. The officers occupied the state rooms and the berths were all full of the privates. The cook and I spread our blankets in the lower cabin under one of the tables and we had a bully place onboard of her 2 nights and one day. We came at anchor off Fortress Monroe early Wednesday morning and about sunrise we started for Newport News which is about 7 miles from the Fortress which can be seen away off in the distance. When I came off of the wharf the first man that I saw was Dan Tolman. He is keeping a kind of store here. Things can be bought here quite reasonable instead of what they could near Fredericksburg. Butter that we used to pay 60 cents per pound can be bought here for 30 and cheese for 20 that used to cost 40 and 50 and apples that used to cost 5 for a quarter can be bought 15 for the same price. The soldiers if they had been paid off I guess would live. We draw soft bread now. We drawed some dried apple and I have soft bread and apple sauce now.

The most of the old Cumberland which was sunk by the Merrimac last year justs sticks above the water and the Congress that was burnt at the same time to the waters edge is still visible and this stick which I put in here is a piece of her. The Moniter lays off to the mouth of the James River and a number of gunboats and war ships. They are expecting the Merrimac No. 2 down the river every night. if she is coming I should like to have her come while we are here so we could see some fighting and not be in it. I do not know how long we shall stay here but I hope we shall stop here a spell. It is a first rate place. It is not so muddy as it was where we came from. I went about 2 miles the other day and got some oysters. This is where they get all of their oysters. There is any quanity of boats out in the stream raking them.

My box has not come yet. There was 40 that came for this regt. night before last and 50 more last night but mine was not with them. I expect it is down to the Port and it will be along in a day or two. I got a letter with a comb in it. It is a first rate one to comb the lice out with. And I got another one also with a 25 cent stamp in it and this morning the cook put 25 more with it and we got a skilet and we can fry slapjacks in good shape now. We used to fry them on an old plate. I should not wonder If both boxes came to once. I had a piece of pie and some doughnuts out of Sergt. Saul Thayer's and a piece of pie out of Sergt Houl's and the man that I tend with (the cook) is and old warrior. He was in the Regular army when the war broke out in Mexico and was there 2 years and when the rebellion broke out he went out as one of the 3 months men and now he is out as one of the 3 years men and he thinks if he gets home now he shall stop there and go to war no more. You must direct my letters to Fortress Monroe and they will come through sooner than to go by Washington.

Ed
I dont know as you can read this but when I get to writing I do it in a hurry

Newport News. VA
Feb. 21st 1863

Father & Mother,
Night before last I received a letter from you and L. A. I have also had one from Grandmother & Lucy. Last Wednesday night both of the boxes came and there was not a thing that was spoiled or jammed at all. And I am living pretty high now, for a private. I am still cooking.

The other day Phinny Burrell came over here. He is in camp about a mile from here. This whole Brigade have got A tents. There is 5 in each tent. The cook & I have a tent by ourselves. There is a boat that runs to the Fort and to Norfolk and all the places of notority and the men can get a furlough and go to any of these places free of expense. We draw a loaf of soft bread per. man every day weighting 22. oz. I generally eat 1 for supper and one for breakfast and about a half one for dinner. That would be about 55 oz per. day of bread besides the rest of the stuff. I am as fat as a hog. I don't believe you would know me if I should walk into the house some night.

I don't know what the Abolitionists are a going to do with us now. I do not care much I should like to stop here my 3 years. It is a nice place. It would be like going down to Nantasket and spending the summer. Some say part of this corps is going to Norfolk and part to the Fortress and we stay here to do Garrison duty and some say the whole corps is going to Newbern and others down on the Penisula. I think that they might as well let us stay here as any where. I think that we shall do as much good here as any where.

You can not find 5 men in the regt. but what are death on the Administration. They say that they never will fire another gun at the Rebs. They were willing to fight till they had got to fight to free the n[----]r and when it come to that they think it is time to stop. it is not only so in this regt. but in all of them.

There is about 3 or 4 hundred thousand 2-years men going home between now and June and I can't see how the goverment are a going to get men to take their place. As for taking the n[----]s to help them, they will be rather poor if they are all like those that I have seen when the shells have been flying around thier heads. They would run and yell and fly around as if they were half killed. I should like to see a n[----]r brigade go into battle once. I don't want any of them to get hurt but I should like to see them run a little.

I get the Courier regular every week and it tells the story about as it is the whole company have to read it. I like my suspenders first rate. I have got on a new suit and feel as big as can be but it is a darned good place to get lousy out here. I have to go and take off all of my clothes and pick all over everyday. If I did not they would crawl over me all night and I could not sleep. I was the first one that had them. It was Sergt. Hawes, the officers and all have them. I have got so I could not do without them.

If they keep us here we shall have a good time and if they send us to Newbern we shall have a good ride so let them go it

Newport News. Va.
March 1st, 1863

Father & Mother,

I received your letter Thursday night with one dollar and twenty cents in it.

There is no chance here at present to get my picture taken but there may be sometime. If we stop here some time I may go down to the Fortress or to Norfolk and I can get one taken there. I dont believe you would know me. I never was so fleshy in my life. I have not been weighed lately but I guess I weigh about 200 lbs. We draw onions and potatoes and soft bread an dried apple, molasses once a week and we are living like princes. I received a letter from Mr Chase night before last. I shall answer in a few days. If you have a chance to send word to Joe & Frank tell them to write to me.

I believe I wrote to them last our Lt. Col. Caruth and Adjutant Nath. Wales who were taken prisoner at Sulpher Springs have got back and Adjutant Wales is Major now. We all like Col. Caruth first rate and always did but the men do not care if Col. Wild never does come back. We have to black our boots every day and clean up and look slick as we can.

Col. Walter Harriman of the 11th N.H. which is the next regt. to ours in this brigade is nominated for Gov. of N.H. I believe, I hope, he will get elected. He is a nice man. He does not feel above the privates as some officers do. If I should go and speak to him he would take just as much notice of me and more to than he would if a commissioned officer spoke to him.

Our Chaplain preached his farwell sermon today. He has got his Discharge and starts for home tomorrow. His health is not very good. I hear that Lt. J. Madden has got his discharge and gone home. He has been in the hospital in Washington for some time past. I have not heard from Henry Munk since you wrote that he had started to join his regiment.

We have not a very large company at the present time. We have about 19 men for duty. There is some difference between that and 101 the number that we started from home with. We draw rations for 38 making about 19 that are home sick and one thing and another.

One night since we have been here we had a great snow storm. It snowed most all night and toward morning it began to rain. We did not get up very early and after it had got to be pretty light I turned over and went into a pond of water all over. The snow had stopped the ditches all up and the water came into our tent six or eight inches deep. It took all the next day to get things dried up but we came out all right in the end.

What do the think of the conscription act in Stoughton? So the wide awakes all coming out to render help fight a little Loranus said he hoped Elijah & Sanford would have to go and get their ears used. I should like to see a good company more come from Stoughton. I should like to have them put in this brigade if they were the right ones.

Ed

Newport News Va.
March 8, 1863

Father & Mother,

I received your letter as usual last Thursday evening. We are still at the old camp enjoying ourselves as well as we can. We have all sorts of weather here in the course of the day. Some days it will rain like June 2 or 3 times and such rain you never see in Mass. We had a very hard thunder shower this morning but it has cleared off and is very pleasant now.

Out on the left of our brigade we have a large market place where 50 or 60 teams come every day from Hampton loaded with all kinds of stuff which they sell or swap off to the soldiers for rations of coffee and the like that they have left over their rations. I suppose that the Gov. has to pay 35 or 40 cents per. pound for coffee now.

I received a town report last night also a letter from Frank. He is still at Fairfax station. It is very muddy there. He has been sick with a slow fever about 3 weeks but did not go into the Hospital. William is to work in the commissary department so I suppose he can live like a king. Frank says Joe is as tough as a little cuss. I should like to have you send me a school report when they get them out. I like to read all such things as them.

My razors I could not tell where they are. They may be in that little closet in Lucys porch or up stairs in that closet or on the shelf over Grammie's butten door next to the stairs, but I could not tell for certain if he find them he must take good care of them.

The apples and potatoes in the box were not froze a bit. I should like to have about a barrell of such apples set up in one corner of my tent. I think I would eat a few of them.

There is a number of minors in this Company and their folks draw a dollar a week from the town where they enlisted and their folks are not dependant on them for support either. These is Edgar Hawes and Geo. P. Gill both of North Stoughton. Williamson Gill is the father of Geo Gill and every body knows that he is not dependant on any of his children for support and the town of Stoughton are paying him a dollar a week for his son. I don't see why they are not obliged to pay you the same for me, if they refuse to pay it at first they will of course try them again

I have been in the service now 7 months and it would amount $28.

Edward

Newport News, Va.
March 13th, (1863)

Father & Mother,

I received your letter last Wednesday with my birthday present in it. It is my birthday today and as I had spare time I thought I would write so you will get this earlier than common. I expect to send home some money before this month is out but I may not get paid off. We were mustered for pay the first of this month. The first of this month, they now owe me fifty two dollars up to March 1st.

They had a fight down to Suffolk yesterday and rather got the best of our troops and today the 3rd Division of this corps went down to reinforce them. It is about 50 miles from here. The troops in the fight yesterday were under the command of Cocoran. The 3rd Division were in wooden barricks and the talk is that we shall go into the place where they came out.

The other night a rebel boat came in sight and when we got up the next morning the old frigate Minnisota which is one of the blockading fleet and has been stationed in Hampton roads was down in front of us and has remained there ever since.

I do not see Daniel Tolman very often. I do not go out of our brigade much. I have not seen D.A.B. yet. It is rather cool here all time being so near to the water.

Sergt. Samuel Thayer of this Company started home on a furlough last Tuesday to be gone 10 days. We have to cook for about forty men at present.

I am going to send home a short piece that I see in the papers about the way that they use the n[----]s in the army. There has been many a warm day when soldiers were sick to my knowledge and tried to get into an Ambulance and it would be full of great fat lazy n[----]s that were able to walk out here. If a fellow has a black face he can go any where without a pass. Alphonso Burrell was not cooking at all the last that I heard from him. He had rather do duty in the ranks. He may have gone at it again by this time though for I have not seen him for quite a while. I have not received any letter from Charles Upham yet but I have the town report about the box. I have got a new knapsack and can carry some things now when I am on the march and I should like to have my other shirt and it will cost more to send it by mail than it will to send a box and if Chas. Upham wants to put in some things you can send one if you have a mind to and put in my shirt and old double brested vest if you can find it. I can not tell where it is. A little salt fish or 2. piece of roast pork would not taste very bad. If you send it get it off as soon as you can conveniently so that I can get rid of it before we have orders to march from here. We may not get from here this summer and we may go before tomorrow night, we can't tell. The whole of the 2nd N.H. regt. they say have gone home on a furlough. They were camped side of us at Falmouth.

Edward

Newport News, Va.
March 22nd, 1863

Father & Mother,

I received your letter Thursday eve. We are still here having a first rate time. I received a letter from Chas. Upham also one from Joe the same night that I got yours. The 29th regt., the one that Phinney is in, started form here yesterday. The rest of his Division went a day or two before. About a fortnight ago, Genl. (Edward) Ferrero our brigadier general was appointed commander of this post and the 21st Mass., 51st Penn,and 51st N.Y. regiments all went into wooden barricks and the 11th N.H. and this regt. expected to go every day. And the prospect was that we should stop here quite a while but the prospect has altered some now and I expect before you get this that we shall be on the move again. They say we are agoing Tenn. and I rather think we are. I may get out there and see James Albert yet. I dont care how much they send us around if they only let us ride. Sergt. Samuel Thayer of this Company was to home on a furlough of 10 days. He got back to-day. He lives in Milton near Blue Hill tavern. He saw a man there that inquired after me. He had black whiskers and wore a black hat. I thought it was Scott and he described the man with him and I thought it answered the description of Ben Atherton.

It snowed here one night and day and yesterday the water was running a stream by our tent and last night if I waked up in the night you could hear it roar like a river.

They captured an infernal machine from the rebels the other day on the James River. It is long and looks like the mast of a ship. They opened a hole in it and took out 14 Rebels. It lays out in the water in front of here now.

The remainder of our knapsacks came the other day but mine did not come. If it did somebody smarter than I was got it. Augustus's came and there was a receipt in it from Dr Gifford that I will put in this and you can give it to his folks. I also forgot to send that piece about the n[----]r and I will put that in this also. We play cards here all night some nights and in the day time to sometimes. We drew new shelter tents yesterday officers and all. They have got to carry their tent on their back as well as a private. There have been two cases of scurvy in this Company. One of them a man from Randolph died and the other Cpl. Young from East Stoughton. The last we heard from him he was in the hospital at Washington.

They can't tuck any of their sicknesses on to me. I am as tough as a door nail and likely to be till I get home. I ain't got but about 2 years and 4 months to stop now. Joe will be a lucky fellow if he get off without hearing some of them blue pills (that the darned Rebels fire) whistle. He will be pretty likely to have a chance this spring.

I saw Dan Tolman the other day. He is as fat as can be and dresses up too.

Edward

Paris, Kentucky
April 2nd, 1863

Father & Mother,

I received a letter from you the last time the day before we left Newport News. We left there one week ago today and have been one the move night and day ever since. We went aboard the Gov. transport John Brooks about five o'clock last Thursday and arrived at Baltimore about Friday noon. We remained on board till night when we marched through the city and took the cars for Pittsburg, Penn. We kept on our way all night only when the engine stopped to take on wood and water. The next morning it began to snow and snowed all day. We passed through a number of cities amongst them was Harrisburg the capitol of Penn. and towards night we arrived at Miflin where we had a dish of coffee furnished by the citizens of that place about 9 Oclock we came to the city of Altoona where we were treated to another dish of coffee and Sunday morning about 9 o'clock we came to Pittsburg which is the last place of any account in Penn. There we were taken to the city hall where we were furnished by the people of that place with a good dinner of soft bread and dried beef apples and coffee. After dinner we took the cars for Cincinnati, Ohio where we arrived Monday night. We were treated to coffee twice along the route and when we got to Cincinnati we were taken to the Market and had a first rate supper of bread and beef, ham, pork, boiled eggs, apples, coffee, onions, lemon pies. When we got through eating and got ready to start again on our Journey about 3 o'clock. We then took the ferry and went across the Ohio River to the city of Covington which is in Kentucky (it is a very large city). It was near 4 o'clock then. Some of the boys spread there blankets on the side walk and others built up good camp fires in the street and passed the time away til day light. It began to snow a little and it did by spells all day. At night our Lt Col commanding the regt. got us into a hall and we had good quarters for the night.

Wednesday morning we started on the Kentucky central R.R. and arrived here about 7 o' clock. We were ordered to stop in the cars, but some of us went out and got into houses that were empty and barns etc. Sergt. Hawes, Wright, Faunce & I found an empty building that was just built. The floor was boarded all over with the exception of a small piece at one end and in that place we built up a good fire and had some coffee and a good nights rest till morning. This morning we put up our tents near the city and here we are at the present time. Lexington is about 10 miles from here. Some say we are going there. We are sent here to protect the union folks from the Guerrillas (I guess that is the way to spell it) that travel around the country here. The 29th is doing Provost duty in this town they say but I have not seen Phinny Burrell since we left Newport News.

If we had not left the day that we did from Newport News I think I should have got my box and should have got it on with the baggage. It will come some time I expect.

You may direct your letters for the present 35th reg. 2nd Brigade 2nd Div. 9th A.C. via Cincinnati, Ohio,and I guess it will come to me

Edward

Winchester, Ky.
April 19th, 1863

Father & Mother,

I have received 3 letters from you since I last wrote. I got 2 of them last night and Friday. We have not got but 2 mails since we left Paris, (the place that I last wrote to you from) which we did the next day after I wrote. The day we left we marched 23 miles to Mount Sterling. We made a forced march of it because we had to go through a Rebel country and we did not want to stop till we got to our destination. There was but six men that came up with the Company and some of them had to have their knapsacks carried on the teams. I went through with mine on my back. When I leave my knapsack I shall leave myself with it. I left my blankets at So. Mountain when we were agoing into the battle and I never got another for about 2 months and the one that I have got now I mean to hold onto or less I shall stop with it. I think I can stand a march about as well as any of them. You thought when I came out here I would be sick on account of the hot weather and hard marches but I ain't dead yet.

I have not cooked any since we left Newport News. While we were on the move to Kentucky we had no need of a cook and since we came to Mt Sterling we have had nothing to cook that we drew from the Gov. so I have done duty as a private. We have not drawn for the last 13 days 3 full days rations but are getting enough now but I have not suffered for the want of food much nor I never mean to while we are in such a country as this. It ain't like old Virginia is one of the handsomest parts of the country I have ever seen. I have been on picket duty about every other day since I came here and the mutton and fresh pork had to take it. The hogs out here and in all parts of South and West they don't keep in Styes but they run in the road or any where have a mind to. We would go out about 10 o'clock and get a hog killed and skinned (for we have no hot water to take off the bristles so we skin them) and all dressed off about 11 and take turns and go to some house and get dinner up and save the pig to carry into camp. We get all of our meals in the same way for the 24 hours that we are on picket. The last time that I was on I ate supper at a Rebel woman's house and she was one of the greatest I ever saw she and her mother both her mother was about as old and looked just like grandmother. I got there at 5 o'clock and stopped til after 9. It was a very nice house and they had things in great style, n[----]r waiters, etc. I stopped in the parlor til supper was ready and then we went into the dining room and took supper. We had silver forks and the cups & plates were china and other things to corresponde to eat. We had fried ham, warm biscuits and butter, slapjacks, tea & white sugar, sweet milk and buttermilk. It is always the fashion to have butter milk on the table here. When I came off (I told her I was agoing to write home that I ate supper with one of the hardest rebel women) I ever saw She sent her respects to you and told me to tell you that she tried to plague me a little. Friday morning we came to this place which is about 20 miles from Mt. Sterling. We were paid off yesterday up to the

1st of March. I have sent home 48 dollars. It was put into a bank here and a draft taken on a New York bank on the 1st and it will be sent from N.Y. to the Mass state treasurer and he will send it by express to you.

Ed

Paint Lick, Ky.
May 9th, 1863

Father & Mother,

I received a letter from you last Satuday night and I should have written to you before but since then we have been on the march. We started from Winchester last Monday morning and we have come through Lexington and Nicholsville and a good many small towns. We have traveled about 100 miles since Monday morning. We crossed the Kentucky River last Wednesday. We are now about 15 miles from Richmond, Ky. where I suppose we shall march the next tramp we take. The 29th Mass is down on the Cumberland and I suppose Phinny is with them. I expect we shall go into Tenn. also before long. They will show us all over the country before we get home I guess.

Isaac Newton Lemfield spent a few days with us while we were at Winchester. I was not very well while he was there. I had a Diareah.

The government allows us 42 dollars for clothing per year and at the end of the year at the last pay day. If they have had more than that amount it is taken out of the last 2 months pay and if they have not had that amount, what they have not had is paid them with the last pay.

I suppose old Hooker before now has had a terrible battle near Fredericksburg. I think he will either use up the army of the Potomac or the rebel army. It is expected that Rossecrans army has engaged the enemy before this and Banks is giving it to them in his department. The Rebel prisoners that are taken here say that the Rebs are in a starving condition and they are the most ragged of any I have ever seen.

Corn and potatoes are up high enough to hoe here but they dont know any thing about hoeing here. They do all of their work here with horse and plough and cultivator.

At Nicholsville I stopped and had dinner. We had roast turkey, fried ham, warm bread and butter, baked beans, peach sause, molasses, onions, tea or coffee, it was a private boarding house.

I get the Courier every week. I suppose the next mail I shall get a letter from you. I expect we shall get one to night.

Henry Monk is in the hospital at Washington. He was coming to the regt. and he was taken sick and had to stop. Direct to Lexington, Ky.

Edward

Lancaster, Ky.
May 10th, 1863

Father & Mother,

I received a letter from you this morning. We marched back to this place at an early hour this morning. I do not know where we are going. Some say that we are to report to Cincinnati and if we do I guess that they will send us to Fredericksburg but can't tell. I threw away my overcoat this morning and I will send home a small piece of the collar and cape and let you see what kind of holes the Rebs make with their darned bullets. The news here tonight is that Hooker has recrossed the Rappahannock with 70,000 fresh troops and has taken Lee's army. And while he was fighting Gen. Dix went down the Peninsula and took Richmond, but it is to good to be true. I have not time to write any more at present. I wrote a letter yesterday.

Direct your Letters to Lexington, Kentucky.

Edward

On board the Steamer Imperial on the Mississippi River
May 11th, 1863

Father and Mother,

I have not received a letter from you this week but suppose there is one on the way but it will take it some time to catch me. 1 week ago yesterday at 6 o'clock P.M. we left Stanford, Ky. for Nicholsville a distance of 35 miles and got there at 4 o'clock the next day being 22 hours marching 35 miles. We then took the cars for Cincinnati where we arrived the next day about 10 o'clock. We then had a good dinner and about dark we went aboard the cars on the Ohio & Mississippi R.R. and went to Cairo, Ill. We had to go through the states of Pa. Ill. We arrived at Cairo which is situated on the Mississippi & Ohio Rivers. Sunday morning and we remained there all day and Monday about 4 o'clock we embarked on this steamer for Memphis, Tenn. We have got stuck on the sand bars twice and that has hindered us some. We shall get there tonight.

We passed Island No. 10 yesterday and Fort Pillow this forenoon.

Yesterday I went on to the Missouri shore and today onto the Arkansas shore and to night I shall go onto the Tenn. shore at Memphis. From that place we are going down to help them take Vicksburg. They can't do any thing without the 35th has a hand in it. Before we get to Vicksburg we shall pass the line of Louisiana and Vicksburg is in Miss so I shall get a glimpse of a good many states. We shall see some more before we get back again.

Henry Monk joined the regt. at Nicholsville and is now with us. He looks as smart as can be.

It rained very hard last night. We had one of the heaviest thunder showers that I ever saw. It has rained some today but it is very pleasant now and hot as tophet.

Monday I received a letter from Hellen. Monday night The Mass 4 regt. of 9 months men is at Port Hudson and some other Mass regiments and we may see some of them before they get home. We are Just a going to stop we have got oppposite the city and the mail is going back and I must stop.

Direct all letter for the present to

35th reg. 2nd Brig.
2nd. Div. 9th A.C.
via Cairo, Ill

Lancaster, Ky.
May 17th (1863)

Father & Mother,

I received letter last night from you. I have got one every week. I dont think that I have had a letter written to me but what I have received and the Courier comes regular every week. I have not missed but one of them and that was while we were over to Fredericksburg (on the 13th of Dec.) There was one that I never got.

We are having a pretty good time here. I suppose that the crops are as forward here as they are in Mass. in the middle of June. We are about as far south as Richmond, Va.

I suppose Hooker got a drove back at Fredericksburg but I guess that the Rebels lost a good many men as well as himself. If the 11 corps (Gen. Howards) had not ran like darned fools before they had fired a gun I guess that Old Hooker would have given it to them good as it was I suppose they have lost one of their best Generals that they have got (Old Stonewall.)

Last Friday we had orders to be ready to march at a moments notice but ain't gone yet. We were agoing down on the Cumberland and reinforce Gen. Carter but he has whipped the Rebels under Marshall and I think we shall not have to go now. You wanted to know if I washed my shirt. I do some times and hire it done some. This morning they wanted me to help cook for the Company again but I think I shall not. I shall keep on doing duty in the ranks. By helping cook before I lost a chance where now I might be earning now 17 dollars per month instead of 13. I think I shall stick to the ranks now. I saw last night by the papers that the spies that were taken by the 35th while at Mount Sterling were hung on Johnson's Island. The 21st Mass, are there now. I heard that the Rebs came in and drove them out and the Rebels were afterwords drove out by the 21st and they still hold the place.

The farm that we are on now was owned by a rebel who burnt his house and then went south at the breaking out of the rebellion. It was sold yesterday. There is 1100 acres of it and it is better looking land than you can find in the east. I should like to have you send me out a war map if you can find one that I can carry in my pocket.

Does Samuel Austin go to school this summer? I suppose that Newton Lemfield has been to see you before this. I am as smart as can be now. I was not very well when he was here.

Edward

Camp near Crab Orchard
May 24th, (1863)

Father & Mother,

I received a letter from you Friday night. We were then at Lancaster but yesterday morning we packed up and took three days rations and started for the Cumberland River where the rebels were about making another raid into this state from Tennessee, but we got as far as this place and the order was countermanded and we are to remain here today and I guess we shall go back to Lancaster. It is the hottest weather I have ever see since I have been out here. It is just nine months ago to day since we came to Washington, so now we have got but about 2 years and 2 months to stop. There is some 9 months troops in our Division whose time is out the 7th of next month. The 9th N.H. Vols. of this Division are all excused from duty. We left them at Lancaster down in the woods. They have all been vaccinated and their arms are so sore that they can hardly lift them to their head. One company have got the small pox.

That John Diamond that used to be in the Dramatic club in Stoughton with Henry Johnson & Major Dutton was in company J (the Dedham Co.) of this regt. He was taken sick at Newport News and was taken to the hospital at Hampton near Fortress Monroe and has since we came to Kentucky died. Col. Carruth has just told the men that Vicksburg has been taken. The news has just been brought in and is official and is to be read on dress parade tonight and Gen. Carter of the army of the Cumberland who sent for us to go and reinforce him does not want us and says the the rebels are retreating before his army so now the Mississippi river will be under our control and Texas where the rebels get the most of their cattle will be cut off from them. I saw in a paper that contained a list of the wounded in the late battles on the Rappahannock that J.S. Waldo of Company C 3rd regt. of Wisconsin Vols. was wounded. I suppose that is cousin John. I have been through the 3rd Wisconsin regt. a number of times but did not know what Company or what regt. he was in. When Burnside got stuck in the mud last winter that regt. stopped on our camp ground 2 or 3 hours and I went and tried to find out if there was any Waldo's in it but I suppose I did not go into the right company.

Edward

Stanford Ky.
May 31st, 1863

Father & Mother,

I received your letter yesterday morning with the cloves in it. We marched to this place last monday night. We started from Crab Orchard about 1/2 past 7 and arrived here about 12 o'clock at night. We were pretty well used up when we got here. The 11th N.H. regt. led us off and they had their napsacks carried and the 35th kept up to them and had theirs on their back. I don't know how long we shall stop here. We expect to move every day. There was a pontoon train went past here day before yesterday. It was going to the Cumberland river so I suppose that our troop are a going to make a movement across there. There is a large flour mill near here so we get some flour. They grind 150 bushels of wheat every day. We have to pay 3 1/2 cents per pound or about $6 per barrell. There is also one of the finest springs of water here that you ever saw. It is in a cave of solid stone that is about 40 feet square.

Lieut. Col. Carruth who has been in command of this regt. ever since Col. Wild was wounded at So. Mountain has received his commission as Col. He is making the officers tread around pretty lively. The officers that were promoted before he got his commission as Col. went through Col. Wilds hands and he says that there has been a good deal of wire pulling to get folks into office and now he says he shall have the handling of it and if he cannot find any Sergants that are fit to hold commissions he shall take them out of the ranks.

Night before last a Sergant of one of our companys who was a going to have a commission was reduced to the ranks and I guess he will make them step around pretty lively. The strawberries and green peas are pretty thick here now. Peas are 25 cents a peck.

You wanted to know who took Sergt. Hawes' place. It was Sergt. Thayer. He is a first rate fellow. The Company all like him. He was out in the 12th reg. about a year and was taken prisoner and got his discharge and was to home about 2 weeks and came out with us.

I have not got this book of mine wrote through yet but it is getting pretty well worn out and if you will send me out one like it and some wafers I will send it home. I am on guard today at the commissary that is where Lt. Hawes stops.

Edward

I am going to have some slapjacks for supper my tent mate and myself. My tent mate is Corporal Wright.

Camp in rear of Vicksburg
June 18, 1863

Father & Mother,

We have received no mail since we left Ky but expect one every day. Last Friday we left Memphis for Vicksburg near which place we arrived Sunday morning. We landed at Shermans Landing and remained till Monday morning when we sent across the bend that the Mississippi makes in front of Vicksburg on the Louisiana shore where we crossed the Mississippi and went on to Grant's left but he did not want us so we came back and stopped over night and the next day we went up the Yazoo to Haynes Bluff and we are now in the rear of the city between there and the big block river where Johnson is reported to be. I think that Grant has got the rebels cooped up there where they will have to surrender. Our sharpshooters are within 150 yards of the city and they can't work their guns in the day time because we pick them off as fast as they show their heads. Our big guns and morters are at work all the time firing on the city so there is considerable noise here all the time.

There was 3 men that went into the Yazoo river the other day and one of them was bit into in the middle of his body and one of them had his arm bit so it had to be amputated and the other one has not been heard from since. This was done by an aligator.

It is very warm down here now. We can not get any water but river water and the Surgeon says that is better for us but I should like to have you send me a little piece of ice and I will send you back some blackberries. There is large quantities of them here. I have just got in from picking them. I got 2 qts in all. I wanted to eat and was not gone but a little while. I put a little sugar on them and they go pretty well on hard tack.

I suppose that James Albert is around here somewhere but have not seen him yet but expect to every day.

When we were marching to this place the western troops all along the road asked what troops we were and we told them 35th Mass. and they say "what you doing way down here." I suppose that the 9 months men are coming home most every week now. I saw the place where Gen. Butler dug the canal across the bed in front of Vicksburg there was a Mass. regt. at work there diging that.

I suppose that Phinney is here somewhere but I do not know where.

Edward

Jackson Miss.
July 18th, 1863

Father & Mother,

I have received two letters from you since we came to this place. One of them I received last Saturday forenoon on the battlefield while we were supporting the 1st Brigade who were out skirmishing with the Rebels. The other one I received last night. I believe I wrote to you last 4 of July we were then in the rear of Vicksburg. The night of the 4th we started for Old Johnson who had been hovering in our rear ever since the seige of Vicksburg had been commenced. We over took him the next day at the Big Black River and since then we have been fighting him every day and night until yesterday when the 35th who were in the front went into the city and planted our Flag up on the breast works the first one and then went double quick and placed them on the capital.

We have lost but 1 man killed and but a few wounded in our regiment. We took about 500 prisoners. We have had a pretty hard time since the 4th. It has been very warm and we have had to be up night and day. We have been in the front 5 days since we got to Jackson and three out of the five we have had to stand behind trees and stumps night and day within 1/4 of a mile of their fortifications and if we stuck our head out in sight in the day time they would send by our heads something that would make us draw it back pretty quick. And their siege guns would rattle their grape and cannister with a solid shot and shell that has the trunks of trees off by the cord— but they did not drive us off. If he had stopped one day longer we would have had all of them prisoners but they took to their legs and old Grant is after them and old Johnson is putting for Mobile as fast as his legs will carry him and 10 to one if Grant don't catch him before he gets there.

I think that we shall start for Vicksburg where we shall take the boats for Ky tomorrow but do not know. Lieut M. B. Hawes was instantly killed about 2 miles from the Big Black river by the falling of a tree while he was riding at the head of his supply train. He was going to report to his company the next day our old Quartermaster having got back.

There is but three from Stoughton left in the Company now and one of them Edgar Hawes of No. Stoughton but Henry Monk and I stick by yet.

Rear of Vicksburg, Miss.
July 29th, 1863

Father & Mother,

We have got back again to our old camp ground in the rear of Vicksburg. We arrived here about noon last Thursday and now are awaiting transportation for Cincinnati. All of the transports that were here have gone to Mobile with Genl. Grant's army. We started from Jackson the 11 of July and we had a pretty hard time coming back. We were on half rations and it was very warm and water was very scarce. There was a good many of this corps that dropped down dead in the ranks owing to the heat. Although we drew but half rations I lived pretty well. I did not draw any rations on the march. I got my living out of the Secesh on the road. We had peaches, figs, hoe cake & molasses, honey and such stuff. We would go along til we came to a good looking house and go in and tell them what we wanted and they would set their n[----]s to work and cook it up. We went to one place and they had about 10 or 12 hives of bees. One of my tent mates and myself thought we should like a little to help a hard tack down so we asked the man of the house which hive was the best one and he said that he guessed that there was not much in any of them but we were not going to give it up. So we went and got a good pile of cotton (there is pleanty of cotton in this state) and set it a fire and got it to smoking then went and picked out a good hive and smoked the bees out and we had a nice mess of honey.

I did not have a very heavy load when I came into camp last thursday. Everything I had was my pants, shirt and cap, Gun & equipments. I lost everything else and my boots I had to throw away. They were all worn out and hurt my feet pretty bad. I came all the way from Jackson bare footed (about 60 miles). (I drew some shoes from the gov yesterday).

I suppose that before this they have drafted in Stoughton Henry Monk. Had a letter Sunday and it stated that there was to be 144 drafted from there. Warren Monk and John Guild of Stoughton have been drafted from Boston. I should like to have you send me a list of the drafted men of Stoughton. I suppose that they had a pretty hard fight at Gettysburg, Penn. I hear that the 12th Mass. suffered considerable. The Sergt. Major told that they were going to fill up the old regiments with the drafted men. If so, I suppose that some of the Stoughton boys will come to this one. I am glad that I am out here now and not have to be drafted. I can have the fun of seeing some of them drill out here in this warm weather. I should like to have you send me a book the name of which is "School of the Guides". It is a Military book and will be found in Boston, where they keep D. Van Nostrands Military Publications. I should think that they would be likely to keep it these time at any book store.

Edward

J D. Van Nostrands Military Publications
School of the Guides
Covington Ky.
Aug 16th 1863

Father & Mother.

I recieved the last letter that I got from you in Miss, we have got back in old Kentuck once more and we are very glad of it you dont know how much better the water is here I never drank so good water in my life as we get in this state, while we was in Miss, we had nothing but cistern water and that was very scarce, when we got to the Big Black, following old Johnson Tip he in his retreat filled up the most of the cisterns and we had a very heave shower as soon as they crossed the river and if it had not been for that we should have died with the thirst this water ran into the holes and ravines and this was where we got our drink there is no springs in the state. We left there 1 week ago last Thirsday and arrived in Cincinnati last friday we had a very pleasant ride up the river in the boat and from Cairo we came on in the cars. We was furnished with refreshments along the rout which was very <u>acceptable</u> to the Soldiers. There was about 48 soldiers that died per day for the last week that we stoped in Miss. out of this corps, we did not loose a man out of this Co with the exception of Lieut Hawes. While we were at Memphis Term, the old 4th came in there on the Steamer No. America. our boat was cuallng up then and I did not get a chance to see any of the boys but Ben Phillips he looked as tough as an <u>ox</u>.

when we arrived at Cario we stoped there one day and the 4th arrived there just before we left. I saw Charles Eaton, Henry Johnson, Gil Bell, George F. Littlefield and Charles Littlefield of E. Stoughton. David Ward was there but I did not get a chance to see him. They thought that they had seen pretty hard times, but I guess if they had been marched around as the 9th Corp has They talk as if they had been in some pretty hard fights But I guess if the 1st one that they went into they had left 300 of there comrads on the field and other fights in propotions would think that they had seen harder times.

I recieved a letter from Ellery while I was in Miss. and I will answer it soon. I also have recieved one from James Albert he is at Corinth Miss now. I have not had one from Georges folks this good while. I saw a list of the drafted men from Stoughton the other day. I have been as tough as could be ever since we left Kentucky. I think the climate of Miss. agrees with me but I dont want to stay there if it does. I have not heard whether or not you recieved the money that I sent home or the Journal.

Edward

Camp Nelson, Ky.
Aug 26th, 1863

Father & Mother,

    The next day after I wrote to you last we started from Covington for Camp Nelson which is near Hickman Ridge about 20 miles beyond Lexington. We are pretty tired. We came all the way over the road as guards on a train of wagons, all the way from Cincinnati which is about 120 miles. The rest of the Brigade came up in the cars. We have not got but 5 commissioned officers in the regt. now. Our Adjutant is promoted and we have three Lieuts. which is all of the commissioned we have with the regt. now. There is but 3 Sargents, 2 Corporals besides myself, and 20 privates in the Company and there is some of them that are not fit for duty. Sergt. Howland is in command of the company.

    This whole army Corps is all used up and will probably stop here a short time and get recruited up a little.

    We have had enough to eat between Cincinnati and this place. We have got a little sheet Iron pail that will hold about 3 qts. and Sergt. Angies, Cpl. Farince Morse and myself manage to get potatoes and onions enough to make it full of soup with the help of a little piece of pork or a chicken and we 4 make out to have a pretty good supper to go to bed upon as a general thing. It is pretty cool here now or it seems so to us. I have got no blanket yet or coat but go in my shirt sleeves and when it comes night I lay down on the ground with my head on my cartridge box and go to sleep. We are going to draw clothing tomorrow and we shall all look like new recruits. A few days before I left Miss, the Lieut. reckoned up my clothing account and it amounted to about 35 dollars. The Gov. allows 45 and that would make 10 dollars due me and then they allow 10 dollars more for the clothes that we lost at So. Mountain & Antietam which would make 20 dollars due me. But the clothing books were all lost in transportation from Mississippi to Kentucky. and as the government has no account of it, they will have to give us the whole 45 dollars or nothing which they will do on the next pay day. If they do not allow anything, I shall draw my 45 dollars worth this year. I will warrant you they will owe us 52 dollars in a few days now. I expect they will pay part of it this week and if they remain here the other 2 months soon.

I wrote a letter to Samuel Austin last Sunday at Paris. Paris is the first place that we stopped the 1st time that we came into Kentucky.

What do they think about the war now at home? Do they think that it looks any more like settling it up?

Edward

Camp Parks, Ky.
Sept. 2nd, 1863

Father & Mother,

I received your last letter last Saturday. I should have wrote to you last Sunday and shall every Sunday if things will permit, but as I wrote to you before the Army Corp is all worn out and you would have thought so if you could have seen them a week ago in clothes as well as in body. But now they have got all dressed up and look as slick in regard to clothes as they did when they first came out and when they will have a little rest they will be all right. I am as well as any of them and for the last week I have felt kind of lazy and have been laying around not knowing whether I had better be sick or not but I concluded that I would not and I am all right again now and got an appetite like a hog.

We can get a plenty of apples, peaches, pears, watermellons, potatoes, onions, eggs, chickens, at pretty reasonable prices and we have some of them once in a while.

Lieut. Stickney of this Company is at home on a furlough and he may possibly come to Stoughton before he comes back. Col. Carruth is also at home and a good many more of our officers.

I did not hear of Phinny's death till I saw it in your letter. I have not seen anything of the 29th Regt. since we left Mississippi. The boy that worked for Lieut. Hawes after he was promoted is dead. He died last night. He has been with the regt. ever since it came out. He came out as Capt. Andrew's servant and was thought a great lot of by the regt. He came very near being killed when Lt. Hawes. was. He was hurt very bad at that time being on the seat with him the time.

You wrote to know if they were agoing to send home Lt. Hawes' body. They will not unless his folks send for it. I do not know where he was burried as he was not with the regt. at the time of the accident but was with the wagon train.

I expect old Burnside is doing a great thing in East Tennessee. He has got across the Tennessee River and driving them like time. He has none of the 9th Army Corps with him. It is the 23rd which is composed mostly of western troops. Henry Monk was left at Cincinnati. I suppose he has gone now to camp Dennison where he can get another furlough if he wants one as all of the sick in this corps is to have one.

Edward

Camp Carruth Crab Orchard

Sept. 28th,1863

Father & Mother,

    I received you letter last Tuesday and I suppose I shall recieve another one from you tomorrow. We get a mail here every morning with the exception of Monday and Sunday the stage does not run so we do not get one the next day. I have just got back from Mount Vernon where I have been since last Tuesday with a detail from this Regt. and one out of the 51st P. V. repairing the road over which Burnside's supplies goes. Mount Vernon is situated in the Cumberland mountains and the road that leads over them is the roughest one that ever was. I like to go out on such excursions as those for we generaly get all we want to eat of that that is good. We find any quanity of hogs & sheep in the woods and it don't take but a few minutes to dress one of them off. We do not stop to heat water and get the hair off but take the hide and all off.

    Some of the boys here have got houses all built up in good shape. They are clap-boarded and shingled. I have not built one yet but shall soon if we stop here. I don't like to work well enough to get one all built and then have to leave it. Sergt. L.G. Thayer our orderly Sergt. and I tent together. He expects to have a commission soon. If our Col. was here I guess he would have got it before this time. He came out in the 12th Mass. as a private and was taken prisoner at Winchester, Va. and was in the Libby prison at Richmond 3 or 4 months and then was paroled and got his discharge. When the 35th was got up he enlisted in this Company and came out as Corporal, was promoted to Sergt. at Falmouth, Va. and when M. B. Hawes received his commission he was promoted to orderly Serg. and in a few weeks he will have some shoulder straps on his shoulder. I call that going up pretty fast. Do you ever here any thing from George Hawes from No. Stoughton that used to be in this company? He got his discharge from Disability.

    George Gill came back to the company last Friday.

    He has not been with us before since we came into Kentucky the 1st time. He is as tough as can be. If you see Mary Crofts you can tell her about him. He used to live there and she used to think a considerable of him.

    Henry Gill is at camp Dennison, Ohio. He will get his discharge I guess.

    It is pretty cool here nights but very warm day times. I must stop now I have got to clean up my old kill devil for inspection. The General is agoing to inspect us this afternoon.

Edward

Tazewell, Tenn.
Oct 15th, 1863

Father & Mother,

It has been just 15 days since we left Crab Orchard. We started with 8 days rations in our haversacks and we were pretty short on for rations before our 8 days rations were out for we can not get 3 days in them. When our 8 days were out we were at London Ky. There we drew nothing but half rations and have not since. It is one of the roughest roads that ever was and they can not get but a small load on a team.

We have had a plenty of apples it is one of the greatest countrys that you ever saw. I go out every night and get a peck to eat for me and my tentmate and they are all gone when we get ready to march in the morning. Some one in the company goes out every day and gets a hog or 2 and we have fresh pork for breakfast most every day. You must not think when we draw half rations that we do not have anything to eat for we are not the boys to let the Grub lay around the country and starve to death. If Uncle Sam don't give us enough to eat, Johnny Reb. must.

I have not had a very heavy load to carry on this march. I had got a new lot of clothing overcoat and all and when we had orders to go down here I thought I should have a pretty hard time of it and was going to send my overcoat home. It was a new one that I never put on but my tentmate Sergt. Thayer is in command of the company and has his baggage carried and I put all of my things with the exception of my blanket into his knapsack and they go with his and I am glad now that I did not send it home for it is pretty cool nights here. We came here last night and are agoing to stop here all day today and rest and tomorrow we go on to Knoxville where we shall get in the course of two or three days. We came through Cumberland Gap yesterday. That is where the States of Ky. Tenn. & Va. come together. When we were marching through we halted to rest and I sat down on a stone in Va. had one foot in Tenn. and the other in Ky.

Parson Bronlow came past here yesterday. He looked about the same as he did when I saw him in Bridgewater. He was going on to Knoxville where he is going to start a paper again. The name of which is the Rebel Avenger. I have got no letters since we left Crab Orchard and I do not expect to get any til we get to Knoxville. The mail went by the way of Nashville.

Edward

Knoxville, Tenn.
Oct 20th, 1863

Father & Mother,

We arrived at this place yesterday and we were very glad to get here. We had been on the march 19 days and the country that we came through was very rough and mountainous and it has rained a great many days and it was a very hard march. This is quite a large place. There was before the war broke out a great lot of business done here. The town being situated on the Tennessee River and it is navigable for Steamboats up to this place. Chattanooga is on the same river about and fifty miles from here. I expect to start for there tomorrow morning.

We got the first mail that we have received for about a month yesterday. I received a letter from Mother dated at Royalton and one from L. A. and 2 from you. Has your foot got well yet? Which foot is it that is sore your, right or left one?

Last night we drew 1/2 rations for the next 3 days. I ate all of my hard tack for supper and for the rest of the 3 days I have got to get my rations from somebody besides Uncle Sam.

I have just got back from town. I saw the house where Parson Bronlow lives and where his daughter hung the Stars & Stripes, and when the Rebels came to pull it down she took a musket and pointed it to them and threatened to shoot the first man that laid his hand on it and they went off with out touching it. This happened when her father was in prison.

I also saw the building where old Parson Bronlow used to print his paper when he was thrust into prison by the Rebs.

Provisions are pretty high in this place now. Bread is 50 cents per loaf, coffee $3.00 per. pound, sugar 30 cents and other things in propotion. Butter is 1 dollar.

I expect old Hooker with part of the army of the Potomac is down with old Rose-crans and part of Grants army is there, and Burnside is on his left flank. So I suppose that they have got men enough to see to Genl. Bragg buy this time. The 9 corps is down there all but this Division and we will go tomorrow I expect. I suppose that Mother will be home by the time you get this letter.

I am in good Health.

Edward Waldo

London, Tenn.
Oct. 26th, 1863

Father & Mother,

We received a mail yesterday. I received a letter from you and one from Joseph & Frank.

We arrived at this place Friday night about 8 o'clock. Genl. Burnside came on in the cars with us. He looks as though he had not seen very hard times. I have not seen him before since we went down to Vicksburg.

This town is on the Virginia & Georgia railroad about 40 miles south from Knox-ville. the road runs to Chatanooga and the Rebels hold the road at Philadelphia and we have got to drive them from it the report is that there is about 30,000 of them at that place now. They have been fighting here every day for about a week sometimes we drive them and then they drive us. we drove them 20 miles the other day (Saturday) and yesterday they drove our men back to within 2 miles of this place. There has none of the 9th Army corps had any fighting to do with then yet but when we get at it I expect we shall clean them out. we have been expecting to have to go over there every day but they have not called for us yet.

We are on half rations yet and shall be I expect till we get this road opened. I went out about 2 miles yesterday morning and this morning and got my haversack full of potatoes each time and I have just had a dinner that tasted just as good at this time as one to home woulda The country around here looks same as it did at Falmouth, Virginia. We are in camp on the east side of the Tennessee River and the town is on the other side and looks some like Fredericksburg and its Fortifications. When it rains it is very muddy indeed, more so I think than it used to be there.

In every army corps in the army there is a signal corps who are stationed around on the hills between the battle ground and the Commanding Generals Headquarters. One of them will be on the battle ground with his flag and another will be on a hill in sight of the one that is on the battle ground and another on a hill over looking the former and so on and one of them will be at Headquarters, so by the motion the commanding General can see and give his directions if he is miles away from the scene of action. There is one of them on a hill in the distance that can be seen from my tent as I sit here writing and if I could only read the motions of the flag I suppose I could tell you some news either good or bad. Sometime ago you wrote about sending me some boots, shirts &etc. but I was so far away that I thought I would draw from the government but I have got on a Government shirt. It is so short that I can not keep it in my pants and I should like to have you send me some shirts by mail and I will get along with Government shoes this winter. I guess it will not be very cold away down here I guess in the day time. I have got to the bottom and I will stop.

Edward

Lenoir, Tenn.
Nov. 1st, 1863

Father & Mother,

We evacuated the town of London last Wednesday. The troops commenced leaving the town Tuesday night but all of the troops did not get across the Pontoon til about 10 o'clock Wednesday forenoon. Our Regt. was the one that took up the Pontoon bridge. We had got it about half taken up and the planks carried about a mile over behind the hills and were to work with all of our might to get the remainder of it up before the Rebs. came into the town and in came about 40 or 50 of them on horseback with a flag of truce. They came in that way so that we should not fire on them. After they went off we expected that they would try and stop us from taking up the rest of it but they did not and we got it all up and on the cars before dark and then went into camp on this side of the river for the night. It rained all day and it was very uncomfortable being out.

This place is situated on the Tennessee River about 6 miles farther north than the town of London but our pickets go down the river as far as that place. Burnside's Headquarters were on the hill back of our camp til yesterday when he took the cars and went on to Knoxville. The Tennessee River is just over the other side of the hill and the rebel pickets are on the other side of the river. There is details out of our Brigade that go over there every day to get cattle & etc. We do not draw any salt meat here all fresh. We get 1 loaf of bread a day about as large as a good size biscuit, a spoonfull of sugar a day and about a spoonfull and a half of coffee and a little piece of fresh meat.

Night before last we were called out into line of battle and stopped there about an hour. The rain poured down in torrents and we were pretty well drenched through before we got into our tents and we had to lay on our arms all night.

The report here is that Meade and Lee have had a fight and Lee has got a good whipping. We don't get much news down here. It takes a good while to get the mail through. After I get done writing I am agoing to go out and see if I can find some good fat hogs some where if I can get a pass from the Major. There is a plenty of them the other side of the river and I don't want Johnny Reb. to get them all. I have got a letter to write to Henry Monk at camp Dennison and one for Morse of this company. I have all of his letters to write and read for him as he can not write.

It takes about a month for a letter to go home and to get an answer to it and I guess I shall get this Memorandum wrote over by that time and if you will send me another one when you get this letter I will send this one home.

Who is agoing to keep school this winter? Is George Agent? Who have they chose for Governor? I suppose they will have a new one before you get this.

The 1st Division is building winter Quarters at this place but I expect the 2nd will go Kingston & Knoxville.

Edward

Knoxville, Tenn.
Dec 19th, 1863

Father & Mother,

I have been waiting to get a mail before I wrote again. I wrote a letter the day that the Rebels left here and I suppose you have received it before this time. We got a mail yesterday and I received 6 or 7 letters and some Courier's. I have got my mittens and they were just the fit. *I have wished that I had a pair a good many times since the Rebels had us surrounded here.* I have not got my memorandum or shirt yet but I guess that I have got all of the rest of the letters. I received Emma & Bett's letter before we retreated to this place. I shall answer Frank's letter soon now and should have done so before if there had been any chance to have sent it. You wrote in one of your letters a good while ago that Henry Gill had sent home his Picture and you did not see why I did not send mine. But you know that he has been spending a few months in or near the city of Cincinnati at the Hospital where he could have it done. It just as well as not and I am away down in the woods of Tennessee where they never heard of such a thing as a picture. I will have it taken as soon as I have a chance to. I received a letter from Charles Upham a few days ago and I answered it day before yesterday.

There is no vacancy in this company now or in the Regiment. It has got to be so small now that they will not allow only 2 commissioned to a company, a Captain or 1st Lieut.

I wrote to Charles Upham that I would take a commission in any regiment. I expected ere this to have been promoted to sergeant. When I was promoted to Corporal. (in Aug last) Capt. Stickney (then Lieut and in command of this company) told me that within three weeks that I should have a Sergt.'s berth, but he expected that our orderly Sergeant would be commissioned and I would have taken his place, but owing to the smallness of the Regiment he did not recieve his promotion.

They are forming regiments to go into the Veteran Corps I see in Mass. (3 or 4 of them). I did not know but through the influence of some of the influencial men, I might obtain a commission in some of them, (that is the way that most of the officers got there commissions).

We were surrounded here in this place 17 days. We had 4 battles with the enemy on the retreat to this place. The loss in our regt. was but 2 killed and 12 wounded and a few taken prisoners. The largest one was at Campbell Station. We fought there from noon till after dark and the Rebels came very near getting us all surrounded. They came down on the sides of us in 3 or 4 lines of battles but old Burnside got away from them with his little Corps. They outnumbered us by thousands. I never saw so many of them in my life on the battle field.

We have had to go on picket say this morning at 4 o'clock and stop till tomorrow at this time and then we would have to go into the rifle pits and stop till 4 the next morning and then go on again (we did not pretend to eat but 1 meal per. day).

Our regt. has made 2 charges since we were here and we drove the enemy out of the Rifle pits both times.

The last charge that we made I was struck by a piece of shell that was nearly spent on my skin. It bruised me a little and that was all (so I guess that they don't mean to kill me after all). I am tough and well and can eat all that I can get. I think that I grow tougher & tougher every day. I have got to the bottom of my paper and it is most dark and I will stop.

Edward

Blanes X roads, Tenn.
Dec 26th, 1863

Father & Mother,

I have not received any letter from you since I last wrote a week ago. The last letter that I received from you was dated Dec 7th. My memorandum or shirt has not got along yet but I expect them every day now. I have got my memorandum all full and am keeping it on paper now.

I received a letter from Elmer yesterday and have just answered it. I will send it home in this.

We are encamped in the woods where we can keep a good fire. the Rebels left here last Wednesday. I do not know which way they have gone. We do not draw but 1/4 rations from the Governmant but we have a chance to go out into the country and buy a little something. We do not have much to do at present but we have had enough to do for the last month to make up for it.

I expect that we shall leave this state this next week. I do not know where we shall go. I think that we shall come back to Kentucky and we may go to Washington and go off on another expedition

I got a goose and some potatoes & onions and set up all night Christmas and Sergt. Thayer & myself had a good soup before we went to bed. It is the first time that I have got filled up this good while.

Henry Monk came back to the regiment just before the fight at Campbell Station. The day before I believe, and Henry Gill came back last week. They are both well.

It is rainy today and I am sitting up in my tent and I can not sit up strait and it makes my back ache and I do not know as you can read this scribbling. I have just wrote a good long letter to Elmer.

We have just had notice that James Osgood has gone into the invalid corps. It came to day.

How many has Stoughton got in their quota now? I should like to be there and get the bounty.

Some of the old regiments in this corps that have been 2 years are enlisting for three more. I wish that this one had been 2 then we could enlist again.

For breakfast this morning I had some hearty pudding & molasses. It was as good a meal as I ever ate.

Our Major has gone home on a furlough and the Col. is to home now and the regiment is in command of Capt. Lyons who used to be an orderly Sergeant in the 12th regiment.

At Knoxville the other day I saw a lot of Rebel Prisoners sweeping the streets. I suppose that that is to make them pay for their board as we have to support our men that is to Richmond.

You wrote that William Capen talked of enlisting. Has he done so yet? If so, what regiment is he going into?

I wonder how Mr. Chase likes to be a soldier. I guess he will find it is not quite so easy a life as keeping school.

I was a going to write to Frank today but it rains so I shall have to put it off as it is rather uncomfortable writing in the rain in these little tents.

I have not had a letter from Lucy since we were down to Miss. I believe. Why don't she write a wad or two once in a while.

It rains so I will not write any more.

Edward

- 1864 -

Blanes Cross Roads, Tenn.
Jan. 4th [1864]

Father & Mother,

I should have written to you yesterday, but I came in from picket in the morning and being up all night I was rather tired so I turned in and had a good sleep instead. (We having been on picket 60 hours).

I have not received a letter from you since the one dated Nov. 7th. We have not received any mail for about 10 days. I hope we shall get one before a great while. It is rather lonesome out here in the woods when we get none for there is no way that we can get any news. We do not know any thing that is going on. They say that we have got old Longstreet surrendered here some where but we can not see any rebels where we are on picket or can not see any body that has.

I am living pretty well now but I cannot thank Uncle Sam for it for last night we only drew one and one half cans of corn for a days ration but we draw a little sugar and coffee now and then. The citizens near here charge 25 cents per. qt. for meal but I have not paid only 10 for any yet. I went out the other day about 6 miles out side of the picket and got a peck of meal and some dried apple and molasses and we have got so that we can cook about equal to the Boston cooks now I guess. We put in a little lye made out of ashes and we can make a cake as light as can be. I dont know but I shall have to get a receipt book for cooking. For dinner yesterday I took some meal and some dried apple and mixed them together and put them in a bag and boiled it the same as you would a suit pudding and when it was done we ate it with molasses on it and you had better believe it was good.

Sergt. Thayer went out yesterday and got half bushel of meal and has just got in and I guess he and I will live for a few days to come if we do not draw any rations.

The 21st Mass. Regiment has all of them reenlisted but about 10 or 12 of them and they start for home tomorrow when they will get a furlough of thirty days and them that don't reenlist will be transfered to this regiment. The 51st P.V. of this Brigade have all enlisted and will start for home in a few days.

I hope my memorandum will come before a great while for I have to write on letter paper now and it is not so heavy as a book. I expect that it will come in the next mail. And my shirt also It was pretty cool here. New Years day the people around here say that they do not very often have any colder weather here.

William Hudson of Randolph who formerly went to Sumner School and you may remember him perhaps, he belonged to the 29th Reg. and the same company that Phinney Burrell did, was shot two or three weeks ago for desertion and forgery.

Tell Samuel Austin that he must write I have not received a letter from him this good while. I answered Emmes & Netts letter a few days ago.

I suppose that it is pretty cool there now. I was telling some of these old farmers what cold weather and large snow storms we have some times in Mass. and it made there eyes stick out a rod. They think that they are having right smart spell of weather here now but they reckon that it will be a heap warmer here soon.

I suppose that today is the last day that they have to get volunteers and will have to draft now if they have not got their quota. Elmer wrote me that he thought that they would get them in Stoughton

Edward

Ering Station, Knoxville, Tenn.
Feb 5th, 1864

Father & Mother,

I received your letter with the cayenne in it but have not got my shirt yet. Yesterday I received a letter from Charles Upham I answered it to day.

We have been in camp here since I last wrote to you. The other night about dark we were ordered to pack up and march in light marching order. We went across the river at Knoxville and stopped over night. They expected that the Rebels were agoing to make a raid but they did not and went back to our old camp the next morning.

We are waiting here expecting every day to start for the North. The report is that we are to go to New York to be recruited up to 50,000.

We draw 1/2 rations now instead of one fourth. Tonight we have drawn some tea which is the first for about 5 months. I do not use any sugar so I swap it off for coffee with Henry Gill and when we draw I get quite a little bag of coffee. I am agoing out tomorrow and swap it off to some of these Farmers and get some meal or something for it.

Charles Upham said that they had got their quota in Stoughton so I suppose that they will not be afraid of the draft.

There was an old Farmer shot near here the other night. He was a Rebel and used all of the means that he could to get the young men around here into the Rebel army when the war first broke out and a good many of them ran off into Kentucky and enlisted and their regiment is here now and they expect that some of them shot him. There is but three regiments in this Division now. The other one all have gone home on a furlough. We are under the command of Gen. Wilcox. The Brigade is under the command of Lt. Col. Collins of the llth N.H. Vol.

I am well as ever I was in the world. This is a very healthy state. The Surgeon does not have but very few callers now mornings. I hope we shall get where the mail goes regular.

Edward

> Camp of the 35th Mass Vol. Knoxville, Tenn.
> Mar 20th, 1864

Father & Mother,
I received a letter from you yesterday with Horaces' picture in it. It looks very natural.

We came to this city yesterday en route for the East. We had stopped here so long I had made up my mind that this Corps would stop here all summer but the order came at last and we will be off I guess shortly.

We have been up to the front for the last two weeks which was at Morristown which is about 42 miles from here. We marched from there in two days and went around through the woods so that the other troops here would not get demoralised and think that we were falling back, but it seems that they have fell back as far as Strawberry Planes since yesterday morning and I do not know but we shall have to go and drive the Rebels back again to Morristown before we get out of it. If the 9th Corps is small it's name is worth more than 50,000 men. If the Rebs. hear that the Corps is coming they take to their legs as fast as possible.

It is not decided yet how we shall go. We may march from here to London a distance of 28 miles and then take the cars and go by the way of Chattanooga and Nashville or Memphis; or we may march over the mountains to Nicholsville a distance of 190 miles and then take the cars for Cincinnati. I do not know but I may get a furlough and come home if we get East before my commission gets along. I do not know when it will come but I shall expect it any time between now and the 1st of May. It is liable to come now any day.

Gov. Andrew said in his note to the commander of this Regiment that I would have to report to Nashville and they say that we are going to Annapolis and if we get there I may get a chance to go by the way of Boston and if it comes while we are here I shall have to go direct to Nashville. Our Col. has got back and is in command of this Division. Gen. Ferrero is in command of the 1st Div. (our old Gen. and Gen. Wilcox of the corps). I have not got my shirt or memorandum do not send another one untill I know where I am agoing to go.

Edward

Annapolis, Md.
April 8th, 1864

Father & Mother,

I should have wrote before but being on the move I have not had a chance. We left Knoxville the 21st of March and arrived at Nicholsville, Ky. on the 31st a distance of 190 mile. We did not come by the way of Cumberland Gap. (the way we went to Knoxville) but by the way of Clinton, Jacksboro & Somerset on what is called the Old Kentucky road. We have marched over a good many different ranges of mountain since we have been in the service, but none that were so high and steep as these. It either rained or snowed about every other day while we were coming over the mountains and made it very hard marching, but the thoughts that we were agoing to get into a country of civilization once more made us trot on through the mud and snow with a good will. We started from Nicholsville on the cars on the 2nd of April passing through Paris on that day just one year from the time we entered it when we first came into KY. We arrived in Covington on the morning of the 3d and received a mail on that day the 1st one that we had had for a long time. I received 2 letters from you and some Couriers.

We started from Cincinnati on the night of the 3d and passing through the cities of Columbus, Pittsburg, Harrisburg and many other smaller ones arriving at Baltimore on the eve of the 6th. We were furnished with refreshments along the road and at Baltimore we had a good breakfast and supper and a night's rest at the soldiers Home... and you had better believe that there was some difference between having an ear of corn for a day's ration and having three good meals at a table.

We started from Baltimore on the morning of the 7th and got to this place yesterday. All of the 9 Corps is here now. The report is here that all of the regiments that was at the Seige of Knoxville are agoing home on a furlough of 7 days but I don't know how true it is.

The mail is agoing now and I shall have to stop.

Edward

Annapolis, Md.
April 17th, 1864

Father & Mother,

Day before yesterday I received a letter from you. It is the only one that I have received since we arrived here with the exception of one from Chas. Upham. We are in A. tents. We have enough to eat once more and we have forgot that we ever suffered for the want of food. We draw for rations Soft bread, sugar, coffee, tea, beef, salt & fresh pork, hominy, rice, beans, molasses, potatoes, candles, straw, and I don't know what else. We get all of the oysters that we want. You know this is where they make them. I can eat about 3 quarts of solid ones in the course of the day.

We had a review the other day by Genls. Burnside & Grant. I have not seen Genl. Grant before since we were down to Vicksburg. He look very natural only he was not smoking. I don't think that any body ever saw him before but what he had a pipe in his mouth.

We do not have anything to do yet but to pass away time the best way that we can. Henry Monk has been promoted to Cpl. vice Charles Wild reduced. I do not know how long that we shall stop here but probably not many weeks. I do not hear anything about moving. We are in camp about one and one half miles from the city. I have been there once since we came here. It is not so large a place as I should think that the capitol of Md. would be. Col. Caruth is in command of the regiment now. Capt. Stickney of this Company was here yesterday but is going back to Boston again. He is recruiting under orders from the War Department. He has got about 60 men for this Regiment and 20 for this company.

I have not received my shirt or memorandum yet. You need not send me another memorandum for I have got one. But I should like to have a pair of shirts and some stockings. If sent by Adams express they will come all right. They have an office up this side of the city. We was paid off 4 months pay the other day. I shall send it home before we leave here (If nothing turns up so that I should want to use it). There was a man here from Randolph yesterday. He went back in the last train last night. If we stop here long I shall weight about 200.

Edward

I send this paper so that you can see what we used to have to do in Tennessee.

Fairfax Court House, Va.
April 27, 1864

Father & Mother,

I have not received a letter from you since I last wrote and I have not time to write but a few lines at present. I do not know when I shall find a another chance for some time as the Army of the Potomac is about to move on to Richmond and the mail is not sent from there now. We shall join them about day after tomorrow.

We left Annapolis last Saturday and arrived in Washington Monday noon where we were received by the President & Gen. Burnside. We then crossed to the Virginia side of the Potomac where we left this morning. Our whole Corps is here 50,000 strong and it does not look much as it did in Tennessee. This is the town near the Bull Run Battlefield where Albiegaull was sick in the Hospital. It is so dark that I can not write any more.

You need not be surprised if I do not write again very soon but will if I can. You must write just the same.

Ed

PS. I have just picked up and old piece of candle and I will mark my paper over.

You have heard I suppose in the papers about Mosby's Guerrillas who have captured so many of our supply trains and Suttler's wagons and are always scouting around in our lines. He was here today so I suppose that Genl. Lee will know of our joining the Army of the Potomac as soon as we get there and will have a good excuse for taking to his heels.

There will be a very large army when they advance this corps has 50,000, the 2nd 50,000, and the 1st 3d 5th & others may each have as many for all that I know. The 56th & 57th Mass. are in the Brigade with us and our Col. commands the Brigade & Genl. Stevenson the Division formally Col. of the 24th Mass. Col. Bartlet of the 57th has got a cork leg and arm both. I don't know but he would stop in the army if he lost the other leg and arm.

I am well as can be and have enough to eat which does not seem much like Tennessee. I drink about 3 qts. of coffee per. day. and you will have to have a good large coffee pot in readyness when I get home. We march early tomorrow morning.

Edward

Direct your letters now to the 1st Brigade 1st Division 9th Corps
Washington, D.C.

[Letter from his parents]

Stoughton [*Massachusetts*]
May 15th, 1864

Edward,

Another week has passed and we have not heard from you but we shall look for a letter the coming week. we have had a cold storm most of the past week. I went to meeting this afternoon Williamson Gill told me one of the neighbors (which I suppose was his son's girl if he has got one) had a letter from Henry he did not expect. He was with the Regt. but he did not know why it is so dark. I cannot see so I must light a lamp or you cannot read what I write. I do not think of much news to write. I have not been out any the past week to hear any. I have been busy sewing straw the man and was in a great hurry for it and I had some custom hats to sew for Mrs Grey's girls so I was pretty busy all the week. Alanson was in here a few days ago. He is quite lame yet. He has not got to work yet. He thought he should have gone to work last week but did not. He does not expect to be able to do anything on the farm himself this summer. He has a horse and wagon so he can ride some. He feels rather poor. It is so long since he has been able to earn much and the children being sick and everything so high. It costs considerable to live. All kinds of clothing and provisions are up to the highest notch.

There has been war meetings two or three evenings of the past week but I have not seen anyone to learn the result. Frances Capen has taken rooms on Washington St. and set up business by himself in the Photograph line so we can all go and have our pictures taken. Elmer has Albert Dickerman's office and boards at home. Albert is in Boston. His New London girl's father has moved to Boston has bought a house and Albert lives with them. They are not married yet. Her father is a very rich man. I have heard he found money and Albert furnished the house as he chose. He has a very good taste for such things so I guess it was done up in good shape. She is an only daughter. I do not recollect what her name is.

Mrs Dennis is assistant teacher in the village Grammer school, Mary Manley Tucker principal. Abby Battle is the next below and I do not know who the other teachers are a Miss Rodgers teaches No 5 this term she commenced last monday and board to Elijah Capens. Saml Austin was here today. He expects to drive a milk cart for George to commence in the course of a week through East Stoughton.

I do not think of anything more to write this time so I will pass it over to headquarters and see what he can do for you this time. I hope we shall get a letter from you before writing day comes along again.

From Mary Waldo

Stoughton, Mass.
May 15th, 1864

Edward,

Drafting commenced in Boston last week. I was in at one of the war meetings here one evening last week. They chose a committee to go to Washington to hire recruits for this Town's quota. On inquiry I was told that they could get veterans there. I have been informed Randolph sent on there and got her quota filled. I think I shall plant my corn tomorrow and finish up planting other things this week. Everything is so high that it stands us in hard to plant as much as we can. I see by the papers that there has been some pretty hard battles last week and week before. Avery has a family in his house. The man is brother to the Jones that lives in the John Turner house. Ezra Churchill is at work for Ira Holmes. He gets 1.50 per day and his dinner. Thomas Swan gives his Irishman twenty five Dollars per month, the brother to the girl that has lived there so long

W.P. Waldo

Mass. Military State Agency,
Corner 7th St. & Pennsylvania Avenue,
Washington, D.C.
May 24, 1864

W. P. Waldo Stoughton, Mass

Sir

Your son, Alfred E. Waldo, Co. E 35th Mass Vols is at Armory Hospital this City. His Arm has been amputated. He is doing well and is receiving every attention.

Yours Respectfully,
Gardiner Tufts
Mass State Agent

Washington
May 25th [1864]

Mr. William P. Waldo,

I am sure you must be very anxious to hear something of your son. I think he told me he had written to you since he was wounded. He only arrived in Washington yesterday (Tuesday) morning. He had a very bad wound in the left arm. It bled a good deal after he got here. He is in the best Hospital in the city & under the best Surgeon Dr. Bliss Armory Square Hospital, it is the "Post Hospital". He was a good deal weakened from the loss of blood. I saw him a short time after he came in. I stayed with him until the Dr. came to examine his wounds. They gave him Chloroform & examined it themselves & I am sorry to have to tell you that he concluded it must come off. So they amputated it immediately & he is now doing very well indeed. I have been with him all day & saw him comfortably fixed for the night & I am sure he will sleep soundly tonight. He has an excelly a nurse to stay with him tonight & I gave him strict charge to watch him closely, not that I think he really requires it for I think he will sleep soundly as he has slept but little since he came in. I wanted to relieve your minds about him & to tell you that he should have the best care & attention for I have become very much interested in his case & I can assume I will do all in my power to make him comfortable. I am a visitor at the Hospital & if there is anything I can do for you shall be very glad to do it. Your son Alfred told me to address the letter to both his Parents but I had forgotten that & wrote to his father he desired me to tell you that he was doing well. Your son seems anxious to hear from home.

Direct to Alfred E. Waldo
Armory Square Hospital
Ward 2. Armory building, Washington D.C.

If I can do any thing for you, that will add in any way to your son's comfort or relieve your minds I shall be very glad indeed to do it.
Direct to Miss F. McSloan
No. 545 17th street
Washington D.C.

Stoughton
May 26th/ 64

Edward,
We received a letter tonight from the State Agent stating you had your arm amputated and was doing well. I was very sorry to hear it was so bad but am very glad your life is spared. I am not going to write but a few lines tonight just to let you know we have heard from you. We received the letter you wrote at Fredericksburg Tuesday night. You must keep up good spirits and get able to come home as soon as you can. If there is any thing you need that you cannot get there let us know and we will send it to you if possible. I suppose you will have to get some one to read your letters for you so I will not write much untill you can read them yourself, so good night for this time.

From your mother,
Mary Waldo

Seventh St., American House, Comer Pennsylvania Avenue and Seventh Street,
Washington, D.C.
May 30, 1864

W.P. Waldo

I got to Washington this morning at 7 oclock went to the Hospital and found Edward. He is in Armory building 3rd story a very good room. He is in good health & spirits. He had his arm amputated halfway between his elbow & shoulder. I have talked with his doctor, He says it is doing tip top. I saw the nurse dress it. It discharges very freely.

I have been with him all the forenoon. The room is twice as large as Chemong Hall. It is full of beds. Did not count them. The nurse is a very good one that takes care of him the best one in the room, there is about 10 of them, one woman. He is in good situation as any in the room. Two good fellows right front of him and one very low spirited one next to them. They have some fun with him. He lost an arm too. I shall stop with him a few days. He appeared to be glad to see me. All they put on to the arm is cold water keep a cloth wet with it all the time. He is next to the window. Good air all the time right by his bed.

Yours truly,
George Talbot

Seventh St. American House, Corner Pennsylvania Avenue and Seventh Street,
Washington, D.C.
June 1, 1864.

2 P.M. I went to the Hospital at 7 1/2 this morning. Edward has not had any chill since last night 7 o'clock. He had the best nights rest that he has had since he has been in the Hospital. Night before last he had the night watch get him up to have his bed made which sitting up he fainted. The watch got him down. If he had fell on to the floor it would have killed him.

He needs watching. It is the most critical time now for 2 days that there will be if he gets over that time well I think he will be safe.

I shall stick by untill I see him out of danger. The doctor gives him special care. He is doing all he can to prevent him from having any more chills. They are very bad for him at this time. The hospital is about 1/4 of a mile from Dan's.

Edward's nurse is a going away tomorow. He is the best nurse in the Hospital. The doctor says if he goes there was never one man so good but another was just as good and that he E. shall have good care if he does it himself.

I am a going up again at 4 P.M.

yours truly,
George Talbot

Seventh St American House, Corner Pennsylvania Avenue and Seventh Street,
Washington, D.C.
June 4, 1864

Edward has not been so well bodily for the last two days. He has a poor apetite. He needs all the care that he can have. He had another Shake the 2nd inst. The medicine he takes for them destroys his apetite.

You can take care of him if you come here.

It is very hot here. Some days the themomet is 108 in the shade. I think there is not much danger from the arm now. I shall stop until next week.

Edward has been change to another bed yesterday and had his bed made. You can imagin how he must feel having to lay on his back without moving for 8 days. His back must be very sore and in great pane. I was sick yesterday, did not go to see him until 3 a.m. I feel some better today, am going after breakfast. If you write to me direct as on the envelope. If to Edward to him Armory Square Hospital 2nd ward Armory building No. 85

George Talbot

PEOPLE'S TELEGRAPH LINES
IQ Dated Wash 4 1864
Rec'd Boston June 1864.
To H Gay
408 Wash.
Send Mary Waldo here Monday.
G. Talbot
5.90

Washington
June 7, 1864

William,

I arrived here last night about seven and went to see Edward. I found him alive. He was very glad to see me, told the doctor when he came along about fifteen minutes afterward that he should get along first rate now for his mother had come but the poor boy did not live until morning. He passed on about one o'clock without a struggle. He stopped breathing. If I had not started Sunday I should not have seen him alive. I was satisfied soon as I saw him he could not last long. He is going to be buried tomorrow at two P.M.

George will go and see him buried if he can get a permit and I think now I shall if but can not tell certain. I shall return home as soon as I get rested so it will answer. It is not nessesary for me to write much and I will not try to write more.

Mary Waldo

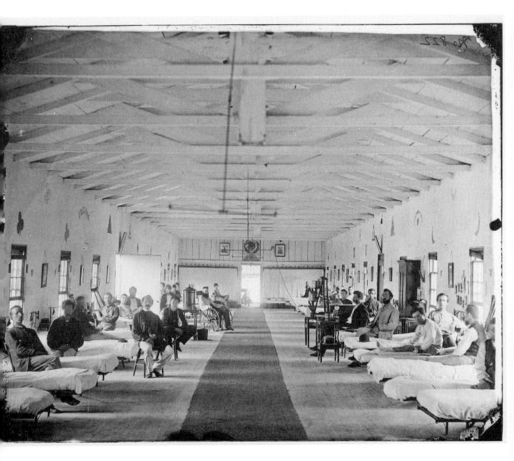

Washington, D.C. Patients in Ward K of Armory Square Hospital

Andersonville:
A Story Of Rebel Military Prisons
By John Mcelroy, Chapters IV - XVI

Fifteen Months A Guest Of The So-Called Southern Confederacy, A Private Soldiers Experience In Richmond, Andersonville, Savannah, Millen, Blackshear And Florence

By John Mcelroy, Late of Co. L. 16th Ill Cav., 1879

Andersonville Prison, Ga., August 17, 1864--Southwest view of stockade showing the dead-line

CHAPTER IV.

A Bitter Cold Morning And A Warm Awakening—Trouble All Along The Line—Fierce Conflicts, Assaults And Defense—Prolonged And Desperate Struggle Ending With A Surrender.

The night had been the most intensely cold that the country had known for many years. Peach and other tender trees had been killed by the frosty rigor, and sentinels had been frozen to death in our neighborhood. The deep snow on which we made our beds, the icy covering of the streams near us, the limbs of the trees above us, had been cracking with loud noises all night, from the bitter cold.

We were camped around Jonesville, each of the four companies lying on one of the roads leading from the town. Company L lay about a mile from the Court House. On a knoll at the end of the village toward us, and at a point where two roads separated,—one of which led to us,—stood a three-inch Rodman rifle, belonging to the Twenty-second Ohio Battery. It and its squad of eighteen men, under command of Lieutenant Alger and Sergeant Davis, had been sent up to us a few days before from the Gap.

The comfortless gray dawn was crawling sluggishly over the mountain-tops, as if numb as the animal and vegetable life which had been shrinking all the long hours under the fierce chill.

The Major's bugler had saluted the morn with the lively, ringing tarr-r-r-a-ta-ara of the Regulation reveille, and the company buglers, as fast as they could thaw out their mouthpieces, were answering him.

I lay on my bed, dreading to get up, and yet not anxious to lie still. It was a question which would be the more uncomfortable. I turned over, to see if there was not another position in which it would be warmer, and began wishing for the thousandth time that the efforts for the amelioration of the horrors of warfare would progress to such a point as to put a stop to all Winter soldiering, so that a fellow could go home as soon as cold weather began, sit around a comfortable stove in a country store; and tell camp stories until the Spring was far enough advanced to let him go back to the front wearing a straw hat and a linen duster.

Then I began wondering how much longer I would dare lie there, before the Orderly Sergeant would draw me out by the heels, and accompany the operation with numerous unkind and sulphurous remarks.

This cogitation, was abruptly terminated by hearing an excited shout from the Captain:

"Turn Out!—COMPANY L!! TURNOUT ! ! !"

Almost at the same instant rose that shrill, piercing Rebel yell, which one who has once heard it rarely forgets, and this was followed by a crashing volley from apparently a regiment of rifles.

I arose-promptly.

Richmond, Va. Castle Thunder, Cary Street

There was evidently something of more interest on hand than the weather.

Cap, overcoat, boots and revolver belt went on, and eyes opened at about the same instant.

As I snatched up my carbine, I looked out in front, and the whole woods appeared to be full of Rebels, rushing toward us, all yelling and some firing. My Captain and First Lieutenant had taken up position on the right front of the tents, and part of the boys were running up to form a line alongside them. The Second Lieutenant had stationed himself on a knoll on the left front, and about a third of the company was rallying around him.

My chum was a silent, sententious sort of a chap, and as we ran forward to the Captain's line, he remarked earnestly:

"Well: this beats hell!"

I thought he had a clear idea of the situation.

All this occupied an inappreciably short space of time. The Rebels had not stopped to reload, but were rushing impetuously toward us. We gave them a hot, rolling volley from our carbines. Many fell, more stopped to load and reply, but the mass surged straight forward at us. Then our fire grew so deadly that they showed a disposition to cover themselves behind the rocks and trees. Again they were urged forward; and a body of them headed by their Colonel, mounted on a white horse, pushed forward through the gap between us and the Second Lieutenant. The Rebel Colonel dashed up to the Second Lieutenant, and ordered him to surrender. The latter-a gallant old graybeard—cursed the Rebel bitterly and snapped his now empty revolver in his face. The Colonel fired and killed him, whereupon his squad, with two of its Sergeants killed and half its numbers on the ground, surrendered.

The Rebels in our front and flank pressed us with equal closeness. It seemed as if it was absolutely impossible to check their rush for an instant, and as we saw the fate of our companions the Captain gave the word for every man to look out for himself. We ran back a little distance, sprang over the fence into the fields, and rushed toward Town, the Rebels encouraging us to make good time by a sharp fire into our backs from the fence.

While we were vainly attempting to stem the onset of the column dashed against us, better success was secured elsewhere. Another column swept down the other road, upon which there was only an outlying picket. This had to come back on the run before the overwhelming numbers, and the Rebels galloped straight for the three-inch Rodman. Company M was the first to get saddled and mounted, and now came up at a steady, swinging gallop, in two platoons, saber and revolver in hand, and led by two Sergeants-Key and McWright,—printer boys from Bloomington, Illinois. They divined the object of the Rebel dash, and strained every nerve to reach the gun first. The Rebels were too near, and got the gun and turned it. Before they could fire it, Company M struck them headlong, but they took the terrible impact without flinching, and for a few minutes there was fierce hand-to-hand work, with sword and pistol. The Rebel leader sank under a half-dozen simultaneous wounds, and fell dead almost under the gun. Men dropped from their horses each instant, and the riderless steeds fled away. The scale of victory was turned by the Major dashing against the Rebel left flank at the head of Company I, and a portion of the artillery squad. The Rebels gave ground slowly, and were packed into a dense mass in the lane up which they had charged. After they had been crowded back, say fifty yards, word was passed through our men to open to the right and left on the sides of the road. The artillerymen had turned the gun and loaded it with a solid shot. Instantly a wide lane opened through our ranks; the man with the lanyard drew the fatal cord, fire burst from the primer and the muzzle, the long gun sprang up and recoiled, and there seemed to be a demoniac yell in its ear-splitting crash, as the heavy ball left the mouth, and tore its bloody way through the bodies of the struggling mass of men and horses.

This ended it. The Rebels gave way in disorder, and our men fell back to give the gun an opportunity to throw shell and canister.

The Rebels now saw that we were not to be run over like a field of cornstalks, and they fell back to devise further tactics, giving us a breathing spell to get ourselves in shape for defense.

The dullest could see that we were in a desperate situation. Critical positions were no new experience to us, as they never are to a cavalry command after a few months in the field, but, though the pitcher goes often to the well, it is broken at last, and our time was evidently at hand. The narrow throat of the Valley, through which lay the road back to the Gap, was held by a force of Rebels evidently much superior to our own, and strongly posted. The road was a slender, tortuous one, winding through rocks and gorges. Nowhere was there room enough to move with even a platoon front against the enemy, and this precluded all chances of cutting out. The best we could do was a slow, difficult movement, in column of fours, and this would have been suicide. On the other side of the Town the Rebels were massed stronger, while to the right and left rose the steep mountain sides. We were caught-trapped as surely as a rat ever was in a wire trap.

As we learned afterwards, a whole division of cavalry, under command of the noted Rebel, Major General Sam Jones, had been sent to effect our capture, to offset in a measure Longstreet's repulse at Knoxville. A gross overestimate of our numbers had caused the sending of so large a force on this errand, and the rough treatment we gave the two columns that attacked us first confirmed the Rebel General's ideas of our strength, and led him to adopt cautious tactics, instead of crushing us out speedily, by a determined advance of all parts of his encircling lines.

The lull in the fight did not last long. A portion of the Rebel line on the east rushed forward to gain a more commanding position.

We concentrated in that direction and drove it back, the Rodman assisting with a couple of well-aimed shells.—This was followed by a similar but more successful attempt by another part of the Rebel line, and so it went on all day—the Rebels rushing up first on this side, and then on that, and we, hastily collecting at the exposed points, seeking to drive them back. We were frequently successful; we were on the inside, and had the advantage of the short interior lines, so that our few men and our breech-loaders told to a good purpose.

There were frequent crises in the struggle, that at some times gave encouragement, but never hope. Once a determined onset was made from the East, and was met by the equally determined resistance of nearly our whole force. Our fire was so galling that a large number of our foes crowded into a house on a knoll, and making loopholes in its walls, began replying to us pretty sharply. We sent word to our faithful artillerists, who trained the gun upon the house. The first shell screamed over the roof, and burst harmlessly beyond. We suspended fire to watch the next. It crashed through the side; for an instant all was deathly still; we thought it had gone on through. Then came a roar and a crash; the clapboards flew off the roof, and smoke poured out; panic-stricken Rebels rushed from the doors and sprang from the windows-like bees from a disturbed hive; the shell had burst among the confined mass of men inside! We afterwards heard that twenty-five were killed there.

At another time a considerable force of rebels gained the cover of a fence in easy range of our main force. Companies L and K were ordered to charge forward on foot and dislodge them. Away we went, under a fire that seemed to drop a man at every step. A hundred yards in front of the Rebels was a little cover, and behind this our men lay down as if by one impulse. Then came a close, desperate duel at short range. It was a question between Northern pluck and Southern courage, as to which could stand the most punishment. Lying as flat as possible on the crusted snow, only raising the head or body enough to load and aim, the men on both sides, with their teeth set, their glaring eyes fastened on the foe, their nerves as tense as tightly-drawn steel wires, rained shot on each other as fast as excited hands could crowd cartridges into the guns and discharge them.

Not a word was said.

The shallower enthusiasm that expresses itself in oaths and shouts had given way to the deep, voiceless rage of men in a death grapple. The Rebel line was a rolling torrent of flame, their bullets shrieked angrily as they flew past, they struck the snow in front of us, and threw its cold flakes in faces that were white with the fires of consuming hate; they buried themselves with a dull thud in the quivering bodies of the enraged combatants.

Minutes passed; they seemed hours.

Would the villains, scoundrels, hell-hounds, sons of vipers never go?

At length a few Rebels sprang up and tried to fly. They were shot down instantly.

Then the whole line rose and ran!

The relief was so great that we jumped to our feet and cheered wildly, forgetting in our excitement to make use of our victory by shooting down our flying enemies.

Nor was an element of fun lacking. A Second Lieutenant was ordered to take a party of skirmishers to the top of a hill and engage those of the Rebels stationed on another hill-top across a ravine. He had but lately joined us from the Regular Army, where he was a Drill Sergeant. Naturally, he was very methodical in his way, and scorned to do otherwise under fire than he would upon the parade ground. He moved his little command to the hill-top, in close order, and faced them to the front. The Johnnies received them with a yell and a volley, whereat the boys winced a little, much to the Lieutenant's disgust, who swore at them; then had them count off with great deliberation, and deployed them as coolly as if them was not an enemy within a hundred miles. After the line deployed, he "dressed" it, commanded "Front!" and "Begin, firing!" his attention was called another way for an instant, and when he looked back again, there was not a man of his nicely formed skirmish line visible. The logs and stones had evidently been put there for the use of skirmishers, the boys thought, and in an instant they availed themselves of their shelter.

Never was there an angrier man than that Second Lieutenant; he brandished his saber and swore; he seemed to feel that all his soldierly reputation was gone, but the boys stuck to their shelter for all that, informing him that when the Rebels would stand out in the open field and take their fire, they would likewise.

Despite all our efforts, the Rebel line crawled up closer an closer to us; we were driven back from knoll to knoll, and from one fence after another. We had maintained the unequal struggle for eight hours; over one-fourth of our number were stretched upon the snow, killed or badly wounded. Our cartridges were nearly all gone; the cannon had fired its last shot long ago, and having a blank cartridge left, had shot the rammer at a gathering party of the enemy.

Just as the Winter sun was going down upon a day of gloom the bugle called us all up on the hillside. Then the Rebels saw for the first time how few there were, and began an almost simultaneous charge all along the line. The Major raised piece of a shelter tent upon a pole. The line halted. An officer rode out from it, followed by two privates.

Approaching the Major, he said, "Who is in command this force?"

The Major replied: "I am."

"Then, Sir, I demand your sword."

"What is your rank, Sir!"

"I am Adjutant of the Sixty-fourth Virginia."

The punctillious soul of the old "Regular"—for such the Major was swelled up instantly, and he answered:

"By ——, sir, I will never surrender to my inferior in rank!"

The Adjutant reined his horse back. His two followers leveled their pieces at the Major and waited orders to fire. They were covered by a dozen carbines in the hands of our men. The Adjutant ordered his men to "recover arms," and rode away with them. He presently returned with a Colonel, and to him the Major handed his saber.

As the men realized what was being done, the first thought of many of them was to snatch out the cylinder's of their revolvers, and the slides of their carbines, and throw them away, so as to make the arms useless.

We were overcome with rage and humiliation at being compelled to yield to an enemy whom we had hated so bitterly. As we stood there on the bleak mountain-side, the biting wind soughing through the leafless branches, the shadows of a gloomy winter night closing around us, the groans and shrieks of our wounded mingling with the triumphant yells of the Rebels plundering our tents, it seemed as if Fate could press to man's lips no cup with bitterer dregs in it than this.

CHAPTER V.

The Reaction—Depression—Bitting Cold—Sharp Hunger And Sad Reflexion.

"Of being taken by the Insolent foe."—Othello.

The night that followed was inexpressibly dreary: The high-wrought nervous tension, which had been protracted through the long hours that the fight lasted, was succeeded by a proportionate mental depression, such as naturally follows any strain upon the mind. This was intensified in our cases by the sharp sting of defeat, the humiliation of having to yield ourselves, our horses and our arms into the possession of the enemy, the uncertainty as to the future, and the sorrow we felt at the loss of so many of our comrades.

Company L had suffered very severely, but our chief regret was for the gallant Osgood, our Second Lieutenant. He, above all others, was our trusted leader. The Captain and First Lieutenant were brave men, and good enough soldiers, but Osgood was the one "whose adoption tried, we grappled to our souls with hooks of steel." There was never any difficulty in getting all the volunteers he wanted for a scouting party. A quiet, pleasant spoken gentleman, past middle age, he looked much better fitted for the office of Justice of the Peace, to which his fellow-citizens of Urbana, Illinois, had elected and reelected him, than to command a troop of rough riders in a great civil war. But none more gallant than he ever vaulted into saddle to do battle for the right. He went into the Army solely as a matter of principle, and did his duty with the unflagging zeal of an olden Puritan fighting for liberty and his soul's salvation. He was a superb horseman—as all the older Illinoisans are and, for all his two-score years and ten, he recognized few superiors for strength and activity in the Battalion. A radical, uncompromising Abolitionist, he had frequently asserted that he would rather die than yield to a Rebel, and he kept his word in this as in everything else.

As for him, it was probably the way he desired to die. No one believed more ardently than he that

> Whether on the scaffold high,
>
> Or in the battle's van;
>
> The fittest place for man to die,
>
> Is where he dies for man.

Among the many who had lost chums and friends was Ned Johnson, of Company K. Ned was a young Englishman, with much of the suggestiveness of the bull-dog common to the lower class of that nation. His fist was readier than his tongue. His chum, Walter Savage was of the same surly type. The two had come from England twelve years before, and had been together ever since. Savage was killed in the struggle for the fence described in the preceding chapter. Ned could not realize for a while that his friend was dead. It was only when the body rapidly stiffened on its icy bed, and the eyes which had been gleaming deadly hate when he was stricken down were glazed over with the dull film of death, that he believed he was gone from him forever. Then his rage was terrible. For the rest of the day he was at the head of every assault upon the enemy. His voice could ever be heard above the firing, cursing the Rebels bitterly, and urging the boys to "Stand up to 'em! Stand right up to 'em! Don't give a inch! Let them have the best you got in the shop! Shoot low, and don't waste a cartridge!"

When we surrendered, Ned seemed to yield sullenly to the inevitable. He threw his belt and apparently his revolver with it upon the snow. A guard was formed around us, and we gathered about the fires that were started. Ned sat apart, his arms folded, his head upon his breast, brooding bitterly upon Walter's death. A horseman, evidently a Colonel or General, clattered up to give some directions concerning us. At the sound of his voice

Ned raised his head and gave him a swift glance; the gold stars upon the Rebel's collar led him to believe that he was the commander of the enemy. Ned sprang to his feet, made a long stride forward, snatched from the breast of his overcoat the revolver he had been hiding there, cocked it and leveled it at the Rebel's breast. Before he could pull the trigger Orderly Sergeant Charles Bentley, of his Company, who was watching him, leaped forward, caught his wrist and threw the revolver up. Others joined in, took the weapon away, and handed it over to the officer, who then ordered us all to be searched for arms, and rode away.

All our dejection could not make us forget that we were intensely hungry. We had eaten nothing all day. The fight began before we had time to get any breakfast, and of course there was no interval for refreshments during the engagement. The Rebels were no better off than we, having been marched rapidly all night in order to come upon us by daylight.

Late in the evening a few sacks of meal were given us, and we took the first lesson in an art that long and painful practice afterward was to make very familiar to us. We had nothing to mix the meal in, and it looked as if we would have to eat it dry, until a happy thought struck some one that our caps would do for kneading troughs. At once every cap was devoted to this. Getting water from an adjacent spring, each man made a little wad of dough—unsalted—and spreading it upon a flat stone or a chip, set it up in front of the fire to bake. As soon as it was browned on one side, it was pulled off the stone, and the other side turned to the fire. It was a very primitive way of cooking and I became thoroughly disgusted with it. It was fortunate for me that I little dreamed that this was the way I should have to get my meals for the next fifteen months.

After somewhat of the edge had been taken off our hunger by this food, we crouched around the fires, talked over the events of the day, speculated as to what was to be done with us, and snatched such sleep as the biting cold would permit.

CHAPTER VI.

"On To Richmond!"—Marching On Foot Over The Mountains—My Horse Has A New Rider—Unsophisticated Mountain Girls—Discussing The Issues Of The War—Parting With "Hiatoga."

At dawn we were gathered together, more meal issued to us, which we cooked in the same way, and then were started under heavy guard to march on foot over the mountains to Bristol, a station at the point where the Virginia and Tennessee Railroad crosses the line between Virginia and Tennessee.

As we were preparing to set out a Sergeant of the First Virginia cavalry came galloping up to us on my horse! The sight of my faithful "Hiatoga" bestrid by a Rebel, wrung my heart. During the action I had forgotten him, but when it ceased I began to worry about his fate. As he and his rider came near I called out to him; he stopped and gave a whinny of recognition, which seemed also a plaintive appeal for an explanation of the changed condition of affairs.

The Sergeant was a pleasant, gentlemanly boy of about my own age. He rode up to me and inquired if it was my horse, to which I replied in the affirmative, and asked permission to take from the saddle pockets some letters, pictures and other trinkets. He granted this, and we became friends from thence on until we separated. He rode by my side as we plodded over the steep, slippery hills, and we beguiled the way by chatting of the thousand things that soldiers find to talk about, and exchanged reminiscences of the service on both sides. But the subject he was fondest of was that which I relished least: my—now his—horse. Into the open ulcer of my heart he poured the acid of all manner of questions concerning my lost steed's qualities and capabilities: would he swim? how was he in fording? did he jump well! how did he stand fire? I smothered my irritation, and answered as pleasantly as I could.

In the afternoon of the third day after the capture, we came up to where a party of rustic belles were collected at "quilting." The "Yankees" were instantly objects of greater interest than the parade of a menagerie would have been. The Sergeant told the girls we were going to camp for the night a mile or so ahead, and if they would be at a certain house, he would have a Yankee for them for close inspection. After halting, the Sergeant obtained leave to take me out with a guard, and I was presently ushered into a room in which the damsels were massed in force, —a carnation-checked, staring, open-mouthed, linsey-clad crowd, as ignorant of corsets and gloves as of Hebrew, and with a propensity to giggle that was chronic and irrepressible. When we entered the room there was a general giggle, and then a shower of comments upon my appearance,—each sentence punctuated with the chorus of feminine cachination. A remark was made about my hair and eyes, and their risibles gave way; judgment was passed on my nose, and then came a ripple of laughter. I got very red in the face, and uncomfortable generally. Attention was called to the size of my feet and hands, and the usual chorus followed. Those useful members of my body seemed to swell up as they do to a young man at his first party.

Then I saw that in the minds of these bucolic maidens I was scarcely, if at all, human; they did not understand that I belonged to the race; I was a "Yankee"—a something of the non-human class, as the gorilla or the chimpanzee. They felt as free to discuss my points before my face as they would to talk of a horse or a wild animal in a show. My equanimity was partially restored by this reflection, but I was still too young to escape embarrassment and irritation at being thus dissected and giggled at by a party of girls, even if they were ignorant Virginia mountaineers.

I turned around to speak to the Sergeant, and in so doing showed my back to the ladies. The hum of comment deepened into surprise, that half stopped and then intensified the giggle.

I was puzzled for a minute, and then the direction of their glances, and their remarks explained it all. At the rear of the lower part of the cavalry jacket, about where the upper ornamental buttons are on the tail of a frock coat, are two funny tabs, about the size of small pin-cushions. They are fastened by the edge, and stick out straight behind. Their use is to support the heavy belt in the rear, as the buttons do in front. When the belt is off it would puzzle the Seven Wise Men to guess what they are for. The unsophisticated young ladies, with that swift intuition which is one of lovely woman's salient mental traits, immediately jumped at the conclusion that the projections covered some peculiar conformation of the Yankee anatomy—some incipient, dromedary-like humps, or perchance the horns of which they had heard so much.

This anatomical phenomena was discussed intently for a few minutes, during which I heard one of the girls inquire whether "it would hurt him to cut 'em off?" and another hazarded the opinion that "it would probably bleed him to death."

Then a new idea seized them, and they said to the Sergeant "Make him sing! Make him sing!"

This was too much for the Sergeant, who had been intensely amused at the girls' wonderment. He turned to me, very red in the face, with:

"Sergeant: the girls want to hear you sing."

I replied that I could not sing a note. Said he:

"Oh, come now. I know better than that; I never seed or heerd of a Yankee that couldn't sing."

I nevertheless assured him that there really were some Yankees that did not have any musical accomplishments, and that I was one of that unfortunate number. I asked him to get the ladies to sing for me, and to this they acceded quite readily. One girl, with a fair soprano, who seemed to be the leader of the crowd, sang "The Homespun Dress," a song very popular in the South, and having the same tune as the "Bonnie Blue Flag." It began

I envy not the Northern girl

Their silks and jewels fine,

and proceeded to compare the homespun habiliments of the Southern women to the finery and frippery of the ladies on the other side of Mason and Dixon's line in a manner very disadvantageous to the latter.

The rest of the girls made a fine exhibition of the lung-power acquired in climbing their precipitous mountains, when they came in on the chorus

Hurra! Hurra! for southern rights Hurra!

Hurra for the homespun dress,

The Southern ladies wear.

This ended the entertainment.

On our journey to Bristol we met many Rebel soldiers, of all ranks, and a small number of citizens. As the conscription had then been enforced pretty sharply for over a year the only able-bodied men seen in civil life were those who had some trade which exempted them from being forced into active service. It greatly astonished us at first to find that nearly all the mechanics were included among the exempts, or could be if they chose; but a very little reflection showed us the wisdom of such a policy. The South is as nearly a purely agricultural country as is Russia or South America. The people have, little inclination or capacity for anything else than pastoral pursuits. Consequently mechanics are very scarce, and manufactories much scarcer. The limited quantity of products of mechanical skill needed by the people was mostly imported from the North or Europe. Both these sources of supply were cutoff by the war, and the country was thrown upon its own slender manufacturing resources. To force its mechanics into the army would therefore be suicidal. The Army would gain a few thousand men, but its operations would be embarrassed, if not stopped altogether, by a want of supplies. This condition of affairs reminded one of the singular paucity of mechanical skill among the Bedouins of the desert, which renders the life of a blacksmith sacred. No matter how bitter the feud between tribes, no one will kill the other's workers of iron, and instances are told of warriors saving their lives at critical periods by falling on their knees and making with their garments an imitation of the action of a smith's bellows.

All whom we met were eager to discuss with us the causes, phases and progress of the war, and whenever opportunity offered or could be made, those of us who were inclined to talk were speedily involved in an argument with crowds of soldiers and citizens. But, owing to the polemic poverty of our opponents, the argument was more in name than in fact. Like all people of slender or untrained intellectual powers they labored under the hallucination that asserting was reasoning, and the emphatic reiteration of bald statements, logic. The narrow round which all from highest to lowest—traveled was sometimes comical, and sometimes irritating, according to one's mood! The dispute invariably began by their asking:

"Well, what are you 'uns down here a-fightin' we 'uns for?"

As this was replied to the newt one followed:

"Why are you'uns takin' our n___s away from we 'uns for?"

Then came:

"What do you 'uns put our n___s to fightin' we'uns for?" The windup always was: "Well, let me tell you, sir, you can never whip people that are fighting for liberty, sir."

Even General Giltner, who had achieved considerable military reputation as commander of a division of Kentucky cavalry, seemed to be as slenderly furnished with logical ammunition as the balance, for as he halted by us he opened the conversation with the well-worn formula:

"Well: what are you 'uns down here a-fighting we'uns for?"

The question had become raspingly monotonous to me, whom he addressed, and I replied with marked acerbity:

"Because we are the Northern mudsills whom you affect to despise, and we came down here to lick you into respecting us."

The answer seemed to tickle him, a pleasanter light came into his sinister gray eyes, he laughed lightly, and bade us a kindly good day.

Four days after our capture we arrived in Bristol. The guards who had brought us over the mountains were relieved by others, the Sergeant bade me good by, struck his spurs into "Hiatoga's" sides, and he and my faithful horse were soon lost to view in the darkness.

A new and keener sense of desolation came over me at the final separation from my tried and true four-footed friend, who had been my constant companion through so many perils and hardships. We had endured together the Winter's cold, the dispiriting drench of the rain, the fatigue of the long march, the discomforts of the muddy camp, the gripings of hunger, the weariness of the drill and review, the perils of the vidette post, the courier service, the scout and the fight. We had shared in common

The whips and scorns of time,

The oppressor's wrong, the proud man's contumely,

The insolence of office, and the spurns

which a patient private and his horse of the unworthy take; we had had our frequently recurring rows with other fellows and their horses, over questions of precedence at watering places, and grass-plots, had had lively tilts with guards of forage piles in surreptitious attempts to get additional rations, sometimes coming off victorious and sometimes being driven off ingloriously. I had often gone hungry that he might have the only ear of corn obtainable. I am not skilled enough in horse lore to speak of his points or pedigree. I only know that his strong limbs never failed me, and that he was always ready for duty and ever willing.

Now at last our paths diverged. I was retired from actual service to a prison, and he bore his new master off to battle against his old friends.

Packed closely in old, dilapidated stock and box cars, as if cattle in shipment to market, we pounded along slowly, and apparently interminably, toward the Rebel capital.

The railroads of the South were already in very bad condition. They were never more than passably good, even in their best estate, but now, with a large part of the skilled men engaged upon them escaped back to the North, with all renewal, improvement, or any but the most necessary repairs stopped for three years, and with a marked absence of even ordinary skill and care in their management, they were as nearly ruined as they could well be and still run.

One of the severe embarrassments under which the roads labored was a lack of oil. There is very little fatty matter of any kind in the South. The climate and the food plants do not favor the accumulation of adipose tissue by animals, and there is no other source of supply. Lard oil and tallow were very scarce and held at exorbitant prices.

Attempts were made to obtain lubricants from the peanut and the cotton seed. The first yielded a fine bland oil, resembling the ordinary grade of olive oil, but it was entirely too expensive for use in the arts. The cotton seed oil could be produced much cheaper, but it had in it such a quantity of gummy matter as to render it worse than useless for employment on machinery.

This scarcity of oleaginous matter produced a corresponding scarcity of soap and similar detergents, but this was a deprivation which caused the Rebels, as a whole, as little inconvenience as any that they suffered from. I have seen many thousands of them who were obviously greatly in need of soap, but if they were rent with any suffering on that account they concealed it with marvelous self-control.

There seemed to be a scanty supply of oil provided for the locomotives, but the cars had to run with unlubricated axles, and the screaking and groaning of the grinding journals in the dry boxes was sometimes almost deafening, especially when we were going around a curve.

Our engine went off the wretched track several times, but as she was not running much faster than a man could walk, the worst consequence to us was a severe jolting. She was small, and was easily pried back upon the track, and sent again upon her wheezy, straining way.

The depression which had weighed us down for a night and a day after our capture had now been succeeded by a more cheerful feeling. We began to look upon our condition as the fortune of war. We were proud of our resistance to overwhelming numbers. We knew we had sold ourselves at a price which, if the Rebels had it to do over again, they would not pay for us. We believed that we had killed and seriously wounded as many of them as they had killed, wounded and captured of us. We had nothing to blame ourselves for. Moreover, we began to be buoyed up with the expectation that we would be exchanged immediately upon our arrival at Richmond, and the Rebel officers confidently assured us that this would be so. There was then a temporary hitch in the exchange, but it would all be straightened out in a few days, and it might not be a month until we were again marching out of Cumberland Gap, on an avenging foray against some of the force which had assisted in our capture.

Fortunately for this delusive hopefulness there was no weird and boding Cassandra to pierce the veil of the future for us, and reveal the length and the ghastly horror of the Valley of the Shadow of Death, through which we must pass for hundreds of sad days, stretching out into long months of suffering and death. Happily there was no one to tell us that of every five in that party four would never stand under the Stars and Stripes again, but succumbing to chronic starvation, long-continued exposure, the bullet of the brutal guard, the loathsome scurvy, the hideous gangrene, and the heartsickness of hope deferred, would find respite from pain low in the barren sands of that hungry Southern soil.

Were every doom foretokened by appropriate omens, the ravens along our route would have croaked themselves hoarse.

But, far from being oppressed by any presentiment of coming evil, we began to appreciate and enjoy the picturesque grandeur of the scenery through which we were moving. The rugged sternness of the Appalachian mountain range, in whose rock-ribbed heart we had fought our losing fight, was now softening into less strong, but more graceful outlines as we approached the pine-clad, sandy plains of the seaboard, upon which Richmond is built. We were skirting along the eastern base of the great Blue Ridge, about whose distant and lofty summits hung a perpetual veil of deep, dark, but translucent blue, which refracted the slanting rays of the morning and evening sun into masses of color more gorgeous than a dreamer's vision of an enchanted land. At Lynchburg we saw the famed Peaks of Otter—twenty miles away—lifting their proud heads far into the clouds, like giant watchtowers sentineling the gateway that the mighty waters of the James had forced through the barriers of solid adamant lying across their path to the far-off sea. What we had seen many miles back start from the mountain sides as slender rivulets, brawling over the worn boulders, were now great, rushing, full-tide streams, enough of them in any fifty miles of our journey to furnish water power for all the factories of New England. Their amazing opulence of mechanical energy has lain unutilized, almost unnoticed; in the two and one-half centuries that the white man has dwelt near them, while in Massachusetts and her near neighbors every rill that can turn a wheel has been put into harness and forced to do its share of labor for the benefit of the men who have made themselves its masters.

Here is one of the differences between the two sections: In the North man was set free, and the elements made to do his work. In the South man was the degraded slave, and the elements wantoned on in undisturbed freedom.

As we went on, the Valleys of the James and the Appomattox, down which our way lay, broadened into an expanse of arable acres, and the faces of those streams were frequently flecked by gem-like little islands.

CHAPTER VII.

Entering Richmond—Disappointment At Its Appearance—Everybody In Uniform— Curled Darlings Of The Capital—The Rebel Flag—Libby Prison —Dick Turner— Searching The New Comers.

Early on the tenth morning after our capture we were told that we were about to enter Richmond. Instantly all were keenly observant of every detail in the surroundings of a City that was then the object of the hopes and fears of thirty-five millions of people—a City assailing which seventy-five thousand brave men had already laid down their lives, defending which an equal number had died, and which, before it fell, was to cost the life blood of another one hundred and fifty thousand valiant assailants and defenders.

So much had been said and written about Richmond that our boyish minds had wrought up the most extravagant expectations of it and its defenses. We anticipated seeing a City differing widely from anything ever seen before; some anomaly of nature displayed in its site, itself guarded by imposing and impregnable fortifications, with powerful forts and heavy guns, perhaps even walls, castles, postern gates, moats and ditches, and all the other panoply of defensive warfare, with which romantic history had made us familiar.

We were disappointed—badly disappointed—in seeing nothing of this as we slowly rolled along. The spires and the tall chimneys of the factories rose in the distance very much as they had in other Cities we had visited. We passed a single line of breastworks of bare yellow sand, but the scrubby pines in front were not cut away, and there were no signs that there had ever been any immediate expectation of use for the works. A redoubt or two—without guns—could be made out, and this was all. Grim-visaged war had few wrinkles on his front in that neighborhood. They were then seaming his brow on the Rappahannock, seventy miles away, where the Army of Northern Virginia and the Army of the Potomac lay confronting each other.

At one of the stopping places I had been separated from my companions by entering a car in which were a number of East Tennesseeans, captured in the operations around Knoxville, and whom the Rebels, in accordance with their usual custom, were treating with studied contumely. I had always had a very warm side for these simple rustics of the mountains and valleys. I knew much of their unwavering fidelity to the Union, of the firm steadfastness with which they endured persecution for their country's sake, and made sacrifices even unto death; and, as in those days I estimated all men simply by their devotion to the great cause of National integrity, (a habit that still clings to me) I rated these men very highly. I had gone into their car to do my little to encourage them, and when I attempted to return to my own I was prevented by the guard.

Crossing the long bridge, our train came to a halt on the other side of the river with the usual clamor of bell and whistle, the usual seemingly purposeless and vacillating, almost dizzying, running backward and forward on a network of sidetracks and switches, that seemed unavoidably necessary, a dozen years ago, in getting a train into a City.

Still unable to regain my comrades and share their fortunes, I was marched off with the Tennesseeans through the City to the office of some one who had charge of the prisoners of war.

The streets we passed through were lined with retail stores, in which business was being carried on very much as in peaceful times. Many people were on the streets, but the greater part of the men wore some sort of a uniform. Though numbers of these were in active service, yet the wearing of a military garb did not necessarily imply this. Nearly every able-bodied man in Richmond was; enrolled in some sort of an organization, and armed, and drilled regularly. Even the members of the Confederate Congress were uniformed and attached, in theory at least, to the Home Guards.

It was obvious even to the casual glimpse of a passing prisoner of war, that the City did not lack its full share of the class which formed so large an element of the society of Washington and other Northern Cities during the war—the dainty carpet soldiers, heros of the promenade and the boudoir, who strutted in uniforms when the enemy was far off, and wore citizen's clothes when he was close at hand. There were many curled darlings displaying their fine forms in the nattiest of uniforms, whose gloss had never suffered from so much as a heavy dew, let alone a rainy day on the march. The Confederate gray could be made into a very dressy garb. With the sleeves lavishly embroidered with gold lace, and the collar decorated with stars indicating the wearer's rank—silver for the field officers, and gold for the higher grade,—the feet compressed into high-heeled, high-instepped boots, (no Virginian is himself without a fine pair of skin-tight boots) and the head covered with a fine, soft, broad-brimmed hat, trimmed with a gold cord, from which a bullion tassel dangled several inches down the wearer's back, you had a military swell, caparisoned for conquest—among the fair sex.

On our way we passed the noted Capitol of Virginia—a handsome marble building,—of the column-fronted Grecian temple style. It stands in the center of the City. Upon the grounds is Crawford's famous equestrian statue of Washington, surrounded by smaller statues of other Revolutionary patriots.

The Confederate Congress was then in session in the Capitol, and also the Legislature of Virginia, a fact indicated by the State flag of Virginia floating from the southern end of the building, and the new flag of the Confederacy from the northern end. This was the first time I had seen the latter, which had been recently adopted, and I examined it with some interest. The design was exceedingly plain. Simply a white banner, with a red field in the corner where the blue field with stars is in ours. The two blue stripes were drawn diagonally across this field in the shape of a letter X, and in these were thirteen white stars, corresponding to the number of States claimed to be in the Confederacy.

The battle-flag was simply the red field. My examination of all this was necessarily very brief. The guards felt that I was in Richmond for other purposes than to study architecture, statuary and heraldry, and besides they were in a hurry to be relieved of us and get their breakfast, so my art-education was abbreviated sharply.

We did not excite much attention on the streets. Prisoners had by that time become too common in Richmond to create any interest. Occasionally passers by would fling opprobrious epithets at "the East Tennessee traitors," but that was all.

The commandant of the prisons directed the Tennesseeans to be taken to Castle Lightning—a prison used to confine the Rebel deserters, among whom they also classed the East Tennesseeans, and sometimes the West Virginians, Kentuckians, Marylanders and Missourians found fighting against them. Such of our men as deserted to them were also lodged there, as the Rebels, very properly, did not place a high estimate upon this class of recruits to their army, and, as we shall see farther along, violated all obligations of good faith with them, by putting them among the regular prisoners of war, so as to exchange them for their own men.

Back we were all marched to a street which ran parallel to the river and canal, and but one square away from them. It was lined on both sides by plain brick warehouses and tobacco factories, four and five stories high, which were now used by the Rebel Government as prisons and military storehouses.

The first we passed was Castle Thunder, of bloody repute. This occupied the same place in Confederate history, that, the dungeons beneath the level of the water did in the annals of the Venetian Council of Ten. It was believed that if the bricks in its somber, dirt-grimed walls could speak, each could tell a separate story of a life deemed dangerous to the State that had gone down in night, at the behest of the ruthless Confederate authorities. It was confidently asserted that among the commoner occurrences within its confines was the stationing of a doomed prisoner against a certain bit of blood-stained, bullet-chipped wall, and relieving the Confederacy of all farther fear of him by the rifles of a firing party. How well this dark reputation was deserved, no one but those inside the inner circle of the Davis Government can say. It is safe to believe that more tragedies were enacted there than the archives of the Rebel civil or military judicature give any account of. The prison was employed for the detention of spies, and those charged with the convenient allegation of "treason against the Confederate States of America." It is probable that many of these were sent out of the world with as little respect for the formalities of law as was exhibited with regard to the 'suspects' during the French Revolution.

Next we came to Castle Lightning, and here I bade adieu to my Tennessee companions.

A few squares more and we arrived at a warehouse larger than any of the others. Over the door was a sign

THOMAS LIBBY & SON,

SHIP CHANDLERS AND GROCERS.

This was the notorious "Libby Prison," whose name was painfully familiar to every Union man in the land. Under the sign was a broad entrance way, large enough to admit a dray or a small wagon. On one side of this was the prison office, in which were a number of dapper, feeble-faced clerks at work on the prison records.

As I entered this space a squad of newly arrived prisoners were being searched for valuables, and having their names, rank and regiment recorded in the books. Presently a clerk addressed as "Majah Tunnah," the man who was superintending these operations, and I scanned him with increased interest, as I knew then that he was the ill-famed Dick Turner, hated all over the North for his brutality to our prisoners.

He looked as if he deserved his reputation. Seen upon the street he would be taken for a second or third class gambler, one in whom a certain amount of cunning is pieced out by a readiness to use brute force. His face, clean-shaved, except a "Bowery-b'hoy" goatee, was white, fat, and selfishly sensual. Small, pig-like eyes, set close together, glanced around continually. His legs were short, his body long, and made to appear longer, by his wearing no vest—a custom common them with Southerners.

His faculties were at that moment absorbed in seeing that no person concealed any money from him. His subordinates did not search closely enough to suit him, and he would run his fat, heavily-ringed fingers through the prisoner's hair, feel under their arms and elsewhere where he thought a stray five dollar greenback might be concealed. But with all his greedy care he was no match for Yankee cunning. The prisoners told me afterward that, suspecting they would be searched, they had taken off the caps of the large, hollow brass buttons of their coats, carefully folded a bill into each cavity, and replaced the cap. In this way they brought in several hundred dollars safely.

There was one dirty old Englishman in the party, who, Turner was convinced, had money concealed about his person. He compelled him to strip off everything, and stand shivering in the sharp cold, while he took up one filthy rag after another, felt over each carefully, and scrutinized each seam and fold. I was delighted to see that after all his nauseating work he did not find so much as a five cent piece.

It came my turn. I had no desire, in that frigid atmosphere, to strip down to what Artemus Ward called "the skanderlous costoom of the Greek Slave;" so I pulled out of my pocket my little store of wealth—ten dollars in greenbacks, sixty dollars in Confederate graybacks—and displayed it as Turner came up with, "There's all I have, sir." Turner pocketed it without a word, and did not search me. In after months, when I was nearly famished, my estimation of "Majah Tunnah" was hardly enhanced by the reflection that what would have purchased me many good meals was probably lost by him in betting on a pair of queens, when his opponent held a "king full."

I ventured to step into the office to inquire after my comrades. One of the whey-faced clerks said with the supercilious asperity characteristic of gnat-brained headquarters attaches:

"Get out of here!" as if I had been a stray cur wandering in in search of a bone lunch.

I wanted to feed the fellow to a pile-driver. The utmost I could hope for in the way of revenge was that the delicate creature might some day make a mistake in parting his hair, and catch his death of cold.

The guard conducted us across the street, and into the third story of a building standing on the next corner below. Here I found about four hundred men, mostly belonging to the Army of the Potomac, who crowded around me with the usual questions to new prisoners: What was my Regiment, where and when captured, and:

What were the prospects of exchange?

It makes me shudder now to recall how often, during the dreadful months that followed, this momentous question was eagerly propounded to every new comer: put with bated breath by men to whom exchange meant all that they asked of this world, and possibly of the next; meant life, home, wife or sweet-heart, friends, restoration to manhood, and self-respect —everything, everything that makes existence in this world worth having.

I answered as simply and discouragingly as did the tens of thousands that came after me:

"I did not hear anything about exchange."

A soldier in the field had many other things of more immediate interest to think about than the exchange of prisoners. The question only became a living issue when he or some of his intimate friends fell into the enemy's hands.

Thus began my first day in prison.

CHAPTER VIII

Introduction To Prison Life—The Pemberton Building And Its Occupants —Neat Sailors—Roll Call—Rations And Clothing—Chivalric "Confiscation."

I began acquainting myself with my new situation and surroundings. The building into which I had been conducted was an old tobacco factory, called the "Pemberton building," possibly from an owner of that name, and standing on the corner of what I was told were Fifteenth and Carey streets. In front it was four stories high; behind but three, owing to the rapid rise of the hill, against which it was built.

It fronted towards the James River and Kanawha Canal, and the James River—both lying side by side, and only one hundred yards distant, with no intervening buildings. The front windows afforded a fine view. To the right front was Libby, with its guards pacing around it on the sidewalk, watching the fifteen hundred officers confined within its walls. At intervals during each day squads of fresh prisoners could be seen entering its dark mouth, to be registered, and searched, and then marched off to the prison assigned them. We could see up the James River for a mile or so, to where the long bridges crossing it bounded the view. Directly in front, across the river, was a flat, sandy plain, said to be General Winfield Scott's farm, and now used as a proving ground for the guns cast at the Tredegar Iron Works.

The view down the river was very fine. It extended about twelve miles, to where a gap in the woods seemed to indicate a fort, which we imagined to be Fort Darling, at that time the principal fortification defending the passage of the James.

Between that point and where we were lay the river, in a long, broad mirror-like expanse, like a pretty little inland lake. Occasionally a busy little tug would bustle up or down, a gunboat move along with noiseless dignity, suggestive of a reserved power, or a schooner beat lazily from one side to the other. But these were so few as to make even more pronounced the customary idleness that hung over the scene. The tug's activity seemed spasmodic and forced—a sort of protest against the gradually increasing lethargy that reigned upon the bosom of the waters —the gunboat floated along as if performing a perfunctory duty, and the schooners sailed about as if tired of remaining in one place. That little stretch of water was all that was left for a cruising ground. Beyond Fort Darling the Union gunboats lay, and the only vessel that passed the barrier was the occasional flag-of-truce steamer.

The basement of the building was occupied as a store-house for the taxes-in-kind which the Confederate Government collected. On the first floor were about five hundred men. On the second floor—where I was—were about four hundred men. These were principally from the First Division, First Corps distinguished by a round red patch on their caps; First Division, Second Corps, marked by a red clover leaf; and the First Division, Third Corps, who wore a red diamond. They were mainly captured at Gettysburg and Mine Run. Besides these there was a considerable number from the Eighth Corps, captured at Winchester, and a large infusion of Cavalry-First, Second and

Third West Virginia—taken in Averill's desperate raid up the Virginia Valley, with the Wytheville Salt Works as an objective.

On the third floor were about two hundred sailors and marines, taken in the gallant but luckless assault upon the ruins of Fort Sumter, in the September previous. They retained the discipline of the ship in their quarters, kept themselves trim and clean, and their floor as white as a ship's deck. They did not court the society of the "sojers" below, whose camp ideas of neatness differed from theirs. A few old barnacle-backs always sat on guard around the head of the steps leading from the lower rooms. They chewed tobacco enormously, and kept their mouths filled with the extracted juice. Any luckless "sojer" who attempted to ascend the stairs usually returned in haste, to avoid the deluge of the filthy liquid.

For convenience in issuing rations we were divided into messes of twenty, each mess electing a Sergeant as its head, and each floor electing a Sergeant-of-the-Floor, who drew rations and enforced what little discipline was observed.

Though we were not so neat as the sailors above us, we tried to keep our quarters reasonably clean, and we washed the floor every morning; getting down on our knees and rubbing it clean and dry with rags. Each mess detailed a man each day to wash up the part of the floor it occupied, and he had to do this properly or no ration would be given him. While the washing up was going on each man stripped himself and made close examination of his garments for the body-lice, which otherwise would have increased beyond control. Blankets were also carefully hunted over for these "small deer."

About eight o'clock a spruce little lisping rebel named Ross would appear with a book, and a body-guard, consisting of a big Irishman, who had the air of a Policeman, and carried a musket barrel made into a cane. Behind him were two or three armed guards. The Sergeant-of-the-Floor commanded:

"Fall in in four ranks for roll-call."

We formed along one side of the room; the guards halted at the head of the stairs; Ross walked down in front and counted the files, closely followed by his Irish aid, with his gun-barrel cane raised ready for use upon any one who should arouse his ruffianly ire. Breaking ranks we returned to our places, and sat around in moody silence for three hours. We had eaten nothing since the previous noon. Rising hungry, our hunger seemed to increase in arithmetical ratio with every quarter of an hour.

These times afforded an illustration of the thorough subjection of man to the tyrant Stomach. A more irritable lot of individuals could scarcely be found outside of a menagerie than these men during the hours waiting for rations. "Crosser than, two sticks" utterly failed as a comparison. They were crosser than the lines of a check apron. Many could have given odds to the traditional bear with a sore head, and run out of the game fifty points ahead of him. It was astonishingly easy to get up a fight at these times. There was no need of going a step out of the way to search for it, as one could have a full fledged article of overwhelming size on his hands at any instant, by a trifling indiscretion of speech or manner. All the old irritating flings between the cavalry, the artillery and the infantry, the older "first-call" men, and the later or "Three-Hundred-Dollar-men," as they were derisively dubbed, between the different corps of the Army of the Potomac, between men of different States, and lastly between the adherents and opponents of McClellan, came to the lips and were answered by a blow with the fist, when a ring would be formed around the combatants by a crowd, which would encourage them with yells to do their best. In a few minutes one of the parties to the fistic debate, who found the point raised by him not well taken, would retire to the sink to wash the blood from his battered face, and the rest would resume their seats and glower at space until some fresh excitement roused them. For the last hour or so of these long waits hardly a word would be spoken. We were too ill-natured to talk for amusement, and there was nothing else to talk for.

This spell was broken about eleven o'clock by the appearance at the head of the stairway of the Irishman with the gun-barrel cane, and his singing out:

"Sargint uv the flure: fourtane min and a bread-box!"

Instantly every man sprang to his feet, and pressed forward to be one of the favored fourteen. One did not get any more gyrations or obtain them any sooner by this, but it was a relief, and a change to walk the half square outside the prison to the cookhouse, and help carry the rations back.

For a little while after our arrival in Richmond, the rations were tolerably good. There had been so much said about the privations of the prisoners that our Government had, after much quibbling and negotiation, succeeded in getting the privilege of sending food and clothing through the lines to us. Of course but a small part of that sent ever reached its destination. There were too many greedy Rebels along its line of passage to let much of it be received by those for whom it was intended. We could see from our windows Rebels strutting about in overcoats, in which the box wrinkles were still plainly visible, wearing new "U. S." blankets as cloaks, and walking in Government shoes, worth fabulous prices in Confederate money.

Fortunately for our Government the rebels decided to out themselves off from this profitable source of supply. We read one day in the Richmond papers that "President Davis and his Cabinet had come to the conclusion that it was incompatible with the dignity of a sovereign power to permit another power with which it was at war, to feed and clothe prisoners in its hands."

I will not stop to argue this point of honor, and show its absurdity by pointing out that it is not an unusual practice with nations at war. It is a sufficient commentary upon this assumption of punctiliousness that the paper went on to say that some five tons of clothing and fifteen tons of food, which had been sent under a flag of truce to City Point, would neither be returned nor delivered to us, but "converted to the use of the Confederate Government."

"And surely they are all honorable men!"

Heaven save the mark.

CHAPTER IX.

Brans Or Peas—Insufficiency Of Darky Testimony—A Guard Kills A Prisoner—
Prisoners Teaze The Guards—Desperate Outbreak.

But, to return to the rations—a topic which, with escape or exchange, were to be the
absorbing ones for us for the next fifteen months. There was now issued to every two men
a loaf of coarse bread—made of a mixture of flour and meal—and about the size and
shape of an ordinary brick. This half loaf was accompanied, while our Government was
allowed to furnish rations, with a small piece of corned beef. Occasionally we got a sweet
potato, or a half-pint or such a matter of soup made from a coarse, but nutritious, bean or
pea, called variously "n___r-pea," "stock-pea," or "cow-pea."

This, by the way, became a fruitful bone of contention during our stay in the South.
One strong party among us maintained that it was a bean, because it was shaped like one,
and brown, which they claimed no pea ever was. The other party held that it was a pea
because its various names all agreed in describing it as a pea, and because it was so full of
bugs —none being entirely free from insects, and some having as many as twelve by actual
count—within its shell. This, they declared, was a distinctive characteristic of the pea family. The contention began with our first instalment of the leguminous ration, and was still
raging between the survivors who passed into our lines in 1865. It waxed hot occasionally,
and each side continually sought evidence to support its view of the case. Once an old
darky, sent into the prison on some errand, was summoned to decide a hot dispute that
was raging in the crowd to which I belonged. The champion of the pea side said, producing one of the objects of dispute:

"Now, boys, keep still, till I put the question fairly. Now, uncle, what do they call that
there?"

The colored gentleman scrutinized the vegetable closely, and replied,

"Well, dey mos' generally calls 'em stock-peas, round hyar aways."

"There," said the pea-champion triumphantly.

"But," broke in the leader of the bean party, "Uncle, don't they also call them beans?"

"Well, yes, chile, I spec dat lots of 'em does."

And this was about the way the matter usually ended.

I will not attempt to bias the reader's judgment by saying which side I believed to
be right. As the historic British showman said, in reply to the question as to whether an
animal in his collection was a rhinoceros or an elephant, "You pays your money and you
takes your choice."

The rations issued to us, as will be seen above, though they appear scanty, were still sufficient to support life and health, and months afterward, in Andersonville, we used to look
back to them as sumptuous. We usually had them divided and eaten by noon, and, with
the gnawings of hunger appeased, we spent the afternoon and evening comfortably. We
told stories, paced up and down, the floor for exercise, played cards, sung, read what few

books were available, stood at the windows and studied the landscape, and watched the Rebels trying their guns and shells, and so on as long as it was daylight. Occasionally it was dangerous to be about the windows. This depended wholly on the temper of the guards. One day a member of a Virginia regiment, on guard on the pavement in front, deliberately left his beat, walked out into the center of the street, aimed his gun at a member of the Ninth West Virginia, who was standing at a window near, and firing, shot him through the heart, the bullet passing through his body, and through the floor above. The act was purely malicious, and was done, doubtless, in revenge for some injury which our men had done the assassin or his family.

We were not altogether blameless, by any means. There were few opportunities to say bitterly offensive things to the guards, let pass unimproved.

The prisoners in the third floor of the Smith building, adjoining us, had their own way of teasing them. Late at night, when everybody would be lying down, and out of the way of shots, a window in the third story would open, a broomstick, with a piece nailed across to represent arms, and clothed with a cap and blouse, would be protruded, and a voice coming from a man carefully protected by the wall, would inquire:

"S-a-y, g-uarr-d, what time is it?"

If the guard was of the long suffering kind he would answer:

"Take yo' head back in, up dah; you kno hits agin all odahs to do dat?"

Then the voice would say, aggravatingly, "Oh, well, go to —— you —— Rebel ——, if you can't answer a civil question."

Before the speech was ended the guard's rifle would be at his shoulder and he would fire. Back would come the blouse and hat in haste, only to go out again the next instant, with a derisive laugh, and,

"Thought you were going to hurt somebody, didn't you, you —— —— —— ——
——. But, Lord, you can't shoot for sour apples; if I couldn't shoot no better than you, Mr. Johnny Reb, I would ——"

By this time the guard, having his gun loaded again, would cut short the remarks with another shot, which, followed up with similar remarks, would provoke still another, when an alarm sounding, the guards at Libby and all the other buildings around us would turn out. An officer of the guard would go up with a squad into the third floor, only to find everybody up there snoring away as if they were the Seven Sleepers. After relieving his mind of a quantity of vigorous profanity, and threats to "buck and gag" and cut off the rations of the whole room, the officer would return to his quarters in the guard house, but before he was fairly ensconced there the cap and blouse would go out again, and the maddened guard be regaled with a spirited and vividly profane lecture on the depravity of Rebels in general, and his own unworthiness in particular.

One night in January things took a more serious turn. The boys on the lower floor of our building had long considered a plan of escape. There were then about fifteen thousand prisoners in Richmond—ten thousand on Belle Isle and five thousand in the

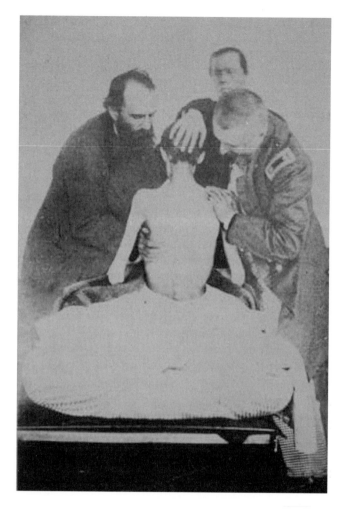

Doctors examining a Federal prisoner returned from prison

buildings. Of these one thousand five hundred were officers in Libby. Besides there were the prisoners in Castles Thunder and Lightning. The essential features of the plan were that at a preconcerted signal we at the second and third floors should appear at the windows with bricks and irons from the tobacco presses, which a should shower down on the guards and drive them away, while the men of the first floor would pour out, chase the guards into the board house in the basement, seize their arms, drive those away from around Libby and the other prisons, release the officers, organize into regiments and brigades, seize the armory, set fire to the public buildings and retreat from the City, by the south side of the James, where there was but a scanty force of Rebels, and more could be prevented from coming over by burning the bridges behind us.

It was a magnificent scheme, and might have been carried out, but there was no one in the building who was generally believed to have the qualities of a leader.

But while it was being debated a few of the hot heads on the lower floor undertook to precipitate the crisis. They seized what they thought was a favorable opportunity, overpowered the guard who stood at the foot of the stairs, and poured into the street. The other guards fell back and opened fire on them; other troops hastened up, and soon drove them back into the building, after killing ten or fifteen. We of the second and third floors did not anticipate the break at that time, and were taken as much by surprise as were the Rebels. Nearly all were lying down and many were asleep. Some hastened to the windows, and dropped missiles out, but before any concerted action could be taken it was seen that the case was hopeless, and we remained quiet.

Among those who led in the assault was a drummer-boy of some New York Regiment, a recklessly brave little rascal. He had somehow smuggled a small four-shooter in with him, and when they rushed out he fired it off at the guards.

After the prisoners were driven back, the Rebel officers came in and vapored around considerably, but confined themselves to big words. They were particularly anxious to find the revolver, and ordered a general and rigorous search for it. The prisoners were all ranged on one side of the room and carefully examined by one party, while another hunted through the blankets and bundles. It was all in vain; no pistol could be found. The boy had a loaf of wheat bread, bought from a baker during the day. It was a round loaf, set together in two pieces like a biscuit. He pulled these apart, laid the fourshooter between them, pressed the two halves together, and went on calmly nibbling away at the loaf while the search was progressing.

Two gunboats were brought up the next morning, and anchored in the canal near us, with their heavy guns trained upon the building. It was thought that this would intimidate as from a repetition of the attack, but our sailors conceived that, as they laid against the shore next to us, they could be easily captured, and their artillery made to assist us. A scheme to accomplish this was being wrought out, when we received notice to move, and it came to naught.

CHAPTER X.

The Exchange And The Cause Of Its Interruption—Brief Resume Of The Different Cartels, And The Difficulties That Led To Their Suspension.

Few questions intimately connected with the actual operations of the Rebellion have been enveloped with such a mass of conflicting statement as the responsibility for the interruption of the exchange. Southern writers and politicians, naturally anxious to diminish as much as possible the great odium resting upon their section for the treatment of prisoners of war during the last year and a half of the Confederacy's existence, have vehemently charged that the Government of the United States deliberately and pitilessly resigned to their fate such of its soldiers as fell into the hands of the enemy, and repelled all advances from the Rebel Government looking toward a resumption of exchange. It is alleged on our side, on the other hand, that our Government did all that was possible, consistent with National dignity and military prudence, to secure a release of its unfortunate men in the power of the Rebels.

Over this vexed question there has been waged an acrimonious war of words, which has apparently led to no decision, nor any convictions—the disputants, one and all, remaining on the sides of the controversy occupied by them when the debate began.

I may not be in possession of all the facts bearing upon the case, and may be warped in judgment by prejudices in favor of my own Government's wisdom and humanity, but, however this may be, the following is my firm belief as to the controlling facts in this lamentable affair:

1. For some time after the beginning of hostilities our Government refused to exchange prisoners with the Rebels, on the ground that this might be held by the European powers who were seeking a pretext for acknowledging the Confederacy, to be admission by us that the war was no longer an insurrection but a revolution, which had resulted in the 'de facto' establishment of a new nation. This difficulty was finally gotten over by recognizing the Rebels as belligerents, which, while it placed them on a somewhat different plane from mere insurgents, did not elevate them to the position of soldiers of a foreign power.

2. Then the following cartel was agreed upon by Generals Dig on our side and Hill on that of the Rebels:

HAXALL'S LANDING, ON JAMES RIVER, July 22, 1882.

The undersigned, having been commissioned by the authorities they respectively represent to make arrangements for a general exchange of prisoners of war, have agreed to the following articles:

ARTICLE I.—It is hereby agreed and stipulated, that all prisoners of war, held by either party, including those taken on private armed vessels, known as privateers, shall be exchanged upon the conditions and terms following:

Prisoners to be exchanged man for man and officer for officer. Privateers to be placed upon the footing of officers and men of the navy.

Men and officers of lower grades may be exchanged for officers of a higher grade, and men and officers of different services may be exchanged according to the following scale of equivalents:

A General-commanding-in-chief, or an Admiral, shall be exchanged for officers of equal rank, or for sixty privates or common seamen.

A Commodore, carrying a broad pennant, or a Brigadier General, shall be exchanged for officers of equal rank, or twenty privates or common seamen.

A Captain in the Navy, or a Colonel, shall be exchanged for officers of equal rank, or for fifteen privates or common seamen.

Confederate prisoners for exchange

A Lieutenant Colonel, or Commander in the Navy, shall be exchanged for officers of equal rank, or for ten privates or common seamen.

A Lieutenant, or a Master in the Navy, or a Captain in the Army or marines shall be exchanged for officers of equal rank, or six privates or common seamen.

Master's-mates in the Navy, or Lieutenants or Ensigns in the Army, shall be exchanged for officers of equal rank, or four privates or common seamen. Midshipmen, warrant officers in the Navy, masters of merchant vessels and commanders of privateers, shall be exchanged for officers of equal rank, or three privates or common seamen; Second Captains, Lieutenants or mates of merchant vessels or privateers, and all petty officers in the Navy, and all noncommissioned officers in the Army or marines, shall be severally exchanged for persons of equal rank, or for two privates or common seamen; and private soldiers or common seamen shall be exchanged for each other man for man.

ARTICLE II.—Local, State, civil and militia rank held by persons not in actual military service will not be recognized; the basis of exchange being the grade actually held in the naval and military service of the respective parties.

ARTICLE III.—If citizens held by either party on charges of disloyalty, or any alleged civil offense, are exchanged, it shall only be for citizens. Captured sutlers, teamsters, and all civilians in the actual service of either party, to be exchanged for persons in similar positions.

ARTICLE IV.—All prisoners of war to be discharged on parole in ten days after their capture; and the prisoners now held, and those hereafter taken, to be transported to the points mutually agreed upon, at the expense of the capturing party. The surplus prisoners not exchanged shall not be permitted to take up arms again, nor to serve as military police or constabulary force in any fort, garrison or field-work, held by either of the respective parties, nor as guards of prisoners, deposits or stores, nor to discharge any duty usually performed by soldiers, until exchanged under the provisions of this cartel. The exchange is not to be considered complete until the officer or soldier exchanged for has been actually restored to the lines to which he belongs.

ARTICLE V.—Each party upon the discharge of prisoners of the other party is authorized to discharge an equal number of their own officers or men from parole, furnishing, at the same time, to the other party a list of their prisoners discharged, and of their own officers and men relieved from parole; thus enabling each party to relieve from parole such of their officers and men as the party may choose. The lists thus mutually furnished, will keep both parties advised of the true condition of the exchange of prisoners.

ARTICLE VI.—The stipulations and provisions above mentioned to be of binding obligation during the continuance of the war, it matters not which party may have the surplus of prisoners; the great principles involved being, First, An equitable exchange of prisoners, man for man, or officer for officer, or officers of higher grade exchanged for officers of lower grade, or for privates, according to scale of equivalents. Second, That privates and officers and men of different services may be exchanged according to the same scale of equivalents. Third, That all prisoners, of whatever arm of service, are to be exchanged or paroled in ten days from the time of their capture, if it be practicable to transfer them to their own lines in that time; if not, so soon thereafter as practicable. Fourth, That no officer, or soldier, employed in the service of either party, is to be considered as exchanged and absolved from his parole until his equivalent has actually reached the lines of his friends. Fifth, That parole forbids the performance of field, garrison, police, or guard or constabulary duty.

JOHN A. DIX, Major General.

D. H. HILL, Major General, C. S. A.

SUPPLEMENTARY ARTICLES.

ARTICLE VII.—All prisoners of war now held on either side, and all prisoners hereafter taken, shall be sent with all reasonable dispatch to A. M. Aiken's, below Dutch Gap, on the James River, in Virginia, or to Vicksburg, on the Mississippi River, in the State of Mississippi, and there exchanged of paroled until such exchange can be effected, notice being previously given by each party of the number of prisoners it will send, and the time when they will be delivered at those points respectively; and in case the vicissitudes of war shall change the military relations of the places designated in this article to the contending parties, so as to render the same inconvenient for the delivery and exchange of prisoners, other places bearing as nearly as may be the present local relations of said places to the lines of said parties, shall be, by mutual agreement, substituted. But nothing in this article contained shall prevent the commanders of the two opposing armies from exchanging prisoners or releasing them on parole, at other points mutually agreed on by said commanders.

ARTICLE VIII.—For the purpose of carrying into effect the foregoing articles of agreement, each party will appoint two agents for the exchange of prisoners of war, whose duty it shall be to communicate with each other by correspondence and otherwise; to prepare the lists of prisoners; to attend to the delivery of the prisoners at the places agreed on, and to carry out promptly, effectually, and in good faith, all the details and provisions of the said articles of agreement.

ARTICLE IX.—And, in case any misunderstanding shall arise in regard to any clause or stipulation in the foregoing articles, it is mutually agreed that such misunderstanding shall not affect the release of prisoners on parole, as herein provided, but shall be made the subject of friendly explanation, in order that the object of this agreement may neither be defeated nor postponed.

JOHN A. DIX, Major General. D. H. HILL, Major General. C. S. A.

This plan did not work well. Men on both sides, who wanted a little rest from soldiering, could obtain it by so straggling in the vicinity of the enemy. Their parole—following close upon their capture, frequently upon the spot—allowed them to visit home, and sojourn awhile where were pleasanter pastures than at the front. Then the Rebels grew into the habit of paroling everybody that they could constrain into being a prisoner of war. Peaceable, unwarlike and decrepit citizens of Kentucky, East Tennessee, West Virginia, Missouri and Maryland were "captured" and paroled, and setoff against regular Rebel soldiers taken by us.

3. After some months of trial of this scheme, a modification of the cartel was agreed upon, the main feature of which was that all prisoners must be reduced to possession, and delivered to the exchange officers either at City Point, Va., or Vicksburg, Miss. This worked very well for some months, until our Government began organizing negro troops. The Rebels then issued an order that neither these troops nor their officers should be held as amenable to the laws of war, but that, when captured, the men should be returned to slavery, and the officers turned over to the Governors of the States in which they were taken, to be dealt with according to the stringent law punishing the incitement of servile insurrection. Our Government could not permit this for a day. It was bound by every consideration of National honor to protect those who wore its uniform and bore its flag. The Rebel Government was promptly informed that rebel officers and men would be held as hostages for the proper treatment of such members of colored regiments as might be taken.

4. This discussion did not put a stop to the exchange, but while it was going on Vicksburg was captured, and the battle of Gettysburg was fought. The first placed one of the exchange points in our hands. At the opening of the fight at Gettysburg Lee captured some six thousand Pennsylvania militia. He sent to Meade to have these exchanged on the field of battle. Meade declined to do so for two reasons: first, because it was against the cartel, which prescribed that prisoners must be reduced to possession; and second, because he was anxious to have Lee hampered with such a body of prisoners, since it was very doubtful if he could get his beaten army back across the Potomac, let alone his prisoners. Lee then sent a communication to General Couch, commanding the Pennsylvania militia, asking him to receive prisoners on parole, and Couch, not knowing what Meade had done, acceded to the request. Our Government disavowed Couch's action instantly,

and ordered the paroles to be treated as of no force, whereupon the Rebel Government ordered back into the field twelve thousand of the prisoners captured by Grant's army at Vicksburg.

5. The paroling now stopped abruptly, leaving in the hands of both sides the prisoners captured at Gettysburg, except the militia above mentioned. The Rebels added considerably to those in their hands by their captures at Chickamauga, while we gained a great many at Mission Ridge, Cumberland Gap and elsewhere, so that at the time we arrived in Richmond the Rebels had about fifteen thousand prisoners in their hands and our Government had about twenty-five thousand.

6. The rebels now began demanding that the prisoners on both sides be exchanged— man for man—as far as they went, and the remainder paroled. Our Government offered to exchange man for man, but declined—on account of the previous bad faith of the Rebels—to release the balance on parole. The Rebels also refused to make any concessions in regard to the treatment of officers and men of colored regiments.

7. At this juncture General B. F. Butler was appointed to the command of the Department of the Blackwater, which made him an ex-officio Commissioner of Exchange. The Rebels instantly refused to treat with him, on the ground that he was outlawed by the proclamation of Jefferson Davis. General Butler very pertinently replied that this only placed him nearer their level, as Jefferson Davis and all associated with him in the Rebel Government had been outlawed by the proclamation of President Lincoln. The Rebels scorned to notice this home thrust by the Union General.

8. On February 12, 1864, General Butler addressed a letter to the Rebel Commissioner Ould, in which be asked, for the sake of humanity, that the questions interrupting the exchange be left temporarily in abeyance while an informal exchange was put in operation. He would send five hundred prisoners to City Point; let them be met by a similar number of Union prisoners. This could go on from day to day until all in each other's hands should be transferred to their respective flags.

The five hundred sent with the General's letter were received, and five hundred Union prisoners returned for them. Another five hundred, sent the next day, were refused, and so this reasonable and humane proposition ended in nothing.

This was the condition of affairs in February, 1864, when the Rebel authorities concluded to send us to Andersonville. If the reader will fix these facts in his minds I will explain other phases as they develop.

CHAPTER XI.

Putting In The Time—Rations—Cooking Utensils—"Fiat" Soup—"Spooning" — African Newspaper Venders—Trading Greenbacks For Confederate Money —Visit From John Morgan.

The Winter days passed on, one by one, after the manner described in a former chapter,—the mornings in ill-nature hunger; the afternoons and evenings in tolerable comfort. The rations kept growing lighter and lighter; the quantity of bread remained the same, but the meat diminished, and occasional days would pass without any being issued. Then we receive a pint or less of soup made from the beans or peas before mentioned, but this, too, suffered continued change, in the gradually increasing proportion of James River water, and decreasing of that of the beans.

The water of the James River is doubtless excellent: it looks well—at a distance—and is said to serve the purposes of ablution and navigation admirably. There seems to be a limit however, to the extent of its advantageous combination with the bean (or pea) for nutritive purposes. This, though, was or view of the case, merely, and not shared in to any appreciably extent by the gentlemen who were managing our boarding house. We seemed to view the matter through allopathic spectacles, they through homoeopathic lenses. We thought that the atomic weight of peas (or beans) and the James River fluid were about equal, which would indicate that the proper combining proportions would be, say a bucket of beans (or peas) to a bucket of water. They held that the nutritive potency was increased by the dilution, and the best results were obtainable when the symptoms of hunger were combated by the trituration of a bucketful of the peas-beans with a barrel of 'aqua jamesiana.'

My first experience with this "flat" soup was very instructive, if not agreeable. I had come into prison, as did most other prisoners, absolutely destitute of dishes, or cooking utensils. The well-used, half-canteen frying-pan, the blackened quart cup, and the spoon, which formed the usual kitchen outfit of the cavalryman in the field, were in the haversack on my saddle, and were lost to me when I separated from my horse. Now, when we were told that we were to draw soup, I was in great danger of losing my ration from having no vessel in which to receive it. There were but few tin cups in the prison, and these were, of course, wanted by their owners. By great good fortune I found an empty fruit can, holding about a quart. I was also lucky enough to find a piece from which to make a bail. I next manufactured a spoon and knife combined from a bit of hoop-iron.

These two humble utensils at once placed myself and my immediate chums on another plane, as far as worldly goods were concerned. We were better off than the mass, and as well off as the most fortunate. It was a curious illustration of that law of political economy which teaches that so-called intrinsic value is largely adventitious. Their possession gave us infinitely more consideration among our fellows than would the possession of a brownstone front in an eligible location, furnished with hot and cold water throughout, and all the modern improvements. It was a place where cooking utensils were in demand, and title-deeds to brown-stone fronts were not. We were in possession of something which every one needed every day, and, therefore, were persons of consequence and consideration to those around us who were present or prospective borrowers.

On our side we obeyed another law of political economy: We clung to our property with unrelaxing tenacity, made the best use of it in our intercourse with our fellows, and only gave it up after our release and entry into a land where the plenitude of cooking utensils of superior construction made ours valueless. Then we flung them into the sea, with little gratitude for the great benefit they had been to us. We were more anxious to get rid of the many hateful recollections clustering around them.

But, to return to the alleged soup: As I started to drink my first ration it seemed to me that there was a superfluity of bugs upon its surface. Much as I wanted animal food, I did not care for fresh meat in that form. I skimmed them off carefully, so as to lose as little soup as possible. But the top layer seemed to be underlaid with another equally dense. This was also skimmed off as deftly as possible. But beneath this appeared another layer, which, when removed, showed still another; and so on, until I had scraped to the bottom of the can, and the last of the bugs went with the last of my soup. I have before spoken of the remarkable bug fecundity of the beans (or peas). This was a demonstration of it. Every scouped out pea (or bean) which found its way into the soup bore inside of its shell from ten to twenty of these hard-crusted little weevil. Afterward I drank my soup without skimming. It was not that I hated the weevil less, but that I loved the soup more. It was only another step toward a closer conformity to that grand rule which I have made the guiding maxim of my life:

'When I must, I had better.'

I recommend this to other young men starting on their career.

The room in which we were was barely large enough for all of us to lie down at once. Even then it required pretty close "spooning" together —so close in fact that all sleeping along one side would have to turn at once. It was funny to watch this operation. All, for instance, would be lying on their right sides. They would begin to get tired, and one of the wearied ones would sing out to the Sergeant who was in command of the row—

"Sergeant: let's spoon the other way."

That individual would reply:

"All right. Attention! LEFT SPOON!!" and the whole line would at once flop over on their left sides.

The feet of the row that slept along the east wall on the floor below us were in a line with the edge of the outer door, and a chalk line drawn from the crack between the door and the frame to the opposite wall would touch, say 150 pairs of feet. They were a noisy crowd down there, and one night their noise so provoked the guard in front of the door that he called out to them to keep quiet or he would fire in upon them. They greeted this threat with a chorus profanely uncomplimentary to the purity of the guard's ancestry; they did not imply his descent a la Darwin, from the remote monkey, but more immediate generation by a common domestic animal. The incensed Rebel opened the door wide enough to thrust his gun in, and he fired directly down the line of toes. His piece was apparently loaded with buckshot, and the little balls must have struck the legs, nipped off the toes, pierced the feet, and otherwise slightly wounded the lower extremities of fifty men. The simultaneous shriek that went up was deafening. It was soon found out that nobody had been hurt seriously, and there was not a little fun over the occurrence.

One of the prisoners in Libby was Brigadier General Neal Dow, of Maine, who had then a National reputation as a Temperance advocate, and the author of the famous

Maine Liquor Law. We, whose places were near the front window, used to see him frequently on the street, accompanied by a guard. He was allowed, we understood, to visit
our sick in the hospital. His long, snowy beard and hair gave him a venerable and commanding appearance.

Newsboys seemed to be a thing unknown in Richmond. The papers were sold on the
streets by negro men. The one who frequented our section with the morning journals had
a mellow; rich baritone for which we would be glad to exchange the shrill cries of our
street Arabs. We long remembered him as one of the peculiar features of Richmond. He
had one unvarying formula for proclaiming his wares. It ran in this wise:

"Great Nooze in de papahs!

"Great Nooze from Orange Coaht House, Virginny!

"Great Nooze from Alexandry, Virginny!

"Great Nooze from Washington City!

"Great Nooze from Chattanoogy, Tennessee!

"Great Nooze from Chahlston, Sou' Cahlina!

"Great Nooze in depapahs!"

It did not matter to him that the Rebels had not been at some of these places for
months. He would not change for such mere trifles as the entire evaporation of all possible interest connected with Chattanooga and Alexandria. He was a true Bourbon South-
erner—he learned nothing and forgot nothing.

There was a considerable trade driven between the prisoners and the guard at the door.
This was a very lucrative position for the latter, and men of a commercial turn of mind
generally managed to get stationed there. The blockade had cut off the Confederacy's
supplies from the outer world, and the many trinkets about a man's person were in good
demand at high prices. The men of the Army of the Potomac, who were paid regularly,
and were always near their supplies, had their pockets filled with combs, silk handkerchiefs, knives, neckties, gold pens, pencils, silver watches, playing cards, dice, etc. Such of
these as escaped appropriation by their captors and Dick Turner, were eagerly bought by
the guards, who paid fair prices in Confederate money, or traded wheat bread, tobacco,
daily papers, etc., for them.

There was also considerable brokerage in money, and the manner of doing this was
an admirable exemplification of the folly of the "fiat" money idea. The Rebels exhausted
their ingenuity in framing laws to sustain the purchasing power of their paper money. It
was made legal tender for all debts public and private; it was decreed that the man who
refused to take it was a public enemy; all the considerations of patriotism were rallied to
its support, and the law provided that any citizens found trafficking in the money of the
enemy—i.e., greenbacks, should suffer imprisonment in the Penitentiary, and any soldier
so offending should suffer death.

Notwithstanding all this, in Richmond, the head and heart of the Confederacy, in
January, 1864—long before the Rebel cause began to look at all desperate—it took a
dollar to buy such a loaf of bread as now sells for ten cents; a newspaper was a half dollar,

and everything else in proportion. And still worse: There was not a day during our stay in Richmond but what one could go to the hole in the door before which the guard was pacing and call out in a loud whisper:

"Say, Guard: do you want to buy some greenbacks?"

And be sure that the reply would be, after a furtive glance around to see that no officer was watching:

"Yes; how much do you want for them?"

The reply was then: "Ten for one."

"All right; how much have you got?"

The Yankee would reply; the Rebel would walk to the farther end of his beat, count out the necessary amount, and, returning, put up one hand with it, while with the other he caught hold of one end of the Yankee's greenback. At the word, both would release their holds simultaneously, the exchange was complete, and the Rebel would pace industriously up and down his beat with the air of the school boy who "ain't been a-doin' nothing."

There was never any risk in approaching any guard with a proposition of this kind. I never heard of one refusing to trade for greenbacks, and if the men on guard could not be restrained by these stringent laws, what hope could there be of restraining anybody else?

One day we were favored with a visit from the redoubtable General John H. Morgan, next to J. E. B. Stuart the greatest of Rebel cavalry leaders. He had lately escaped from the Ohio Penitentiary. He was invited to Richmond to be made a Major General, and was given a grand ovation by the citizens and civic Government. He came into our building to visit a number of the First Kentucky Cavalry (loyal)—captured at New Philadelphia, East Tennessee—whom he was anxious to have exchanged for men of his own regiment—the First Kentucky Cavalry (Rebel)—who were captured at the same time he was. I happened to get very close to him while he was standing there talking to his old acquaintances, and I made a mental photograph of him, which still retains all its original distinctness. He was a tall, heavy man, with a full, coarse, and somewhat dull face, and lazy, sluggish gray eyes. His long black hair was carefully oiled, and turned under at the ends, as was the custom with the rural beaux some years ago. His face was clean shaved, except a large, sandy goatee. He wore a high silk hat, a black broadcloth coat, Kentucky jeans pantaloons, neatly fitting boots, and no vest. There was nothing remotely suggestive of unusual ability or force of character, and I thought as I studied him that the sting of George D. Prentice's bon mot about him was in its acrid truth. Said Mr. Prentice:

"Why don't somebody put a pistol to Basil Duke's head, and blow John Morgan's brains out!" [Basil Duke was John Morgan's right hand man.]

CHAPTER XII.

Remarks As To Nomenclature—Vaccination And Its Effects—"N'yaarker's" —Their Characteristics And Their Methods Of Operating.

Before going any further in this narrative it may be well to state that the nomenclature employed is not used in any odious or disparaging sense. It is simply the adoption of the usual terms employed by the soldiers of both sides in speaking to or of each other. We habitually spoke of them and to them, as "Rebels," and "Johnnies ;" they of and to us, as "Yanks," and "Yankees." To have said "Confederates," "Southerners," "Secessionists," or "Federalists," "Unionists," "Northerners" or "Nationalists," would have seemed useless euphemism. The plainer terms suited better, and it was a day when things were more important than names.

For some inscrutable reason the Rebels decided to vaccinate us all. Why they did this has been one of the unsolved problems of my life. It is true that there was small pox in the City, and among the prisoners at Danville; but that any consideration for our safety should have led them to order general inoculation is not among the reasonable inferences. But, be that as it may, vaccination was ordered, and performed. By great good luck I was absent from the building with the squad drawing rations, when our room was inoculated, so I escaped what was an infliction to all, and fatal to many. The direst consequences followed the operation. Foul ulcers appeared on various parts of the bodies of the vaccinated. In many instances the arms literally rotted off; and death followed from a corruption of the blood. Frequently the faces, and other parts of those who recovered, were disfigured by the ghastly cicatrices of healed ulcers. A special friend of mine, Sergeant Frank Beverstock—then a member of the Third Virginia Cavalry, (loyal), and after the war a banker in Bowling Green, O.,—bore upon his temple to his dying day, (which occurred a year ago), a fearful scar, where the flesh had sloughed off from the effects of the virus that had tainted his blood.

This I do not pretend to account for. We thought at the time that the Rebels had deliberately poisoned the vaccine matter with syphilitic virus, and it was so charged upon them. I do not now believe that this was so; I can hardly think that members of the humane profession of medicine would be guilty of such subtle diabolism—worse even than poisoning the wells from which an enemy must drink. The explanation with which I have satisfied myself is that some careless or stupid practitioner took the vaccinating lymph from diseased human bodies, and thus infected all with the blood venom, without any conception of what he was doing. The low standard of medical education in the South makes this theory quite plausible.

We now formed the acquaintance of a species of human vermin that united with the Rebels, cold, hunger, lice and the oppression of distraint, to leave nothing undone that could add to the miseries of our prison life.

These were the fledglings of the slums and dives of New York—graduates of that metropolitan sink of iniquity where the rogues and criminals of the whole world meet for mutual instruction in vice.

They were men who, as a rule, had never known, a day of honesty and cleanliness in their misspent lives; whose fathers, brothers and constant companions were roughs, malefactors and, felons; whose mothers, wives and sisters were prostitutes, procuresses and thieves; men who had from infancy lived in an atmosphere of sin, until it saturated every fiber of their being as a dweller in a jungle imbibes malaria by every one of his, millions of pores, until his very marrow is surcharged with it.

They included representatives from all nationalities, and their descendants, but the English and Irish elements predominated. They had an argot peculiar to themselves. It was partly made up of the "flash" language of the London thieves, amplified and enriched by the cant vocabulary and the jargon of crime of every European tongue. They spoke it with a peculiar accent and intonation that made them instantly recognizable from the roughs of all other Cities. They called themselves "N'Yaarkers;" we came to know them as "Raiders."

If everything in the animal world has its counterpart among men, then these were the wolves, jackals and hyenas of the race at once cowardly and fierce—audaciously bold when the power of numbers was on their side, and cowardly when confronted with resolution by anything like an equality of strength.

Like all other roughs and rascals of whatever degree, they were utterly worthless as soldiers. There may have been in the Army some habitual corner loafer, some fistic champion of the bar-room and brothel, some Terror of Plug Uglyville, who was worth the salt in the hard tack he consumed, but if there were, I did not form his acquaintance, and I never heard of any one else who did. It was the rule that the man who was the readiest in the use of fist and slungshot at home had the greatest diffidence about forming a close acquaintance with cold lead in the neighborhood of the front. Thousands of the so-called "dangerous classes" were recruited, from whom the Government did not receive so much service as would pay for the buttons on their uniforms. People expected that they would make themselves as troublesome to the Rebels as they were to good citizens and the Police, but they were only pugnacious to the provost guard, and terrible to the people in the rear of the Army who had anything that could be stolen.

The highest type of soldier which the world has yet produced is the intelligent, self-respecting American boy, with home, and father and mother and friends behind him, and duty in front beckoning him on. In the sixty centuries that war has been a profession no man has entered its ranks so calmly resolute in confronting danger, so shrewd and energetic in his aggressiveness, so tenacious of the defense and the assault, so certain to rise swiftly to the level of every emergency, as the boy who, in the good old phrase, had been "well-raised" in a Godfearing home, and went to the field in obedience to a conviction of duty. His unfailing courage and good sense won fights that the incompetency or cankering jealousy of commanders had lost. High officers were occasionally disloyal, or willing to sacrifice their country to personal pique; still more frequently they were ignorant and inefficient; but the enlisted man had more than enough innate soldiership to make amends for these deficiencies, and his superb conduct often brought honors and promotions to those only who deserved shame and disaster.

Our "N'Yaarkers," swift to see any opportunity for dishonest gain, had taken to bounty-jumping, or, as they termed it, "leppin' the bounty," for a livelihood. Those who were thrust in upon us had followed this until it had become dangerous, and then deserted to the Rebels. The latter kept them at Castle Lightning for awhile, and then, rightly estimating their character, and considering that it was best to trade them off for a genuine Rebel soldier, sent them in among us, to be exchanged regularly with us. There was not so much good faith as good policy shown by this. It was a matter of indifference to the Rebels how soon our Government shot these deserters after getting them in its hands again. They were only anxious to use them to get their own men back.

The moment they came into contact with us our troubles began. They stole whenever opportunities offered, and they were indefatigable in making these offer; they robbed by actual force, whenever force would avail; and more obsequious lick-spittles to power never existed—they were perpetually on the look-out for a chance to curry favor by betraying some plan or scheme to those who guarded us.

I saw one day a queer illustration of the audacious side of these fellows' characters, and it shows at the same time how brazen effrontery will sometimes get the better of courage. In a room in an adjacent building were a number of these fellows, and a still greater number of East Tennesseeans. These latter were simple, ignorant folks, but reasonably courageous. About fifty of them were sitting in a group in one corner of the room, and near them a couple or three "N'Yaarkers." Suddenly one of the latter said with an oath:

"I was robbed last night; I lost two silver watches, a couple of rings, and about fifty dollars in greenbacks. I believe some of you fellers went through me."

This was all pure invention; he no more had the things mentioned than he had purity of heart and a Christian spirit, but the unsophisticated Tennesseeans did not dream of disputing his statement, and answered in chorus:

"Oh, no, mister; we didn't take your things; we ain't that kind."

This was like the reply of the lamb to the wolf, in the fable, and the N'Yaarker retorted with a simulated storm of passion, and a torrent of oaths:

"—— —— I know ye did; I know some uv yez has got them; stand up agin the wall there till I search yez!"

And that whole fifty men, any one of whom was physically equal to the N'Yaarker, and his superior in point of real courage, actually stood against the wall, and submitted to being searched and having taken from them the few Confederate bills they had, and such trinkets as the searcher took a fancy to.

I was thoroughly disgusted.

CHAPTER XIII.

Belle Isle—Terrible Suffering From Cold And Hunger—Fate Of Lieutenant Boisseux's Dog—Our Company Mystery—Termination Of All Hopes Of Its Solution.

In February my chum—B. B. Andrews, now a physician in Astoria, Illinois —was brought into our building, greatly to my delight and astonishment, and from him I obtained the much desired news as to the fate of my comrades. He told me they had been sent to Belle Isle, whither he had gone, but succumbing to the rigors of that dreadful place, he had been taken to the hospital, and, upon his convalesence, placed in our prison.

Our men were suffering terribly on the island. It was low, damp, and swept by the bleak, piercing winds that howled up and down the surface of the James. The first prisoners placed on the island had been given tents that afforded them some shelter, but these were all occupied when our battalion came in, so that they were compelled to lie on the snow and frozen ground, without shelter, covering of any kind, or fire. During this time the cold had been so intense that the James had frozen over three times.

The rations had been much worse than ours. The so-called soup had been diluted to a ridiculous thinness, and meat had wholly disappeared. So intense became the craving for animal food, that one day when Lieutenant Boisseux—the Commandant—strolled into the camp with his beloved white bull-terrier, which was as fat as a Cheshire pig, the latter was decoyed into a tent, a blanket thrown over him, his throat cut within a rod of where his master was standing, and he was then skinned, cut up, cooked, and furnished a savory meal to many hungry men.

When Boisseux learned of the fate of his four-footed friend he was, of course, intensely enraged, but that was all the good it did him. The only revenge possible was to sentence more prisoners to ride the cruel wooden horse which he used as a means of punishment.

Four of our company were already dead. Jacob Lowry and John Beach were standing near the gate one day when some one snatched the guard's blanket from the post where he had hung it, and ran. The enraged sentry leveled his gun and fired into the crowd. The balls passed through Lowry's and Beach's breasts. Then Charley Osgood, son of our Lieutenant, a quiet, fair-haired, pleasant-spoken boy, but as brave and earnest as his gallant father, sank under the combination of hunger and cold. One stinging morning he was found stiff and stark, on the hard ground, his bright, frank blue eyes glazed over in death.

One of the mysteries of our company was a tall, slender, elderly Scotchman, who appeared on the rolls as William Bradford. What his past life had been, where he had lived, what his profession, whether married or single, no one ever knew. He came to us while in Camp of Instruction near Springfield, Illinois, and seemed to have left all his past behind him as he crossed the line of sentries around the camp. He never received any letters, and never wrote any; never asked for a furlough or pass, and never expressed a wish to be elsewhere than in camp. He was courteous and pleasant, but very reserved. He interfered with no one, obeyed orders promptly and without remark, and was always present for duty. Scrupulously neat in dress, always as clean-shaved as an old-fashioned gentleman of the world, with manners and conversation that showed him to have belonged to a refined and polished circle, he was evidently out of place as a private soldier in a company of reckless and none-too-refined young Illinois troopers, but he never availed himself of any of the numerous opportunities offered to change his associations. His elegant penmanship would have secured him an easy berth and better society at headquarters, but he declined to accept a detail. He became an exciting mystery to a knot of us imaginative young cubs, who sorted up out of the reminiscential rag-bag of high colors and strong contrasts with which the sensational literature that we most affected had plentifully stored our minds, a half-dozen intensely emotional careers for him. We spent much time in mentally trying these on, and discussing which fitted him best. We were always expecting a denouement that would come like a lightning flash and reveal his whole mysterious past, showing him to have been the disinherited scion of some noble house, a man of high station, who was expiating some fearful crime; an accomplished villain eluding his pursuers—in short, a Somebody who would be a fitting hero for Miss Braddon's or Wilkie Collins's literary purposes. We never got but two clues of his past, and they were faint ones. One day, he left lying near me a small copy of "Paradise Lost," that he always carried with him. Turning over its leaves I found all of Milton's bitter invectives against women heavily underscored. Another time, while on guard with him, he spent much of his time in writing some Latin verses in very elegant chirography upon the white painted boards of a fence along which his beat ran. We pressed in all the available knowledge of Latin about camp, and found that the tenor of the verses was very uncomplimentary to that charming sex which does us the honor of being our mothers and sweethearts. These evidences we accepted as sufficient demonstration that there was a woman at the bottom of the mystery, and made us more impatient for further developments. These were never to come. Bradford pined away an Belle Isle, and grew weaker, but no less reserved, each day. At length, one bitter cold night ended it all. He was found in the morning stone dead, with his iron-gray hair frozen fast to the ground, upon which he lay. Our mystery had to remain unsolved. There was nothing about his person to give any hint as to his past.

CHAPTER XIV.

Hoping For Exchange—An Exposition Of The Doctrine Of Chances —Off For Andersonville—Uncertainty As To Our Destination—Arrival At Andersonville.

As each lagging day closed, we confidently expected that the next would bring some news of the eagerly-desired exchange. We hopefully assured each other that the thing could not be delayed much longer; that the Spring was near, the campaign would soon open, and each government would make an effort to get all its men into the field, and this would bring about a transfer of prisoners. A Sergeant of the Seventh Indiana Infantry stated his theory to me this way:

"You know I'm just old lightnin' on chuck-a-luck. Now the way I bet is this: I lay down, say on the ace, an' it don't come up; I just double my bet on the ace, an' keep on doublin' every time it loses, until at last it comes up an' then I win a bushel o' money, and mebbe bust the bank. You see the thing's got to come up some time; an' every time it don't come up makes it more likely to come up the next time. It's just the same way with this 'ere exchange. The thing's got to happen some day, an' every day that it don't happen increases the chances that it will happen the next day."

Some months later I folded the sanguine Sergeant's stiffening hands together across his fleshless ribs, and helped carry his body out to the dead-house at Andersonville, in order to get a piece of wood to cook my ration of meal with.

On the evening of the 17th of February, 1864, we were ordered to get ready to move at daybreak the next morning. We were certain this could mean nothing else than exchange, and our exaltation was such that we did little sleeping that night. The morning was very cold, but we sang and joked as we marched over the creaking bridge, on our way to the cars. We were packed so tightly in these that it was impossible to even sit down, and we rolled slow ly away after a wheezing engine to Petersburg, whence we expected to march to the exchange post. We reached Petersburg before noon, and the cars halted there along time, we momentarily expecting an order to get out. Then the train started up and moved out of the City toward the southeast. This was inexplicable, but after we had proceeded this way for several hours some one conceived the idea that the Rebels, to avoid treating with Butler, were taking us into the Department of some other commander to exchange us. This explanation satisfied us, and our spirits rose again.

Night found us at Gaston, N. C., where we received a few crackers for rations, and changed cars. It was dark, and we resorted to a little strategy to secure more room. About thirty of us got into a tight box car, and immediately announced that it was too full to admit any more. When an officer came along with another squad to stow away, we would yell out to him to take some of the men out, as we were crowded unbearably. In the mean time everybody in the car would pack closely around the door, so as to give the impression that the car was densely crowded. The Rebel would look convinced, and demand:

"Why, how many men have you got in de cah?"

Then one of us would order the imaginary host in the invisible recesses to—

"Stand still there, and be counted," while he would gravely count up to one hundred or one hundred and twenty, which was the utmost limit of the car, and the Rebel would hurry off to put his prisoners somewhere else. We managed to play this successfully during the whole journey, and not only obtained room to lie down in the car, but also drew three or four times as many rations as were intended for us, so that while we at no time had enough, we were farther from starvation than our less strategic companions.

The second afternoon we arrived at Raleigh, the capitol of North Carolina, and were camped in a piece of timber, and shortly after dark orders were issued to us all to lie flat on the ground and not rise up till daylight. About the middle of the night a man belong-ing to a New Jersey regiment, who had apparently forgotten the order, stood up, and was immediately shot dead by the guard.

For four or five days more the decrepit little locomotive strained along, dragging after it the rattling' old cars. The scenery was intensely monotonous. It was a flat, almost unending, stretch of pine barrens and the land so poor that a disgusted Illinoisan, used to the fertility of the great American Bottom, said rather strongly, that,

"By George, they'd have to manure this ground before they could even make brick out of it."

It was a surprise to all of us who had heard so much of the wealth of Virginia, North Carolina, South Carolina and Georgia, to find the soil a sterile sand bank, interspersed with swamps.

We had still no idea of where we were going. We only knew that our general course was southward, and that we had passed through the Carolinas, and were in Georgia. We furbished up our school knowledge of geography and endeavored to recall something of the location of Raleigh, Charlotte, Columbia and Augusta, through which we passed, but the attempt was not a success.

Late on the afternoon of the 25th of February the Seventh Indiana Sergeant approached me with the inquiry:

"Do you know where Macon is?"

The place had not then become as well known as it was afterward.

It seemed to me that I had read something of Macon in Revolutionary history, and that it was a fort on the sea coast. He said that the guard had told him that we were to be taken to a point near that place, and we agreed that it was probably a new place of exchange. A little later we passed through the town of Macon, Ga, and turned upon a road that led almost due south.

About midnight the train stopped, and we were ordered off. We were in the midst of a forest of tall trees that loaded the air with the heavy balsamic odor peculiar to pine trees. A few small rude houses were scattered around near.

Stretching out into the darkness was a double row of great heaps of burning pitch pine, that smoked and flamed fiercely, and lit up a little space around in the somber forest with a ruddy glare. Between these two rows lay a road, which we were ordered to take.

The scene was weird and uncanny. I had recently read the "Iliad," and the long lines of huge fires reminded me of that scene in the first book, where the Greeks burn on the sea shore the bodies of those smitten by Apollo's

For nine long nights, through all the dusky air,

The pyres, thick flaming shot a dismal glare.

Five hundred weary men moved along slowly through double lines of guards. Five hundred men marched silently towards the gates that were to shut out life and hope from most of them forever. A quarter of a mile from the railroad we came to a massive palisade of great squared logs standing upright in the ground. The fires blazed up and showed us a section of these, and two massive wooden gates, with heavy iron hinges and bolts. They swung open as we stood there and we passed through into the space beyond.

We were in Andersonville.

CHAPTER XV.

Georgia—A Lean And Hungry Land—Difference Between Upper And Lower Georgia—The Pillage Of Andersonville.

As the next nine months of the existence of those of us who survived were spent in intimate connection with the soil of Georgia, and, as it exercised a potential influence upon our comfort and well-being, or rather lack of these—a mention of some of its peculiar characteristics may help the reader to a fuller comprehension of the conditions surrounding us—our environment, as Darwin would say.

Georgia, which, next to Texas, is the largest State in the South, and has nearly twenty-five per cent. more area than the great State of New York, is divided into two distinct and widely differing sections, by a geological line extending directly across the State from Augusta, on the Savannah River, through Macon, on the Ocmulgee, to Columbus, on the Chattahoochie. That part lying to the north and west of this line is usually spoken of as "Upper Georgia;" while that lying to the south and east, extending to the Atlantic Ocean and the Florida line, is called "Lower Georgia." In this part of the State—though far removed from each other—were the prisons of Andersonville, Savannah, Millen and Blackshear, in which we were incarcerated one after the other.

Upper Georgia—the capital of which is Atlanta—is a fruitful, productive, metalliferous region, that will in time become quite wealthy. Lower Georgia, which has an extent about equal to that of Indiana, is not only poorer now than a worn-out province of Asia Minor, but in all probability will ever remain so.

It is a starved, sterile land, impressing one as a desert in the first stages of reclamation into productive soil, or a productive soil in the last steps of deterioration into a desert. It is a vast expanse of arid, yellow sand, broken at intervals by foul swamps, with a jungle-life growth of unwholesome vegetation, and teeming With venomous snakes, and all manner of hideous crawling thing.

The original forest still stands almost unbroken on this wide stretch of thirty thousand square miles, but it does not cover it as we say of forests in more favored lands. The tall, solemn pines, upright and symmetrical as huge masts, and wholly destitute of limbs, except the little, umbrella-like crest at the very top, stand far apart from each other in an unfriendly isolation. There is no fraternal interlacing of branches to form a kindly, umbrageous shadow. Between them is no genial undergrowth of vines, shrubs, and demi-trees, generous in fruits, berries and nuts, such as make one of the charms of Northern forests. On the ground is no rich, springing sod of emerald green, fragrant with the elusive sweetness of white clover, and dainty flowers, but a sparse, wiry, famished grass, scattered thinly over the surface in tufts and patches, like the hair on a mangy cur.

The giant pines seem to have sucked up into their immense boles all the nutriment in the earth, and starved out every minor growth. So wide and clean is the space between them, that one can look through the forest in any direction for miles, with almost as little interference with the view as on a prairie. In the swampier parts the trees are lower, and their limbs are hung with heavy festoons of the gloomy Spanish moss, or "death moss," as it is more frequently called, because where it grows rankest the malaria is the deadliest. Everywhere Nature seems sad, subdued and somber.

I have long entertained a peculiar theory to account for the decadence and ruin of countries. My reading of the world's history seems to teach me that when a strong people take possession of a fertile land, they reduce it to cultivation, thrive upon its bountifulness, multiply into millions the mouths to be fed from it, tax it to the last limit of production of the necessities of life, take from it continually, and give nothing back, starve and overwork it as cruel, grasping men do a servant or a beast, and when at last it breaks down under the strain, it revenges itself by starving many of them with great famines, while the others go off in search of new countries to put through the same process of exhaustion. We have seen one country after another undergo this process as the seat of empire took its westward way, from the cradle of the race on the banks of the Oxus to the fertile plains in the Valley of the Euphrates. Impoverishing these, men next sought the Valley of the Nile, then the Grecian Peninsula; next Syracuse and the Italian Peninsula, then the Iberian Peninsula, and the African shores of the Mediterranean. Exhausting all these, they were deserted for the French, German and English portions of Europe. The turn of the latter is now come; famines are becoming terribly frequent, and mankind is pouring into the virgin fields of America.

Lower Georgia, the Carolinas and Eastern Virginia have all the characteristics of these starved and worn-out lands. It would seem as if, away back in the distance of ages, some numerous and civilized race had drained from the soil the last atom of food-producing constituents, and that it is now slowly gathering back, as the centuries pass, the elements that have been wrung from the land.

Lower Georgia is very thinly settled. Much of the land is still in the hands of the Government. The three or four railroads which pass through it have little reference to local traffic. There are no towns along them as a rule; stations are made every ten miles, and not named, but numbered, as "Station No. 4"—"No. 10", etc. The roads were built as through lines, to bring to the seaboard the rich products of the interior.

Andersonville is one of the few stations dignified with a same, probably because it contained some half dozen of shabby houses, whereas at the others there was usually nothing more than a mere open shed, to shelter goods and travelers. It is on a rudely constructed, rickety railroad, that runs from Macon to Albany, the head of navigation on the Flint River, which is, one hundred and six miles from Macon, and two hundred and fifty from the Gulf of Mexico. Andersonville is about sixty miles from Macon, and, consequently, about three hundred miles from the Gulf. The camp was merely a hole cut in the wilderness. It was as remote a point from, our armies, as they then lay, as the Southern Confederacy could give. The nearest was Sherman, at Chattanooga, four hundred miles away, and on the other side of a range of mountains hundreds of miles wide.

To us it seemed beyond the last forlorn limits of civilization. We felt that we were more completely at the mercy of our foes than ever. While in Richmond we were in the heart of the Confederacy; we were in the midst of the Rebel military and, civil force, and were surrounded on every hand by visible evidences of the great magnitude of that power, but this, while it enforced our ready submission, did not overawe us depressingly, We knew that though the Rebels were all about us in great force, our own men were also near, and in still greater force—that while they were very strong our army was still stronger, and there was no telling what day this superiority of strength, might be demonstrated in such a way as to decisively benefit us.

But here we felt as did the Ancient Mariner:

> Alone on a wide, wide sea,
>
> So lonely 'twas that God himself
>
> Scarce seemed there to be.

CHAPTER XVI.

Waking Up In Andersonville—Some Description Of The Place—Our First Mail—Building Shelter—Gen. Winder—Himself And Lineage.

We roused up promptly with the dawn to take a survey of our new abiding place. We found ourselves in an immense pen, about one thousand feet long by eight hundred wide, as a young surveyor—a member of the Thirty-fourth Ohio—informed us after he had paced it off. He estimated that it contained about sixteen acres. The walls were formed by pine logs twenty-five feet long, from two to three feet in diameter, hewn square, set into the ground to a depth of five feet, and placed so close together as to leave no crack through which the country outside could be seen. There being five feet of the logs in the ground, the wall was, of course, twenty feet high. This manner of enclosure was in some respects superior to a wall of masonry. It was equally unscalable, and much more difficult to undermine or batter down.

The pen was longest due north and south. It was divided in the center by a creek about a yard wide and ten inches deep, running from west to east. On each side of this was a quaking bog of slimy ooze one hundred and fifty feet wide, and so yielding that one attempting to walk upon it would sink to the waist. From this swamp the sand-hills sloped north and south to the stockade. All the trees inside the stockade, save two, had been cut down and used in its construction. All the rank vegetation of the swamp had also been cut off.

There were two entrances to the stockade, one on each side of the creek, midway between it and the ends, and called respectively the "North Gate" and the "South Gate." These were constructed double, by building smaller stockades around them on the outside, with another set of gates. When prisoners or wagons with rations were brought in, they were first brought inside the outer gates, which were carefully secured, before the inner gates were opened. This was done to prevent the gates being carried by a rush by those confined inside.

At regular intervals along the palisades were little perches, upon which stood guards, who overlooked the whole inside of the prison.

The only view we had of the outside was that obtained by looking from the highest points of the North or South Sides across the depression where the stockade crossed the swamp. In this way we could see about forty acres at a time of the adjoining woodland, or say one hundred and sixty acres altogether, and this meager landscape had to content us for the next half year.

Before our inspection was finished, a wagon drove in with rations, and a quart of meal, a sweet potato and a few ounces of salt beef were issued to each one of us.

In a few minutes we were all hard at work preparing our first meal in Andersonville. The debris of the forest left a temporary abundance of fuel, and we had already a cheerful fire blazing for every little squad. There were a number of tobacco presses in the rooms we occupied in Richmond, and to each of these was a quantity of sheets of tin, evidently used to put between the layers of tobacco. The deft hands of the mechanics among us bent these up into square pans, which were real handy cooking utensils, holding about—a quart. Water was carried in them from the creek; the meal mixed in them to a dough, or else boiled as mush in the same vessels; the potatoes were boiled; and their final service was to hold a little meal to be carefully browned, and then water boiled upon it, so as to form a feeble imitation of coffee. I found my education at Jonesville in the art of baking a hoe-cake now came in good play, both for myself and companions. Taking one of the pieces of tin which had not yet been made into a pan, we spread upon it a layer of dough about a half-inch thick. Propping this up nearly upright before the fire, it was soon nicely browned over. This process made it sweat itself loose from the tin, when it was turned over and the bottom browned also. Save that it was destitute of salt, it was quite a toothsome bit of nutriment for a hungry man, and I recommend my readers to try making a "pone" of this kind once, just to see what it was like.

The supreme indifference with which the Rebels always treated the matter of cooking utensils for us, excited my wonder. It never seemed to occur to them that we could have any more need of vessels for our food than cattle or swine. Never, during my whole prison life, did I see so much as a tin cup or a bucket issued to a prisoner. Starving men were driven to all sorts of shifts for want of these. Pantaloons or coats were pulled off and their sleeves or legs used to draw a mess's meal in. Boots were common vessels for carrying water, and when the feet of these gave way the legs were ingeniously closed up with pine pegs, so as to form rude leathern buckets. Men whose pocket knives had escaped the search at the gates made very ingenious little tubs and buckets, and these devices enabled us to get along after a fashion.

After our meal was disposed of, we held a council on the situation. Though we had been sadly disappointed in not being exchanged, it seemed that on the whole our condition had been bettered. This first ration was a decided improvement on those of the Pemberton building; we had left the snow and ice behind at Richmond—or rather at some place between Raleigh, N. C., and Columbia, S. C.—and the air here, though chill, was not nipping, but bracing. It looked as if we would have a plenty of wood for shelter and fuel, it was certainly better to have sixteen acres to roam over than the stiffing confines of a building; and, still better, it seemed as if there would be plenty of opportunities to get beyond the stockade, and attempt a journey through the woods to that blissful land —"Our lines."

We settled down to make the best of things. A Rebel Sergeant came in presently and arranged us in hundreds. We subdivided these into messes of twenty-five, and began devising means for shelter. Nothing showed the inborn capacity of the Northern soldier to take care of himself better than the way in which we accomplished this with the rude materials at our command. No ax, spade nor mattock was allowed us by the Rebels, who treated us in regard to these the same as in respect to culinary vessels. The only tools were a few pocket-knives, and perhaps half-a-dozen hatchets which some infantrymen-principally members of the Third Michigan—were allowed to retain. Yet, despite all these drawbacks, we had quite a village of huts erected in a few days,—nearly enough, in fact, to afford tolerable shelter for the whole five hundred of us first-comers.

The wither and poles that grew in the swamp were bent into the shape of the semicircular bows that support the canvas covers of army wagons, and both ends thrust in the ground. These formed the timbers of our dwellings. They were held in place by weaving in, basket-wise, a network of briers and vines. Tufts of the long leaves which are the distinguishing characteristic of the Georgia pine (popularly known as the "long-leaved pine") were wrought into this network until a thatch was formed, that was a fair protection against the rain—it was like the Irishman's unglazed window-sash, which "kep' out the coarsest uv the cold."

The results accomplished were as astonishing to us as to the Rebels, who would have lain unsheltered upon the sand until bleached out like field-rotted flax, before thinking to protect themselves in this way. As our village was approaching completion, the Rebel Sergeant who called the roll entered. He was very odd-looking. The cervical muscles were distorted in such a way as to suggest to us the name of "Wry-necked Smith," by which we always designated him. Pete Bates, of the Third Michigan, who was the wag of our squad, accounted for Smith's condition by saying that while on dress parade once the Colonel of Smith's regiment had commanded "eyes right," and then forgot to give the order "front." Smith, being a good soldier, had kept his eyes in the position of gazing at the buttons of the third man to the right, waiting for the order to restore them to their natural direction, until they had become permanently fixed in their obliquity and he was compelled to go through life taking a biased view of all things.

Smith walked in, made a diagonal survey of the encampment, which, if he had ever seen "Mitchell's Geography," probably reminded him of the picture of a Kaffir village, in that instructive but awfully dull book, and then expressed the opinion that usually welled up to every Rebel's lips:

"Well, I'll be durned, if you Yanks don't just beat the devil."

Of course, we replied with the well-worn prison joke, that we supposed we did, as we beat the Rebels, who were worse than the devil.

There rode in among us, a few days after our arrival, an old man whose collar bore the wreathed stars of a Major General. Heavy white locks fell from beneath his slouched hat, nearly to his shoulders. Sunken gray eyes, too dull and cold to light up, marked a hard, stony face, the salient feature of which was a thin-upped, compressed mouth, with corners drawn down deeply—the mouth which seems the world over to be the index of selfish, cruel, sulky malignance. It is such a mouth as has the school-boy—the coward of the play ground, who delights in pulling off the wings of flies. It is such a mouth as we can imagine some remorseless inquisitor to have had—that is, not an inquisitor filled with holy zeal for what he mistakenly thought the cause of Christ demanded, but a spleeny, envious, rancorous shaveling, who tortured men from hatred of their superiority to him, and sheer love of inflicting pain.

The rider was John H. Winder, Commissary General of Prisoners, Baltimorean renegade and the malign genius to whose account should be charged the deaths of more gallant men than all the inquisitors of the world ever slew by the less dreadful rack and wheel. It was he who in August could point to the three thousand and eighty-one new made graves for that month, and exultingly tell his hearer that he was "doing more for the Confederacy than twenty regiments."

His lineage was in accordance with his character. His father was that General William H. Winder, whose poltroonery at Bladensburg, in 1814, nullified the resistance of the gallant Commodore Barney, and gave Washington to the British.

The father was a coward and an incompetent; the son, always cautiously distant from the scene of hostilities, was the tormentor of those whom the fortunes of war, and the arms of brave men threw into his hands.

Winder gazed at us stonily for a few minutes without speaking, and, turning, rode out again.

Our troubles, from that hour, rapidly increased.

The Battle of Shiloh
by *Warren Olney, Late Captain 65ᵗʰ U.S.C. Inf.*

The Battle of Shiloh

"Shiloh" as Seen by a Private Soldier
by *Warren Olney*

A paper read before California Commandery of the Military Order of the Loyal Legion of the United States, May, 31, 1889

WAR PAPER No. 5.

Commandery of the State of California

Military Order of the Loyal Legion of the United States

Very interesting descriptions of the great battles of the late war, written by prominent generals, have been lately published and widely read. It seems to me, however, that it is time for the private soldier to be heard from.

Of course, his field of vision is much more limited than that of his general. On the other hand, it is of vital importance to the latter to gloss over his mistakes, and draw attention only to those things which will add to his reputation. The private soldier has no such feeling. It is only to the officers of high rank engaged that a battle can bring glory and renown. To the army of common soldiers, who do the actual fighting, and risk mutilation and death, there is no reward except the consciousness of duty bravely performed. This was peculiarly the case in the late war, when more than a million of young men, the flower of our country, left their workshops and farms, their schools and colleges, to endure the hardships of the march and the camp, to risk health, limb and life, that their country might live, expecting nothing, hoping nothing for themselves, but all for their fatherland.

The first really great battle of the war was that of Pittsburg Landing, or Shiloh, and I shall not only attempt to give a general account of the battle, but also describe it from the point of view of a man in the ranks.

In respect to the general features of this desperate struggle between our own countrymen, my statements are derived from many reports and accounts carefully collated, and from many conversations with soldiers engaged, both from the Union and Confederate armies.

Who of us, having reached middle life, does not recall the exultation and enthusiasm aroused by the news of the capture of Fort Donelson? What a thrill of pride and patriotism was felt through all the loyal North! The soldiers of the great Northwest had attacked a citadel of the rebellion, and captured it, with sixteen thousand of its defenders.

At this time the Third Iowa Infantry was strung along the North Missouri Railroad, guarding bridges and doing other police work. Company B, which had the honor of having on its muster roll private Olney, was stationed at that time in the little town of Sturgeon, Missouri, where our principal occupation was to keep from freezing. We had then spent eight months campaigning in that border State—that is, if you call guarding railways and bridges, and attempting to overawe the disaffected, enlivened now and then by a brisk skirmish, campaigning. The Second Iowa had led the charge which captured the hostile breastworks at Donelson, and General Grant had telegraphed to General Halleck at St. Louis, who had repeated the message to the Governor of our State, that the Second Iowa was the bravest of the brave. The First Iowa had distinguished itself at Wilson's Creek, near Springfield, under General Lyon, while we—well, we hadn't done much of anything but to get a licking at Blue Mills. Therefore, when a message to move came, and we found ourselves on the way to join General Grant's army, we felt quite hilarious.

At St. Louis we were put on board the steamer "Iatan." Down the Mississippi, up the Ohio, up the Tennessee. As we proceeded up the Tennessee we were continually overtaking or being joined by other steamboats loaded with troops, until presently the river was alive with transports, carrying the army of the West right into the heart of the Confederacy. It was a beautiful and stirring sight; mild weather had set in (it was now the second week of March), the flotilla of steamboats, black with soldiers, bands playing, flags flying, all combined to arouse and interest. It was the "pomp and circumstance of glorious war."

Frequent stoppages were made, giving us a chance to run ashore. About the thirteenth we reached the landing-place, which soon afterwards became famous. The river was very high, and at first there seemed to be doubts as to where a landing should be effected, but in a few days the question was settled. Our boat was moored as near the shore as possible, and we joined the immense throng painfully making their way through the unfathomable mud to camps in the dense woods. The first things I observed after reaching the high bluff, were trees that had been torn and shattered by shells from our gunboats, which, it seems, had dislodged a company of Confederates, who had dug rifle-pits on the bluff, from whence they had fired on our steamboats.

We first camped on the bluff near the landing, but shortly moved back about a mile from the river, and camped on the edge of a small cotton field with dense forests all around. The Hamburg road ran past the left of our line, between us and the Forty-first Illinois; while on the right was a small ravine, which ran into a little creek, and that into Snake Creek.

The mud—well, it was indescribable. Though we were only a mile from our base of supplies, the greatest difficulty was experienced in getting camp equipage and provisions. We found that other divisions of the army had landed before us, moving farther out to the front towards Corinth, and had so cut up the roads that they were quagmires their whole length. Teams were stalled in the mud in every direction. The principal features of the landscape were trees, mud, wagons buried to the hub, and struggling, plunging mule teams. The shouts of teamsters and resounding whacks filled the air; and as to profanity—well, you could see the air about an enraged teamster turn blue as he exhorted his impenitent mules. And the rain! how it did come down! As I recall it, the spring of 1862 did not measure its rainfall in Western Tennessee by inches, but by feet.

But in time our camp was fairly established. Sibley tents were distributed, one for fourteen men. They protected us from the rain, but they had their drawbacks. Several of us were schoolmates from a Western college, and, of course, in some respects, constituted a little aristocracy. We had had a small tent to ourselves, and the socialistic grayback, as yet, had not crawled therein. Now, we were required to share our tent with others, and that might mean a great many. But when it came to a question of sleeping out in the cold rain, or camping down in a crowded tent in true democratic equality and taking the chances of immigration from our neighbors' clothing, we did not prefer the rain.

Of course, the private soldier has not much opportunity for exploration about his camp, however strong may be his passion in that direction. I did what I could, but my knowledge of the general encampment was much enlarged when, during the days following the battle, all discipline being relaxed, I tramped the field over in every direction and talked with the men of numerous regiments on their camp grounds. Further on, I shall refer to the position occupied by our army more at length, and shall only refer now to the general position of our encampment, as on a wooded plateau, accessible to attack only from the direction of Corinth, the river being in our rear, Snake Creek and Owl Creek on our right flank, and Lick Creek on our left. In places there were small fields with their adjuncts of deserted cabins. Our troops were camped wherever there was an opening in the woods or underbrush sufficiently large for a regiment. There seemed to be no order or system about the method of encampment, but each regiment occupied such suitable ground as presented itself in the neighborhood of the rest of the brigade; and the same was true of the brigades composing the divisions.

Our regiment was brigaded with the Twenty-eighth, Thirty-second, and Forty-first Illinois. The division was commanded by Brigadier-General Stephen A. Hurlbut (since somewhat noted as United States Minister to Peru). We had served under him in Missouri, and our principal recollection of him was an event which occurred at Macon. We had got aboard a train of cattle cars for the purpose of going to the relief of some point threatened by the enemy. After waiting on the train two or three hours, expecting every moment to start, we noticed a couple of staff officers supporting on each side the commanding general, and leading him to the car I was in. Getting him to the side of the car, they boosted him in at the door, procured a soldier's knapsack for him to sit on, and left him. He was so drunk he couldn't sit upright. The consequence was that the regimental officers refused to move. A court-martial followed, and we heard no more of our general until we found him at Pittsburg Landing in command of a division. He showed so much coolness and bravery in the battle which followed, that we forgave him his first scandalous appearance. But the distrust of him before the battle can readily be imagined.

No one who has not been through the experience can realize the anxiety of the private soldier respecting the character and capacity of his commanding officer. His life is in the general's hand. Whether he shall be uselessly sacrificed, may depend wholly upon the coolness or readiness for an emergency of the commander; whether he has had two drinks or three; whether he has had a good night's rest, or a good cigar. The private soldier regards a new and unknown commander very much as a slave does a new owner, and with good reason. Without confidence on the part of the rank and file, victory is impossible. Their soldiers' confidence in Stonewall Jackson and Lee doubled the effective strength of their armies. When in the Franco-Prussian war a German regiment was called upon for a charge, each man felt that the order was given because it was necessary, and that what he was doing was part of a comprehensive scheme, whose success might very likely depend upon whether he did his assigned part manfully. The French soldier in that war had no such feeling and, of course, the result of that campaign was not long in doubt. In Napoleon's time, the confidence of the rank and file was such that time and again he was saved from defeat by the feeling of the attacked corps or detachment that it must hold its ground, or probably imperil the army. Oh, the sickening doubt and distrust of our generals during the first years of the war! Our soldiers were as brave as ever trod the earth, and thoroughly imbued with the cause for which they were fighting; but the suspicion that at headquarters there might be inefficiency or drunkenness; that marches and counter-marches had no definite purpose; that their lives might be uselessly thrown away—you would have to go through it to realize it! At the beginning of the war, the Southerners had a vast advantage over us in that respect. Generally speaking, they started out with the same able commanders they had at the end.

Our colonel was thoroughly disliked and distrusted. As he was the ranking colonel of the brigade, he was placed in command of it; so you see we did not feel particularly happy over the situation, especially as we knew the Confederate army was only twenty-two miles off.

The steady, cold rains of the first week or two was most depressing. On account, probably, of the bad weather and exposure, the soldiers' worst enemy, diarrhœa, took possession of our camps, and for a week or ten days we literally had no stomachs for fighting. But after a little the rain let up, the sun came out warm, our spirits revived, the roads, and consequently the supplies improved; and on the whole, we thought it rather jolly.

If you had been there of a warm, sunny day you would have noticed every log and stump serving as a seat for a soldier, who had taken off his shirt and was diligently hunting it all over. It was not safe to ask him what he was looking for.

Troops were continually arriving, some of them freshly recruited, and not yet familiar with their arms, or the simplest elements of regimental maneuvers. It was said there were some regiments who had just received their guns, and had never fired them. Badeau says they came on the field without cartridges. I know that improved rifles were scarce, for my own regiment at that time did not have rifles, but old smooth bore muskets with buck-and-ball ammunition—that is, the cartridge had next to the powder a large ball, and then next to it three buck shot. Of course, we should have had no show against rifles at long range, but at short range, in woods and brush, these weapons were fearfully destructive, as we shall presently see.

Strange to say, these freshly recruited regiments were assigned to Sherman's division and to Prentiss' division, whose camps were scattered in the woods farthest out towards Corinth. As might have been expected, these new soldiers did not stand on the order of their going, when they suddenly discovered a hostile army on top of them.

A map of the place selected for the concentration of our army shows that with proper precautions and such defensive works as, later in the war, would have been constructed within a few hours, the place was impregnable. The river which ran in the rear was controlled by our gunboats, and furnished us the means of obtaining abundant supplies. Creeks with marshy banks protected either flank. The only possible avenue of attack upon this position was directly in front, and across that ran little creeks and ravines, with here and there open fields affording fine vantage-ground. A general anticipating the possibility of attack, would not have scattered his divisions so widely, and would have marked a line of defense upon which the troops should rally. Advantage would have been taken of the ground, and trees felled with the tops outwards, through which an attacking force would have, with great difficulty, to struggle. And later in the war, as a matter of precaution, and because of the proximity of the enemy, breastworks would have been thrown up. All this could have been done in a few hours. Our flanks were so well protected that no troops were needed there, and in case of attack, each division commander should have had his place in the front, to which to immediately march his command; while, the line being not more than three miles long at the very outside estimate, there were abundant forces to man it thoroughly, leaving a large force in the reserve to reinforce a point imperiled.

Why was not this done? It is hard to find an answer. General Sherman's division was at the extreme front. It was being organized. The enemy was not more than twenty-two miles away, and was known to be concentrating from all the West. Yet this general, who afterwards acquired such fame as a consummate master of the art of war, took no precautions whatever, not even thoroughly scouting the ground in his front. His pickets could not have been out more than a mile. General Prentiss' division was also in process of organization, and he, like Sherman, was in advance, and on Sherman's left. The complete absence of the ordinary precautions, always taken by military commanders since the beginning of history, is inexplicable. The only reason I can conjecture for it grows out of the character of General Grant and his distinguished subordinate, and their inexperience. They had had then little practical knowledge of actual warfare. General Sherman, except on one occasion, had never heard a hostile gun fired. They had to learn their art, and the country and their army had to pay the cost of their teaching. Happily, they were able to profit by every lesson, and soon had no equals among our commanders. But because they have since deserved so well of their country, is no reason why history should be silent as to their mistakes. The Confederates would have made a great mistake in attacking us at all in such a position, if we had been prepared to receive them. But this want of preparation prevented us from taking advantage of the opportunity, and inflicting a crushing defeat upon the South. By it the war was prolonged, and every village and hamlet in the West had its house of mourning.

Immediately in the right rear of General Sherman was camped the veteran division of General McClernand. About two miles further back, and about a mile from the river, was stationed the reserve, consisting of two divisions, Hurlbut's and W. H. L. Wallace's, formerly C. F. Smith's. Across Owl Creek, and seven or eight miles off, was camped General Lew Wallace's division. It was so far away as not to be in easy supporting distance.

On April 1st, our division was marched to an open field, and there carefully reviewed by General Grant. This was our first sight of the victor of Donelson. Friday, the 4th of April, was a sloppy day, and just before sundown we heard firing off towards Sherman's division. We fell into line and started toward the front. After we had marched about a mile, pitch darkness came on. Presently, a staff officer directed a counter-march back to camp, saying it was only a rebel reconnoisance. It was a nasty march back in the mud, dense woods, and thick darkness.

All this day the Confederate army was struggling through the woods and mud, on its march from Corinth to attack us. It was the expectation of General Johnston and his subordinates to cover the intervening space between the two armies in this one day and attack early Saturday morning; but the difficulties of the march was such, that he did not make more than half the distance, and had to go into camp for the night. Saturday was a reasonably pleasant day, but General Johnston's troops had got so entangled in the forests, he did not feel justified in attacking until all his preparations were made, which took the whole of Saturday. He then moved up to within a mile or two of Sherman and Prentiss, and went into camp within sound of our drums.

The delay had been so great that Beauregard now advised a countermarch back to Corinth. He represented that our forces had surely been appraised of their march, and it would be too late now to effect a surprise; that they would undoubtedly find us all prepared, and probably behind breastworks and other obstructions. General Johnston was smarting under the criticisms of the campaign which resulted in the loss of Donelson. His courage and military instinct told him that now was the time to strike. He felt, too, that a bold stroke was necessary to redeem the fortunes of the Confederacy and his own reputation. His resolution was to conquer or die; and he replied to Beauregard: "We shall attack at daylight to-morrow."

Here was an army of a little over 40,000 men, as brave as ever shouldered muskets, fighting on their own soil, and, as they believed, for homes and liberty, resting for the night at about two miles from the invading army, and all prepared to attack at dawn, and sweep the invaders of their country back into the Tennessee river. Upon the favoring breeze, the sound of our drums at evening parade came floating to their ears. They heard the bugle note enjoying quiet and repose in the camp of their unsuspecting foe. They, themselves, were crouching in the thick woods and darkness, all prepared to spring on their prey. No camp-fire was lighted; no unnecessary sound was permitted; but silent, watchful, with mind and heart prepared for conflict, the Southern hosts waited for the morning.

Such was the situation, so far as our enemies were concerned. But how was it with the army fighting for the integrity and preservation of the nation? Let us begin with the commanding General. That day (Saturday) he dispatched General Halleck as follows: "The main force of the army is at Corinth. * * * The number at Corinth and within supporting distance of it cannot be far from 80,000 men." Later in the day he dispatched the news of the enemy's reconnoisance the night before, and added: "I have scarcely the faintest idea of an attack (general one) being made upon us, but will be prepared should a thing take place."

Grant had less than 50,000 men fit for battle. He thinks the enemy at Corinth, twenty-two miles away, has 80,000 men. He must know that the enemy knows Buell, with his army, will soon reach the Tennessee, and when united with his own will nearly double his effective strength; that now, and before Buell joins him, if ever, must the Confederates strike an effective blow. His pickets have been driven in the night before, the enemy using a piece or two of artillery; yet he does not expect an attack, and makes not the slightest preparation to receive or repel one. He leaves General Lew Wallace with over 7,000 good troops at Crump's Landing, out of easy supporting distance, Nelson's division and Crittenden's division of Buell's army at Savannah; and has no thought of moving them up that day to repel an overwhelming attack about to be made on him. On Saturday he visits his army and Sherman, and then goes back to Savannah, unsuspicious of the presence of the enemy.

How was it with General Sherman, who had the advance on the right, and was probably more relied upon by Grant and Halleck than was Prentiss? In fact it is not at all improbable that Grant wholly relied upon the two division commanders at the front, particularly Sherman, to keep him posted as to the movements of the hostile army. General Sherman reported on Saturday that he thought there were about two regiments of infantry and a battery of artillery about six miles out. As a matter of fact, the whole rebel army was not more than six miles out. Later in the day he dispatches: "The enemy is saucy, but got the worst of it yesterday, and will not press our pickets far. I do not apprehend anything like an attack on our position."

A tolerably extensive reading of campaigns and military histories justifies me in saying that such an exhibition of unsuspicious security in the presence of a hostile army is without a parallel in the history of warfare.

How was it with our army? We knew the enemy to be at Corinth, but there had been no intimation of advance; and no army could get over the intervening space in less than two days, of which, of course, it was the duty of our generals to have ample notice. Usually, before a battle, there seems to be something in the very air that warns the soldier and officer of what is coming, and to nerve themselves for the struggle; but most of us retired this Saturday night to our blankets in as perfect fancied security as ever enveloped an army.

But this was not true of all. A sense of uneasiness pervaded a portion of the advance line. Possibly there had been too much noise in the woods in front, possibly that occult sense, which tells us of the proximity of another, warned them of the near approach of a hostile army. Some of the officers noticed that the woods beyond the pickets seemed to be full of Rebel cavalry. General Prentiss was infected with this uneasiness, and at daylight on Sunday morning sent out the Twenty-first Missouri to make an observation towards Corinth.

This regiment, proceeding through the forest, ran plump upon the Confederate skirmish line, which it promptly attacked. Immediately the Missourians saw an army behind the skirmish line advancing upon them. They could hold their ground but for a moment. The enemy's advance swept them back, and, like an avalanche, the Confederate army poured into the camps of Sherman's and Prentiss' divisions.

At the first fire our men sprang to arms. By the time the enemy had reached our camps many regiments had become partially formed, but they were all unnerved by the shock. Some were captured by the enemy before they could get their clothes on. Some, without firing a shot, broke for the river-landing, three miles away, and cowered beneath its banks. General Sherman and his staff mounted their horses, and as they galloped past the Fifty-third Ohio, which was getting into line, one of the officers called out to him not to go any farther, for the rebel army was just beyond the rising ground. The general made use of some expression about not getting frightened at a reconnoisance, and went ahead. As he reached the slight elevation he beheld the Confederate army sweeping down upon him. Their skirmish line fired at him, killing his orderly. He realized at last that he was in the presence of a hostile army. From that moment he did everything that mortal man could do to retrieve his fatal mistake. Wounded twice, several horses successively killed under him, chaos and defeat all around, yet his clear intelligence and steady courage stamped him a born leader of men. The other generals and officers yielded to his superior force and obeyed his orders. He was everywhere, encouraging, threatening, organizing, and succeeded in establishing a tolerable line in the rear of his camps.

General Prentiss' troops were more demoralized than Sherman's. Whole regiments broke away, and were not reorganized until after the battle. A tide of fugitives set in toward the landing, carrying demoralization and terror with them.

Our camp was so far back that we heard nothing of this early uproar. The morning was a beautiful one, and after our early breakfast I started down the little creek, hunting for some first flowers of spring. I had scarcely got out of sight of camp, when the firing toward the front, though faintly heard, seemed too steady to be caused by the pernicious habit which prevailed of the pickets firing off their guns on returning from duty, preparatory to cleaning them. A sense of apprehension took possession of me. Presently artillery was heard, and then I turned toward camp, getting more alarmed at every step. When I reached camp a startled look was on every countenance. The musketry firing had become loud and general, and whole batteries of artillery were joining in the dreadful chorus. The men rushed to their tents and seized their guns, but as yet no order to fall in was given. Nearer and nearer sounded the din of a tremendous conflict. Presently the long roll was heard from the regiments on our right. A staff officer came galloping up, spoke a word to the Major in command, the order to fall in was shouted, the drummers began to beat the long roll, and it was taken up by the regiments on our left. The men, with pale faces, wild eyes, compressed lips, quickly accoutered themselves for battle. The shouts of the officers, the rolling of the drums, the hurrying to and fro of the men, the uproar of approaching but unexpected battle, all together produced sensations which cannot be described. Soon, teams with shouting drivers came tearing along the road toward the landing. Crowds of fugitives and men slightly wounded went hurrying past in the same direction. Uproar and turmoil were all around; but we, having got into line, stood quietly with scarcely a word spoken. Each man was struggling with himself and nerving himself for what bid fair to be a dreadful conflict. What thoughts of home and kindred and all that makes life dear come to one at such a moment.

Presently a staff officer rode up, the command to march was given, and with the movement came some relief to the mental and moral strain. As we passed in front of the Forty-first Illinois, a field officer of that regiment, in a clear, ringing voice, was speaking to his men, and announced that if any man left the ranks on pretense of caring for the wounded he should be shot on the spot; that the wounded must be left till the fight was over. His men cheered him, and we took up the cheer. Blood was beginning to flow through our veins again, and we could even comment to one another upon the sneaks who remained in camp, on pretense of being sick. As we moved toward the front the fugitives and the wounded increased in numbers. Poor wretches, horribly mutilated, would drop down, unable to go farther. Wagons full of wounded, filling the air with their groans, went hurrying by. As we approached the scene of conflict, we moved off to the left of the line of the rear-ward going crowd, crossed a small field and halted in the open woods beyond.

As we halted, we saw right in front of us, but about three hundred or four hundred yards off, a dense line of Confederate infantry, quietly standing in ranks. In our excitement, and without a word of command, we turned loose and with our smooth bore muskets opened fire upon them. After three or four rounds, the absurdity of firing at the enemy at that distance with our guns dawned upon us, and we stopped. As the smoke cleared up we saw the enemy still there, not having budged or fired a shot in return. But though our action was absurd, it was a relief to us to do something, and we were rapidly becoming toned up to the point of steady endurance.

As we gazed at the enemy so coolly standing there, an Ohio battery of artillery came galloping up in our rear, and what followed I don't believe was equalled by anything of the kind during the war. As the artillery came up we moved off by the right flank a few steps, to let it come in between us and the Illinois regiment next on our left. Where we were standing was in open, low-limbed oak timber. The line of Southern infantry was in tolerably plain view through the openings in the woods, and were still standing quietly. Of course, we all turned our heads away from them to look at the finely equipped battery, as it came galloping from the rear to our left flank, its officers shouting directions to the riders where to stop their guns. It was the work of but an instant to bring every gun into position. Like a flash the gunners leaped from their seats and unlimbered the cannon. The fine six-horse teams began turning round with the caissons, charges were being rammed home, and the guns pointed toward the dense ranks of the enemy, when, from right in front, a dense puff of smoke, a tearing of shot and shell through the trees, a roar from half a dozen cannon, hitherto unseen, and our brave battery was knocked into smithereens. Great limbs of trees, torn off by cannon shot, came down on horse and rider, crushing them to earth. Shot and shell struck cannon, upsetting them; caissons exploded them. Not a shot was fired from our side.

But how those astounded artillery men—those of them who could run at all—did scamper out of there. Like Mark Twain's dog, they may be running yet. At least, it is certain that no attempt was ever made to reorganize that battery—it was literally wiped out then and there.

This made us feel mightily uncomfortable—in fact, we had been feeling quite uncomfortable all the morning. It did not particularly add to the cheerfulness of the prospect, to reflect that our division was the reserve of the army, and should not be called into action, ordinarily, until towards the close of the battle; while here we were, early in the forenoon, face to face with the enemy, our battery of artillery gobbled up at one mouthful, and the rest of the army in great strait, certainly, and probably demoralized.

One of the cannon shot had gone through our Colonel's horse, and the rider had been carried off the field. Colonel Pugh, of the Forty-first Illinois, then took command of the brigade, about-faced us, and marched us back across the little field, and halted us just behind the fence, the enemy during this maneuver leaving us wholly undisturbed.

The rails were thrown down and we lay flat upon the ground, while another battery came up and opened on the enemy, who had moved up almost to the wreck of our first battery.

Here, then, began a fierce artillery duel. Shot and shell went over us and crashing through the trees to the rear of us, and I suppose that shot and shell went crashing through the trees above the enemy; but if they didn't suffer any more from shot and shell than we did, there was a great waste of powder and iron that day. But how a fellow does hug the ground under such circumstances! As a shell goes whistling over him he flattens out, and presses himself into the earth, almost. Pity the sorrows of a big fat man under such a fire.

Later in the war we should have dug holes for ourselves with bayonets. We must have lain there hugging the ground for more than two hours, with now and then an intermission, listening to the flight of dreaded missiles above us; but, as nobody in our immediate neighborhood was hurt, we at length voted the performance of the artillery to be, on the whole, rather fine. During intermissions, while the scenes were shifting, as it were, we began to feel a disposition to talk and joke over the situation.

The reason why we were not subjected to an infantry fire, was because the enemy's forces, tangled in the wooded country, and in places beaten back by the stubborn gallantry of our surprised but not demoralized men, needed to be reorganized. All the Southern accounts agree that their brigades and divisions had become mixed in apparently hopeless confusion. The battlefield was so extensive that fighting was going on at some point all the time, so that at no time was there a complete cessation of the roar of artillery or the rattle of musketry.

Two or three times General Hurlbut came riding along our line; and once, during a lull, General Grant and staff came slowly riding by, the General with a cigar in his mouth, and apparently as cool and unconcerned as if inspection was the sole purpose of visiting us. The General's apparent indifference had, undoubtedly, a good influence on the men. They saw him undisturbed, and felt assured that the worst was over, and the attack had spent its force. This must have been soon after he reached the field; for, upon hearing the roar of battle in the morning at Savannah he went aboard a steamer, came up the river eight or nine miles, and did not reach the scene of action much, if any, before 10 o'clock. By that time, Sherman, McClernand and Prentiss had been driven more than a mile beyond their camps, and with such of their command as they could hold together had formed on the flanks of the two reserve divisions of Hurlbut and W. H. L. Wallace, who had moved forward beyond their own camps to meet them.

While General Johnston and his adjutants were reorganizing their command after their first great triumph, to complete the conquest so well begun, Grant and his generals were attempting to organize resistance out of defeat, to establish their lines, to connect the divisions with each other, and improve the situation of the different commands by seizing the most favorable ground. Sherman and McClernand, with what remained of their divisions, were on the extreme right; W. H. L. Wallace, whose division had not yet come into action, on their left, and on the left center of our army; Prentiss on his left. Then came Hurlbut; then a small force under Stuart, on the extreme left of our line.

Fortunately for us, General Johnston's plan was to attack our left. If, when he was ready to renew the battle, he had assailed our right, where were Sherman's and McClernand's divisions, who had already done almost as much as flesh and blood could stand, nothing would have stopped him, and by two o'clock we should have been where we were at dark—that is, huddled about the landing. Then there would have been nothing to do but to surrender. Happily, most happily, when he renewed the assaults upon our lines, it was upon those portions manned by reserve divisions, troops that had not been seriously engaged, and had had time to steady their nerves, and to select favorable positions.

As for myself and comrades, we had become accustomed to the situation somewhat. The lull in the fighting in our immediate vicinity, and the reports which reached us that matters were now progressing favorably on the rest of the field, reassured us. We were becoming quite easy in mind. I had always made it a rule to keep a supply of sugar and some hard tack in my haversack, ready for an emergency. It stood me in good stead just then, for I alone had something besides fighting for lunch. I nibbled my hard tack, and ate my sugar with comfort and satisfaction, for I don't believe three men of our regiment were hurt by this artillery fire upon us, which had been kept up with more or less fury for two or three hours.

One of the little episodes of the battle happened about this time. We noticed that a Confederate, seated on one of the abandoned cannon I have mentioned, was leisurely taking an observation. He was out of range of our guns, but our First Lieutenant got a rifle from a man who happened to have one, took deliberate aim, and Johnny Reb tumbled.

But soon after noon the Confederate forces were ready to hurl themselves on our lines. There had been more or less fighting on our right all the time, but now Johnston had collected his troops and massed them in front of the Union army's left. Language is inadequate to give an idea of the situation. Cannon and musketry roared and rattled, not in volleys, but in one continual din. Charge after charge was made upon the Union lines, and every time repulsed. By concentrating the main body of his troops on our left, General Johnston was superior there to us in numbers, and there was no one upon whom we could call for help. General Lew Wallace had not taken the precaution to learn the roads between his division at Crump's Landing and the main body, and he and his 7,000 men were lost in the woods, instead of being where they could support us in this our dire extremity. The left wing of our brigade was the Hornet's Nest, mentioned in the Southern accounts of the battle. On the immediate right of my regiment was timber with growth of underbrush, and the dreadful conflict set the woods on fire, burning the dead and the wounded who could not crawl away. At one point not burned over, I noticed, after the battle, a strip of low underbrush which had evidently been the scene of a most desperate contest. Large patches of brush had been cut off by bullets at about as high as a man's waist, as if mowed with a scythe, and I could not find in the whole thicket a bush which had not at some part of it been touched by a ball. Of course, human beings could not exist in such a scene, save by closely hugging the ground, or screening themselves behind trees.

Hour after hour passed. Time and again the Confederate hordes threw themselves on our lines, and were repulsed; but our ranks were becoming dangerously thinned. If a few thousand troops could have been brought from Lew Wallace's division to our sorely-tried left the battle would have been won. His failure to reach us was fatal.

Yet, during all this terrible ordeal through which our comrades on the immediate right and the left of us were passing, we were left undisturbed until about two o'clock. Then there came from the woods on the other side of the field, to the edge of it, and then came trotting across it, as fine looking a body of men as I ever expect to see under arms. They came with their guns at what soldiers call right shoulder shift. Lying on the ground there, with the rails of the fence thrown down in front of us, we beheld them, as they started in beautiful line; then increasing their speed as they neared our side of the field, they came on till they reached the range of our smooth bore guns, loaded with buck and ball. Then we rose with a volley right in their faces. Of course, the smoke then entirely obscured the vision, but with eager, bloodthirsty energy, we loaded and fired our muskets at the top of our speed, aiming low, until, from not noticing any return fire, the word passed along from man to man to stop firing. As the smoke rose so that we could see over the field, that splendid body of men presented to my eyes more the appearance of a wind-row of hay than anything else. They seemed to be piled up on each other in a long row across the field. Probably the obscurity caused by the smoke, as well as the slight slope of the ground towards us, accounted for this piled up appearance, for it was something which could not possibly occur. But the slaughter had been fearful. Here and there you could see a squad of men running off out of range; now and then a man lying down, probably wounded or stunned, would rise and try to run, soon to tumble from the shots we sent after him. After the action I went all over the field of battle, visiting every part of it; but in no place was there anything like the number of dead upon the same space of ground as here in this little field. Our old fashioned guns, loaded as they were, and at such close quarters, had done fearful execution. This is undoubtedly the same field General Grant speaks of in the Century article, but he is mistaken when he speaks of the dead being from both sides. There were no Union dead in that field.

Our casualties were small. In our little set of college boys only one, was hurt; he receiving a wound in the leg, which caused its amputation. The bayonet of my gun was shot off, but possibly that was done by some man behind me, firing just as I threw the muzzle of my gun into his way. I didn't notice it until, in loading my gun, I struck my hand against the jagged end of the broken piece.

The Confederates had all they wanted of charging across the field, and let us alone. But just to our left General Johnston had personally organized and started a heavy assaulting column. Overwhelmed by numbers, the Forty-first and Thirty-second Illinois gave way from the position they had so tenaciously held, but one of their last shots mortally wounded the Confederate general. The gallant Lieutenant-Colonel of the Forty-first, whom we had cheered as we moved out in the morning, was killed, and his regiment, broken and cut to pieces, did not renew the fight. Making that break in our line, after four or five hours of as hard fighting as ever occurred on this continent, was the turning point of the day. American had met American in fair, stand-up fight, and our side was beaten, because we could not reinforce the point which was assailed by the concentrated forces of the enemy.

Of course, the giving way on our left necessitated our abandoning the side of the field from whence we had annihilated an assaulting column. We moved back a short distance in the woods, and a crowd of our enemies promptly occupied the position we had left. Then began the first real, prolonged fighting experienced by our regiment that day. Our success in crushing the first attack had exhilarated us. We had tasted blood and were thoroughly aroused. Screening ourselves behind every log and tree, all broken into squads, the enemy broken up likewise, we gave back shot for shot and yell for yell. The very madness of bloodthirstiness possessed us. To kill, to exterminate the beings in front of us was our whole desire. Such energy and force was too much for our enemies, and ere long we saw squads of them rising from the ground and running away. Again there was no foe in our front. Ammunition was getting short, but happily a wagon came up with cartridges, and we took advantage of the lull to fill our boxes. We had not yet lost many men and were full of fight.

This contest exploded all my notions derived from histories and pictures, of the way men stand up in the presence of the enemy. Unless in making an assault or moving forward, both sides hugged the ground as closely as they possibly could and still handle their guns. I doubt if a human being could have existed three minutes, if standing erect in open ground under such a fire as we here experienced. As for myself, at the beginning I jumped behind a little sapling not more than six inches in diameter, and instantly about six men ranged themselves behind me, one behind the other. I thought they would certainly shoot my ears off, and I would be in luck if the side of my head didn't go. The reports of their guns were deafening. A savage remonstrance was unheeded. I was behind a sapling and proposed to stay there. They were behind me and proposed to stay there.

The sapling did me a good turn, small as it was. It caught some Rebel bullets, as I ascertained for a certainty afterwards. I fancied at the time that I heard the spat of the bullets as they struck.

Here my particular chum was wounded by a spent ball, and crawled off the field. I can see him yet, writhing at my feet, grasping the leaves and sticks in the horrible pain which the blow from a spent ball inflicts. A bullet struck the top of the forehead of the wit of the company, plowing along the skull without breaking it. His dazed expression, as he turned instinctively to crawl to the rear, was so comical as to cause a laugh even there.

The lull caused by the death of General Johnston did not last long, and again on our left flank great masses of the enemy appeared, and we had to fall back two or three hundred yards.

Then began another fight. But this time the odds were overwhelmingly against us. At it we went, but in front and quartering on the left thick masses of the enemy slowly but steadily advanced upon us. This time it was a log I got behind, kneeling, loading and firing into the dense ranks of the enemy advancing right in front, eager to kill, kill! I lost thought of companions, until a ball struck me fair in the side, just under the arm, knocking me over. I felt it go clear through my body, struggled on the ground with the effect of the blow for an instant, recovered myself, sprang to my feet, saw I was alone, my comrades already on the run, the enemy close in on the left as well as front—saw it all at a glance, felt I was mortally wounded, and—took to my heels. Run! such time was never made before; overhauled my companions in no time; passed them; began to wonder that a man shot through the body could run so fast, and to suspect that perhaps I was not mortally wounded after all; felt for the hole the ball had made, found it in the blouse and shirt, bad bruise on the ribs, nothing more—spent ball; never relaxed my speed; saw everything around—see it yet. I see the enemy close in on the flank, pouring in their fire at short range. I see our men running for their lives, men every instant tumbling forward limp on their faces, men falling wounded and rolling on the ground, the falling bullets raising little puffs of dust on apparently every foot of ground, a bullet through my hair, a bullet through my trousers. I hear the cruel iz, iz, of the minie balls everywhere. Ahead I see artillery galloping for the landing, and crowds of men running with almost equal speed, and all in the same direction. I even see the purple tinge given by the setting sun to the dust and smoke of battle. I see unutterable defeat, the success of the rebellion, a great catastrophe, a moral and physical cataclysm.

No doubt, in less time than it takes to recall these impressions, we ran out of this horrible gauntlet—a party who shall be nameless still in the lead of the regiment.

Before getting out of it we crossed our camp ground, and here one of our college set, the captain of the company fell, with several holes through his body, while two others of our set were wounded. In that short race at least one-third of our little command were stricken down.

Immediately behind us the Confederates closed in, and the brave General Prentiss and the gallant remains of his command were cut off and surrendered. As we passed out of range of the enemy's fire we mingled with the masses of troops skurrying towards the landing, all semblance of organization lost. It was a great crowd of beaten troops. Pell-mell we rushed towards the landing. As we approached it we saw a row of siege guns, manned and ready for action, while a dense mass of unorganized infantry were rallied to their support. No doubt they were men from every regiment on the field, rallied by brave officers for the last and final stand.

We passed them—or, at least, I did. As I reached the top of the bluff I saw, marching up, in well dressed lines, the advance of General Nelson's division of Buell's army, then being ferried across the river. They moved up the bluff and took part in repulsing the last, rather feeble assault made at dark by a small portion of the enemy, though the main defense was made by brave men collected from every quarter of the field, determined to fight to the last.

As for myself, I was alone in the crowd. My regiment was thoroughly scattered. I was considerably hurt and demoralized, and didn't take a hand in the last repulse of the enemy. Darkness came on, and then, for the first time since morning, the horrid din of fire-arms ceased. An examination showed that the ball, though it had hit me fair on the rib, was so far spent that it only made a bad bruise and respiration painful. A requisition on the sugar and hard tack followed, and then, as I happened to be near an old house filled with wounded, most of the night was spent in carrying them water.

Every fifteen minutes the horizon was lighted up by the flash of a great gun from one of our gunboats, as it sent a shell over towards the Confederate bivouacs in the woods. General Lew Wallace's division at last reached the battle field, and was placed by General

Grant on the right, preparatory to renewing the fight in the morning. All night long the fresh divisions of Buell's army were being ferried across the river, and placed in position. A light rain came on, putting out the fires kindled by the battle.

The next morning the contest was begun by Wallace's division of Buell's army. The remnants of Grant's army that had any fight left in them, slowly collected together on the right.

My own regiment, when I found its colors, had as many men together, probably, as any in Hurlbut's division, but there could not have been more than one hundred and fifty. It was the same, I suspect, with every regiment that had been hotly engaged. The men were thoroughly scattered. Soldiers of pluck joined us who could not find their own command, and no doubt some of ours joined other regiments.

When our general was again about to lead our division to the front, I was only too glad to avail myself of permission to join a body of men to support a battery in reserve. Badly bruised, sore and worn out, I sat or lay on the ground near the guns, while Monday's battle progressed, the sound of it getting farther and farther away. About two o'clock we saw the cavalry moving to the front, and knew the enemy had retreated.

That night, as we collected on our old camp ground, what eager inquiries were made! With what welcome did we greet each new arrival; how excitedly the events of the last two days were discussed! We found that from the fourteen in our tent, one was killed, one mortally wounded, and seven others more or less severely wounded, only five escaping unhurt. This proportion, of course, was very unusual. The regiment itself, which had not lost many in the first two fights we made, was still, on account of the disastrous retreat under a flank fire, one of the heaviest losers, in proportion to the numbers engaged, in the whole army.

The feeling in the army after the battle was very bitter. All felt that even a few hours' notice of the impending attack, spent in preparation to receive it, would have been ample to have enabled us to give the Confederates such a reception as Beauregard feared and expected, and to have defeated them. It was long before General Grant regained the confidence of the army and country that he lost that day. He and Sherman here learned a lesson that they never forgot, but they learned it at fearful cost to the country and to us.

It has been many times claimed that Buell's opportune arrival Sunday night saved Grant and his army from annihilation on Monday. This is probably correct. Still, it is possible, that without this aid, the arrival on the ground of Lew Wallace's fresh and strong division, to aid the thousands of brave men determined to fight to the last, would have resulted in the repulse of an enemy which had suffered so severely on Sunday.

But I have long been inclined to agree with these Southerners, who contend, that if the gallant Johnston had not been killed so early in the afternoon, our defeat would have been accomplished long enough before dark, to have rendered our reinforcements useless.

One word more, as to the numbers of the armies engaged on Sunday. A careful comparison of the returns will show that at the beginning the two armies were about equally matched in numbers; but by the time our stampeded men had got out of the way, and the two reserve divisions were in line with the remnants of the three other divisions, the preponderance was largely with the Confederates. They could choose their own point of attack, and we had no reserve with which to strengthen a shattered line.

The literature of the battle is quite extensive. The Count of Paris gives in his history the best preliminary description; but as a whole, and making reasonable allowances, the best account yet written is contained in the life of Albert Sidney Johnston, by his son. The account by General Force, contained in the Scribner series of "Campaigns of the Civil War," is good.

But no study of the battle can be complete without the aid of General Buell's articles in the Century Magazine, and the maps of the field, which he has so carefully prepared.

What were the results of this first great battle of the war? Its influence upon the gigantic contest which was to be waged for three years longer was probably not great. It was too near a drawn battle. But if it was necessary to demonstrate to the world and to ourselves the courage of our people, that generations of peace and peaceful pursuits had not one whit lessened the force or the enthusiasm of the race that peopled this Western Continent, then here was demonstration the most positive.

The people of the South for the first time realized the nature of the conflict they had provoked. Until this campaign, the great mass of the Southerners could not be made to believe that the students and farmers and mechanics and merchants of the North loved their country and its institutions more than they loved the gains of peace; nay, more than they loved their lives. They saw here an army of young men representing their kindred of the North, fighting, not for their own homes and firesides, but for the perpetuity of the Nation, with a courage and pertinacity which showed that this generation was resolved to transmit what it had received from the fathers of the country. They saw this army attacked at every disadvantage, rally at the call of a chief worthy of it, and who was a type of its character and its lofty motives, and then bravely endure a storm unparalleled on this continent.

The thousands of youthful dead left on that bloody battlefield demonstrated that we have a country and a race worthy to take the lead in the march of human advancement.

Warren Olney.

Abraham Lincoln raising a flag at Independence Hall, Philadelphia, in honor of the admission of Kansas to the Union on Washington's Birthday, February 22, 1861

*Scene on the dock at the Rip Raps. Testing the Sawyer gun and projectile,
a shell bursting on the rebel batteries at Sewell's Point*

Bull Run, Ruins of Mrs. Judith Henry's house

C. W. Reed illustration of Union soldier

The Battle of New Orleans

Soldier seated on crate containing hard tack. Box says "50 lbs. net.
Army Bread from the Union Mechanic Baking Company, 45 Leonard St."

Andersonville Military Prison Series
"Nine sleeping under two gun blanket"

100th Pennsylvania Regiment at Falmouth, Virginia

Confederate prisoners captured at the battle of Fisher's Hill, Virginia.
Sent to the rear under guard of Union troops

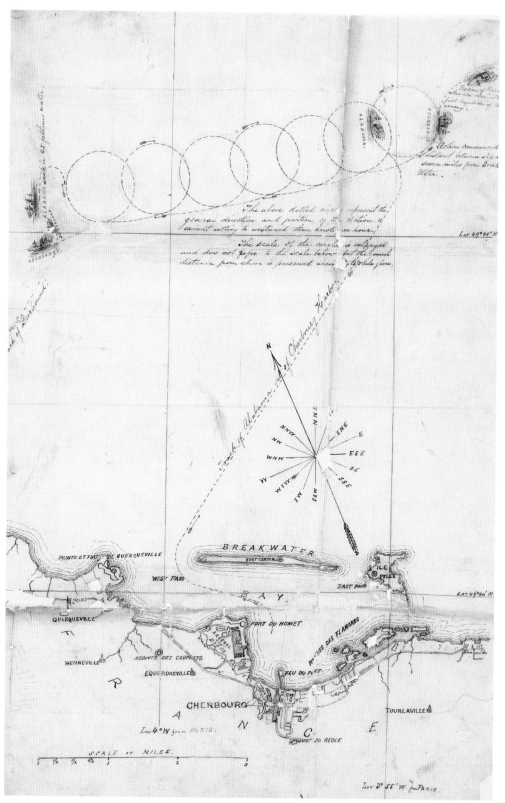

Blockade Runner map

Sullivan's Island, South Carolina, Wreck of blockade-runner near the shore

Blockade runner TEASER off Fort Monroe, Virginia

Photograph from the main eastern theater of the war, Battle of Antietam, September-October 1862. Allan Pinkerton, President Lincoln, and Major General John McClellan at Antietam

THE LITTLE RECRUIT.

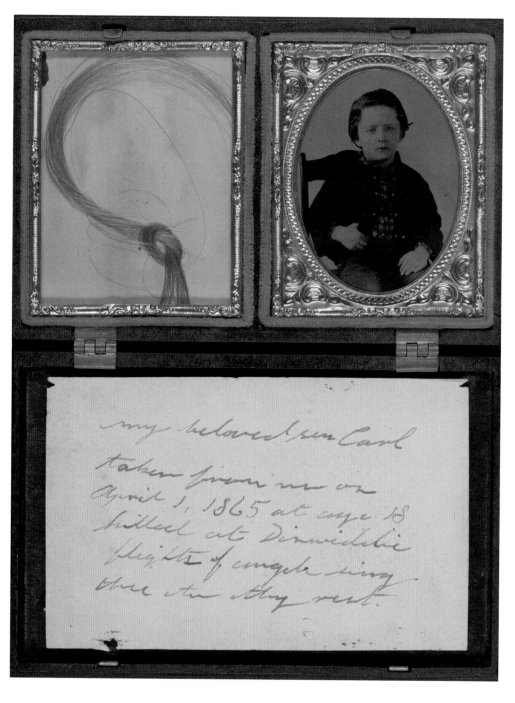

Photo from The Liljenquist Collection, Library of Congress. Photo shows a childhood image of a soldier named Carl. He was killed in combat during the fighting at Dinwiddie Court House (March 31) and Five Forks (April 1), shortly before Lee surrendered at Appomattox Court House on April 9, 1865. Inscription on handwritten note: "My beloved son Carl taken from me on April 1, 1865, at age 18, killed at Dinwiddie. Flights of angels sing thee to thy rest." (Hamlet, Act 5, Scene 2)

Castle Pinkney, Charleston, S.C. Garrison of South Carolina Troops, August 1861.

George A. Custer, Nicolas Bowen, and William G. Jones

DEATH OF GEN. JAMES B. McPHERSON- JULY 22º 1864, ARMY OF THE TENNESSEE ENGAGED.

BAT-TLE

LANTA.

Surrender of General Lee, at Appomattox, April 9th. 1865

Behind The Scenes
By Elizabeth Keckley, Chapters IV - XII

Formerly A Slave, But More Recently Modiste, and Friend to Mrs. Abraham Lincoln or Thirty Years a Slave, and Four Years in the White House

PREFACE

I have often been asked to write my life, as those who know me know that it has been an eventful one. At last I have acceded to the importunities of my friends, and have hastily sketched some of the striking incidents that go to make up my history. My life, so full of romance, may sound like a dream to the matter-of-fact reader, nevertheless everything I have written is strictly true; much has been omitted, but nothing has been exaggerated. In writing as I have done, I am well aware that I have invited criticism; but before the critic judges harshly, let my explanation be carefully read and weighed. If I have portrayed the dark side of slavery, I also have painted the bright side. The good that I have said of human servitude should be thrown into the scales with the evil that I have said of it. I have kind, true-hearted friends in the South as well as in the North, and I would not wound those Southern friends by sweeping condemnation, simply because I was once a slave. They were not so much responsible for the curse under which I was born, as the God of nature and the fathers who framed the Constitution for the United States. The law descended to them, and it was but natural that they should recognize it, since it manifestly was their interest to do so. And yet a wrong was inflicted upon me; a cruel custom deprived me of my liberty, and since I was robbed of my dearest right, I would not have been human had I not rebelled against the robbery. God rules the Universe. I was a feeble instrument in His hands, and through me and the enslaved millions of my race, one of the problems was solved that belongs to the great problem of human destiny; and the solution was developed so gradually that there was no great convulsion[Pg 4] of the harmonies of natural laws. A solemn truth was thrown to the surface, and what is better still, it was recognized as a truth by those who give force to moral laws. An act may be wrong, but unless the ruling power recognizes the wrong, it is useless to hope for a correction of it. Principles may be right, but they are not established within an hour. The masses are slow to reason, and each principle, to acquire moral force, must come to us from the fire of the crucible; the fire may inflict unjust punishment, but then it purifies and renders stronger the principle, not in itself, but in the eyes of those who arrogate judgment to themselves. When the war of the Revolution established the independence of the American colonies, an evil was perpetuated, slavery was more firmly established; and since the evil had been planted, it must pass through certain stages before it could be eradicated. In fact, we give but little thought to the plant of evil until it grows to such monstrous proportions that it overshadows important interests; then the efforts to destroy it become earnest. As one of the victims of slavery I drank of the bitter water; but then, since destiny willed it so, and since I aided in bringing a solemn truth to the surface as a truth, perhaps I have no right to complain. Here, as in all things pertaining to life, I can afford to be charitable.

It may be charged that I have written too freely on some questions, especially in regard to Mrs. Lincoln. I do not think so; at least I have been prompted by the purest motive. Mrs. Lincoln, by her own acts, forced herself into notoriety. She stepped beyond the formal lines which hedge about a private life, and invited public criticism. The people have judged her harshly, and no woman was ever more traduced in the public prints of the country. The people knew nothing of the secret history of her transactions, therefore they judged her by what was thrown to the surface. For an act may be wrong judged purely by itself, but when the motive that prompted the act is understood, it is construed differently. I lay it down as an axiom, that only that is criminal in the sight of God where crime is meditated. Mrs. Lincoln may have been imprudent, but since her intentions were good, she should be judged more kindly than she has been. But the world do not know what her intentions were; they have only been made acquainted with her acts without knowing what feeling guided her actions. If the world are to judge her as I have judged her, they must be introduced to the secret history of her transactions. The veil of mystery must be drawn aside; the origin of a fact must be brought to light with the naked fact itself. If I have betrayed confidence in anything I have published, it has been to place Mrs. Lincoln in a better light before the world. A breach of trust—if breach it can be called—of this kind is always excusable. My own character, as well as the character of Mrs. Lincoln, is at stake, since I have been intimately associated with that lady in the most eventful periods of her life. I have been her confidante, and if evil charges are laid at her door, they also must be laid at mine, since I have been a party to all her movements. To defend myself I must defend the lady that I have served. The world have judged Mrs. Lincoln by the facts which float upon the surface, and through her have partially judged me, and the only way to convince them that wrong was not meditated is to explain the motives that actuated us. I have written nothing that can place Mrs. Lincoln in a worse light before the world than the light in which she now stands, therefore the secret history that I publish can do her no harm. I have excluded everything of a personal character from her letters; the extracts introduced only refer to public men, and are such as to throw light upon her unfortunate adventure in New York. These letters were not written for publication, for which reason they are all the more valuable; they are the frank overflowings of the heart, the outcropping of impulse, the key to genuine motives. They prove the motive to have been pure, and if they shall help to stifle the voice of calumny, I am content. I do not forget, before the public journals vilified Mrs. Lincoln, that ladies who moved in the Washington circle in which she moved, freely canvassed her character among themselves. They gloated over many a tale of scandal that grew out of gossip in their own circle. If these ladies, could say everything bad of the wife of the President, why should I not be permitted to lay her secret history bare, especially when that history plainly shows that her life, like all lives, has its good side as well as its bad side! None of us are[Pg 6] perfect, for which reason we should heed the voice of charity when it whispers in our ears, "Do not magnify the imperfections of others." Had Mrs. Lincoln's acts never become public property, I should not have published to the world the secret chapters of her life. I am not the special champion of the widow of our lamented President; the reader of the pages which follow will discover that I have written with the utmost frankness in regard to her—have exposed her faults as well as given her credit for honest motives. I wish the world to judge her as she is, free from the exaggerations of praise or scandal, since I have been associated with her in so many things that have provoked hostile criticism; and the judgment that the world may pass upon her, I flatter myself, will present my own actions in a better light.

Elizabeth Keckley. 14 Carroll Place, New York, March 14, 1868.

Chapter IV In The Family Of Senator Jefferson Davis

The twelve hundred dollars with which I purchased the freedom of myself and son I consented to accept only as a loan. I went to work in earnest, and in a short time paid every cent that was so kindly advanced by my lady patrons of St. Louis. All this time my husband was a source of trouble to me, and a burden. Too close occupation with my needle had its effects upon my health, and feeling exhausted with work, I determined to make a change. I had a conversation with Mr. Keckley; informed him that since he persisted in dissipation we must separate; that I was going North, and that I should never live with him again, at least until I had good evidence of his reform. He was rapidly debasing himself, and although I was willing to work for him, I was not willing to share his degradation. Poor man; he had his faults, but over these faults death has drawn a veil. My husband is now sleeping in his grave, and in the silent grave I would bury all unpleasant memories of him.

I left St. Louis in the spring of 1860, taking the cars direct for Baltimore, where I stopped six weeks, attempting to realize a sum of money by forming classes of young colored women, and teaching them my system of cutting and fitting dresses. The scheme was not successful, for after six weeks of labor and vexation, I left Baltimore with scarcely money enough to pay my fare to Washington. Arriving in the capital, I sought and obtained work at two dollars and a half per day. However, as I was notified that I could only remain in the city ten days without obtaining a license to do so, such being the law, and as I did not know whom to apply to for assistance, I was sorely troubled. I also had to have some one vouch to the authorities that I was a free woman. My means were too scanty, and my profession too precarious to warrant my purchasing [a] license. In my perplexity I called on a lady for whom I was sewing, Miss Ringold, a member of Gen. Mason's family, from Virginia. I stated my case, and she kindly volunteered to render me all the assistance in her power. She called on Mayor Burritt with me, and Miss Ringold succeeded in making an arrangement for me to remain in Washington without paying the sum required for a license; moreover, I was not to be molested. I rented apartments in a good locality, and soon had a good run of custom. The summer passed, winter came, and I was still in Washington. Mrs. Davis, wife of Senator Jefferson Davis, came from the South in November of

1860, with her husband. Learning that Mrs. Davis wanted a modiste, I presented myself, and was employed by her on the recommendation of one of my patrons and her intimate friend, Mrs. Captain Hetsill. I went to the house to work, but finding that they were such late risers, and as I had to fit many dresses on Mrs. Davis, I told her that I should prefer giving half the day to her, working the other in my own room for some of my other lady patrons. Mrs. D. consented to the proposition, and it was arranged that I should come to her own house every day after 12 m. It was the winter before the breaking out of that fierce and bloody war between the two sections of the country; and as Mr. Davis occupied a leading position, his house was the resort of politicians and statesmen from the South. Almost every night, as I learned from the servants and other members of the family, secret meetings were held at the house; and some of these meetings were protracted to a very late hour. The prospects of war were freely discussed in my presence by Mr. and Mrs. Davis and their friends. The holidays were approaching, and Mrs. Davis kept me busy in manufacturing articles of dress for herself and children. She desired to present Mr. Davis on Christmas with a handsome dressing-gown. The material was purchased, and for weeks the work had been under way. Christmas eve came, and the gown had been laid aside so often that it was still unfinished. I saw that Mrs. D. was anxious to have it completed, so I volunteered to remain and work on it. Wearily the hours dragged on, but there was no rest for my busy fingers. I persevered in my task, notwithstanding my head was aching. Mrs. Davis was busy in the adjoining room, arranging the Christmas tree for the children. I looked at the clock, and the hands pointed to a quarter of twelve. I was arranging the cords on the gown when the Senator came in; he looked somewhat careworn, and his step seemed to be a little nervous. He leaned against the door, and expressed his admiration of the Christmas tree, but there was no smile on his face. Turning round, he saw me sitting in the adjoining room, and quickly exclaimed:

"That you, Lizzie! why are you here so late? Still at work; I hope that Mrs. Davis is not too exacting!"

"No, sir," I answered. "Mrs. Davis was very anxious to have this gown finished to-night, and I volunteered to remain and complete it."

"Well, well, the case must be urgent," and he came slowly towards me, took the gown in his hand, and asked the color of the silk, as he said the gas-light was so deceptive to his old eyes.

"It is a drab changeable silk, Mr. Davis," I answered; and might have added that it was rich and handsome, but did not, well knowing that he would make the discovery in the morning.

He smiled curiously, but turned and walked from the room without another question. He inferred that the gown was for him, that it was to be the Christmas present from his wife, and he did not wish to destroy the pleasure that she would experience in believing that the gift would prove a surprise. In this respect, as in many others, he always appeared to me as a thoughtful, considerate man in the domestic circle. As the clock struck twelve I finished the gown, little dreaming of the future that was before it. It was worn, I have not the shadow of a doubt, by Mr. Davis during the stormy years that he was the President of the Confederate States.

The holidays passed, and before the close of January the war was discussed in Mr. Davis's family as an event certain to happen in the future. Mrs. Davis was warmly attached to Washington, and I often heard her say that she disliked the idea of breaking up old associations, and going South to suffer from trouble and deprivation. One day, while discussing the question in my presence with one of her intimate friends, she exclaimed: "I would rather remain in Washington and be kicked about, than go South and be Mrs. President." Her friend expressed surprise at the remark, and Mrs. Davis insisted that the opinion was an honest one.

While dressing her one day, she said to me: "Lizzie, you are so very handy that I should like to take you South with me."

"When do you go South, Mrs. Davis?" I inquired.

"Oh, I cannot tell just now, but it will be soon. You know there is going to be war, Lizzie?"

"No!"

"But I tell you yes."

"Who will go to war?" I asked.

"The North and South," was her ready reply. "The Southern people will not submit to the humiliating demands of the Abolition party; they will fight first."

"And which do you think will whip?"

"The South, of course. The South is impulsive, is in earnest, and the Southern soldiers will fight to conquer. The North will yield, when it sees the South is in earnest, rather than engage in a long and bloody war."

"But, Mrs. Davis, are you certain that there will be war?"

"Certain!—I know it. You had better go South with me; I will take good care of you. Besides, when the war breaks out, the colored people will suffer in the North. The Northern people will look upon them as the cause of the war, and I fear, in their exasperation, will be inclined to treat you harshly. Then, I may come back to Washington in a few months, and live in the White House. The Southern people talk of choosing Mr. Davis for their President. In fact, it may be considered settled that he will be their President. As soon as we go South and secede from the other States, we will raise an army and march on Washington, and then I shall live in the White House."

I was bewildered with what I heard. I had served Mrs. Davis faithfully, and she had learned to place the greatest confidence in me. At first I was almost tempted to go South with her, for her reasoning seemed plausible. At the time the conversation was closed, with my promise to consider the question.

I thought over the question much, and the more I thought the less inclined I felt to accept the proposition so kindly made by Mrs. Davis. I knew the North to be strong, and believed that the people would fight for the flag that they pretended to venerate so

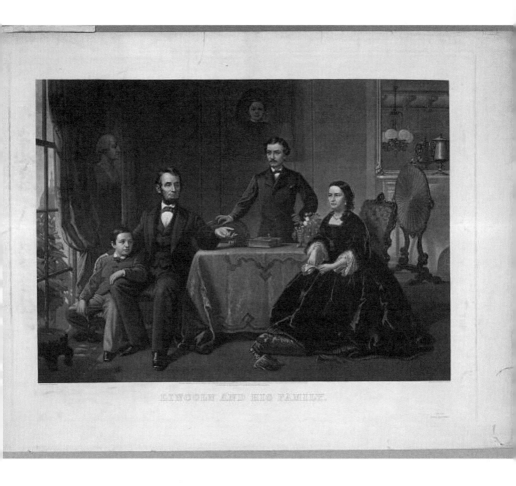

Lincoln and his family

highly. The Republican party had just emerged from a heated campaign, flushed with victory, and I could not think that the hosts composing the party would quietly yield all they had gained in the Presidential canvass. A show of war from the South, I felt, would lead to actual war in the North; and with the two sections bitterly arrayed against each other, I preferred to cast my lot among the people of the North.

I parted with Mrs. Davis kindly, half promising to join her in the South if further deliberation should induce me to change my views. A few weeks before she left Washington I made two chintz wrappers for her. She said that she must give up expensive dressing for a while; and that she, with the Southern people, now that war was imminent, must learn to practise lessons of economy. She left some fine needle-work in my hands, which I finished, and forwarded to her at Montgomery, Alabama, in the month of June, through the assistance of Mrs. Emory, one of her oldest and best friends.

Since bidding them good-by at Washington, early in the year 1860, I have never met any of the Davis family. Years of excitement, years of bloodshed, and hundreds of thousands of graves intervene between the months I spent in the family and now. The years have brought many changes; and in view of these terrible changes even I, who was once a slave, who have been punished with the cruel lash, who have experienced the heart and soul tortures of a slave's life, can say to Mr. Jefferson Davis, "Peace! you have suffered! Go in peace."

In the winter of 1865 I was in Chicago, and one day visited the great charity fair held for the benefit of the families of those soldiers who were killed or wounded during the war. In one part of the building was a wax figure of Jefferson Davis, wearing over his other garments the dress in which it was reported that he was captured. There was always a great crowd around this figure, and I was naturally attracted towards it. I worked my way to the figure, and in examining the dress made the pleasing discovery that it was one of the chintz wrappers that I had made for Mrs. Davis, a short time before she departed from Washington for the South. When it was announced that I recognized the dress as one that I had made for the wife of the late Confederate President there was great cheering and excitement, and I at once became the object of the deepest curiosity. Great crowds followed me, and in order to escape from the embarrassing situation I left the building.

I believe it now is pretty well established that Mr. Davis had on a water-proof cloak instead of a dress, as first reported, when he was captured. This does not invalidate any portion of my story. The dress on the wax figure at the fair in Chicago unquestionably was one of the chintz wrappers that I made for Mrs. Davis in January, 1860, in Washington; and I infer, since it was not found on the body of the fugitive President of the South, it was taken from the trunks of Mrs. Davis, captured at the same time. Be this as it may, the coincidence is none the less striking and curious.

Chapter V My Introduction To Mrs. Lincoln

Ever since arriving in Washington I had a great desire to work for the ladies of the White House, and to accomplish this end I was ready to make almost any sacrifice consistent with propriety. Work came in slowly, and I was beginning to feel very much embarrassed, for I did not know how I was to meet the bills staring me in the face. It is true, the bills were small, but then they were formidable to me, who had little or nothing to pay them with. While in this situation I called at the Ringolds, where I met Mrs. Captain Lee. Mrs. L. was in a state bordering on excitement, as the great event of the season, the dinner-party given in honor of the Prince of Wales, was soon to come off, and she must have a dress suitable for the occasion. The silk had been purchased, but a dress-maker had not yet been found. Miss Ringold recommended me, and I received the order to make the dress. When I called on Mrs. Lee the next day, her husband was in the room, and handing me a roll of bank bills, amounting to one hundred dollars, he requested me to purchase the trimmings, and to spare no expense in making a selection. With the money in my pocket I went out in the street, entered the store of Harper & Mitchell, and asked to look at their laces. Mr. Harper waited on me himself, and was polite and kind. When I asked permission to carry the laces to Mrs. Lee, in order to learn whether she could approve my selection or not, he gave a ready assent. When I reminded him that I was a stranger, and that the goods were valuable, he remarked that he was not afraid to trust me—that he believed my face was the index to an honest heart. It was pleasant to be spoken to thus, and I shall never forget the kind words of Mr. Harper. I often recall them, for they are associated with the dawn of a brighter period in my dark life. I purchased the trimmings, and Mr. Harper allowed me a commission of twenty-five dollars on the purchase. The dress was done in time, and it gave complete satisfaction. Mrs. Lee attracted great attention at the dinner-party, and her elegant dress proved a good card for me. I received numerous orders, and was relieved from all pecuniary embarrassments. One of my patrons was Mrs. Gen. McClean, a daughter of Gen. Sumner. One day when I was very busy, Mrs. McC. drove up to my apartments, came in where I was engaged with my needle, and in her emphatic way said:

"Lizzie, I am invited to dine at Willard's on next Sunday, and positively I have not a dress fit to wear on the occasion. I have just purchased material, and you must commence work on it right away."

"But Mrs. McClean," I replied, "I have more work now promised than I can do. It is impossible for me to make a dress for you to wear on Sunday next."

"Pshaw! Nothing is impossible. I must have the dress made by Sunday;" and she spoke with some impatience.

"I am sorry," I began, but she interrupted me.

"Now don't say no again. I tell you that you must make the dress. I have often heard you say that you would like to work for the ladies of the White House. Well, I have it in my power to obtain you this privilege. I know Mrs. Lincoln well, and you shall make a dress for her provided you finish mine in time to wear at dinner on Sunday."

The inducement was the best that could have been offered. I would undertake the dress if I should have to sit up all night—every night, to make my pledge good. I sent out and employed assistants, and, after much worry and trouble, the dress was completed to the satisfaction of Mrs. McClean. It appears that Mrs. Lincoln had upset a cup of coffee on the dress she designed wearing on the evening of the reception after the inauguration of Abraham Lincoln as President of the United States, which rendered it necessary that she should have a new one for the occasion. On asking Mrs. McClean who her dress-maker was, that lady promptly informed her,

"Lizzie Keckley."

"Lizzie Keckley? The name is familiar to me. She used to work for some of my lady friends in St. Louis, and they spoke well of her. Can you recommend her to me?"

"With confidence. Shall I send her to you?"

"If you please. I shall feel under many obligations for your kindness."

The next Sunday Mrs. McClean sent me a message to call at her house at four o'clock P.M., that day. As she did not state why I was to call, I determined to wait till Monday morning. Monday morning came, and nine o'clock found me at Mrs. McC.'s house. The streets of the capital were thronged with people, for this was Inauguration day. A new President, a man of the people from the broad prairies of the West, was to accept the solemn oath of office, was to assume the responsibilities attached to the high position of Chief Magistrate of the United States. Never was such deep interest felt in the inauguration proceedings as was felt today; for threats of assassination had been made, and every breeze from the South came heavily laden with the rumors of war. Around Willard's hotel swayed an excited crowd, and it was with the utmost difficulty that I worked my way to the house on the opposite side of the street, occupied by the McCleans. Mrs. McClean was out, but presently an aide on General McClean's staff called, and informed me that I was wanted at Willard's. I crossed the street, and on entering the hotel was met by Mrs. McClean, who greeted me:

"Lizzie, why did you not come yesterday, as I requested? Mrs. Lincoln wanted to see you, but I fear that now you are too late."

"I am sorry, Mrs. McClean. You did not say what you wanted with me yesterday, so I judged that this morning would do as well."

"You should have come yesterday," she insisted. "Go up to Mrs. Lincoln's room"—giving me the number—"she may find use for you yet."

With a nervous step I passed on, and knocked at Mrs. Lincoln's door. A cheery voice bade me come in, and a lady, inclined to stoutness, about forty years of age, stood before me.

"You are Lizzie Keckley, I believe."

I bowed assent.

"The dress-maker that Mrs. McClean recommended?"

"Yes, madam."

"Very well; I have not time to talk to you now, but would like to have you call at the White House, at eight o'clock to-morrow morning, where I shall then be."

I bowed myself out of the room, and returned to my apartments. The day passed slowly, for I could not help but speculate in relation to the appointed interview for the morrow. My long-cherished hope was about to be realized, and I could not rest.

Tuesday morning, at eight o'clock, I crossed the threshold of the White House for the first time. I was shown into a waiting-room, and informed that Mrs. Lincoln was at breakfast. In the waiting-room I found no less than three mantua-makers waiting for an interview with the wife of the new President. It seems that Mrs. Lincoln had told several of her lady friends that she had urgent need for a dress-maker, and that each of these friends had sent her mantua-maker to the White House. Hope fell at once. With so many rivals for the position sought after, I regarded my chances for success as extremely doubtful. I was the last one summoned to Mrs. Lincoln's presence. All the others had a hearing, and were dismissed. I went up-stairs timidly, and entering the room with nervous step, discovered the wife of the President standing by a window, looking out, and engaged in lively conversation with a lady, Mrs. Grimsly, as I afterwards learned. Mrs. L. came forward, and greeted me warmly.

"You have come at last. Mrs. Keckley, who have you worked for in the city?"

"Among others, Mrs. Senator Davis has been one of my best patrons," was my reply.

"Mrs. Davis! So you have worked for her, have you? Of course you gave satisfaction; so far, good. Can you do my work?"

"Yes, Mrs. Lincoln. Will you have much work for me to do?"

"That, Mrs. Keckley, will depend altogether upon your prices. I trust that your terms are reasonable. I cannot afford to be extravagant. We are just from the West, and are poor. If[Pg 38] you do not charge too much, I shall be able to give you all my work."

"I do not think there will be any difficulty about charges, Mrs. Lincoln; my terms are reasonable."

"Well, if you will work cheap, you shall have plenty to do. I can't afford to pay big prices, so I frankly tell you so in the beginning."

The terms were satisfactorily arranged, and I measured Mrs. Lincoln, took the dress with me, a bright rose-colored moiré-antique, and returned the next day to fit it on her. A number of ladies were in the room, all making preparations for the levee to come off on Friday night. These ladies, I learned, were relatives of Mrs. L.'s, Mrs. Edwards and Mrs. Kellogg, her own sisters, and Elizabeth Edwards and Julia Baker, her nieces. Mrs. Lincoln this morning was dressed in a cashmere wrapper, quilted down the front; and she wore a simple head-dress. The other ladies wore morning robes.

I was hard at work on the dress, when I was informed that the levee had been postponed from Friday night till Tuesday night. This, of course, gave me more time to complete my task. Mrs. Lincoln sent for me, and suggested some alteration in style, which was made. She also requested that I make a waist of blue watered silk for Mrs. Grimsly, as work on the dress would not require all my time.

Tuesday evening came, and I had taken the last stitches on the dress. I folded it and carried it to the White House, with the waist for Mrs. Grimsly. When I went up-stairs, I found the ladies in a terrible state of excitement. Mrs. Lincoln was protesting that she could not go down, for the reason that she had nothing to wear.

"Mrs. Keckley, you have disappointed me—deceived me. Why do you bring my dress at this late hour?"

"Because I have just finished it, and I thought I should be in time."

"But you are not in time, Mrs. Keckley; you have bitterly disappointed me. I have no time now to dress, and, what is more, I will not dress, and go down-stairs."

"I am sorry if I have disappointed you, Mrs. Lincoln, for I in[Pg 39]tended to be in time. Will you let me dress you? I can have you ready in a few minutes."

"No, I won't be dressed. I will stay in my room. Mr. Lincoln can go down with the other ladies."

"But there is plenty of time for you to dress, Mary," joined in Mrs. Grimsly and Mrs. Edwards. "Let Mrs. Keckley assist you, and she will soon have you ready."

Thus urged, she consented. I dressed her hair, and arranged the dress on her. It fitted nicely, and she was pleased. Mr. Lincoln came in, threw himself on the sofa, laughed with Willie and little Tad, and then commenced pulling on his gloves, quoting poetry all the while.

"You seem to be in a poetical mood to-night," said his wife.

"Yes, mother, these are poetical times," was his pleasant reply. "I declare, you look charming in that dress. Mrs. Keckley has met with great success." And then he proceeded to compliment the other ladies.

Mrs. Lincoln looked elegant in her rose-colored moiré-antique. She wore a pearl necklace, pearl ear-rings, pearl bracelets, and red roses in her hair. Mrs. Baker was dressed in lemon-colored silk; Mrs. Kellogg in a drab silk, ashes of rose; Mrs. Edwards in a brown and black silk; Miss Edwards in crimson, and Mrs. Grimsly in blue watered silk. Just before starting downstairs, Mrs. Lincoln's lace handkerchief was the object of search. It had been displaced by Tad, who was mischievous, and hard to restrain. The handkerchief found, all became serene. Mrs. Lincoln took the President's arm, and with smiling face led the train below. I was surprised at her grace and composure. I had heard so much, in current and malicious report, of her low life, of her ignorance and vulgarity, that I expected to see her embarrassed on this occasion. Report, I soon saw, was wrong. No queen, accustomed to the usages of royalty all her life, could have comported herself with more calmness and dignity than did the wife of the President. She was confident and self-possessed, and confidence always gives grace.

This levee was a brilliant one, and the only one of the season. I became the regular modiste of Mrs. Lincoln. I made fifteen or sixteen dresses for her during the spring and early part of the summer, when she left Washington; spending the hot weather at Saratoga, Long Branch, and other places. In the mean time I was employed by Mrs. Senator Douglas, one of the loveliest ladies that I ever met, Mrs. Secretary Wells, Mrs. Secretary Stanton, and others. Mrs. Douglas always dressed in deep mourning, with excellent taste, and several of the leading ladies of Washington society were extremely jealous of her superior attractions.

Willie Lincoln's Death-Bed

Mrs. Lincoln returned to Washington in November, and again duty called me to the White House. The war was now in progress, and every day brought stirring news from the front—the front, where the Gray opposed the Blue, where flashed the bright sabre in the sunshine, where were heard the angry notes of battle, the deep roar of cannon, and the fearful rattle of musketry; where new graves were being made every day, where brother forgot a mother's early blessing and sought the lifeblood of brother, and friend raised the deadly knife against friend. Oh, the front, with its stirring battle-scenes! Oh, the front, with its ghastly heaps of dead! The life of the nation was at stake; and when the land was full of sorrow, there could not be much gayety at the capital. The days passed quietly with me. I soon learned that some people had an intense desire to penetrate the inner circle of the White House. No President and his family, heretofore occupying this mansion, ever excited so much curiosity as the present incumbents. Mr. Lincoln had grown up in the wilds of the West, and evil report had said much of him and his wife. The polite world was shocked, and the tendency to exaggerate intensified curiosity. As soon as it was known that I was the modiste of Mrs. Lincoln, parties crowded around and affected friendship for me, hoping to induce me to betray the secrets of the domestic circle. One day a woman, I will not call her a lady, drove up to my rooms, gave me an order to make a dress, and insisted on partly paying me in advance. She called on me every day, and was exceedingly kind. When she came to take her dress away, she cautiously remarked:

"Mrs. Keckley, you know Mrs. Lincoln?"

"Yes."

"You are her modiste; are you not?"

"Yes."

"You know her very well; do you not?"

"I am with her every day or two."

"Don't you think you would have some influence with her?"

"I cannot say. Mrs. Lincoln, I presume, would listen to anything I should suggest, but whether she would be influenced by a suggestion of mine is another question."

"I am sure that you could influence her, Mrs. Keckley. Now listen; I have a proposition to make. I have a great desire to become an inmate of the White House. I have heard so much of Mr. Lincoln's goodness that I should like to be near him; and if I can enter the White House no other way, I am willing to go as a menial. My dear Mrs. Keckley, will you not recommend me to Mrs. Lincoln as a friend of yours out of employment, and ask her to take me as a chambermaid? If you will do this you shall be well rewarded. It may be worth several thousand dollars to you in time."

I looked at the woman in amazement. A bribe, and to betray the confidence of my employer! Turning to her with a glance of scorn, I said:

"Madam, you are mistaken in regard to my character. Sooner than betray the trust of a friend, I would throw myself into the Potomac river. I am not so base as that. Pardon me, but there is the door, and I trust that you will never enter my room again."

She sprang to her feet in deep confusion, and passed through the door, murmuring: "Very well; you will live to regret your action today."

"Never, never!" I exclaimed, and closed the door after her with a bang. I afterwards learned that this woman was an actress, and that her object was to enter the White House as a servant, learn its secrets, and then publish a scandal to the world. I do not give her name, for such publicity would wound the sensitive feelings of friends, who would have to share her disgrace, without being responsible for her faults. I simply record the incident to show how I often was approached by unprincipled parties. It is unnecessary to say that I indignantly refused every bribe offered.

The first public appearance of Mrs. Lincoln that winter was at the reception on New Year's Day. This reception was shortly followed by a brilliant levee. The day after the levee I went to the White House, and while fitting a dress to Mrs. Lincoln, she said:

"Lizabeth"—she had learned to drop the E Lizabeth, I have an idea. These are war times, and we must be as economical as possible. You know the President is expected to give a series of state dinners every winter, and these dinners are very costly; Now I want to avoid this expense; and my idea is, that if I give three large receptions, the state dinners can be scratched from the programme. What do you think, Lizabeth?"

"I think that you are right, Mrs. Lincoln."

"I am glad to hear you say so. If I can make Mr. Lincoln take the same view of the case, I shall not fail to put the idea into practice."

Before I left her room that day, Mr. Lincoln came in. She at once stated the case to him. He pondered the question a few moments before answering.

"Mother, I am afraid your plan will not work."

"But it will work, if you will only determine that it shall work."

"It is breaking in on the regular custom," he mildly replied.

"But you forget, father, these are war times, and old customs can be done away with for the once. The idea is economical, you must admit."

"Yes, mother, but we must think of something besides economy."

"I do think of something else. Public receptions are more democratic than stupid state dinners—are more in keeping with the spirit of the institutions of our country, as you would say if called upon to make a stump speech. There are a great many strangers in the city, foreigners and others, whom we can entertain at our receptions, but whom we cannot invite to our dinners."

"I believe you are right, mother. You argue the point well. I think that we shall have to decide on the receptions."

So the day was carried. The question was decided, and arrangements were made for the first reception. It now was January, and cards were issued for February.

The children, Tad and Willie, were constantly receiving presents. Willie was so delighted with a little pony, that he insisted on riding it every day. The weather was changeable, and exposure resulted in a severe cold, which deepened into fever. He was very sick, and I was summoned to his bedside. It was sad to see the poor boy suffer. Always of a delicate constitution, he could not resist the strong inroads of disease. The days dragged wearily by, and he grew weaker and more shadow-like. He was his mother's favorite child, and she doted on him. It grieved her heart sorely to see him suffer. When able to be about, he was almost constantly by her side. When I would go in her room, almost always I found blue-eyed Willie there, reading from an open book, or curled up in a chair with pencil and paper in hand. He had decidedly a literary taste, and was a studious boy. A short time before his death he wrote this simple little poem:

"WASHINGTON, D. C., October 30, 1861.

DEAR SIR: I enclose you my first attempt at poetry.

"Yours truly,

"WM. W. LINCOLN.

"To the Editor of the National Republican."

LINES ON THE DEATH OF COLONEL EDWARD BAKER. THERE was no patriot like Baker, So noble and so true; He fell as a soldier on the field, His face to the sky of blue. His voice is silent in the hall Which oft his presence graced; No more he'll hear the loud acclaim Which rang from place to place. No squeamish notions filled his breast, The Union was his theme; "No surrender and no compromise," His day-thought and night's dream. His Country has her part to pay To'rds those he has left behind; His widow and his children all, She must always keep in mind.

Finding that Willie continued to grow worse, Mrs. Lincoln determined to withdraw her cards of invitation and postpone the reception. Mr. Lincoln thought that the cards had better not be withdrawn. At least he advised that the doctor be consulted before any steps were taken. Accordingly Dr. Stone was called in. He pronounced Willie better, and said that there was every reason for an early recovery. He thought, since the invitations had been issued, it would be best to go on with the reception. Willie, he insisted, was in no immediate danger. Mrs. Lincoln was guided by these counsels, and no postponement was announced. On the evening of the reception Willie was suddenly taken worse. His mother sat by his bedside a long while, holding his feverish hand in her own, and watching his labored breathing. The doctor claimed there was no cause for alarm. I arranged Mrs. Lincoln's hair, then assisted her to dress. Her dress was white satin, trimmed with black lace. The trail was very long, and as she swept through the room, Mr. Lincoln was standing with his back to the fire, his hands behind him, and his eyes on the carpet. His face wore a thoughtful, solemn look. The rustling of the satin dress attracted his attention. He looked at it a few moments; then, in his quaint, quiet way remarked—

"Whew! our cat has a long tail to-night."

Mrs. Lincoln did not reply. The President added:

"Mother, it is my opinion, if some of that tail was nearer the head, it would be in better style;" and he glanced at her bare arms and neck. She had a beautiful neck and arm, and low dresses were becoming to her. She turned away with a look of offended dignity, and presently took the President's arm, and both went down-stairs to their guests, leaving me alone with the sick boy.

The reception was a large and brilliant one, and the rich notes of the Marine Band in the apartments below came to the sick-room in soft, subdued murmurs, like the wild, faint sobbing of far-off spirits. Some of the young people had suggested dancing, but Mr. Lincoln met the suggestion with an emphatic veto. The brilliance of the scene could not dispel the sadness that rested upon the face of Mrs. Lincoln. During the evening she came upstairs several times, and stood by the bedside of the suffering boy. She loved him with a mother's heart, and her anxiety was great. The night passed slowly; morning came, and Willie was worse. He lingered a few days, and died. God called the beautiful spirit home, and the house of joy was turned into the house of mourning. I was worn out with watching, and was not in the room when Willie died, but was immediately sent for. I assisted in washing him and dressing him, and then laid him on the bed, when Mr. Lincoln came in. I never saw a man so bowed down with grief. He came to the bed, lifted the cover from the face of his child, gazed at it long and earnestly, murmuring, "My poor boy, he was too good for this earth. God has called him home. I know that he is much better off in heaven, but then we loved him so. It is hard, hard to have him die!"

Great sobs choked his utterance. He buried his head in his hands, and his tall frame was convulsed with emotion. I stood at the foot of the bed, my eyes full of tears, looking at the man in silent, awe-stricken wonder. His grief unnerved him, and made him a weak, passive child. I did not dream that his rugged nature could be so moved. I shall never forget those solemn moments—genius and greatness weeping over love's idol lost. There is a grandeur as well as a simplicity about the picture that will never fade. With me it is immortal—I really believe that I shall carry it with me across the dark, mysterious river of death.

Mrs. Lincoln's grief was inconsolable. The pale face of her dead boy threw her into convulsions. Around him love's tendrils had been twined, and now that he was dressed for the tomb, it was like tearing the tendrils out of the heart by their roots. Willie, she often said, if spared by Providence, would be the hope and stay of her old age. But Providence had not spared him. The light faded from his eyes, and the death-dew had gathered on his brow.

In one of her paroxysms of grief the President kindly bent over his wife, took her by the arm, and gently led her to the window. With a stately, solemn gesture, he pointed to the lunatic asylum.

"Mother, do you see that large white building on the hill yonder? Try and control your grief, or it will drive you mad, and we may have to send you there."

Mrs. Lincoln was so completely overwhelmed with sorrow that she did not attend the funeral. Willie was laid to rest in the cemetery, and the White House was draped in mourning. Black crape everywhere met the eye, contrasting strangely with the gay and brilliant colors of a few days before. Party dresses were laid aside, and every one who crossed the threshold of the Presidential mansion spoke in subdued tones when they thought of the sweet boy at rest—

"Under the sod and the dew."

Previous to this I had lost my son. Leaving Wilberforce, he went to the battle-field with the three months troops, and was killed in Missouri—found his grave on the battle-field where the gallant General Lyon fell. It was a sad blow to me, and the kind womanly letter that Mrs. Lincoln wrote to me when she heard of my bereavement was full of golden words of comfort.

Nathaniel Parker Willis, the genial poet, now sleeping in his grave, wrote this beautiful sketch of Willie Lincoln, after the sad death of the bright-eyed boy:

"This little fellow had his acquaintances among his father's friends, and I chanced to be one of them. He never failed to seek me out in the crowd, shake hands, and make some pleasant remark; and this, in a boy of ten years of age, was, to say the least, endearing to a stranger. But he had more than mere affectionateness. His self-possession—aplomb, as the French call it—was extraordinary. I was one day passing the White House, when he was outside with a play-fellow on the side-walk. Mr. Seward drove in, with Prince Napoleon and two of his suite in the carriage; and, in a mock-heroic way—terms of intimacy evidently existing between the boy and the Secretary—the official gentleman took off his hat, and the Napoleon did the same, all making the young Prince President a ceremonious salute. Not a bit staggered with the homage, Willie drew himself up to his full height, took off his little cap with graceful self-possession, and bowed down formally to the ground, like a little ambassador. They drove past, and he went on unconcernedly with his play: the impromptu readiness and good judgment being clearly a part of his nature. His genial and open expression of countenance was none the less ingenuous and fearless for a certain tincture of fun; and it was in this mingling of qualities that he so faithfully resembled his father.

"With all the splendor that was around this little fellow in his new home, he was so bravely and beautifully himself—and that only. A wild flower transplanted from the prairie to the hot-house, he retained his prairie habits, unalterably pure and simple, till he died. His leading trait seemed to be a fearless and kindly frankness, willing that everything should be as different as it pleased, but resting unmoved in his own conscious single-heartedness. I found I was studying him irresistibly, as one of the sweet problems of childhood that the world is blessed with in rare places; and the news of his death (I was absent from Washington, on a visit to my own children, at the time) came to me like a knell heard unexpectedly at a merry-making.

"On the day of the funeral I went before the hour, to take a near farewell look at the dear boy; for they had embalmed him to send home to the West—to sleep under the sod of his own valley—and the coffin-lid was to be closed before the service. The family had just taken their leave of him, and the servants and nurses were seeing him for the last time—and with tears and sobs wholly unrestrained, for he was loved like an idol by every one of them. He lay with eyes closed—his brown hair parted as we had known it—pale in the slumber of death; but otherwise unchanged, for he was dressed as if for the evening, and held in one of his hands, crossed upon his breast, a bunch of exquisite flowers—a message coming from his mother, while we were looking upon him, that those flowers might be preserved for her. She was lying sick in her bed, worn out with grief and over-watching.

"The funeral was very touching. Of the entertainments in the East Room the boy had been—for those who now assembled more especially—a most life-giving variation. With his bright face, and his apt greetings and replies, he was remembered in every part of that crimson-curtained hall, built only for pleasure—of all the crowds, each night, certainly the one least likely to be death's first mark. He was his father's favorite. They were intimates—often seen hand in hand. And there sat the man, with a burden on his brain at which the world marvels—bent now with the load at both heart and brain—staggering under a blow like the taking from him of his child! His men of power sat around him—McClellan, with a moist eye when he bowed to the prayer, as I could see from where I stood; and Chase and Seward, with their austere features at work; and senators, and ambassadors, and soldiers, all struggling with their tears—great hearts sorrowing with the President as a stricken man and a brother. That God may give him strength for all his burdens is, I am sure, at present the prayer of a nation."

This sketch was very much admired by Mrs. Lincoln. I copy it from the scrap-book in which she pasted it, with many tears, with her own hands.

Chapter VII Washington In 1862-3

In the summer of 1862, freedmen began to flock into Washington from Maryland and Virginia. They came with a great hope in their hearts, and with all their worldly goods on their backs. Fresh from the bonds of slavery, fresh from the benighted regions of the plantation, they came to the Capital looking for liberty, and many of them not knowing it when they found it. Many good friends reached forth kind hands, but the North is not warm and impulsive. For one kind word spoken, two harsh ones were uttered; there was something repelling in the atmosphere, and the bright joyous dreams of freedom to the slave faded—were sadly altered, in the presence of that stern, practical mother, reality. Instead of flowery paths, days of perpetual sunshine, and bowers hanging with golden fruit, the road was rugged and full of thorns, the sunshine was eclipsed by shadows, and the mute appeals for help too often were answered by cold neglect. Poor dusky children of slavery, men and women of my own race—the transition from slavery to freedom was too sudden for you! The bright dreams were too rudely dispelled; you were not prepared for the new life that opened before you, and the great masses of the North learned to look upon your helplessness with indifference—learned to speak of you as an idle, dependent race. Reason should have prompted kinder thoughts. Charity is ever kind.

One fair summer evening I was walking the streets of Washington, accompanied by a friend, when a band of music was heard in the distance. We wondered what it could mean, and curiosity prompted us to find out its meaning. We quickened our steps, and discovered that it came from the house of Mrs. Farnham. The yard was brilliantly lighted, ladies and gentlemen were moving about, and the band was playing some of its sweetest airs. We approached the sentinel on duty at the gate, and asked what was going on. He told us that it was a festival given for the benefit of the sick and wounded soldiers in the city. This suggested an idea to me. If the white people can give festivals to raise funds for the relief of suffering soldiers, why should not the well-to-do colored people go to work to do something for the benefit of the suffering blacks? I could not rest. The thought was ever present with me, and the next Sunday I made a suggestion in the colored church, that a society of colored people be formed to labor for the benefit of the unfortunate freedmen. The idea proved popular, and in two weeks "the Contraband Relief Association" was organized, with forty working members.

In September of 1862, Mrs. Lincoln left Washington for New York, and requested me to follow her in a few days, and join her at the Metropolitan Hotel. I was glad of the opportunity to do so, for I thought that in New York I would be able to do something in the interests of our society. Armed with credentials, I took the train for New York, and went to the Metropolitan, where Mrs. Lincoln had secured accommodations for me. The next morning I told Mrs. Lincoln of my project; and she immediately headed my list with a subscription of $200. I circulated among the colored people, and got them thoroughly interested in the subject, when I was called to Boston by Mrs. Lincoln, who wished to visit her son Robert, attending college in that city. I met Mr. Wendell Phillips, and other Boston philanthropists, who gave me all the assistance in their power. We held a mass meeting at the Colored Baptist Church, Rev. Mr. Grimes, in Boston, raised a sum of money, and organized there a branch society. The society was organized by Mrs. Grimes, wife of the pastor, assisted by Mrs. Martin, wife of Rev. Stella Martin. This branch of the main society, during the war, was able to send us over eighty large boxes of goods, contributed exclusively by the colored people of Boston. Returning to New York, we held a successful meeting at the Shiloh Church, Rev. Henry Highland Garnet, pastor. The Metropolitan Hotel, at that time as now, employed colored help. I suggested the object of my mission to Robert Thompson, Steward of the Hotel, who immediately raised quite a sum of money among the dining-room waiters. Mr. Frederick Douglass contributed $200, besides lecturing for us. Other prominent colored men sent in liberal contributions. From England a large quantity of stores was received. Mrs. Lincoln made frequent contributions, as also did the President. In 1863 I was re-elected President of the Association, which office I continue to hold.

For two years after Willie's death the White House was the scene of no fashionable display. The memory of the dead boy was duly respected. In some things Mrs. Lincoln was an altered woman. Sometimes, when in her room, with no one present but myself, the mere mention of Willie's name would excite her emotion, and any trifling memento that recalled him would move her to tears. She could not bear to look upon his picture; and after his death she never crossed the threshold of the Guest's Room in which he died, or the Green Room in which he was embalmed. There was something supernatural in her dread of these things, and something that she could not explain. Tad's nature was the opposite of Willie's, and he was always regarded as his father's favorite child. His black eyes fairly sparkled with mischief.

The war progressed, fair fields had been stained with blood, thousands of brave men had fallen, and thousands of eyes were weeping for the fallen at home. There were desolate hearthstones in the South as well as in the North, and as the people of my race watched the sanguinary struggle, the ebb and flow of the tide of battle, they lifted their faces Zionward, as if they hoped to catch a glimpse of the Promised Land beyond the sulphureous clouds of smoke which shifted now and then but to reveal ghastly rows of new-made graves. Sometimes the very life of the nation seemed to tremble with the fierce shock of arms. In 1863 the Confederates were flushed with victory, and sometimes it looked as if the proud flag of the Union, the glorious old Stars and Stripes, must yield half its nationality to the tri-barred flag that floated grandly over long columns of gray. These were sad, anxious days to Mr. Lincoln, and those who saw the man in privacy only could tell how much he suffered. One day he came into the room where I was fitting a dress on Mrs. Lincoln. His step was slow and heavy, and his face sad. Like a tired child he threw himself upon a sofa, and shaded his eyes with his hands. He was a complete picture of dejection. Mrs. Lincoln, observing his troubled look, asked:

"Where have you been, father?"

"To the War Department," was the brief, almost sullen answer.

"Any news?"

"Yes, plenty of news, but no good news. It is dark, dark everywhere."

He reached forth one of his long arms, and took a small Bible from a stand near the head of the sofa, opened the pages of the holy book, and soon was absorbed in reading them. A quarter of an hour passed, and on glancing at the sofa the face of the President seemed more cheerful. The dejected look was gone, and the countenance was lighted up with new resolution and hope. The change was so marked that I could not but wonder at it, and wonder led to the desire to know what book of the Bible afforded so much comfort to the reader. Making the search for a missing article an excuse, I walked gently around the sofa, and looking into the open book, I discovered that Mr. Lincoln was reading that divine comforter, Job. He read with Christian eagerness, and the courage and hope that he derived from the inspired pages made him a new man. I almost imagined that I could hear the Lord speaking to him from out the whirlwind of battle: "Gird up thy loins now like a man: I will demand of thee, and declare thou unto me." What a sublime picture was this! A ruler of a mighty nation going to the pages of the Bible with simple Christian earnestness for comfort and courage, and finding both in the darkest hours of a nation's calamity. Ponder it, O ye scoffers at God's Holy Word, and then hang your heads for very shame!

Frequent letters were received warning Mr. Lincoln of assassination, but he never gave a second thought to the mysterious warnings. The letters, however, sorely troubled his wife. She seemed to read impending danger in every rustling leaf, in every whisper of the wind.

"Where are you going now, father?" she would say to him, as she observed him putting on his overshoes and shawl.

"I am going over to the War Department, mother, to try and learn some news."

"But, father, you should not go out alone. You know you are surrounded with danger."

"All imagination. What does any one want to harm me for? Don't worry about me, mother, as if I were a little child, for no one is going to molest me;" and with a confident, unsuspecting air he would close the door behind him, descend the stairs, and pass out to his lonely walk.

For weeks, when trouble was anticipated, friends of the President would sleep in the White House to guard him from danger.

Robert would come home every few months, bringing new joy to the family circle. He was very anxious to quit school and enter the army, but the move was sternly opposed by his mother.

"We have lost one son, and his loss is as much as I can bear, without being called upon to make another sacrifice," she would say, when the subject was under discussion.

"But many a poor mother has given up all her sons," mildly suggested Mr. Lincoln, "and our son is not more dear to us than the sons of other people are to their mothers."

"That may be; but I cannot bear to have Robert exposed to danger. His services are not required in the field, and the sacrifice would be a needless one."

"The services of every man who loves his country are required in this war. You should take a liberal instead of a selfish view of the question, mother."

Argument at last prevailed, and permission was granted Robert to enter the army. With the rank of Captain and A. D. C. he went to the field, and remained in the army till the close of the war.

I well recollect a little incident that gave me a clearer insight into Robert's character. He was at home at the time the Tom Thumb combination was at Washington. The marriage of little Hopo'-my-thumb—Charles Stratton—to Miss Warren created no little excitement in the world, and the people of Washington participated in the general curiosity. Some of Mrs. Lincoln's friends made her believe that it was the duty of Mrs. Lincoln to show some attention to the remarkable dwarfs. Tom Thumb had been caressed by royalty in the Old World, and why should not the wife of the President of his native country smile upon him also? Verily, duty is one of the greatest bugbears in life. A hasty reception was arranged, and cards of invitation issued. I had dressed Mrs. Lincoln, and she was ready to go below and receive her guests, when Robert entered his mother's room.

"You are at leisure this afternoon, are you not, Robert?"

"Yes, mother."

"Of course, then, you will dress and come down-stairs."

"No, mother, I do not propose to assist in entertaining Tom Thumb. My notions of duty, perhaps, are somewhat different from yours."

Robert had a lofty soul, and he could not stoop to all of the follies and absurdities of the ephemeral current of fashionable life.

Mrs. Lincoln's love for her husband sometimes prompted her to act very strangely. She was extremely jealous of him, and if a lady desired to court her displeasure, she could select no surer way to do it than to pay marked attention to the President. These little jealous freaks often were a source of perplexity to Mr. Lincoln. If it was a reception for which they were dressing, he would come into her room to conduct her downstairs, and while pulling on his gloves ask, with a merry twinkle in his eyes:

"Well, mother, who must I talk with to-night—shall it be Mrs. D.?"

"That deceitful woman! No, you shall not listen to her flattery."

"Well, then, what do you say to Miss C.? She is too young and handsome to practise deceit."

"Young and handsome, you call her! You should not judge beauty for me. No, she is in league with Mrs. D., and you shall not talk with her."

"Well, mother, I must talk with some one. Is there any one that you do not object to?" trying to button his glove, with a mock expression of gravity.

"I don't know as it is necessary that you should talk to anybody in particular. You know well enough, Mr. Lincoln, that I do not approve of your flirtations with silly women, just as if you were a beardless boy, fresh from school."

"But, mother, I insist that I must talk with somebody. I can't stand around like a simpleton, and say nothing. If you will not tell me who I may talk with, please tell me who I may not talk with."

"There is Mrs. D. and Miss C. in particular. I detest them both. Mrs. B. also will come around you, but you need not listen to her flattery. These are the ones in particular."

"Very well, mother; now that we have settled the question to your satisfaction, we will go down-stairs;" and always with stately dignity, he proffered his arm and led the way.

The Sheffield Anti-Slavery Society of England contributed through Mr. Frederick Douglass, to the Freedmen's Relief Association, $24.00; Aberdeen Ladies' Society, $40.00; Anti-Slavery Society of Edinburgh, Scotland, $48.00; Friends at Bristol, England, $176.00; Birmingham Negro's Friend Society, $50.00. Also received through Mr. Charles R. Douglass, from the Birmingham Society, $33.00.

Chapter VIII Candid Opinions

Often Mr. and Mrs. Lincoln discussed the relations of Cabinet officers, and gentlemen prominent in politics, in my presence. I soon learned that the wife of the President had no love for Mr. Salmon P. Chase, at that time Secretary of the Treasury. She was well versed in human character, was somewhat suspicious of those by whom she was surrounded, and often her judgment was correct. Her intuition about the sincerity of individuals was more accurate than that of her husband. She looked beyond, and read the reflection of action in the future. Her hostility to Mr. Chase was very bitter. She claimed that he was a selfish politician instead of a true patriot, and warned Mr. Lincoln not to trust him too far. The daughter of the Secretary was quite a belle in Washington, and Mrs. Lincoln, who was jealous of the popularity of others, had no desire to build up her social position through political favor to her father. Miss Chase, now Mrs. Senator Sprague, was a lovely woman, and was worthy of all the admiration she received. Mr. Lincoln was more confiding than his wife. He never suspected the fidelity of those who claimed to be his friends. Honest to the very core himself, and frank as a child, he never dreamed of questioning the sincerity of others.

"Father, I do wish that you would inquire a little into the motives of Chase," said his wife one day.

The President was lying carelessly upon a sofa, holding a newspaper in his hands. "Mother, you are too suspicious. I give you credit for sagacity, but you are disposed to magnify trifles. Chase is a patriot, and one of my best friends."

"Yes, one of your best friends because it is his interest to be so. He is anything for Chase. If he thought he could make anything by it, he would betray you to-morrow."

"I fear that you are prejudiced against the man, mother. I know that you do him injustice."

"Mr. Lincoln, you are either blind or will not see. I am not the only one that has warned you against him."

"True, I receive letters daily from all parts of the country, telling me not to trust Chase; but then these letters are written by the political enemies of the Secretary, and it would be unjust and foolish to pay any attention to them."

"Very well, you will find out some day, if you live long enough, that I have read the man correctly. I only hope that your eyes may not be opened to the truth when it is too late." The President, as far as I could judge from his conversation with his wife, continued to confide in Mr. Chase to the time of his tragic death.

Mrs. Lincoln was especially severe on Mr. Wm. H. Seward, Secretary of State. She but rarely lost an opportunity to say an unkind word of him.

One morning I went to the White House earlier than usual. Mr. Lincoln was sitting in a chair, reading a paper, stroking with one hand the head of little Tad. I was basting a dress for Mrs. Lincoln. A servant entered, and handed the President a letter just brought by a messenger. He broke the seal, and when he had read the contents his wife asked:

"Who is the letter from, father?"

"Seward; I must go over and see him today."

"Seward! I wish you had nothing to do with that man. He cannot be trusted."

"You say the same of Chase. If I listened to you, I should soon be without a Cabinet."

"Better be without it than to confide in some of the men that you do. Seward is worse than Chase. He has no principle."

"Mother, you are mistaken; your prejudices are so violent that you do not stop to reason. Seward is an able man, and the country as well as myself can trust him."

"Father, you are too honest for this world! You should have been born a saint. You will generally find it a safe rule to distrust a disappointed, ambitious politician. It makes me mad to see you sit still and let that hypocrite, Seward, twine you around his finger as if you were a skein of thread."

"It is useless to argue the question, mother. You cannot change my opinion."

Mrs. Lincoln prided herself upon her ability to read character. She was shrewd and far-seeing, and had no patience with the frank, confiding nature of the President.

When Andrew Johnson was urged for military Governor of Tennessee, Mrs. Lincoln bitterly opposed the appointment.

"He is a demagogue," she said, almost fiercely, "and if you place him in power, Mr. Lincoln, mark my words, you will rue it some day."

General McClellan, when made Commander-in-Chief, was the idol of the soldiers, and never was a general more universally popular. "He is a humbug," remarked Mrs. Lincoln one day in my presence.

"What makes you think so, mother?" good-naturedly inquired the President.

"Because he talks so much and does so little. If I had the power I would very soon take off his head, and put some energetic man in his place."

"But I regard McClellan as a patriot and an able soldier. He has been much embarrassed. The troops are raw, and the subordinate officers inclined to be rebellious. There are too many politicians in the army with shoulder-straps. McClellan is young and popular, and they are jealous of him. They will kill him off if they can."

"McClellan can make plenty of excuse for himself, therefore he needs no advocate in you. If he would only do something, and not promise so much, I might learn to have a little faith in him. I tell you he is a humbug, and you will have to find some man to take his place, that is, if you wish to conquer the South."

Mrs. Lincoln could not tolerate General Grant. "He is a butcher," she would often say, "and is not fit to be at the head of an army."

"But he has been very successful in the field," argued the President.

"Yes, he generally manages to claim a victory, but such a victory! He loses two men to the enemy's one. He has no management, no regard for life. If the war should continue four years longer, and he should remain in power, he would depopulate the North. I could fight an army as well myself. According to his tactics, there is nothing under the heavens to do but to march a new line of men up in front of the rebel breastworks to be shot down as fast as they take their position, and keep marching until the enemy grows tired of the slaughter. Grant, I repeat, is an obstinate fool and a butcher."

"Well, mother, supposing that we give you command of the army. No doubt you would do much better than any general that has been tried." There was a twinkle in the eyes, and a ring of irony in the voice.

I have often heard Mrs. Lincoln say that if Grant should ever be elected President of the United States she would desire to leave the country, and remain absent during his term of office.

It was well known that Mrs. Lincoln's brothers were in the Confederate army, and for this reason it was often charged that her sympathies were with the South. Those who made the hasty charge were never more widely mistaken.

One morning, on my way to the White House, I heard that Captain Alexander Todd, one of her brothers, had been killed. I did not like to inform Mrs. Lincoln of his death, judging that it would be painful news to her. I had been in her room but a few minutes when she said, with apparent unconcern, "Lizzie, I have just heard that one of my brothers has been killed in the war."

"I also heard the same, Mrs. Lincoln, but hesitated to speak of it, for fear the subject would be a painful one to you."

"You need not hesitate. Of course, it is but natural that I should feel for one so nearly related to me, but not to the extent that you suppose. He made his choice long ago. He decided against my husband, and through him against me. He has been fighting against us; and since he chose to be our deadly enemy, I see no special reason why I should bitterly mourn his death."

I felt relieved, and in subsequent conversations learned that Mrs. Lincoln had no sympathy for the South. "Why should I sympathize with the rebels," she would say; "are they not against me? They would hang my husband to-morrow if it was in their power, and perhaps gibbet me with him. How then can I sympathize with a people at war with me and mine?" She always objected to being thought Southern in feeling.

Mr. Lincoln was generous by nature, and though his whole heart was in the war, he could not but respect the valor of those opposed to him. His soul was too great for the narrow, selfish views of partisanship. Brave by nature himself, he honored bravery in others, even his foes. Time and again I have heard him speak in the highest terms of the soldierly qualities of such brave Confederate generals as Lee, Stonewall Jackson, and Joseph E. Johns[t]on. Jackson was his ideal soldier. "He is a brave, honest Presbyterian soldier," were his words; "what a pity that we should have to fight such a gallant fellow! If we only had such a man to lead the armies of the North, the country would not be appalled with so many disasters."

As this is a rambling chapter, I will here record an incident showing his feeling toward Robert E. Lee. The very morning of the day on which he was assassinated, his son, Capt. Robert Lincoln, came into the room with a portrait of General Lee in his hand. The President took the picture, laid it on a table before him, scanned the face thoughtfully, and said: "It is a good face; it is the face of a noble, noble, brave man. I am glad that the war is over at last." Looking up at Robert, he continued: "Well, my son, you have returned safely from the front. The war is now closed, and we soon will live in peace with the brave men that have been fighting against us. I trust that the era of good feeling has returned with the war, and that henceforth we shall live in peace. Now listen to me, Robert: you must lay aside your uniform, and return to college. I wish you to read law for three years, and at the end of that time I hope that we will be able to tell whether you will make a lawyer or not." His face was more cheerful than I had seen it for a long while, and he seemed to be in a generous, forgiving mood.

Chapter IX Behind The Scenes

Some of the freedmen and freedwomen had exaggerated ideas of liberty. To them it was a beautiful vision, a land of sunshine, rest and glorious promise. They flocked to Washington, and since their extravagant hopes were not realized, it was but natural that many of them should bitterly feel their disappointment. The colored people are wedded to associations, and when you destroy these you destroy half of the happiness of their lives.

They make a home, and are so fond of it that they prefer it, squalid though it be, to the comparative ease and luxury of a shifting, roaming life. Well, the emancipated slaves, in coming North, left old associations behind them, and the love for the past was so strong that they could not find much beauty in the new life so suddenly opened to them. Thousands of the disappointed, huddled together in camps, fretted and pined like children for the "good old times." In visiting them in the interests of the Relief Society of which I was president, they would crowd around me with pitiful stories of distress. Often I heard them declare that they would rather go back to slavery in the South, and be with their old masters, than to enjoy the freedom of the North. I believe they were sincere in these declarations, because dependence had become a part of their second nature, and independence brought with it the cares and vexations of poverty.

I was very much amused one day at the grave complaints of a good old, simple-minded woman, fresh from a life of servitude. She had never ventured beyond a plantation until coming North. The change was too radical for her, and she could not exactly understand it. She thought, as many others thought, that Mr. and Mrs. Lincoln were the government, and that the President and his wife had nothing to do but to supply the extravagant wants of every one that applied to them. The wants of this old woman, however, were not very extravagant.

"Why, Missus Keckley," said she to me one day, "I is been here eight months, and Missus Lingom an't even give me one shife. Bliss God, childen, if I had ar know dat de Government, and Mister and Missus Government, was going to do dat ar way, I neber would 'ave comed here in God's wurld. My old missus us't gib me two shifes eber year."

I could not restrain a laugh at the grave manner in which this good old woman entered her protest. Her idea of freedom was two or more old shifts every year. Northern readers may not fully recognize the pith of the joke. On the Southern plantation, the mistress, according to established custom, every year made a present of certain under-garments to her slaves, which articles were always anxiously looked forward to, and thankfully received. The old woman had been in the habit of receiving annually two shifts from her mistress, and she thought the wife of the President of the United States very mean for overlooking this established custom of the plantation.

While some of the emancipated blacks pined for the old associations of slavery, and refused to help themselves, others went to work with commendable energy, and planned with remarkable forethought. They built themselves cabins, and each family cultivated for itself a small patch of ground. The colored people are fond of domestic life, and with them domestication means happy children, a fat pig, a dozen or more chickens, and a garden. Whoever visits the Freedmen's Village now in the vicinity of Washington will discover all of these evidences of prosperity and happiness. The schools are objects of much interest. Good teachers, white and colored, are employed, and whole brigades of bright-eyed dusky children are there taught the common branches of education. These children are studious, and the teachers inform me that their advancement is rapid. I number among my personal friends twelve colored girls employed as teachers in the schools at Washington. The Colored Mission Sabbath School, established through the influence of Gen. Brown at the

Fifteenth Street Presbyterian Church, is always an object of great interest to the residents of the Capital, as well as to the hundreds of strangers visiting the city.

In 1864 the receptions again commenced at the White House. For the first two years of Mr. Lincoln's administration, the President selected a lady to join in the promenade with him, which left Mrs. Lincoln free to choose an escort from among the distinguished gentlemen that always surrounded her on such occasions. This custom at last was discontinued by Mrs. Lincoln.

"Lizabeth!"—I was sewing in her room, and she was seated in a comfortable arm-chair—"Lizabeth, I have been thinking over a little matter. As you are well aware, the President, at every reception, selects a lady to lead the promenade with him. Now it occurs to me that this custom is an absurd one. On such occasions our guests recognize the position of the President as first of all; consequently, he takes the lead in everything; well, now, if they recognize his position they should also recognize mine. I am his wife, and should lead with him. And yet he offers his arm to any other lady in the room, making her first with him and placing me second. The custom is an absurd one, and I mean to abolish it. The dignity that I owe to my position, as Mrs. President, demands that I should not hesitate any longer to act."

Mrs. Lincoln kept her word. Ever after this, she either led the promenade with the President, or the President walked alone or with a gentleman. The change was much remarked, but the reason why it was made, I believe, was never generally known.

In 1864 much doubt existed in regard to the re-election of Mr. Lincoln, and the White House was besieged by all grades of politicians. Mrs. Lincoln was often blamed for having a certain class of men around her.

"I have an object in view, Lizabeth," she said to me in reference to this matter. "In a political canvass it is policy to cultivate every element of strength. These men have influence, and we require influence to re-elect Mr. Lincoln. I will be clever to them until after the election, and then, if we remain at the White House, I will drop every one of them, and let them know very plainly that I only made tools of them. They are an unprincipled set, and I don't mind a little double-dealing with them."

"Does Mr. Lincoln know what your purpose is?" I asked.

"God! no; he would never sanction such a proceeding, so I keep him in the dark, and will tell him of it when all is over. He is too honest to take the proper care of his own interests, so I feel it to be my duty to electioneer for him."

Mr. Lincoln, as every one knows, was far from handsome. He was not admired for his graceful figure and finely moulded face, but for the nobility of his soul and the greatness of his heart. His wife was different. He was wholly unselfish in every respect, and I believe that he loved the mother of his children very tenderly. He asked nothing but affection from her, but did not always receive it. When in one of her wayward impulsive moods, she was apt to say and do things that wounded him deeply. If he had not loved her, she would have been powerless to cloud his thoughtful face, or gild it with a ray of sunshine as she pleased. We are indifferent to those we do not love, and certainly the President was not indifferent to his wife. She often wounded him in unguarded moments, but calm reflection never failed to bring regret.

Mrs. Lincoln was extremely anxious that her husband should be re-elected President of the United States. In endeavoring to make a display becoming her exalted position, she had to incur many expenses. Mr. Lincoln's salary was inadequate to meet them, and she was forced to run in debt, hoping that good fortune would favor her, and enable her to extricate herself from an embarrassing situation. She bought the most expensive goods on credit, and in the summer of 1864 enormous unpaid bills stared her in the face.

"What do you think about the election, Lizabeth?" she said to me one morning.

"I think that Mr. Lincoln will remain in the White House four years longer," I replied, looking up from my work.

"What makes you think so? Somehow I have learned to fear that he will be defeated."

"Because he has been tried, and has proved faithful to the best interests of the country. The people of the North recognize in him an honest man, and they are willing to confide in him, at least until the war has been brought to a close. The Southern people made his election a pretext for rebellion, and now to replace him by some one else, after years of sanguinary war, would look too much like a surrender of the North. So, Mr. Lincoln is certain to be re-elected. He represents a principle, and to maintain this principle the loyal people of the loyal States will vote for him, even if he had no merits to commend him."

"Your view is a plausible one, Lizabeth, and your confidence gives me new hope. If he should be defeated, I do not know what would become of us all. To me, to him, there is more at stake in this election than he dreams of."

"What can you mean, Mrs. Lincoln? I do not comprehend."

"Simply this. I have contracted large debts, of which he knows nothing, and which he will be unable to pay if he is defeated."

"What are your debts, Mrs. Lincoln?"

"They consist chiefly of store bills. I owe altogether about twenty-seven thousand dollars; the principal portion at Stewart's, in New York. You understand, Lizabeth, that Mr. Lincoln has but little idea of the expense of a woman's wardrobe. He glances at my rich dresses, and is happy in the belief that the few hundred dollars that I obtain from him supply all my wants. I must dress in costly materials. The people scrutinize every article that I wear with critical curiosity. The very fact of having grown up in the West, subjects me to more searching observation. To keep up appearances, I must have money—more than Mr. Lincoln can spare for me. He is too honest to make a penny outside of his salary; consequently I had, and still have, no alternative but to run in debt."

"And Mr. Lincoln does not even suspect how much you owe?"

"God, no!"—this was a favorite expression of hers—"and I would not have him suspect. If he knew that his wife was involved to the extent that she is, the knowledge would drive him mad. He is so sincere and straightforward himself, that he is shocked by the duplicity of others. He does not know a thing about any debts and I value his happiness, not to speak of my own, too much to allow him to know anything. This is what troubles me so much. If he is re-elected, I can keep him in ignorance of my affairs; but if he is defeated, then the bills will be sent in, and he will know all;" and something like a hysterical sob escaped her.

Mrs. Lincoln sometimes feared that the politicians would get hold of the particulars of her debts, and use them in the Presidential campaign against her husband; and when this thought occurred to her, she was almost crazy with anxiety and fear.

When in one of these excited moods, she would fiercely exclaim—

"The Republican politicians must pay my debts. Hundreds of them are getting immensely rich off the patronage of my husband, and it is but fair that they should help me out of my embarrassment. I will make a demand of them, and when I tell them the facts they cannot refuse to advance whatever money I require."

Chapter X The Second Inauguration

Mrs. Lincoln came to my apartments one day towards the close of the summer of 1864, to consult me in relation to a dress. And here let me remark, I never approved of ladies, attached to the Presidential household, coming to my rooms. I always thought that it would be more consistent with their dignity to send for me, and let me come to them, instead of their coming to me. I may have peculiar notions about some things, and this may be regarded as one of them. No matter, I have recorded my opinion. I cannot forget the associations of my early life. Well, Mrs. Lincoln came to my rooms, and, as usual, she had much to say about the Presidential election.

After some conversation, she asked: "Lizzie, where do you think I will be this time next summer?"

"Why, in the White House, of course."

"I cannot believe so. I have no hope of the re-election of Mr. Lincoln. The canvass is a heated one, the people begin to murmur at the war, and every vile charge is brought against my husband."

"No matter," I replied, "Mr. Lincoln will be re-elected. I am so confident of it, that I am tempted to ask a favor of you."

"A favor! Well, if we remain in the White House I shall be able to do you many favors. What is the special favor?"

"Simply this, Mrs. Lincoln—I should like for you to make me a present of the right-hand glove that the President wears at the first public reception after his second inaugural."

"You shall have it in welcome. It will be so filthy when he pulls it off, I shall be tempted to take the tongs and put it in the fire. I cannot imagine, Lizabeth, what you want with such a glove."

"I shall cherish it as a precious memento of the second inauguration of the man who has done so much for my race. He has been a Jehovah to my people—has lifted them out of bondage, and directed their footsteps from darkness into light. I shall keep the glove, and hand it down to posterity."

"You have some strange ideas, Lizabeth. Never mind, you shall have the glove; that is, if Mr. Lincoln continues President after the 4th of March next."

I held Mrs. Lincoln to her promise. That glove is now in my possession, bearing the marks of the thousands of hands that grasped the honest hand of Mr. Lincoln on that eventful night. Alas! it has become a prouder, sadder memento than I ever dreamed—prior to making the request—it would be.

In due time the election came off, and all of my predictions were verified. The loyal States decided that Mr. Lincoln should continue at the nation's helm. Autumn faded, winter dragged slowly by, and still the country resounded with the clash of arms. The South was suffering, yet suffering was borne with heroic determination, and the army continued to present a bold, defiant front. With the first early breath of spring, thousands of people gathered in Washington to witness the second inauguration of Abraham Lincoln as President of the United States. It was a stirring day in the National Capital, and one that will never fade from the memory of those who witnessed the imposing ceremonies. The morning was dark and gloomy; clouds hung like a pall in the sky, as if portending some great disaster. But when the President stepped forward to receive the oath of office, the clouds parted, and a ray of sunshine streamed from the heavens to fall upon and gild his face. It is also said that a brilliant star was seen at noon-day. It was the noon-day of life with Mr. Lincoln, and the star, as viewed in the light of subsequent events, was emblematic of a summons from on high. This was Saturday, and on Monday evening I went to the White House to dress Mrs. Lincoln for the first grand levee. While arranging Mrs. L.'s hair, the President came in. It was the first time I had seen him since the inauguration, and I went up to him, proffering my hand with words of congratulation.

He grasped my outstretched hand warmly, and held it while he spoke: "Thank you. Well, Madam Elizabeth"—he always called me Madam Elizabeth—"I don't know whether I should feel thankful or not. The position brings with it many trials. We do not know what we are destined to pass through. But God will be with us all. I put my trust in God." He dropped my hand, and with solemn face walked across the room and took his seat on the sofa. Prior to this I had congratulated Mrs. Lincoln, and she had answered with a sigh, "Thank you, Elizabeth; but now that we have won the position, I almost wish it were otherwise. Poor Mr. Lincoln is looking so broken-hearted, so completely worn out, I fear he will not get through the next four years." Was it a presentiment that made her take a sad view of the future? News from the front was never more cheering. On every side the Confederates were losing ground, and the lines of blue were advancing in triumph. As I would look out my window almost every day, I could see the artillery going past on its way to the open space of ground, to fire a salute in honor of some new victory. From every point came glorious news of the success of the soldiers that fought for the Union. And yet, in their private chamber, away from the curious eyes of the world, the President and his wife wore sad, anxious faces.

I finished dressing Mrs. Lincoln, and she took the President's arm and went below. It was one of the largest receptions ever held in Washington. Thousands crowded the halls and rooms of the White House, eager to shake Mr. Lincoln by his hand, and receive a gracious smile from his wife. The jam was terrible, and the enthusiasm great. The President's hand was well shaken, and the next day, on visiting Mrs. Lincoln, I received the soiled glove that Mr. Lincoln had worn on his right hand that night.

Many colored people were in Washington, and large numbers had desired to attend the levee, but orders were issued not to admit them. A gentleman, a member of Congress, on his way to the White House, recognized Mr. Frederick Douglass, the eloquent colored orator, on the outskirts of the crowd.

"How do you do, Mr. Douglass? A fearful jam to-night. You are going in, of course?"

"No—that is, no to your last question."

"Not going in to shake the President by the hand! Why, pray?"

"The best reason in the world. Strict orders have been issued not to admit people of color."

"It is a shame, Mr. Douglass, that you should thus be placed under ban. Never mind; wait here, and I will see what can be done."

The gentleman entered the White House, and working his way to the President, asked permission to introduce Mr. Douglass to him.

"Certainly," said Mr. Lincoln. "Bring Mr. Douglass in, by all means. I shall be glad to meet him."

The gentleman returned, and soon Mr. Douglass stood face to face with the President. Mr. Lincoln pressed his hand warmly, saying: "Mr. Douglass, I am glad to meet you. I have long admired your course, and I value your opinions highly."

Mr. Douglass was very proud of the manner in which Mr. Lincoln received him. On leaving the White House he came to a friend's house where a reception was being held, and he related the incident with great pleasure to myself and others.

On the Monday following the reception at the White House, everybody was busy preparing for the grand inaugural ball to come off that night. I was in Mrs. Lincoln's room the greater portion of the day. While dressing her that night, the President came in, and I remarked to him how much Mr. Douglass had been pleased on the night he was presented to Mr. Lincoln. Mrs. L. at once turned to her husband with the inquiry, "Father, why was not Mr. Douglass introduced to me?"

"I do not know. I thought he was presented."

"But he was not."

"It must have been an oversight then, mother; I am sorry you did not meet him."

I finished dressing her for the ball, and accompanied her to the door. She was dressed magnificently, and entered the ball-room leaning on the arm of Senator Sumner, a gentleman that she very much admired. Mr. Lincoln walked into the ball-room accompanied by two gentlemen. This ball closed the season. It was the last time that the President and his wife ever appeared in public.

Some days after, Mrs. Lincoln, with a party of friends, went to City Point on a visit.

Mrs. Lincoln had returned to Washington prior to the 2d of April. On Monday, April 3d, Mrs. Secretary Harlan came into my room with material for a dress. While conversing with her, I saw artillery pass the window; and as it was on its way to fire a salute, I inferred that good news had been received at the War Department. My reception-room was on one side of the street, and my work-room on the other side. Inquiring the cause of the demonstration, we were told that Richmond had fallen. Mrs. Harlan took one of my hands in each of her own, and we rejoiced together. I ran across to my work-room, and on entering it, discovered that the girls in my employ also had heard the good news. They were particularly elated, as it was reported that the rebel capital had surrendered to colored troops. I had promised my employees a holiday when Richmond should fall; and now that Richmond had fallen, they reminded me of my promise.

I recrossed to my reception-room, and Mrs. Harlan told me that the good news was enough for her—she could afford to wait for her dress, and to give the girls a holiday and a treat, by all means. She returned to her house, and I joined my girls in the joy of the long-promised holiday. We wandered about the streets of the city with happy faces, and hearts overflowing with joy. The clerks in the various departments also enjoyed a holiday, and they improved it by getting gloriously fuddled. Towards evening I saw S., and many other usually clear-headed men, in the street, in a confused, uncertain state of mind.

Mrs. Lincoln had invited me to accompany her to City Point. I went to the White House, and told her that if she intended to return, I would regard it as a privilege to go with her, as City Point was near Petersburg, my old home. Mrs. L. said she designed returning, and would be delighted to take me with her; so it was arranged that I should accompany her.

A few days after we were on board the steamer, en route for City Point. Mrs. Lincoln was joined by Mrs. Secretary Harlan and daughter, Senator Sumner, and several other gentlemen.

Prior to this, Mr. Lincoln had started for City Point, and before we reached our destination he had visited Richmond, Petersburg, and other points. We arrived on Friday, and Mrs. Lincoln was much disappointed when she learned that the President had visited the late Confederate capital, as she had greatly desired to be with him when he entered the conquered stronghold. It was immediately arranged that the entire party on board the River Queen should visit Richmond, and other points, with the President. The next morning, after the arrangement was perfected, we were steaming up James River—the river that so long had been impassable, even to our gunboats. The air was balmy, and the banks of the river were beautiful, and fragrant with the first sweet blossoms of spring. For hours I stood on deck, breathing the pure air, and viewing the landscape on either side of the majestically flowing river. Here stretched fair fields, emblematic of peace—and here deserted camps and frowning forts, speaking of the stern vicissitudes of war. Alas! how many changes had taken place since my eye had wandered over the classic fields of dear old Virginia! A birthplace is always dear, no matter under what circumstances you were born, since it revives in memory the golden hours of childhood, free from philosophy, and the warm kiss of a mother. I wondered if I should catch a glimpse of a familiar face; I wondered what had become of those I once knew; had they fallen in battle, been scattered by the relentless tide of war, or were they still living as they lived when last I saw them? I wondered, now that Richmond had fallen, and Virginia been restored to the clustering stars of the Union, if the people would come together in the bonds of peace; and as I gazed and wondered, the River Queen rapidly carried us to our destination.

The Presidential party were all curiosity on entering Richmond. They drove about the streets of the city, and examined every object of interest. The Capitol presented a desolate appearance—desks broken, and papers scattered promiscuously in the hurried flight of the Confederate Congress. I picked up a number of papers, and, by curious coincidence, the resolution prohibiting all free colored people from entering the State of Virginia. In the Senate chamber I sat in the chair that Jefferson Davis sometimes occupied; also in the chair of the Vice-President, Alexander H. Stephens. We paid a visit to the mansion occupied by Mr. Davis and family during the war, and the ladies who were in charge of it scowled darkly upon our party as we passed through and inspected the different rooms. After a delightful visit we returned to City Point.

That night, in the cabin of the River Queen, smiling faces gathered around the dinner-table. One of the guests was a young officer attached to the Sanitary Commission. He was seated near Mrs. Lincoln, and, by way of pleasantry, remarked: "Mrs. Lincoln, you should have seen the President the other day, on his triumphal entry into Richmond. He was the cynosure of all eyes. The ladies kissed their hands to him, and greeted him with the waving of handkerchiefs. He is quite a hero when surrounded by pretty young ladies."

The young officer suddenly paused with a look of embarrassment. Mrs. Lincoln turned to him with flashing eyes, with the remark that his familiarity was offensive to her. Quite a scene followed, and I do not think that the Captain who incurred Mrs. Lincoln's displeasure will ever forget that memorable evening in the cabin of the River Queen, at City Point.

Saturday morning the whole party decided to visit Petersburg, and I was only too eager to accompany them.

When we arrived at the city, numbers crowded around the train, and a little ragged negro boy ventured timidly into the car occupied by Mr. Lincoln and immediate friends, and in replying to numerous questions, used the word "tote."

"Tote," remarked Mr. Lincoln; "what do you mean by tote?"

"Why, massa, to tote um on your back."

"Very definite, my son; I presume when you tote a thing, you carry it. By the way, Sumner," turning to the Senator, "what is the origin of tote?"

"Its origin is said to be African. The Latin word totum, from totus, means all—an entire body—the whole."

"But my young friend here did not mean an entire body, or anything of the kind, when he said he would tote my things for me," interrupted the President.

"Very true," continued the Senator. "He used the word tote in the African sense, to carry, to bear. Tote in this sense is defined in our standard dictionaries as a colloquial word of the Southern States, used especially by the negroes."

"Then you regard the word as a good one?"

"Not elegant, certainly. For myself, I should prefer a better word; but since it has been established by usage, I cannot refuse to recognize it."

Thus the conversation proceeded in pleasant style.

Getting out of the car, the President and those with him went to visit the forts and other scenes, while I wandered off by myself in search of those whom I had known in other days. War, grim-visaged war, I soon discovered had brought many changes to the city so well known to me in the days of my youth. I found a number of old friends, but the greater portion of the population were strange to me. The scenes suggested painful memories, and I was not sorry to turn my back again upon the city. A large, peculiarly shaped oak tree, I well remember, attracted the particular attention of the President; it grew upon the outskirts of Petersburg, and as he had discovered it on his first visit, a few days previous to the second, he insisted that the party should go with him to take a look at the isolated and magnificent specimen of the stately grandeur of the forest. Every member of the party was only too willing to accede to the President's request, and the visit to the oak was made, and much enjoyed.

On our return to City Point from Petersburg the train moved slowly, and the President, observing a terrapin basking in the warm sunshine on the wayside, had the conductor stop the train, and one of the brakemen bring the terrapin in to him. The movements of the ungainly little animal seemed to delight him, and he amused himself with it until we reached James River, where our steamer lay. Tad stood near, and joined in the happy laugh with his father.

For a week the River Queen remained in James River, anchored the greater portion of the time at City Point, and a pleasant and memorable week was it to all on board. During the whole of this time a yacht lay in the stream about a quarter of a mile distant, and its peculiar movements attracted the attention of all on board. General Grant and Mrs. Grant were on our steamer several times, and many distinguished officers of the army also were entertained by the President and his party.

Mr. Lincoln, when not off on an excursion of any kind lounged about the boat, talking familiarly with every one that approached him.

The day before we started on our journey back to Washington, Mr. Lincoln was engaged in reviewing the troops in camp. He returned to the boat in the evening, with a tired, weary look.

"Mother," he said to his wife, "I have shaken so many hands to-day that my arms ache tonight. I almost wish that I could go to bed now."

As the twilight shadows deepened the lamps were lighted, and the boat was brilliantly illuminated; as it lay in the river, decked with many-colored lights, it looked like an enchanted floating palace. A military band was on board, and as the hours lengthened into night it discoursed sweet music. Many officers came on board to say good-by, and the scene was a brilliant one indeed. About 10 o'clock Mr. Lincoln was called upon to make a speech. Rising to his feet, he said:

"You must excuse me, ladies and gentlemen. I am too tired to speak to-night. On next Tuesday night I make a speech in Washington, at which time you will learn all I have to say. And now, by way of parting from the brave soldiers of our gallant army, I call upon the band to play Dixie. It has always been a favorite of mine, and since we have captured it, we have a perfect right to enjoy it." On taking his seat the band at once struck up with Dixie, that sweet, inspiring air; and when the music died away, there were clapping of hands and other manifestations of applause.

At 11 o'clock the last good-by was spoken, the lights were taken down, the River Queen rounded out into the water and we were on our way back to Washington. We arrived at the Capital at 6 o'clock on Sunday evening, where the party separated, each going to his and her own home. This was one of the most delightful trips of my life, and I always revert to it with feelings of genuine pleasure.

Chapter XI The Assassination Of President Lincoln

I had never heard Mr. Lincoln make a public speech, and, knowing the man so well, was very anxious to hear him. On the morning of the Tuesday after our return from City Point, Mrs. Lincoln came to my apartments, and before she drove away I asked permission to come to the White House that night and hear Mr. Lincoln speak.

"Certainly, Lizabeth; if you take any interest in political speeches, come and listen in welcome."

"Thank you, Mrs. Lincoln. May I trespass further on your kindness by asking permission to bring a friend with me?"

"Yes, bring your friend also. By the way, come in time to dress me before the speaking commences."

"I will be in time. You may rely upon that. Good morning," I added, as she swept from my room, and, passing out into the street, entered her carriage and drove away.

About 7 o'clock that evening I entered the White House. As I went up-stairs I glanced into Mr. Lincoln's room through the half-open door, and seated by a desk was the President, looking over his notes and muttering to himself. His face was thoughtful, his manner abstracted, and I knew, as I paused a moment to watch him, that he was rehearsing the part that he was to play in the great drama soon to commence.

Proceeding to Mrs. Lincoln's apartment, I worked with busy fingers, and in a short time her toilette was completed.

Washington, D.C. President Lincoln's funeral procession on Pennsylvania Avenue

Great crowds began to gather in front of the White House, and loud calls were made for the President. The band stopped playing, and as he advanced to the centre window over the door to make his address, I looked out, and never saw such a mass of heads before. It was like a black, gently swelling sea. The swaying motion of the crowd, in the dim uncertain light, was like the rising and falling of billows—like the ebb and flow of the tide upon the stranded shore of the ocean. Close to the house the faces were plainly discernible, but they faded into mere ghostly outlines on the outskirts of the assembly; and what added to the weird, spectral beauty of the scene, was the confused hum of voices that rose above the sea of forms, sounding like the subdued, sullen roar of an ocean storm, or the wind soughing through the dark lonely forest. It was a grand and imposing scene, and when the President, with pale face and his soul flashing through his eyes, advanced to speak, he looked more like a demigod than a man crowned with the fleeting days of mortality.

The moment the President appeared at the window he was greeted with a storm of applause, and voices re-echoed the cry, "A light! a light!"

A lamp was brought, and little Tad at once rushed to his father's side, exclaiming:

"Let me hold the light, Papa! let me hold the light!"

Mrs. Lincoln directed that the wish of her son be gratified, and the lamp was transferred to his hands. The father and son standing there in the presence of thousands of free citizens, the one lost in a chain of eloquent ideas, the other looking up into the speaking face with a proud, manly look, formed a beautiful and striking tableau.

There were a number of distinguished gentlemen, as well as ladies, in the room, nearly all of whom remarked the picture.

I stood a short distance from Mr. Lincoln, and as the light from the lamp fell full upon him, making him stand out boldly in the darkness, a sudden thought struck me, and I whispered to the friend at my side:

"What an easy matter would it be to kill the President, as he stands there! He could be shot down from the crowd, and no one be able to tell who fired the shot."

I do not know what put such an idea into my head, unless it was the sudden remembrance of the many warnings that Mr. Lincoln had received.

The next day, I made mention to Mrs. Lincoln of the idea that had impressed me so strangely the night before, and she replied with a sigh:

"Yes, yes, Mr. Lincoln's life is always exposed. Ah, no one knows what it is to live in constant dread of some fearful tragedy. The President has been warned so often, that I tremble for him on every public occasion. I have a presentiment that he will meet with a sudden and violent end. I pray God to protect my beloved husband from the hands of the assassin."

Mr. Lincoln was fond of pets. He had two goats that knew the sound of his voice, and when he called them they would come bounding to his side. In the warm bright days, he and Tad would sometimes play in the yard with these goats, for an hour at a time. One Saturday afternoon I went to the White House to dress Mrs. Lincoln. I had nearly completed my task when the President came in. It was a bright day, and walking to the window, he looked down into the yard, smiled, and, turning to me, asked:

"Madam Elizabeth, you are fond of pets, are you not?"

"O yes, sir," I answered.

"Well, come here and look at my two goats. I believe they are the kindest and best goats in the world. See how they sniff the clear air, and skip and play in the sunshine. Whew! what a jump," he exclaimed as one of the goats made a lofty spring. "Madam Elizabeth, did you ever before see such an active goat?" Musing a moment, he continued: "He feeds on my bounty, and jumps with joy. Do you think we could call him a bounty-jumper? But I flatter the bounty-jumper. My goat is far above him. I would rather wear his horns and hairy coat through life, than demean myself to the level of the man who plunders the national treasury in the name of patriotism. The man who enlists into the service for a consideration, and deserts the moment he receives his money but to repeat the play, is bad enough; but the men who manipulate the grand machine and who simply make the bounty-jumper their agent in an outrageous fraud are far worse. They are beneath the worms that crawl in the dark hidden places of earth."

His lips curled with haughty scorn, and a cloud was gathering on his brow. Only a moment the shadow rested on his face. Just then both goats looked up at the window and shook their heads as if they would say "How d'ye do, old friend?"

"See, Madam Elizabeth," exclaimed the President in a tone of enthusiasm, "my pets recognize me. How earnestly they look! There they go again; what jolly fun!" and he laughed outright as the goats bounded swiftly to the other side of the yard. Just then Mrs. Lincoln called out, "Come, Lizabeth; if I get ready to go down this evening I must finish dressing myself, or you must stop staring at those silly goats."

Mrs. Lincoln was not fond of pets, and she could not understand how Mr. Lincoln could take so much delight in his goats. After Willie's death, she could not bear the sight of anything he loved, not even a flower. Costly bouquets were presented to her, but she turned from them with a shudder, and either placed them in a room where she could not see them, or threw them out of the window. She gave all of Willie's toys—everything connected with him—away, as she said she could not look upon them without thinking of her poor dead boy, and to think of him, in his white shroud and cold grave, was maddening. I never in my life saw a more peculiarly constituted woman. Search the world over, and you will not find her counterpart. After Mr. Lincoln's death, the goats that he loved so well were given away—I believe to Mrs. Lee, née Miss Blair, one of the few ladies with whom Mrs. Lincoln was on intimate terms in Washington.

During my residence in the Capital I made my home with Mr. and Mrs. Walker Lewis, people of my own race, and friends in the truest sense of the word.

The days passed without any incident of particular note disturbing the current of life. On Friday morning, April 14th—alas! what American does not remember the day—I saw Mrs. Lincoln but for a moment. She told me that she was to attend the theatre that night with the President, but I was not summoned to assist her in making her toilette. Sherman had swept from the northern border of Georgia through the heart of the Confederacy down to the sea, striking the death-blow to the rebellion. Grant had pursued General Lee beyond Richmond, and the army of Virginia, that had made such stubborn resistance, was crumbling to pieces. Fort Sumter had fallen;—the stronghold first wrenched from the Union; and which had braved the fury of Federal guns for so many years, was restored to the Union; the end of the war was near at hand, and the great pulse of the loyal North thrilled with joy. The dark war-cloud was fading, and a white-robed angel seemed to hover in the sky, whispering "Peace—peace on earth, good-will toward men!" Sons, brothers, fathers, friends, sweethearts were coming home. Soon the white tents would be folded, the volunteer army be disbanded, and tranquillity again reign. Happy, happy day!—happy at least to those who fought under the banner of the Union. There was great rejoicing throughout the North. From the Atlantic to the Pacific, flags were gayly thrown to the breeze, and at night every city blazed with its tens of thousand lights. But scarcely had the fireworks ceased to play, and the lights been taken down from the windows, when the lightning flashed the most appalling news over the magnetic wires. "The President has been murdered!" spoke the swift-winged messenger, and the loud huzza died upon the lips. A nation suddenly paused in the midst of festivity, and stood paralyzed with horror—transfixed with awe.

Oh, memorable day! Oh, memorable night! Never before was joy so violently contrasted with sorrow.

At 11 o'clock at night I was awakened by an old friend and neighbor, Miss M. Brown, with the startling intelligence that the entire Cabinet had been assassinated, and Mr. Lincoln shot, but not mortally wounded. When I heard the words I felt as if the blood had been frozen in my veins, and that my lungs must collapse for the want of air. Mr. Lincoln shot! the Cabinet assassinated! What could it mean? The streets were alive with wondering, awe-stricken people. Rumors flew thick and fast, and the wildest reports came with every new arrival. The words were repeated with blanched cheeks and quivering lips. I waked Mr. and Mrs. Lewis, and told them that the President was shot, and that I must go to the White House. I could not remain in a state of uncertainty. I felt that the house would not hold me. They tried to quiet me, but gentle words could not calm the wild tempest. They quickly dressed themselves, and we sallied out into the street to drift with the excited throng. We walked rapidly towards the White House, and on our way passed the residence of Secretary Seward, which was surrounded by armed soldiers, keeping back all intruders with the point of the bayonet. We hurried on, and as we approached the White House, saw that it too was surrounded with soldiers. Every entrance was strongly guarded, and no one was permitted to pass. The guard at the gate told us that Mr. Lincoln had not been brought home, but refused to give any other information. More excited than ever, we wandered down the street. Grief and anxiety were making me weak, and as we joined the outskirts of a large crowd, I began to feel as meek and humble as a penitent child. A gray-haired old man was passing. I caught a glimpse of his face, and it seemed so full of kindness and sorrow that I gently touched his arm, and imploringly asked:

"Will you please, sir, to tell me whether Mr. Lincoln is dead or not?"

"Not dead," he replied, "but dying. God help us!" and with a heavy step he passed on.

"Not dead, but dying! then indeed God help us!"

We learned that the President was mortally wounded—that he had been shot down in his box at the theatre, and that he was not expected to live till morning; when we returned home with heavy hearts. I could not sleep. I wanted to go to Mrs. Lincoln, as I pictured her wild with grief; but then I did not know where to find her, and I must wait till morning. Never did the hours drag so slowly. Every moment seemed an age, and I could do nothing but walk about and hold my arms in mental agony.

Morning came at last, and a sad morning was it. The flags that floated so gayly yesterday now were draped in black, and hung in silent folds at half-mast. The President was dead, and a nation was mourning for him. Every house was draped in black, and every face wore a solemn look. People spoke in subdued tones, and glided whisperingly, wonderingly, silently about the streets.

About eleven o'clock on Saturday morning a carriage drove up to the door, and a messenger asked for "Elizabeth Keckley."

"Who wants her?" I asked.

"I come from Mrs. Lincoln. If you are Mrs. Keckley, come with me immediately to the White House."

I hastily put on my shawl and bonnet, and was driven at a rapid rate to the White House. Everything about the building was sad and solemn. I was quickly shown to Mrs. Lincoln's room, and on entering, saw Mrs. L. tossing uneasily about upon a bed. The room was darkened, and the only person in it besides the widow of the President was Mrs. Secretary Welles, who had spent the night with her. Bowing to Mrs. Welles, I went to the bedside.

"Why did you not come to me last night, Elizabeth—I sent for you?" Mrs. Lincoln asked in a low whisper.

"I did try to come to you, but I could not find you," I answered, as I laid my hand upon her hot brow.

I afterwards learned, that when she had partially recovered from the first shock of the terrible tragedy in the theatre, Mrs. Welles asked:

"Is there no one, Mrs. Lincoln, that you desire to have with you in this terrible affliction?"

"Yes, send for Elizabeth Keckley. I want her just as soon as she can be brought here."

Three messengers, it appears, were successively despatched for me, but all of them mistook the number and failed to find me.

Shortly after entering the room on Saturday morning, Mrs. Welles excused herself, as she said she must go to her own family, and I was left alone with Mrs. Lincoln.

She was nearly exhausted with grief, and when she became a little quiet, I asked and received permission to go into the Guests' Room, where the body of the President lay in state. When I crossed the threshold of the room, I could not help recalling the day on which I had seen little Willie lying in his coffin where the body of his father now lay. I remembered how the President had wept over the pale beautiful face of his gifted boy, and now the President himself was dead. The last time I saw him he spoke kindly to me, but alas! the lips would never move again. The light had faded from his eyes, and when the light went out the soul went with it. What a noble soul was his—noble in all the noble attributes of God! Never did I enter the solemn chamber of death with such palpitating heart and trembling footsteps as I entered it that day. No common mortal had died. The Moses of my people had fallen in the hour of his triumph. Fame had woven her choicest chaplet for his brow. Though the brow was cold and pale in death, the chaplet should not fade, for God had studded it with the glory of the eternal stars.

When I entered the room, the members of the Cabinet and many distinguished officers of the army were grouped around the body of their fallen chief. They made room for me, and, approaching the body, I lifted the white cloth from the white face of the man that I had worshipped as an idol—looked upon as a demi-god. Notwithstanding the violence of the death of the President, there was something beautiful as well as grandly solemn in the expression of the placid face. There lurked the sweetness and gentleness of childhood, and the stately grandeur of godlike intellect. I gazed long at the face, and turned away with tears in my eyes and a choking sensation in my throat. Ah! never was man so widely mourned before. The whole world bowed their heads in grief when Abraham Lincoln died.

Returning to Mrs. Lincoln's room, I found her in a new paroxysm of grief. Robert was bending over his mother with tender affection, and little Tad was crouched at the foot of the bed with a world of agony in his young face. I shall never forget the scene—the wails of a broken heart, the unearthly shrieks, the terrible convulsions, the wild, tempestuous outbursts of grief from the soul. I bathed Mrs. Lincoln's head with cold water, and soothed the terrible tornado as best I could. Tad's grief at his father's death was as great as the grief of his mother, but her terrible outbursts awed the boy into silence. Sometimes he would throw his arms around her neck, and exclaim, between his broken sobs, "Don't cry so, Mamma! don't cry, or you will make me cry, too! You will break my heart."

Mrs. Lincoln could not bear to hear Tad cry, and when he would plead to her not to break his heart, she would calm herself with a great effort, and clasp her child in her arms.

Every room in the White House was darkened, and every one spoke in subdued tones, and moved about with muffled tread. The very atmosphere breathed of the great sorrow which weighed heavily upon each heart. Mrs. Lincoln never left her room, and while the body of her husband was being borne in solemn state from the Atlantic to the broad prairies of the West, she was weeping with her fatherless children in her private chamber. She denied admittance to almost every one, and I was her only companion, except her children, in the days of her great sorrow.

There were many surmises as to who was implicated with J. Wilkes Booth in the assassination of the President. A new messenger had accompanied Mr. and Mrs. Lincoln to the theatre on that terrible Friday night. It was the duty of this messenger to stand at the door of the box during the performance, and thus guard the inmates from all intrusion. It appears that the messenger was carried away by the play, and so neglected his duty that Booth gained easy admission to the box. Mrs. Lincoln firmly believed that this messenger was implicated in the assassination plot.

One night I was lying on a lounge near the bed occupied by Mrs. Lincoln. One of the servants entering the room, Mrs. L. asked:

"Who is on watch to-night?"

"The new messenger," was the reply.

"What! the man who attended us to the theatre on the night my dear, good husband was murdered! He, I believe, is one of the murderers. Tell him to come in to me."

The messenger had overheard Mrs. Lincoln's words through the half-open door, and when he came in he was trembling violently.

She turned to him fiercely: "So you are on guard to-night—on guard in the White House after helping to murder the President!"

"Pardon me, but I did not help to murder the President. I could never stoop to murder—much less to the murder of so good and great a man as the President."

"But it appears that you did stoop to murder."

"No, no! don't say that," he broke in. "God knows that I am innocent."

"I don't believe you. Why were you not at the door to keep the assassin out when he rushed into the box?"

"I did wrong, I admit, and I have bitterly repented it, but I did not help to kill the President. I did not believe that any one would try to kill so good a man in such a public place, and the belief made me careless. I was attracted by the play, and did not see the assassin enter the box."

"But you should have seen him. You had no business to be careless. I shall always believe that you are guilty. Hush! I shan't hear another word," she exclaimed, as the messenger essayed to reply. "Go now and keep your watch," she added, with an imperious wave of her hand. With mechanical step and white face the messenger left the room, and Mrs. Lincoln fell back on her pillow, covered her face with her hands, and commenced sobbing.

Robert was very tender to his mother in the days of her sorrow.

He suffered deeply, as his haggard face indicated, but he was ever manly and collected when in the presence of his mother. Mrs. Lincoln was extremely nervous, and she refused to have anybody about her but myself. Many ladies called, but she received none of them. Had she been less secluded in her grief, perhaps she would have had many warmer friends to-day than she has. But far be it from me to harshly judge the sorrow of any one. Could the ladies who called to condole with Mrs. Lincoln, after the death of her husband, and who were denied admittance to her chamber, have seen how completely prostrated she was with grief, they would have learned to speak more kindly of her. Often at night, when Tad would hear her sobbing, he would get up, and come to her bed in his white sleeping-clothes: "Don't cry, Mamma; I cannot sleep if you cry! Papa was good, and he has gone to heaven. He is happy there. He is with God and brother Willie. Don't cry, Mamma, or I will cry too."

The closing appeal always proved the most effectual, as Mrs. Lincoln could not bear to hear her child cry.

Tad had been petted by his father, but petting could not spoil such a manly nature as his. He seemed to realize that he was the son of a President—to realize it in its loftiest and noblest sense. One morning, while being dressed, he looked up at his nurse, and said: "Pa is dead. I can hardly believe that I shall never see him again. I must learn to take care of myself now." He looked thoughtful a moment, then added, "Yes, Pa is dead, and I am only Tad Lincoln now, little Tad, like other little boys. I am not a President's son now. I won't have many presents any more. Well, I will try and be a good boy, and will hope to go some day to Pa and brother Willie, in heaven." He was a brave, manly child, and knew that influence had passed out of their hands with the death of his father, and that his position in life was altered. He seemed to feel that people petted him, and gave him presents, because they wanted to please the President of the United States. From that period forward he became more independent, and in a short time learned to dispense with the services of a nurse. While in Chicago, I saw him get out his clothes one Sunday morning and dress himself, and the change was such a great one to me—for while in the White House, servants obeyed his every nod and bid—that I could scarcely refrain from shedding tears. Had his father lived, I knew it would have been different with his favorite boy. Tad roomed with Robert, and he always took pride in pleasing his brother.

After the Committee had started West with the body of the President, there was quite a breeze of excitement for a few days as to where the remains should be interred. Secretary Stanton and others held frequent conferences with Robert, Mr. Todd, Mrs. Lincoln's cousin, and Dr. Henry, an old schoolmate and friend of Mr. Lincoln. The city authorities of Springfield had purchased a beautiful plat of ground in a prosperous portion of the city, and work was rapidly progressing on the tomb, when Mrs. Lincoln made strenuous objection to the location. She declared that she would stop the body in Chicago before it should be laid to rest in the lot purchased for the purpose by the City of Springfield. She gave as a reason, that it was her desire to be laid by the side of her husband when she died, and that such would be out of the question in a public place of the kind. As is well known, the difficulty was finally settled by placing the remains of the President in the family vault at Oak Ridge, a charming spot for the home of the dead.

After the President's funeral Mrs. Lincoln rallied, and began to make preparations to leave the White House. One day she suddenly exclaimed: "God, Elizabeth, what a change! Did ever woman have to suffer so much and experience so great a change? I had an ambition to be Mrs. President; that ambition has been gratified, and now I must step down from the pedestal. My poor husband! had he never been President, he might be living to-day. Alas! all is over with me!"

Folding her arms for a few moments, she rocked back and forth, then commenced again, more vehemently than ever: "My God, Elizabeth, I can never go back to Springfield! no, never, until I go in my shroud to be laid by my dear husband's side, and may Heaven speed that day! I should like to live for my sons, but life is so full of misery that I would rather die." And then she would go off into a fit of hysterics.

Chapter XII Mrs. Lincoln Leaves The White House

For five weeks Mrs. Lincoln was confined to her room. Packing afforded quite a relief, as it so closely occupied us that we had not much time for lamentation.

Letters of condolence were received from all parts of the country, and even from foreign potentates, but Mr. Andrew Johnson, the successor of Mr. Lincoln, never called on the widow, or even so much as wrote a line expressing sympathy for her grief and the loss of her husband. Robert called on him one day to tell him that his mother would turn the White House over to him in a few days, and he never even so much as inquired after their welfare. Mrs. Lincoln firmly believes that Mr. Johnson was concerned in the assassination plot.

In packing, Mrs. Lincoln gave away everything intimately connected with the President, as she said that she could not bear to be reminded of the past. The articles were given to those who were regarded as the warmest of Mr. Lincoln's admirers. All of the presents passed through my hands. The dress that Mrs. Lincoln wore on the night of the assassination was given to Mrs. Slade, the wife of an old and faithful messenger. The cloak, stained with the President's blood, was given to me, as also was the bonnet worn on the same memorable night. Afterwards I received the comb and brush that Mr. Lincoln used during his residence at the White House. With this same comb and brush I had often combed his head. When almost ready to go down to a reception, he would turn to me with a quizzical look: "Well, Madam Elizabeth, will you brush my bristles down to-night?"

"Yes, Mr. Lincoln."

Then he would take his seat in an easy-chair, and sit quietly while I arranged his hair. As may well be imagined, I was only too glad to accept this comb and brush from the hands of Mrs. Lincoln. The cloak, bonnet, comb, and brush, the glove worn at the first reception after the second inaugural, and Mr. Lincoln's over-shoes, also given to me, I have since donated for the benefit of Wilberforce University, a colored college near Xenia, Ohio, destroyed by fire on the night that the President was murdered.

There was much surmise, when Mrs. Lincoln left the White House, what her fifty or sixty boxes, not to count her score of trunks, could contain. Had the government not been so liberal in furnishing the boxes, it is possible that there would have been less demand for so much transportation. The boxes were loosely packed, and many of them with articles not worth carrying away. Mrs. Lincoln had a passion for hoarding old things, believing, with Toodles, that they were "handy to have about the house."

The bonnets that she brought with her from Springfield, in addition to every one purchased during her residence in Washington, were packed in the boxes, and transported to Chicago. She remarked that she might find use for the material some day, and it was prudent to look to the future. I am sorry to say that Mrs. Lincoln's foresight in regard to the future was only confined to cast-off clothing, as she owed, at the time of the President's death, different store bills amounting to seventy thousand dollars. Mr. Lincoln knew nothing of these bills, and the only happy feature of his assassination was that he died in ignorance of them. Had he known to what extent his wife was involved, the fact would have embittered the only pleasant moments of his life. I disclose this secret in regard to Mrs. Lincoln's debts, in order to explain why she should subsequently have labored under pecuniary embarrassment. The children, as well as herself, had received a vast number of presents during Mr. Lincoln's administration, and these presents constituted a large item in the contents of the boxes. The only article of furniture, so far as I know, taken away from the White House by Mrs. Lincoln, was a little dressing-stand used by the President. I recollect hearing him say one day:

"Mother, this little stand is so handy, and suits me so well, that I do not know how I shall get along without it when we move away from here." He was standing before a mirror, brushing his hair, when he made the remark.

"Well, father," Mrs. Lincoln replied, "if you like the stand so well, we will take it with us when we go away."

"Not for the world," he exclaimed; but she interrupted him:

"I should like to know what difference it makes if we put a better one in its place."

"That alters the question. If you will put a stand in its place worth twice as much as this one, and the Commissioner consents, then I have no objection."

Mrs. Lincoln remembered these words, and, with the consent of the Commissioner, took the stand to Chicago with her for the benefit of little Tad. Another stand, I must not forget to add, was put in its place.

It is charged that a great deal of furniture was lost from the White House during Mr. Lincoln's occupation of it. Very true, and it can be accounted for in this way: In some respects, to put the case very plainly, Mrs. Lincoln was "penny wise and pound foolish." When she moved into the White House, she discharged the Steward, whose business it was to look after the affairs of the household. When the Steward was dismissed, there was no one to superintend affairs, and the servants carried away many pieces of furniture. In this manner the furniture rapidly disappeared.

Robert was frequently in the room where the boxes were being packed, and he tried without avail to influence his mother to set fire to her vast stores of old goods. "What are you going to do with that old dress, mother?" he would ask.

"Never mind, Robert, I will find use for it. You do not understand this business."

"And what is more, I hope I never may understand it. I wish to heaven the car would take fire in which you place these boxes for transportation to Chicago, and burn all of your old plunder up;" and then, with an impatient gesture, he would turn on his heel and leave the room.

"Robert is so impetuous," his mother would say to me, after the closing of the door. "He never thinks about the future. Well, I hope that he will get over his boyish notions in time.

Many of the articles that Mrs. Lincoln took away from the White House were given, after her arrival in Chicago, for the benefit of charity fairs.

At last everything was packed, and the day for departure for the West came. I can never forget that day; it was so unlike the day when the body of the President was borne from the hall in grand and solemn state. Then thousands gathered to bow the head in reverence as the plumed hearse drove down the line. There was all the pomp of military display— drooping flags, battalions with reversed arms, and bands playing dirge-like airs. Now, the wife of the President was leaving the White House, and there was scarcely a friend to tell her good-by. She passed down the public stairway, entered her carriage, and quietly drove to the depot where we took the cars. The silence was almost painful.

It had been arranged that I should go to Chicago. When Mrs. Lincoln first suggested her plan, I strongly objected; but I had been with her so long, that she had acquired great power over me.

"I cannot go West with you, Mrs. Lincoln," I said, when the idea was first advanced.

"But you must go to Chicago with me, Elizabeth; I cannot do without you."

"You forget my business, Mrs. Lincoln. I cannot leave it. Just now I have the spring trousseau to make for Mrs. Douglas, and I have promised to have it done in less than a week."

"Never mind. Mrs. Douglas can get some one else to make her trousseau. You may find it to your interest to go. I am very poor now, but if Congress makes an appropriation for my benefit, you shall be well rewarded."

"It is not the reward, but—" I commenced, by way of reply, but she stopped me:

"Now don't say another word about it, if you do not wish to distress me. I have determined that you shall go to Chicago with me, and you must go."

When Mrs. Douglas learned that Mrs. Lincoln wished me to accompany her West, she sent me word:

"Never mind me. Do all you can for Mrs. Lincoln. My heart's sympathy is with her."

Finding that no excuse would be accepted, I made preparations to go to Chicago with Mrs. L.

The green car had specially been chartered for us, and in this we were conveyed to the West. Dr. Henry accompanied us, and he was remarkably attentive and kind. The first night out, Mrs. Lincoln had a severe headache; and while I was bathing her temples, she said to me:

"Lizabeth, you are my best and kindest friend, and I love you as my best friend. I wish it were in my power to make you comfortable for the balance of your days. If Congress provides for me, depend upon it, I will provide for you."

The trip was devoid of interest. We arrived in Chicago without accident or delay, and apartments were secured for us at the Tremont House, where we remained one week. At the expiration of this time Mrs. Lincoln decided that living at the hotel was attended with too much expense, so it was arranged that we should go to the country. Rooms were selected at Hyde Park, a summer resort.

Robert and Tad accompanied their mother to Hyde Park. We arrived about 3 o'clock in the afternoon of Saturday. The place had just been opened the summer before, and there was a newness about everything. The accommodations were not first-class, the rooms being small and plainly furnished. It was a lively day for us all. Robert occupied himself unpacking his books, and arranging them on the shelves in the corner of his small but neat room. I assisted him, he talking pleasantly all the while. When we were through, he folded his arms, stood off a little distance from the mantel, with an abstracted look as if he were thinking of the great change in his fortunes—contrasting the present with the past. Turning to me, he asked: "Well, Mrs. Keckley, how do you like our new quarters?"

"This is a delightful place, and I think you will pass your time pleasantly," I answered.

He looked at me with a quizzical smile, then remarked: "You call it a delightful place! Well, perhaps it is. Since you do not have to stay here, you can safely say as much about the charming situation as you please. I presume that I must put up with it, as mother's pleasure must be consulted before my own. But candidly, I would almost as soon be dead as be compelled to remain three months in this dreary house."

He seemed to feel what he said, and going to the window, he looked out upon the view with moody countenance. I passed into Mrs. Lincoln's room, and found her lying upon the bed, sobbing as if her heart would break.

"What a dreary place, Lizzie! And to think that I should be compelled to live here, because I have not the means to live elsewhere. Ah! what a sad change has come to us all." I had listened to her sobbing for eight weeks, therefore I was never surprised to find her in tears. Tad was the only cheerful one of the party. He was a child of sunshine, and nothing seemed to dampen the ardor of his spirits.

Sunday was a very quiet day. I looked out of my window in the morning, upon the beautiful lake that formed one of the most delightful views from the house. The wind was just strong enough to ripple the broad bosom of the water, and each ripple caught a jewel from the sunshine, and threw it sparkling up towards the sky. Here and there a sail-boat silently glided into view, or sank below the faint blue line that marked the horizon—glided and melted away like the spectral shadows that sometimes haunt the white snow-fields in the cold, tranquil light of a winter's moon. As I stood by my window that morning, looking out upon the lake, my thoughts were etherealized—the reflected sunbeams suggested visions of crowns studded with the jewels of eternal life, and I wondered how any one could call Hyde Park a dreary place. I had seen so much trouble in my life, that I was willing to fold my arms and sink into a passive slumber—slumber anywhere, so the great longing of the soul was gratified—rest.

Robert spent the day in his room with his books, while I remained in Mrs. Lincoln's room, talking with her, contrasting the present with the past, and drawing plans for the future. She held no communication, by letter or otherwise, with any of her relatives or old friends, saying that she wished to lead a secluded life for the summer. Old faces, she claimed, would only bring back memories of scenes that she desired to forget; and new faces, she felt assured, could not sympathize with her distress, or add to the comforts of her situation.

On Monday morning, Robert was getting ready to ride into Chicago, as business called him to the city.

"Where you goin', brother Bob?"—Tad generally called Robert, brother Bob.

"Only into town!" was the brief reply.

"Mayn't I go with you?"

"Ask mother. I think that she will say no."

Just then Mrs. Lincoln came in, and Tad ran to her, with the eager question:

"Oh, Ma! can't I go to town with brother Bob? I want to go so badly."

"Go to town! No; you must stay and keep me company. Besides, I have determined that you shall get a lesson every day, and I am going to commence to-day with you."

"I don't want to get a lesson—I won't get a lesson," broke in the impetuous boy. "I don't want to learn my book; I want to go to town!"

"I suppose you want to grow up to be a great dunce. Hush, Tad; you shall not go to town until you have said a lesson;" and the mother looked resolute.

"May I go after I learn my book?" was the next question.

"Yes; if Robert will wait for you."

"Oh, Bob will wait; won't you, Bob?"

"No, I cannot wait; but the landlord is going in this afternoon, and you can go with him. You must do as mother tells you, Tad. You are getting to be a big boy now, and must start to school next fall; and you would not like to go to school without knowing how to read."

"Where's my book, Ma? Get my book quick. I will say my lesson," and he jumped about the room, boisterously, boy-like.

"Be quiet, Tad. Here is your book, and we will now begin the first lesson," said his mother, as she seated herself in an easy-chair.

Tad had always been much humored by his parents, especially by his father. He suffered from a slight impediment in his speech, and had never been made to go to school; consequently his book knowledge was very limited. I knew that his education had been neglected, but had no idea he was so deficient as the first lesson at Hyde Park proved him to be.

Drawing a low chair to his mother's side, he opened his book, and began to slowly spell the first word, "A-P-E."

"Well, what does A-p-e spell?"

"Monkey," was the instant rejoinder. The word was illustrated by a small wood-cut of an ape, which looked to Tad's eyes very much like a monkey; and his pronunciation was guided by the picture, and not by the sounds of the different letters.

"Nonsense!" exclaimed his mother. "A-p-e does not spell monkey."

"Does spell monkey! Isn't that a monkey?" and Tad pointed triumphantly to the picture.

"No, it is not a monkey."

"Not a monkey! what is it, then?"

"An ape."

"An ape! 'taint an ape. Don't I know a monkey when I see it?"

"No, if you say that is a monkey."

"I do know a monkey. I've seen lots of them in the street with the organs. I know a monkey better than you do, 'cause I always go out into the street to see them when they come by, and you don't."

"But, Tad, listen to me. An ape is a species of the monkey. It looks like a monkey, but it is not a monkey."

"It shouldn't look like a monkey, then. Here, Yib"—he always called me Yib—"isn't this a monkey, and don't A-p-e spell monkey? Ma don't know anything about it;" and he thrust his book into my face in an earnest, excited manner.

I could not longer restrain myself, and burst out laughing. Tad looked very much offended, and I hastened to say: "I beg your pardon, Master Tad; I hope that you will excuse my want of politeness."

He bowed his head in a patronizing way, and returned to the original question: "Isn't this a monkey? Don't A-p-e spell monkey?"

"No, Tad; your mother is right. A-p-e spells ape."

"You don't know as much as Ma. Both of you don't know anything;" and Master Tad's eyes flashed with indignation.

Robert entered the room, and the question was referred to him. After many explanations, he succeeded in convincing Tad that A-p-e does not spell monkey, and the balance of the lesson was got over with less difficulty.

Whenever I think of this incident I am tempted to laugh; and then it occurs to me that had Tad been a negro boy, not the son of a President, and so difficult to instruct, he would have been called thick-skulled, and would have been held up as an example of the inferiority of race. I know many full negro boys, able to read and write, who are not older than Tad Lincoln was when he persisted that A-p-e spelt monkey. Do not imagine that I desire to reflect upon the intellect of little Tad. Not at all; he is a bright boy, a son that will do honor to the genius and greatness of his father; I only mean to say that some incidents are about as damaging to one side of the question as to the other. If a colored boy appears dull, so does a white boy sometimes; and if a whole race is judged by a single example of apparent dulness, another race should be judged by a similar example.

I returned to Washington, with Mrs. Lincoln's best wishes for my success in business. The journey was devoid of incident. After resting a few days, I called at the White House, and transacted some business for Mrs. Lincoln. I had no desire to enter the house, for everything about it bitterly reminded me of the past; and when I came out of the door, I hoped that I had crossed the threshold for the last time. I was asked by some of my friends if I had sent my business cards to Mr. Johnson's family, and my answer was that I had not, as I had no desire to work for the President's family. Mr. Johnson was no friend to Mr. Lincoln, and he had failed to treat Mrs. Lincoln, in the hour of her greatest sorrow, with even common courtesy.

Having promised to make a spring trousseau for Mrs. Senator Douglas as soon as I should return from Chicago, I called on her to meet the engagement. She appeared pleased to see me, and in greeting me, asked, with evident surprise:

"Why, Keckley"—she always called me Keckley—"is this you? I did not know you were coming back. It was reported that you designed remaining with Mrs. Lincoln all summer."

"Mrs. Lincoln would have been glad to have kept me with her had she been able."

"Able! What do you mean by that?"

"Simply this: Already she is laboring under pecuniary embarrassment, and was only able to pay my expenses, and allow me nothing for my time."

"You surprise me. I thought she was left in good circumstances."

"So many think, it appears. Mrs. Lincoln, I assure you, is now practising the closest economy. I must do something for myself, Mrs. Douglas, so I have come back to Washington to open my shop."

The next day I collected my assistants, and my business went on as usual. Orders came in more rapidly than I could fill them. One day, in the middle of the month of June, the girl who was attending the door came into the cutting-room, where I was hard at work:

"Mrs. Keckley, there is a lady below, who wants to see you."

"Who is she?"

"I don't know. I did not learn her name."

"Is her face familiar? Does she look like a regular customer?"

"No, she is a stranger. I don't think she was ever here before. She came in an open carriage, with a black woman for an attendant."

"It may be the wife of one of Johnson's new secretaries. Do go down, Mrs. Keckley," exclaimed my work-girls in a chorus. I went below, and on entering the parlor, a plainly dressed lady rose to her feet, and asked:

"Is this the dressmaker?"

"Yes, I am a dressmaker."

"Mrs. Keckley?"

"Yes."

"Mrs. Lincoln's former dressmaker, were you not?"

"Yes, I worked for Mrs. Lincoln."

"Are you very busy now?"

"Very, indeed."

"Can you do anything for me?"

"That depends upon what is to be done, and when it is to be done."

"Well, say one dress now, and several others a few weeks later."

"I can make one dress for you now, but no more. I cannot finish the one for you in less than three weeks."

"That will answer. I am Mrs. Patterson, the daughter of President Johnson. I expect my sister, Mrs. Stover, here in three weeks, and the dress is for her. We are both the same size, and you can fit the dress to me."

The terms were satisfactorily arranged, and after measuring Mrs. Patterson, she bade me good morning, entered her carriage, and drove away.

When I went up-stairs into the work-room, the girls were anxious to learn who my visitor was.

"It was Mrs. Patterson, the daughter of President Johnson," I answered, in response to several questions.

"What! the daughter of our good Moses. Are you going to work for her?"

"I have taken her order."

"I fear that Johnson will prove a poor Moses, and I would not work for any of the family," remarked one of the girls. None of them appeared to like Mr. Lincoln's successor.

I finished the dress for Mrs. Patterson, and it gave satisfaction. I afterwards learned that both Mrs. Patterson and Mrs. Stover were kindhearted, plain, unassuming women, making no pretensions to elegance. One day when I called at the White House, in relation to some work that I was doing for them, I found Mrs. Patterson busily at work with a sewing-machine. The sight was a novel one to me for the White House, for as long as I remained with Mrs. Lincoln, I do not recollect ever having seen her with a needle in her hand. The last work done for the Johnsons by me were two dresses, one for each of the sisters. Mrs. Patterson subsequently wrote me a note, requesting me to cut and fit a dress for her; to which I replied that I never cut and fitted work to be made up outside of my work-room. This brought our business relations to an abrupt end.

The months passed, and my business prospered. I continually received letters from Mrs. Lincoln, and as the anniversary of her husband's death approached, she wrote in a sadder strain. Before I left Chicago she had exacted the promise that should Congress make an appropriation for her benefit, I must join her in the West, and go with her to visit the tomb of the President for the first time. The appropriation was made one of the conditions of my visit, for without relief from Congress she would be unable to bear my expenses. The appropriation was not made; and so I was unable to join Mrs. Lincoln at the appointed time. She wrote me that her plan was to leave Chicago in the morning with Tad, reach Springfield at night, stop at one of the hotels, drive out to Oak Ridge the next day, and take the train for Chicago the same evening, thus avoiding a meeting with any of her old friends. This plan, as she afterwards wrote me, was carried out. When the second anniversary approached, President Johnson and party were "swinging round the circle," and as they were to visit Chicago, she was especially anxious to be away from the city when they should arrive; accordingly she hurried off to Springfield, and spent the time in weeping over the tomb where repose the hallowed ashes of her husband.

During all this time I was asked many questions about Mrs. Lincoln, some prompted by friendship, but a greater number by curiosity; but my brief answers, I fear, were not always accepted as the most satisfactory.

Memoirs Of General W. T. Sherman
By *William T. Sherman*

Atlanta, Ga. Gen. William T. Sherman on horseback at Federal Fort No. 7

Chapter XXV Conclusion--Military Lessons Of The War

Having thus recorded a summary of events, mostly under my own personal supervision, during the years from 1846 to 1865, it seems proper that I should add an opinion of some of the useful military lessons to be derived therefrom.

That civil war, by reason of the existence of slavery, was apprehended by most of the leading statesmen of the half-century preceding its outbreak, is a matter of notoriety. General Scott told me on my arrival at New York, as early as 1850, that the country was on the eve of civil war; and the Southern politicians openly asserted that it was their purpose to accept as a casus belli the election of General Fremont in 1856; but, fortunately or unfortunately, he was beaten by Mr. Buchanan, which simply postponed its occurrence for four years. Mr. Seward had also publicly declared that no government could possibly exist half slave and half free; yet the Government made no military preparation, and the Northern people generally paid no attention, took no warning of its coming, and would not realize its existence till Fort Sumter was fired on by batteries of artillery, handled by declared enemies, from the surrounding islands and from the city of Charleston.

General Bragg, who certainly was a man of intelligence, and who, in early life, ridiculed a thousand times, in my hearing, the threats of the people of South Carolina to secede from the Federal Union, said to me in New Orleans, in February, 1861, that he was convinced that the feeling between the slave and free States had become so embittered that it was better to part in peace; better to part anyhow; and, as a separation was inevitable, that the South should begin at once, because the possibility of a successful effort was yearly lessened by the rapid and increasing inequality between the two sections, from the fact that all the European immigrants were coming to the Northern States and Territories, and none to the Southern.

The slave population m 1860 was near four millions, and the money value thereof not far from twenty-five hundred million dollars. Now, ignoring the moral side of the question, a cause that endangered so vast a moneyed interest was an adequate cause of anxiety and preparation, and the Northern leaders surely ought to have foreseen the danger and prepared for it. After the election of Mr. Lincoln in 1860, there was no concealment of the declaration and preparation for war in the South. In Louisiana, as I have related, men were openly enlisted, officers were appointed, and war was actually begun, in January, 1861. The forts at the mouth of the Mississippi were seized, and occupied by garrisons that hauled down the United States flag and hoisted that of the State. The United States Arsenal at Baton Rouge was captured by New Orleans militia, its garrison ignominiously sent off, and the contents of the arsenal distributed. These were as much acts of war as was the subsequent firing on Fort Sumter, yet no public notice was taken thereof; and when, months afterward, I came North, I found not one single sign of preparation. It was for this reason, somewhat, that the people of the South became convinced that those of the North were pusillanimous and cowardly, and the Southern leaders were thereby enabled to commit their people to the war, nominally in defense of their slave property. Up to the hour of the firing on Fort Sumter, in April, 1861, it does seem to me that our public men, our politicians, were blamable for not sounding the note of alarm.

Then, when war was actually begun, it was by a call for seventy-five thousand "ninety-day" men, I suppose to fulfill Mr. Seward's prophecy that the war would last but ninety days.

The earlier steps by our political Government were extremely wavering and weak, for which an excuse can be found in the fact that many of the Southern representatives remained in Congress, sharing in the public councils, and influencing legislation. But as soon as Mr. Lincoln was installed, there was no longer any reason why Congress and the cabinet should have hesitated. They should have measured the cause, provided the means, and left the Executive to apply the remedy.

At the time of Mr. Lincoln's inauguration, viz., March 4, 1861, the Regular Army, by law, consisted of two regiments of dragoons, two regiments of cavalry, one regiment of mounted rifles, four regiments of artillery, and ten regiments of infantry, admitting of an aggregate strength of thirteen thousand and twenty-four officers and men. On the subsequent 4th of May the President, by his own orders (afterward sanctioned by Congress), added a regiment of cavalry, a regiment of artillery, and eight regiments of infantry, which, with the former army, admitted of a strength of thirty-nine thousand nine hundred and seventy-three; but at no time during the war did the Regular Army attain a strength of twenty-five thousand men.

To the new regiments of infantry was given an organization differing from any that had heretofore prevailed in this country--of three battalions of eight companies each; but at no time did more than one of these regiments attain its full standard; nor in the vast army of volunteers that was raised during the war were any of the regiments of infantry formed on the three-battalion system, but these were universally single battalions of ten companies; so that, on the reorganization of the Regular Army at the close of the war, Congress adopted the form of twelve companies for the regiments of cavalry and artillery, and that of ten companies for the infantry, which is the present standard.

Inasmuch as the Regular Army will naturally form the standard of organization for any increase or for new regiments of volunteers, it becomes important to study this subject in the light of past experience, and to select that form which is best for peace as well as war.

A cavalry regiment is now composed of twelve companies, usually divided into six squadrons, of two companies each, or better subdivided into three battalions of four companies each. This is an excellent form, easily admitting of subdivision as well as union into larger masses.

A single battalion of four companies, with a field-officer, will compose a good body for a garrison, for a separate expedition, or for a detachment; and, in war, three regiments would compose a good brigade, three brigades a division, and three divisions a strong cavalry corps, such as was formed and fought by Generals Sheridan and Wilson during the war.

In the artillery arm, the officers differ widely in their opinion of the true organization. A single company forms a battery, and habitually each battery acts separately, though sometimes several are united or "massed;" but these always act in concert with cavalry or infantry.

Nevertheless, the regimental organization for artillery has always been maintained in this country for classification and promotion. Twelve companies compose a regiment, and, though probably no colonel ever commanded his full regiment in the form of twelve batteries, yet in peace they occupy our heavy sea-coast forts or act as infantry; then the regimental organization is both necessary and convenient.

But the infantry composes the great mass of all armies, and the true form of the regiment or unit has been the subject of infinite discussion; and, as I have stated, during the civil war the regiment was a single battalion of ten companies. In olden times the regiment was composed of eight battalion companies and two flank companies. The first and tenth companies were armed with rifles, and were styled and used as "skirmishers;" but during 'the war they were never used exclusively for that special purpose, and in fact no distinction existed between them and the other eight companies.

The ten-company organization is awkward in practice, and I am satisfied that the infantry regiment should have the same identical organization as exists for the cavalry and artillery, viz., twelve companies, so as to be susceptible of division into three battalions of four companies each.

These companies should habitually be about a hundred one men strong, giving twelve hundred to a regiment, which in practice would settle down to about one thousand men.

Three such regiments would compose a brigade, three brigades a division, and three divisions a corps. Then, by allowing to an infantry corps a brigade of cavalry and six batteries of field-artillery, we would have an efficient corps d'armee of thirty thousand men, whose organization would be simple and most efficient, and whose strength should never be allowed to fall below twenty-five thousand men.

The corps is the true unit for grand campaigns and battle, should have a full and perfect staff, and every thing requisite for separate action, ready at all times to be detached and sent off for any nature of service. The general in command should have the rank of lieutenant-general, and should be, by experience and education, equal to any thing in war. Habitually with us he was a major-general, specially selected and assigned to the command by an order of the President, constituting, in fact, a separate grade.

The division is the unit of administration, and is the legitimate command of a major general.

The brigade is the next subdivision, and is commanded by a brigadier-general.

The regiment is the family. The colonel, as the father, should have a personal acquaintance with every officer and man, and should instill a feeling of pride and affection for himself, so that his officers and men would naturally look to him for personal advice and instruction. In war the regiment should never be subdivided, but should always be maintained entire. In peace this is impossible.

The company is the true unit of discipline, and the captain is the company. A good captain makes a good company, and he should have the power to reward as well as punish.

The fact that soldiers world naturally like to have a good fellow for their captain is the best reason why he should be appointed by the colonel, or by some superior authority, instead of being elected by the men.

In the United States the people are the "sovereign," all power originally proceeds from them, and therefore the election of officers by the men is the common rule. This is wrong, because an army is not a popular organization, but an animated machine, an instrument in the hands of the Executive for enforcing the law, and maintaining the honor and dignity of the nation; and the President, as the constitutional commander-in-chief of the army and navy, should exercise the power of appointment (subject to the confirmation of the Senate) of the officers of "volunteers," as well as of "regulars."

No army can be efficient unless it be a unit for action; and the power must come from above, not from below: the President usually delegates his power to the commander-in-chief, and he to the next, and so on down to the lowest actual commander of troops, however small the detachment. No matter how troops come together, when once united, the highest officer in rank is held responsible, and should be consequently armed with the fullest power of the Executive, subject only to law and existing orders. The more simple the principle, the greater the likelihood of determined action; and the less a commanding officer is circumscribed by bounds or by precedent, the greater is the probability that he will make the best use of his command and achieve the best results.

The Regular Army and the Military Academy at West Point have in the past provided, and doubtless will in the future provide an ample supply of good officers for future wars; but, should their numbers be insufficient, we can always safely rely on the great number of young men of education and force of character throughout the country, to supplement them. At the close of our civil war, lasting four years, some of our best corps and division generals, as well as staff-officers, were from civil life; but I cannot recall any of the most successful who did not express a regret that he had not received in early life instruction in the elementary principles of the art of war, instead of being forced to acquire this knowledge in the dangerous and expensive school of actual war.

But the vital difficulty was, and will be again, to obtain an adequate number of good soldiers. We tried almost every system known to modern nations, all with more or less success--voluntary enlistments, the draft, and bought substitutes--and I think that all officers of experience will confirm my assertion that the men who voluntarily enlisted at the outbreak of the war were the best, better than the conscript, and far better than the bought substitute. When a regiment is once organized in a State, and mustered into the service of the United States, the officers and men become subject to the same laws of discipline and government as the regular troops. They are in no sense "militia," but compose a part of the Army of the United States, only retain their State title for convenience, and yet may be principally recruited from the neighborhood of their original organization: Once organized, the regiment should be kept full by recruits, and when it becomes difficult to obtain more recruits the pay should be raised by Congress, instead of tempting new men by exaggerated bounties. I believe it would have been more economical to have raised the pay of the soldier to thirty or even fifty dollars a month than to have held out the promise of three hundred and even six hundred dollars in the form of bounty. Toward the close of the war, I have often heard the soldiers complain that the "stay at-home" men got better pay, bounties, and food, than they who were exposed to all the dangers and vicissitudes of the battles and marches at the front. The feeling of the soldier should be that, in every event, the sympathy and preference of his government is for him who fights, rather than for him who is on provost or guard duty to the rear, and, like most men, he measures this by the amount of pay. Of course, the soldier must be trained to obedience, and should be "content with his wages;" but whoever has commanded an army in the field knows the difference between a willing, contented mass of men, and one that feels a cause of grievance. There is a soul to an army as well as to the individual man, and no general can accomplish the full work of his army unless he commands the soul of his men, as well as their bodies and legs.

The greatest mistake made in our civil war was in the mode of recruitment and promotion. When a regiment became reduced by the necessary wear and tear of service, instead of being filled up at the bottom, and the vacancies among the officers filled from the best noncommissioned officers and men, the habit was to raise new regiments, with new colonels, captains, and men, leaving the old and experienced battalions to dwindle away into mere skeleton organizations. I believe with the volunteers this matter was left to the States exclusively, and I remember that Wisconsin kept her regiments filled with recruits, whereas other States generally filled their quotas by new regiments, and the result was that we estimated a Wisconsin regiment equal to an ordinary brigade. I believe that five hundred new men added to an old and experienced regiment were more valuable than a thousand men in the form of a new regiment, for the former by association with good, experienced captains, lieutenants, and non-commissioned officers, soon became veterans, whereas the latter were generally unavailable for a year. The German method of recruitment is simply perfect, and there is no good reason why we should not follow it substantially.

On a road, marching by the flank, it would be considered "good order" to have five thousand men to a mile, so that a full corps of thirty thousand men would extend six miles, but with the average trains and batteries of artillery the probabilities are that it would draw out to ten miles. On a long and regular march the divisions and brigades should alternate in the lead, the leading division should be on the road by the earliest dawn, and march at the rate of about two miles, or, at most, two and a half miles an hour, so as to reach camp by noon. Even then the rear divisions and trains will hardly reach camp much before night. Theoretically, a marching column should preserve such order that by simply halting and facing to the right or left, it would be in line of battle; but this is rarely the case, and generally deployments are made "forward," by conducting each brigade by the flank obliquely to the right or left to its approximate position in line of battle, and there deployed. In such a line of battle, a brigade of three thousand infantry would occupy a mile of "front;" but for a strong line of battle five-thousand men with two batteries should be allowed to each mile, or a division would habitually constitute a double line with skirmishers and a reserve on a mile of "front."

The "feeding" of an army is a matter of the most vital importance, and demands the earliest attention of the general intrusted with a campaign. To be strong, healthy, and capable of the largest measure of physical effort, the soldier needs about three pounds gross of food per day, and the horse or mule about twenty pounds. When a general first estimates the quantity of food and forage needed for an army of fifty or one hundred thousand men, he is apt to be dismayed, and here a good staff is indispensable, though the general cannot throw off on them the responsibility. He must give the subject his personal attention, for the army reposes in him alone, and should never doubt the fact that their existence overrides in importance all other considerations. Once satisfied of this, and that all has been done that can be, the soldiers are always willing to bear the largest measure of privation. Probably no army ever had a more varied experience in this regard than the one I commanded in 1864'65.

Our base of supply was at Nashville, supplied by railways and the Cumberland River, thence by rail to Chattanooga, a "secondary base," and thence forward a single-track railroad. The stores came forward daily, but I endeavored to have on hand a full supply for twenty days in advance. These stores were habitually in the wagon-trains, distributed to corps, divisions, and regiments, in charge of experienced quartermasters and commissaries, and became subject to the orders of the generals commanding these bodies. They were generally issued on provision returns, but these had to be closely scrutinized, for too often the colonels would make requisitions for provisions for more men than they reported for battle. Of course, there are always a good many non-combatants with an army, but, after careful study, I limited their amount to twenty-five per cent. of the "effective strength," and that was found to be liberal. An ordinary army-wagon drawn by six mules may be counted on to carry three thousand pounds net, equal to the food of a full regiment for one day, but, by driving along beef-cattle, a commissary may safely count the contents of one wagon as sufficient for two days' food for a regiment of a thousand men; and as a corps should have food on hand for twenty days ready for detachment, it should have three hundred such wagons, as a provision-train; and for forage, ammunition, clothing, and other necessary stores, it was found necessary to have three hundred more wagons, or six hundred wagons in all, for a corps d'armee.

These should be absolutely under the immediate control of the corps commander, who will, however, find it economical to distribute them in due proportion to his divisions, brigades, and even regiments. Each regiment ought usually to have at least one wagon for convenience to distribute stores, and each company two pack-mules, so that the regiment may always be certain of a meal on reaching camp without waiting for the larger trains.

On long marches the artillery and wagon-trains should always have the right of way, and the troops should improvise roads to one side, unless forced to use a bridge in common, and all trains should have escorts to protect them, and to assist them in bad places. To this end there is nothing like actual experience, only, unless the officers in command give the subject their personal attention, they will find their wagon-trains loaded down with tents, personal baggage, and even the arms and knapsacks of the escort. Each soldier should, if not actually "sick or wounded," carry his musket and equipments containing from forty to sixty rounds of ammunition, his shelter-tent, a blanket or overcoat, and an extra pair of pants, socks, and drawers, in the form of a scarf, worn from the left shoulder to the right side in lieu of knapsack, and in his haversack he should carry some bread, cooked meat, salt, and coffee. I do not believe a soldier should be loaded down too much, but, including his clothing, arms, and equipment, he can carry about fifty pounds without impairing his health or activity. A simple calculation will show that by such a distribution a corps will-thus carry the equivalent of five hundred wagon-loads--an immense relief to the trains.

Where an army is near one of our many large navigable rivers, or has the safe use of a railway, it can usually be supplied with the full army ration, which is by far the best furnished to any army in America or Europe; but when it is compelled to operate away from such a base, and is dependent on its own train of wagons, the commanding officer must exercise a wise discretion in the selection of his stores. In my opinion, there is no better food for man than beef-cattle driven on the hoof, issued liberally, with salt, bacon, and bread. Coffee has also become almost indispensable, though many substitutes were found for it, such as Indian-corn, roasted, ground, and boiled as coffee; the sweet-potato, and the seed of the okra plant prepared in the same way. All these were used by the people of the South, who for years could procure no coffee, but I noticed that the women always begged of us some real coffee, which seems to satisfy a natural yearning or craving more powerful than can be accounted for on the theory of habit. Therefore I would always advise that the coffee and sugar ration be carried along, even at the expense of bread, for which there are many substitutes. Of these, Indian-corn is the best and most abundant. Parched in a frying-pan, it is excellent food, or if ground, or pounded and boiled with meat of any sort, it makes a most nutritious meal. The potato, both Irish and sweet, forms an excellent substitute for bread, and at Savannah we found that rice (was) also suitable, both for men and animals. For the former it should be cleaned of its husk in a hominy block, easily prepared out of a log, and sifted with a coarse corn bag; but for horses it should be fed in the straw. During the Atlanta campaign we were supplied by our regular commissaries with all sorts of patent compounds, such as desiccated vegetables, and concentrated milk, meat-biscuit, and sausages, but somehow the men preferred the simpler and more familiar forms of food, and usually styled these "desecrated vegetables and consecrated milk." We were also supplied liberally with lime-juice, sauerkraut, and pickles, as an antidote to scurvy, and I now recall the extreme anxiety of my medical director, Dr. Kittoe, about the scurvy, which he reported at one time as spreading and imperiling the army. This occurred at a crisis about Kenesaw, when the railroad was taxed to its utmost capacity to provide the necessary ammunition, food, and forage, and could not possibly bring us an adequate supply of potatoes and cabbage, the usual anti-scorbutics, when providentially the black berries ripened and proved an admirable antidote, and I have known the skirmish-line, without orders, to fight a respectable battle for the possession of some old fields that were full of blackberries. Soon, thereafter, the green corn or roasting-ear came into season, and I heard no more of the scurvy. Our country abounds with plants which can be utilized for a prevention to the scurvy; besides the above are the persimmon, the sassafras root and bud, the wild-mustard, the "agave," turnip tops, the dandelion cooked as greens, and a decoction of the ordinary pine-leaf.

For the more delicate and costly articles of food for the sick we relied mostly on the agents of the Sanitary Commission. I do not wish to doubt the value of these organizations, which gained so much applause during our civil war, for no one can question the motives of these charitable and generous people; but to be honest I must record an opinion that the Sanitary Commission should limit its operations to the hospitals at the rear, and should never appear at the front. They were generally local in feeling, aimed to furnish their personal friends and neighbors with a better class of food than the Government supplied, and the consequence was, that one regiment of a brigade would receive potatoes and fruit which would be denied another regiment close by: Jealousy would be the inevitable result, and in an army all parts should be equal; there should be no "partiality, favor, or affection." The Government should supply all essential wants, and in the hospitals to the rear will be found abundant opportunities for the exercise of all possible charity and generosity. During the war I several times gained the ill-will of the agents of the Sanitary Commission because I forbade their coming to the front unless they would consent to distribute their stores equally among all, regardless of the parties who had contributed them.

The sick, wounded, and dead of an army are the subjects of the greatest possible anxiety, and add an immense amount of labor to the well men. Each regiment in an active campaign should have a surgeon and two assistants always close at hand, and each brigade and division should have an experienced surgeon as a medical director. The great majority of wounds and of sickness should be treated by the regimental surgeon, on the ground, under the eye of the colonel. As few should be sent to the brigade or division hospital as possible, for the men always receive better care with their own regiment than with strangers, and as a rule the cure is more certain; but when men receive disabling wounds, or have sickness likely to become permanent, the sooner they go far to the rear the better for all. The tent or the shelter of a tree is a better hospital than a house, whose walls absorb fetid and poisonous emanations, and then give them back to the atmosphere. To men accustomed to the open air, who live on the plainest food, wounds seem to give less pain, and are attended with less danger to life than to ordinary soldiers in barracks.

Wounds which, in 1861, would have sent a man to the hospital for months, in 1865 were regarded as mere scratches, rather the subject of a joke than of sorrow. To new soldiers the sight of blood and death always has a sickening effect, but soon men become accustomed to it, and I have heard them exclaim on seeing a dead comrade borne to the rear, "Well, Bill has turned up his toes to the daisies." Of course, during a skirmish or battle, armed men should never leave their ranks to attend a dead or wounded comrade--this should be seen to in advance by the colonel, who should designate his musicians or company cooks as hospital attendants, with a white rag on their arm to indicate their office. A wounded man should go himself (if able) to the surgeon near at hand, or, if he need help, he should receive it from one of the attendants and not a comrade. It is wonderful how soon the men accustom themselves to these simple rules. In great battles these matters call for a more enlarged attention, and then it becomes the duty of the division general to see that proper stretchers and field hospitals are ready for the wounded, and trenches are dug for the dead. There should be no real neglect of the dead, because it has a bad effect on the living; for each soldier values himself and comrade as highly as though he were living in a good house at home.

Atlanta, Ga. City Hall; camp of 2d Massachusetts Infantry on the grounds

The regimental chaplain, if any, usually attends the burials from the hospital, should make notes and communicate details to the captain of the company, and to the family at home. Of course it is usually impossible to mark the grave with names, dates, etc., and consequently the names of the "unknown" in our national cemeteries equal about one-half of all the dead.

Very few of the battles in which I have participated were fought as described in European text-books, viz., in great masses, in perfect order, manoeuvring by corps, divisions, and brigades. We were generally in a wooded country, and, though our lines were deployed according to tactics, the men generally fought in strong skirmish-lines, taking advantage of the shape of ground, and of every cover. We were generally the assailants, and in wooded and broken countries the "defensive" had a positive advantage over us, for they were always ready, had cover, and always knew the ground to their immediate front; whereas we, their assailants, had to grope our way over unknown ground, and generally found a cleared field or prepared entanglements that held us for a time under a close and withering fire. Rarely did the opposing lines in compact order come into actual contact, but when, as at Peach-Tree Creek and Atlanta, the lines did become commingled, the men fought individually in every possible style, more frequently with the musket clubbed than with the bayonet, and in some instances the men clinched like wrestlers, and went to the ground together. Europeans frequently criticised our war, because we did not always take full advantage of a victory; the true reason was, that habitually the woods served as a screen, and we often did not realize the fact that our enemy had retreated till he was already miles away and was again intrenched, having left a mere skirmish-line to cover the movement, in turn to fall back to the new position.

Our war was fought with the muzzle-loading rifle. Toward the close I had one brigade (Walcutt's) armed with breech-loading "Spencer's;" the cavalry generally had breach-loading carbines, "Spencer's" and "Sharp's," both of which were good arms.

The only change that breech-loading arms will probably make in the art and practice of war will be to increase the amount of ammunition to be expended, and necessarily to be carried along; to still further "thin out" the lines of attack, and to reduce battles to short, quick, decisive conflicts. It does not in the least affect the grand strategy, or the necessity for perfect organization, drill, and discipline. The companies and battalions will be more dispersed, and the men will be less under the immediate eye of their officers, and therefore a higher order of intelligence and courage on the part of the individual soldier will be an element of strength.

When a regiment is deployed as skirmishers, and crosses an open field or woods, under heavy fire, if each man runs forward from tree to tree, or stump to stump, and yet preserves a good general alignment, it gives great confidence to the men themselves, for they always keep their eyes well to the right and left, and watch their comrades; but when some few hold back, stick too close or too long to a comfortable log, it often stops the line and defeats the whole object. Therefore, the more we improve the fire-arm the more will be the necessity for good organization, good discipline and intelligence on the part of the individual soldier and officer. There is, of course, such a thing as individual courage, which has a value in war, but familiarity with danger, experience in war and its common attendants, and personal habit, are equally valuable traits, and these are the qualities with which we usually have to deal in war. All men naturally shrink from pain and danger, and only incur their risk from some higher motive, or from habit; so that I would define true courage to be a perfect sensibility of the measure of danger, and a mental willingness to incur it, rather than that insensibility to danger of which I have heard far more than I have seen. The most courageous men are generally unconscious of possessing the quality; therefore, when one professes it too openly, by words or bearing, there is reason to mistrust it. I would further illustrate my meaning by describing a man of true courage to be one who possesses all his faculties and senses perfectly when serious danger is actually present.

Modern wars have not materially changed the relative values or proportions of the several arms of service: infantry, artillery, cavalry, and engineers. If any thing, the infantry has been increased in value. The danger of cavalry attempting to charge infantry armed with breech-loading rifles was fully illustrated at Sedan, and with us very frequently. So improbable has such a thing become that we have omitted the infantry-square from our recent tactics. Still, cavalry against cavalry, and as auxiliary to infantry, will always be valuable, while all great wars will, as heretofore, depend chiefly on the infantry. Artillery is more valuable with new and inexperienced troops than with veterans. In the early stages of the war the field-guns often bore the proportion of six to a thousand men; but toward the close of the war one gun; or at most two, to a thousand men, was deemed enough. Sieges; such as characterized the wars of the last century, are too slow for this period of the world, and the Prussians recently almost ignored them altogether, penetrated France between the forts, and left a superior force "in observation," to watch the garrison and accept its surrender when the greater events of the war ahead made further resistance useless; but earth-forts, and especially field-works, will hereafter play an important part in war, because they enable a minor force to hold a superior one in check for a time, and time is a most valuable element in all wars. It was one of Prof. Mahan's maxims that the spade was as useful in war as the musket, and to this I will add the axe. The habit of intrenching certainly does have the effect of making new troops timid. When a line of battle is once covered by a good parapet, made by the engineers or by the labor of the men themselves, it does require an effort to make them leave it in the face of danger; but when the enemy is intrenched, it becomes absolutely necessary to permit each brigade and division of the troops immediately opposed to throw up a corresponding trench for their own protection in case of a sudden sally. We invariably did this in all our recent campaigns, and it had no ill effect, though sometimes our troops were a little too slow in leaving their well-covered lines to assail the enemy in position or on retreat. Even our skirmishers were in the habit of rolling logs together, or of making a lunette of rails, with dirt in front, to cover their bodies; and, though it revealed their position, I cannot say that it worked a bad effect; so that, as a rule, it may safely be left to the men themselves: On the "defensive," there is no doubt of the propriety of fortifying; but in the assailing army the general must watch closely to see that his men do not neglect an opportunity to drop his precautionary defenses, and act promptly on the "offensive" at every chance.

I have many a time crept forward to the skirmish-line to avail myself of the cover of the pickets "little fort," to observe more closely some expected result; and always talked familiarly with the men, and was astonished to see how well they comprehended the general object, and how accurately they were informed of the sate of facts existing miles away from their particular corps. Soldiers are very quick to catch the general drift and purpose of a campaign, and are always sensible when they are well commanded or well cared for. Once impressed with this fact, and that they are making progress, they bear cheerfully any amount of labor and privation.

In camp, and especially in the presence of an active enemy, it is much easier to maintain discipline than in barracks in time of peace. Crime and breaches of discipline are much less frequent, and the necessity for courts-martial far less. The captain can usually inflict all the punishment necessary, and the colonel should always. The field-officers' court is the best form for war, viz., one of the field-officers-the lieutenant-colonel or major --can examine the case and report his verdict, and the colonel should execute it. Of course, there are statutory offenses which demand a general court-martial, and these must be ordered by the division or corps commander; but, the presence of one of our regular civilian judge-advocates in an army in the field would be a first-class nuisance, for technical courts always work mischief. Too many courts-martial in any command are evidence of poor discipline and inefficient officers.

For the rapid transmission of orders in an army covering a large space of ground, the magnetic telegraph is by far the best, though habitually the paper and pencil, with good mounted orderlies, answer every purpose. I have little faith in the signal-service by flags and torches, though we always used them; because, almost invariably when they were most needed, the view was cut off by intervening trees, or by mists and fogs. There was one notable instance in my experience, when the signal-flags carried a message. of vital importance over the heads of Hood's army, which had interposed between me and Allatoona, and had broken the telegraph-wires--as recorded in Chapter XIX.; but the value of the magnetic telegraph in war cannot be exaggerated, as was illustrated by the perfect concert of action between the armies in Virginia and Georgia during 1864. Hardly a day intervened when General Grant did not know the exact state of facts with me, more than fifteen hundred miles away as the wires ran. So on the field a thin insulated wire may be run on improvised stakes or from tree to tree for six or more miles in a couple of hours, and I have seen operators so skillful, that by cutting the wire they would receive a message with their tongues from a distant station. As a matter of course, the ordinary commercial wires along the railways form the usual telegraph-lines for an army, and these are easily repaired and extended as the army advances, but each army and wing should have a small party of skilled men to put up the field-wire, and take it down when done. This is far better than the signal-flags and torches. Our commercial telegraph-lines will always supply for war enough skillful operators.

The value of railways is also fully recognized in war quite as much as, if not more so than, in peace. The Atlanta campaign would simply have been impossible without the use of the railroads from Louisville to Nashville--one hundred and eighty-five miles--from Nashville to Chattanooga--one hundred and fifty-one miles--and from Chattanooga to Atlanta--one hundred and thirty-seven miles. Every mile of this "single track" was so delicate, that one man could in a minute have broken or moved a rail, but our trains usually carried along the tools and means to repair such a break. We had, however, to maintain strong guards and garrisons at each important bridge or trestle--the destruction of which would have necessitated time for rebuilding. For the protection of a bridge, one or two log block houses, two stories high, with a piece of ordnance and a small infantry guard, usually sufficed. The block-house had a small parapet and ditch about it, and the roof was made shot proof by earth piled on. These points could usually be reached only by a dash of the enemy's cavalry, and many of these block houses successfully resisted serious attacks by both cavalry and artillery. The only block-house that was actually captured on the main was the one described near Allatoona. Our trains from Nashville forward were operated under military rules, and ran about ten miles an hour in gangs of four trains of ten cars each. Four such groups of trains daily made one hundred and sixty cars, of ten tons each, carrying sixteen hundred tons, which exceeded the absolute necessity of the army, and allowed for the accidents that were common and inevitable. But, as I have recorded, that single stem of railroad, four hundred and seventy-three miles long, supplied an army of one hundred thousand men and thirty-five thousand animals for the period of one hundred and ninety-six days, viz., from May 1 to November 12, 1864. To have delivered regularly that amount of food and forage by ordinary wagons would have required thirty-six thousand eight hundred wagons of six mules each, allowing each wagon to have hauled two tons twenty miles each day, a simple impossibility in roads such as then existed in that region of country. Therefore, I reiterate that the Atlanta campaign was an impossibility without these railroads; and only then, because we had the men and means to maintain and defend them, in addition to what were necessary to overcome the enemy. Habitually, a passenger-car will carry fifty men with their necessary baggage. Box-cars, and even platform-cars, answer the purpose well enough, but they, should always have rough board-seats. For sick and wounded men, box-cars filled with straw or bushes were usually employed. Personally, I saw but little of the practical working of the railroads, for I only turned back once as far as Resaca; but I had daily reports from the engineer in charge, and officers who came from the rear often explained to me the whole thing, with a description of the wrecked trains all the way from Nashville to Atlanta. I am convinced that the risk to life to the engineers and men on that railroad fully equaled that on the skirmish-line, called for as high an order of courage, and fully equaled it in importance. Still, I doubt if there be any necessity in time of peace to organize a corps specially to work the military railroads in time of war, because in peace these same men gain all the necessary experience, possess all the daring and courage of soldiers, and only need the occasional protection and assistance of the necessary train-guard, which may be composed of the furloughed men coming and going, or of details made from the local garrisons to the rear.

For the transfer of large armies by rail, from one theatre of action to another by the rear--the cases of the transfer of the Eleventh and Twelfth Corps--General Hooker, twenty-three thousand men--from the East to Chattanooga, eleven hundred and ninety-two miles in seven days, in the fall of 1863; and that of the Army of the Ohio--General Schofield, fifteen thousand men--from the valley of the Tennessee to Washington, fourteen hundred miles in eleven days, en route to North Carolina in January, 1865, are the best examples of which I have any knowledge, and reference to these is made in the report of the Secretary of War, Mr. Stanton, dated November 22, 1865.

Engineer troops attached to an army are habitually employed in supervising the construction of forts or field works of a nature more permanent than the lines need by the troops in motion, and in repairing roads and making bridges. I had several regiments of this kind that were most useful, but as a rule we used the infantry, or employed parties of freedmen, who worked on the trenches at night while the soldiers slept, and these in turn rested by day. Habitually the repair of the railroad and its bridges was committed to hired laborers, like the English navies, under the supervision of Colonel W. W. Wright, a railroad-engineer, who was in the military service at the time, and his successful labors were frequently referred to in the official reports of the campaign.

For the passage of rivers, each army corps had a pontoon-train with a detachment of engineers, and, on reaching a river, the leading infantry division was charged with the labor of putting it down. Generally the single pontoon-train could provide for nine hundred feet of bridge, which sufficed; but when the rivers were very wide two such trains would be brought together, or the single train was supplemented by a trestle-bridge, or bridges made on crib-work, out of timber found near the place. The pontoons in general use were skeleton frames, made with a hinge, so as to fold back and constitute a wagon-body. In this same wagon were carried the cotton canvas cover, the anchor and chains, and a due proportion of the balks, cheeses, and lashings. All the troops became very familiar with their mechanism and use, and we were rarely delayed by reason of a river, however broad. I saw, recently, in Aldershot, England, a very complete pontoon-train; the boats were sheathed with wood and felt, made very light; but I think these were more liable to chafing and damage in rough handling than were our less expensive and rougher boats. On the whole, I would prefer the skeleton frame and canvas cover to any style of pontoon that I have ever seen.

In relation to guards, pickets, and vedettes, I doubt if any discoveries or improvements were made during our war, or in any of the modern wars in Europe. These precautions vary with the nature of the country and the situation of each army. When advancing or retreating in line of battle, the usual skirmish-line constitutes the picket-line, and may have "reserves," but usually the main line of battle constitutes the reserve; and in this connection I will state that the recent innovation introduced into the new infantry tactics by General Upton is admirable, for by it each regiment, brigade, and division deployed, sends forward as "skirmishers" the one man of each set of fours, to cover its own front, and these can be recalled or reenforced at pleasure by the bugle-signal.

For flank-guards and rear-guards, one or more companies should be detached under their own officers, instead of making up the guard by detailing men from the several companies.

For regimental or camp guards, the details should be made according to existing army regulations; and all the guards should be posted early in the evening, so as to afford each sentinel or vedette a chance to study his ground before it becomes too dark.

In like manner as to the staff. The more intimately it comes into contact with the troops, the more useful and valuable it becomes. The almost entire separation of the staff from the line, as now practised by us, and hitherto by the French, has proved mischievous, and the great retinues of staff-officers with which some of our earlier generals began the war were simply ridiculous. I don't believe in a chief of staff at all, and any general commanding an army, corps, or division, that has a staff-officer who professes to know more than his chief, is to be pitied. Each regiment should have a competent adjutant, quartermaster, and commissary, with two or three medical officers. Each brigade commander should have the same staff, with the addition of a couple of young aides-de-camp, habitually selected from the subalterns of the brigade, who should be good riders, and intelligent enough to give and explain the orders of their general.

The same staff will answer for a division. The general in command of a separate army, and of a corps d'armee, should have the same professional assistance, with two or more good engineers, and his adjutant-general should exercise all the functions usually ascribed to a chief of staff, viz., he should possess the ability to comprehend the scope of operations, and to make verbally and in writing all the orders and details necessary to carry into effect the views of his general, as well as to keep the returns and records of events for the information of the next higher authority, and for history. A bulky staff implies a division of responsibility, slowness of action, and indecision, whereas a small staff implies activity and concentration of purpose. The smallness of General Grant's staff throughout the civil war forms the best model for future imitation. So of tents, officers furniture, etc., etc. In real war these should all be discarded, and an army is efficient for action and motion exactly in the inverse ratio of its impedimenta. Tents should be omitted altogether, save one to a regiment for an office, and a few for the division hospital. Officers should be content with a tent fly, improvising poles and shelter out of bushes. The tents d'abri, or shelter-tent, carried by the soldier himself, is all-sufficient. Officers should never seek for houses, but share the condition of their men.

A recent message (July 18, 1874) made to the French Assembly by Marshal MacMahon, President of the French Republic, submits a projet de loi, with a report prepared by a board of French generals on "army administration," which is full of information, and is as applicable to us as to the French. I quote from its very beginning: "The misfortunes of the campaign of 1870 have demonstrated the inferiority of our system.... Two separate organizations existed with parallel functions--the 'general' more occupied in giving direction to his troops than in providing for their material wants, which he regarded as the special province of the staff, and the 'intendant' (staff) often working at random, taking on his shoulders a crushing burden of functions and duties, exhausting himself with useless efforts, and aiming to accomplish an insufficient service, to the disappointment of everybody. This separation of the administration and command, this coexistence of two wills, each independent of the other, which paralyzed both and annulled the dualism, was condemned. It was decided by the board that this error should be "proscribed" in the new military system. The report then goes on at great length discussing the provisions. of the "new law," which is described to be a radical change from the old one on the same subject. While conceding to the Minister of War in Paris the general control and supervision of the entire military establishment primarily, especially of the annual estimates or budget, and the great depots of supply, it distributes to the commanders of the corps d'armee in time of peace, and to all army commanders generally in time of war, the absolute command of the money, provisions, and stores, with the necessary staff-officers to receive, issue, and account for them. I quote further: "The object of this law is to confer on the commander of troops whatever liberty of action the case demands. He has the power even to go beyond the regulations, in circumstances of urgency and pressing necessity. The extraordinary measures he may take on these occasions may require their execution without delay. The staff-officer has but one duty before obeying, and that is to submit his observations to the general, and to ask his orders in writing.

With this formality his responsibility ceases, and the responsibility for the extraordinary act falls solely on the general who gives the order. The officers and agents charged with supplies are placed under the orders of the general in command of the troops, that is, they are obliged both in war and peace to obey, with the single qualification above named, of first making their observations and securing the written order of the general.

With us, to-day, the law and regulations are that, no matter what may be the emergency, the commanding general in Texas, New Mexico, and the remote frontiers, cannot draw from the arsenals a pistol-cartridge, or any sort of ordnance-stores, without first procuring an order of the Secretary of War in Washington. The commanding general--though intrusted with the lives of his soldiers and with the safety of a frontier in a condition of chronic war--cannot touch or be trusted with ordnance-stores or property, and that is declared to be the law! Every officer of the old army remembers how, in 1861, we were hampered with the old blue army regulations, which tied our hands, and that to do any thing positive and necessary we had to tear it all to pieces--cut the red-tape, as it was called, a dangerous thing for an army to do, for it was calculated to bring the law and authority into contempt; but war was upon us, and overwhelming necessity overrides all law.

This French report is well worth the study of our army-officers, of all grades and classes, and I will only refer again, casually, to another part, wherein it discusses the subject of military correspondence: whether the staff-officer should correspond directly with his chief in Paris, submitting to his general copies, or whether he should be required to carry on his correspondence through his general, so that the latter could promptly forward the communication, indorsed with his own remarks and opinions. The latter is declared by the board to be the only safe rule, because "the general should never be ignorant of any thing that is transpiring that concerns his command."

In this country, as in France, Congress controls the great questions of war and peace, makes all laws for the creation and government of armies, and votes the necessary supplies, leaving to the President to execute and apply these laws, especially the harder task of limiting the expenditure of public money to the amount of the annual appropriations. The executive power is further subdivided into the seven great departments, and to the Secretary of War is confided the general care of the military establishment, and his powers are further subdivided into ten distinct and separate bureaus.

The chiefs of these bureaus are under the immediate orders of the Secretary of War, who, through them, in fact commands the army from "his office," but cannot do so "in the field"--an absurdity in military if not civil law.

The subordinates of these staff-corps and departments are selected and chosen from the army itself, or fresh from West Point, and too commonly construe themselves into the elite, as made of better clay than the common soldier. Thus they separate themselves more and more from their comrades of the line, and in process of time realize the condition of that old officer of artillery who thought the army would be a delightful place for a gentleman if it were not for the d-d soldier; or, better still, the conclusion of the young lord in

"Henry IV.," who told Harry Percy (Hotspur) that "but for these vile guns he would himself have been a soldier." This is all wrong; utterly at variance with our democratic form of government and of universal experience; and now that the French, from whom we had copied the system, have utterly "proscribed" it, I hope that our Congress will follow suit. I admit, in its fullest force, the strength of the maxim that the civil law should be superior to the military in time of peace; that the army should be at all times subject to the direct control of Congress; and I assert that, from the formation of our Government to the present day, the Regular Army has set the highest example of obedience to law and authority; but, for the very reason that our army is comparatively so very small, I hold that it should be the best possible, organized and governed on true military principles, and that in time of peace we should preserve the "habits and usages of war," so that, when war does come, we may not again be compelled to suffer the disgrace, confusion, and disorder of 1861.

The commanding officers of divisions, departments, and posts, should have the amplest powers, not only to command their troops, but all the stores designed for their use, and the officers of the staff necessary to administer them, within the area of their command; and then with fairness they could be held to the most perfect responsibility. The President and Secretary of War can command the army quite as well through these generals as through the subordinate staff-officers. Of course, the Secretary would, as now, distribute the funds according to the appropriation bills, and reserve to himself the absolute control and supervision of the larger arsenals and depots of supply. The error lies in the law, or in the judicial interpretation thereof, and no code of army regulations can be made that meets the case, until Congress, like the French Corps Legislatif, utterly annihilates and "proscribes" the old law and the system which has grown up under it.

It is related of Napoleon that his last words were, "Tete d'armee!" Doubtless, as the shadow of death obscured his memory, the last thought that remained for speech was of some event when he was directing an important "head of column." I believe that every general who has handled armies in battle most recall from his own experience the intensity of thought on some similar occasion, when by a single command he had given the finishing stroke to some complicated action; but to me recurs another thought that is worthy of record, and may encourage others who are to follow us in our profession. I never saw the rear of an army engaged in battle but I feared that some calamity had happened at the front the apparent confusion, broken wagons, crippled horses, men lying about dead and maimed, parties hastening to and fro in seeming disorder, and a general apprehension of something dreadful about to ensue; all these signs, however, lessened as I neared the front, and there the contrast was complete--perfect order, men and horses--full of confidence, and it was not unusual for general hilarity, laughing, and cheering. Although cannon might be firing, the musketry clattering, and the enemy's shot hitting close, there reigned a general feeling of strength and security that bore a marked contrast to the bloody signs that had drifted rapidly to the rear; therefore, for comfort and safety, I surely would rather be at the front than the rear line of battle. So also on the march, the head of a column moves on steadily, while the rear is alternately halting and then rushing forward to close up the gap; and all sorts of rumors, especially the worst, float back to the rear. Old troops invariably deem it a special privilege to be in the front --to be at the "head of column"--

because experience has taught them that it is the easiest and most comfortable place, and danger only adds zest and stimulus to this fact.

The hardest task in war is to lie in support of some position or battery, under fire without the privilege of returning it; or to guard some train left in the rear, within hearing but out of danger; or to provide for the wounded and dead of some corps which is too busy ahead to care for its own.

To be at the head of a strong column of troops, in the execution of some task that requires brain, is the highest pleasure of war--a grim one and terrible, but which leaves on the mind and memory the strongest mark; to detect the weak point of an enemy's line; to break through with vehemence and thus lead to victory; or to discover some key-point and hold it with tenacity; or to do some other distinct act which is afterward recognized as the real cause of success. These all become matters that are never forgotten. Other great difficulties, experienced by every general, are to measure truly the thousand-and-one reports that come to him in the midst of conflict; to preserve a clear and well-defined purpose at every instant of time, and to cause all efforts to converge to that end.

To do these things he must know perfectly the strength and quality of each part of his own army, as well as that of his opponent, and must be where he can personally see and observe with his own eyes, and judge with his own mind. No man can properly command an army from the rear, he must be "at its front;" and when a detachment is made, the commander thereof should be informed of the object to be accomplished, and left as free as possible to execute it in his own way; and when an army is divided up into several parts, the superior should always attend that one which he regards as most important. Some men think that modern armies may be so regulated that a general can sit in an office and play on his several columns as on the keys of a piano; this is a fearful mistake. The directing mind must be at the very head of the army--must be seen there, and the effect of his mind and personal energy must be felt by every officer and man present with it, to secure the best results. Every attempt to make war easy and safe will result in humiliation and disaster.

Lastly, mail facilities should be kept up with an army if possible, that officers and men may receive and send letters to their friends, thus maintaining the home influence of infinite assistance to discipline. Newspaper correspondents with an army, as a rule, are mischievous. They are the world's gossips, pick up and retail the camp scandal, and gradually drift to the headquarters of some general, who finds it easier to make reputation at home than with his own corps or division. They are also tempted to prophesy events and state facts which, to an enemy, reveal a purpose in time to guard against it. Moreover, they are always bound to see facts colored by the partisan or political character of their own patrons, and thus bring army officers into the political controversies of the day, which are always mischievous and wrong. Yet, so greedy are the people at large for war news, that it is doubtful whether any army commander can exclude all reporters, without bringing down on himself a clamor that may imperil his own safety. Time and moderation must bring a just solution to this modern difficulty.

Sherman's men tearing up railroad track

Chapter XXVI After The War

In the foregoing pages I have endeavored to describe the public events in which I was an actor or spectator before and during the civil war of 1861-'65, and it now only remains for me to treat of similar matters of general interest subsequent to the civil war. Within a few days of the grand review of May 24, 1865, I took leave of the army at Washington, and with my family went to Chicago to attend a fair held in the interest of the families of soldiers impoverished by the war. I remained there about two weeks; on the 22d of June was at South Bend, Indiana, where two of my children were at school, and reached my native place, Lancaster, Ohio, on the 24th. On the 4th of July I visited at Louisville, Kentucky, the Fourteenth, Fifteenth, Sixteenth, and Seventeenth Army Corps, which had come from Washington, under the command of General John A. Logan, for "muster out," or "further orders." I then made a short visit to General George H. Thomas at Nashville, and returned to Lancaster, where I remained with the family till the receipt of General Orders No. 118 of June 27, 1865, which divided the whole territory of the United States into nineteen departments and five military divisions, the second of which was the military division of the "Mississippi," afterward changed to "Missouri," Major-General W. T.

Sherman to command, with, headquarters at St. Louis, to embrace the Departments of the Ohio, Missouri, and Arkansas.

This territorial command included the States north of the Ohio River, and the States and Territories north of Texas, as far west as the Rocky Mountains, including Montana, Utah, and New Mexico, but the part east of the Mississippi was soon transferred to another division. The department commanders were General E. O. C. Ord, at Detroit; General John Pope, at Fort Leavenworth; and General J. J. Reynolds, at Little Rock, but these also were soon changed. I at once assumed command, and ordered my staff and headquarters from Washington to St. Louis, Missouri, going there in person on the 16th of July.

My thoughts and feelings at once reverted to the construction of the great Pacific Railway, which had been chartered by Congress in the midst of war, and was then in progress. I put myself in communication with the parties engaged in the work, visiting them in person, and assured them that I would afford them all possible assistance and encouragement. Dr. Durant, the leading man of the Union Pacific, seemed to me a person of ardent nature, of great ability and energy, enthusiastic in his undertaking, and determined to build the road from Omaha to San Francisco. He had an able corps of assistants, collecting materials, letting out contracts for ties, grading, etc., and I attended the celebration of the first completed division of sixteen and a half miles, from Omaha to Papillon. When the orators spoke so confidently of the determination to build two thousand miles of railway across the plains, mountains, and desert, devoid of timber, with no population, but on the contrary raided by the bold and bloody Sioux and Cheyennes, who had almost successfully defied our power for half a century, I was disposed to treat it jocularly, because I could not help recall our California experience of 1855-'56, when we celebrated the completion of twenty-two and a half miles of the same road eastward of Sacramento; on which occasion Edward Baker had electrified us by his unequalled oratory, painting the glorious things which would result from uniting the Western coast with the East by bands of iron. Baker then, with a poet's imagination, saw the vision of the mighty future, but not the gulf which meantime was destined to swallow up half a million of the brightest and best youth of our land, and that he himself would be one of the first victims far away on the banks of the Potomac (he was killed in battle at Balls Bluff, October 21, 1861).

The Kansas Pacific was designed to unite with the main branch about the 100 deg. meridian, near Fort Kearney. Mr. Shoemaker was its general superintendent and building contractor, and this branch in 1865 was finished about forty miles to a point near Lawrence, Kansas. I may not be able to refer to these roads again except incidentally, and will, therefore, record here that the location of this branch afterward was changed from the Republican to the Smoky Hill Fork of the Kansas River, and is now the main line to Denver. The Union and Central Railroads from the beginning were pushed with a skill, vigor, and courage which always commanded my admiration, the two meeting at Promontory Point, Utah, July 15, 1869, and in my judgment constitute one of the greatest and most beneficent achievements of man on earth.

The construction of the Union Pacific Railroad was deemed so important that the President, at my suggestion, constituted on the 5th of March, 1866, the new Department of the Platte, General P. St. George Cooke commanding, succeeded by General C. C. Augur, headquarters at Omaha, with orders to give ample protection to the working-parties, and to afford every possible assistance in the construction of the road; and subsequently in like manner the Department of Dakota was constituted, General A. H. Terry commanding, with headquarters at St. Paul, to give similar protection and encouragement to the Northern Pacific Railroad. These departments, with changed commanders, have continued up to the present day, and have fulfilled perfectly the uses for which they were designed.

During the years 1865 and 1866 the great plains remained almost in a state of nature, being the pasture-fields of about ten million buffalo, deer, elk, and antelope, and were in full possession of the Sioux, Cheyennes, Arapahoes, and Kiowas, a race of bold Indians, who saw plainly that the construction of two parallel railroads right through their country would prove destructive to the game on which they subsisted, and consequently fatal to themselves.

The troops were posted to the best advantage to protect the parties engaged in building these roads, and in person I reconnoitred well to the front, traversing the buffalo regions from south to north, and from east to west, often with a very small escort, mingling with the Indians whenever safe, and thereby gained personal knowledge of matters which enabled me to use the troops to the best advantage. I am sure that without the courage and activity of the department commanders with the small bodies of regular troops on the plains during the years 1866-'69, the Pacific Railroads could not have been built; but once built and in full operation the fate of the buffalo and Indian was settled for all time to come.

At the close of the civil war there were one million five hundred and sixteen names on the muster-rolls, of which seven hundred and ninety-seven thousand eight hundred and seven were present, and two hundred and two thousand seven hundred and nine absent, of which twenty-two thousand nine hundred and twenty-nine were regulars, the others were volunteers, colored troops, and veteran reserves. The regulars consisted of six regiments of cavalry, five of artillery, and nineteen of infantry. By the act of July 28, 1866, the peace establishment was fixed at one general (Grant), one lieutenant-general (Sherman), five major-generals (Halleck, Meade, Sheridan, Thomas, and Hancock), ten brigadiers (McDowell, Cooke, Pope, Hooker, Schofield, Howard, Terry, Ord, Canby, and Rousseau), ten regiments of cavalry, five of artillery, and forty-five of infantry, admitting of an aggregate force of fifty-four thousand six hundred and forty-one men.

All others were mustered out, and thus were remanded to their homes nearly a million of strong, vigorous men who had imbibed the somewhat erratic habits of the soldier; these were of every profession and trade in life, who, on regaining their homes, found their places occupied by others, that their friends and neighbors were different, and that they themselves had changed. They naturally looked for new homes to the great West, to the new Territories and States as far as the Pacific coast, and we realize to-day that the vigorous men who control Kansas, Nebraska, Dakota, Montana, Colorado, etc., etc., were soldiers of the civil war. These men flocked to the plains, and were rather stimulated than retarded by the danger of an Indian war. This was another potent agency in producing the result we enjoy to-day, in having in so short a time replaced the wild buffaloes by more numerous herds of tame cattle, and by substituting for the useless Indians the intelligent owners of productive farms and cattle-ranches.

While these great changes were being wrought at the West, in the East politics had resumed full sway, and all the methods of anti-war times had been renewed. President Johnson had differed with his party as to the best method of reconstructing the State governments of the South, which had been destroyed and impoverished by the war, and the press began to agitate the question of the next President. Of course, all Union men naturally turned to General Grant, and the result was jealousy of him by the personal friends of President Johnson and some of his cabinet. Mr. Johnson always seemed very patriotic and friendly, and I believed him honest and sincere in his declared purpose to follow strictly the Constitution of the United States in restoring the Southern States to their normal place in the Union; but the same cordial friendship subsisted between General Grant and myself, which was the outgrowth of personal relations dating back to 1839. So I resolved to keep out of this conflict. In September, 1866, I was in the mountains of New Mexico, when a message reached me that I was wanted at Washington. I had with me a couple of officers and half a dozen soldiers as escort, and traveled down the Arkansas, through the Kiowas, Comanches, Cheyennes, and Arapahoes, all more or less disaffected, but reached St. Louis in safety, and proceeded to Washington, where I reported to General Grant.

He explained to me that President Johnson wanted to see me. He did not know the why or wherefore, but supposed it had some connection with an order he (General Grant) had received to escort the newly appointed Minister, Hon. Lew Campbell, of Ohio, to the court of Juarez, the President-elect of Mexico, which country was still in possession of the Emperor Maximilian, supported by a corps of French troops commanded by General Bazaine. General Grant denied the right of the President to order him on a diplomatic mission unattended by troops; said that he had thought the matter over, world disobey the order, and stand the consequences. He manifested much feeling; and said it was a plot to get rid of him. I then went to President Johnson, who treated me with great cordiality, and said that he was very glad I had come; that General Grant was about to go to Mexico on business of importance, and he wanted me at Washington to command the army in General Grant's absence. I then informed him that General Grant would not go, and he seemed amazed; said that it was generally understood that General Grant construed the occupation of the territories of our neighbor, Mexico, by French troops, and the establishment of an empire therein, with an Austrian prince at its head, as hostile to republican America, and that the Administration had arranged with the French Government for the withdrawal of Bazaine's troops, which would leave the country free for the President-elect Juarez to reoccupy the city of Mexico, etc., etc.; that Mr. Campbell had been accredited to Juarez, and the fact that he was accompanied by so distinguished a soldier as General Grant would emphasize the act of the United States. I simply reiterated that General Grant would not go, and that he, Mr. Johnson, could not afford to quarrel with him at that time. I further argued that General Grant was at the moment engaged on the most delicate and difficult task of reorganizing the army under the act of July 28, 1866; that if the real object was to put Mr. Campbell in official communication with President Juarez, supposed to be at El Paso or Monterey, either General Hancock, whose command embraced New Mexico, or General Sheridan, whose command included Texas, could fulfill the object perfectly; or, in the event of neither of these alternates proving satisfactory to the Secretary of State, that I could be easier spared than General Grant. "Certainly," answered the President, "if you will go, that will answer perfectly."

The instructions of the Secretary of State, W. H. Seward, to Hon. Lewis D. Campbell, Minister to Mexico, dated October 25, 1866; a letter from President Johnson to Secretary of War Stanton, dated October 26, 1866; and the letter of Edwin M. Stanton, Secretary of War, to General Grant, dated October 27th, had been already prepared and printed, and the originals or copies were furnished me; but on the 30th of October, 1866, the following letter passed

EXECUTIVE MANSION
WASHINGTON, D. C., October 30,1866.

SIR: General Ulysses S. Grant having found it inconvenient to assume the duties specified in my letter to you of the 26th inst., you will please relieve him, and assign them in all respects to William T. Sherman, Lieutenant-General of the Army of the United States. By way of guiding General Sherman in the performance of his duties, you will furnish him with a copy of your special orders to General Grant made in compliance with my letter of the 26th inst., together with a copy of the instructions of the Secretary of State to Lewis D. Campbell, Esq., therein mentioned.

The lieutenant-general will proceed to the execution of his duties without delay.
Very respectfully yours,
ANDREW JOHNSON

To the Hon. EDWIN M. STANTON, Secretary of War.
At the Navy Department I learned that the United States ship Susquehanna, Captain Alden, was fitting out in New York for the use of this mission, and that there would be time for me to return to St. Louis to make arrangements for a prolonged absence, as also to communicate with Mr. Campbell, who was still at his home in Hamilton, Ohio. By correspondence we agreed to meet in New York, November 8th, he accompanied by Mr. Plumb, secretary of legation, and I by my aide, Colonel Audenried.

We embarked November 10th, and went to sea next day, making for Havana and Vera Cruz, and, as soon as we were outside of Sandy Hook, I explained to Captain Alden that my mission was ended, because I believed by substituting myself for General Grant I had prevented a serious quarrel between him and the Administration, which was unnecessary. We reached Havana on the 18th, with nothing to vary the monotony of an ordinary sea-voyage, except off Hatteras we picked up one woman and twenty men from open boats, who had just abandoned a propeller bound from Baltimore to Charleston which foundered. The sea was very rough, but by the personal skill and supervision of Captain Alden every soul reached our deck safely, and was carried to our consul at Havana. At Havana we were very handsomely entertained, especially by Senor Aldama, who took us by rail to his sugar-estates at Santa Ross, and back by Matanzas.

We took our departure thence on the 25th, and anchored under Isla Verde, off Vera Cruz, on the 29th.

Everything about Vera Cruz indicated the purpose of the French to withdraw, and also that the Emperor Maximilian would precede them, for the Austrian frigate Dandolo was in port, and an Austrian bark, on which were received, according to the report of our consul, Mr. Lane, as many as eleven hundred packages of private furniture to be transferred to Miramar, Maximilian's home; and Lieutenant Clarin, of the French navy, who visited the Susquehanna from the French commodore, Clouet, told me, without reserve, that, if we had delayed eight days more, we would have found Maximilian gone. General Bazaine was reported to be in the city of Mexico with about twenty-eight thousand French troops; but instead of leaving Mexico in three detachments, viz., November, 1866, March, 1867, and November, 1867, as described in Mr. Seward's letter to Mr. Campbell, of October 25, 1866, it looked to me that, as a soldier, he would evacuate at some time before November, 1867, all at once, and not by detachments. Lieutenant Clarin telegraphed Bazaine at the city of Mexico the fact of our arrival, and he sent me a most courteous and pressing invitation to come up to the city; but, as we were accredited to the government of Juarez, it was considered undiplomatic to establish friendly relations with the existing authorities. Meantime we could not hear a word of Juarez, and concluded to search for him along the coast northward. When I was in Versailles, France, July, 1872, learning that General Bazaine was in arrest for the surrender of his army and post at Metz, in 1870, I wanted to call on him to thank him for his courteous invitation to me at Vera Cruz in 1866. I inquired of President Thiera if I could with propriety call on the marshal. He answered that it would be very acceptable, no doubt, but suggested for form's sake that I should consult the Minister of War, General de Cissey, which I did, and he promptly assented. Accordingly, I called with my aide, Colonel Audenried, on Marshal Bazaine, who occupied a small, two-story stone house at Versailles, in an inclosure with a high garden wall, at the front gate or door of which was a lodge, in which was a military guard. We were shown to a good room on the second floor, where was seated the marshal in military half-dress, with large head, full face, short neck, and evidently a man of strong physique. He did not speak English, but spoke Spanish perfectly. We managed to carry on a conversation in which I endeavored to convey my sense of his politeness in inviting me so cordially up to the city of Mexico, and my regret that the peculiar duty on which I was engaged did not admit of a compliance, or even of an intelligent explanation, at the time. He spoke of the whole Mexican business as a "sad affair," that the empire necessarily fell with the result of our civil war, and that poor Maximilian was sacrificed to his own high sense of honor.

While on board the Susquehanna, on the 1st day of December, 1866, we received the proclamation made by the Emperor Maximilian at Orizaba, in which, notwithstanding the near withdrawal of the French troops, he declared his purpose to remain and "shed the last drop of his blood in defense of his dear country." Undoubtedly many of the most substantial people of Mexico, having lost all faith in the stability of the native government, had committed themselves to what they considered the more stable government of Maximilian, and Maximilian, a man of honor, concluded at the last moment he could not abandon them; the consequence was his death.

Failing to hear of Juarez, we steamed up the coast to the Island of Lobos, and on to Tampico, off which we found the United States steamer Paul Jones, which, drawing less water than the Susquehanna, carried us over the bar to the city, then in possession of the Liberal party, which recognized Juarez as their constitutional President, but of Juarez and his whereabout we could hear not a word; so we continued up the coast and anchored off Brazos Santiago, December 7th. Going ashore in small boats, we found a railroad, under the management of General J. R. West, now one of the commissioners of the city of Washington, who sent us up to Brownsville, Texas. We met on the way General Sheridan, returning from a tour of inspection of the Rio Grande frontier. On Sunday, December 9th, we were all at Matamoras, Mexico, where we met General Escobedo, one of Juarez's trusty lieutenants, who developed to us the general plan agreed on for the overthrow of the empire, and the reestablishment of the republican government of Mexico. He asked of us no assistance, except the loan of some arms, ammunition, clothing, and camp-equipage. It was agreed that Mr. Campbell should, as soon as he could get his baggage off the Susquehanna, return to Matamoras, and thence proceed to Monterey, to be received by Juarez in person as, the accredited Minister of the United States to the Republic of Mexico. Meantime the weather off the coast was stormy, and the Susquehanna parted a cable, so that we were delayed some days at Brazos; but in due time Mr. Campbell got his baggage, and we regained the deck of the Susquehanna, which got up steam and started for New Orleans. We reached New Orleans December 20th, whence I reported fully everything to General Grant, and on the 21st received the following dispatch:

WASHINGTON, December 21,1866.
Lieutenant-General SHERMAN, New Orleans.

Your telegram of yesterday has been submitted to the President. You are authorized to proceed to St. Louis at your convenience. Your proceedings in the special and delicate duties assigned you are cordially approved by the President and Cabinet and this department.
EDWIN M. STANTON.

And on the same day I received this dispatch

GALVESTON, December 21, 1866.
To General SHERMAN, or General SHERIDAN.

Will be in New Orleans to-morrow. Wish to see you both on arrival, on matters of importance. LEWIS D. CAMPBELL, Minister to Mexico.

Mr. Campbell arrived on the 22d, but had nothing to tell of the least importance, save that he was generally disgusted with the whole thing, and had not found Juarez at all. I am sure this whole movement was got up for the purpose of getting General Grant away from Washington, on the pretext of his known antagonism to the French occupation of Mexico, because he was looming up as a candidate for President, and nobody understood the animus and purpose better than did Mr. Stanton. He himself was not then on good terms with President Johnson, and with several of his associates in the Cabinet. By Christmas I was back in St. Louis.

By this time the conflict between President Johnson and Congress had become open and unconcealed. Congress passed the bill known as the "Tenure of Civil Office" on the 2d of March, 1867 (over the President's veto), the first clause of which, now section 1767 of the Revised Statutes, reads thus: "Every person who holds any civil office to which he has been or hereafter may be appointed, by and with the advice and consent of the Senate, and who shall have become duly qualified to act therein, shall be entitled to hold such office during the term for which he was appointed, unless sooner removed by and with the advice and consent of the Senate, or by the appointment with the like advice and consent of a successor in his place, except as herein otherwise provided."

General E. D. Townsend, in his "Anecdotes of the Civil War," states tersely and correctly the preliminary circumstances of which I must treat. He says: "On Monday morning, August 5, 1867, President Johnson invited Mr. Stanton to resign as Secretary of War. Under the tenure-of-civil-office law, Mr. Stanton declined. The President a week after suspended him, and appointed General Grant, General-in-Chief of the Army, to exercise the functions. This continued until January 13, 1868, when according to the law the Senate passed a resolution not sustaining the President's action. The next morning General Grant came to my office and handed me the key of the Secretary's room, saying: 'I am to be found over at my office at army headquarters. I was served with a copy of the Senate resolution last evening.' I then went up-stairs and delivered the key of his room to Mr. Stanton."

The mode and manner of Mr. Stanton's regaining his office, and of General Grant's surrendering it, were at the time subjects of bitter controversy. Unhappily I was involved, and must bear testimony. In all January, 1868, I was a member of a board ordered to compile a code of articles of war and army regulations, of which Major-General Sheridan and Brigadier-General C. C. Augur were associate members. Our place of meeting was in the room of the old War Department, second floor, next to the corner room occupied by the Secretary of War, with a door of communication. While we were at work it was common for General Grant and, afterward, for Mr. Stanton to drop in and chat with us on the social gossip of the time.

On Saturday, January 11th, General Grant said that he had more carefully read the law (tenure of civil office), and it was different from what he had supposed; that in case the Senate did not consent to the removal of Secretary of War Stanton, and he (Grant) should hold on, he should incur a liability of ten thousand dollars and five years' imprisonment.

We all expected the resolution of Senator Howard, of Michigan, virtually restoring Mr. Stanton to his office, would pass the Senate, and knowing that the President expected General Grant to hold on, I inquired if he had given notice of his change of purpose; he answered that there was no hurry, because he supposed Mr. Stanton would pursue toward him (Grant) the same course which he (Stanton) had required of him the preceding August, viz., would address him a letter claiming the office, and allow him a couple of days for the change. Still, he said he would go to the White House the same day and notify the President of his intended action.

That afternoon I went over to the White House to present General Pope, who was on a visit to Washington, and we found the President and General Grant together. We made our visit and withdrew, leaving them still together, and I always supposed the subject of this conference was the expected decision of the Senate, which would in effect restore Mr. Stanton to his civil office of Secretary of War. That evening I dined with the Hon. Reverdy Johnson, Senator from Maryland, and suggested to him that the best way to escape a conflict was for the President to nominate some good man as Secretary of War whose confirmation by the Senate would fall within the provisions of the law, and named General J. D. Cox, then Governor of Ohio, whose term of office was drawing to a close, who would, I knew, be acceptable to General Grant and the army generally. Mr. Johnson was most favorably impressed with this suggestion, and promised to call on the President the next day (Sunday), which he did, but President Johnson had made up his mind to meet the conflict boldly. I saw General Grant that afternoon at his house on I Street, and told him what I had done, and so anxious was he about it that he came to our room at the War Department the next morning (Monday), the 13th, and asked me to go in person to the White House to urge the President to send in the name of General Cox. I did so, saw the President, and inquired if he had seen Mr. Reverdy Johnson the day before about General Cox. He answered that he had, and thought well of General Cox, but would say no further.

Tuesday, January 14, 1868, came, and with it Mr. Stanton. He resumed possession of his former office; came into that where General Sheridan, General Augur, and I were at work, and greeted us very cordially. He said he wanted to see me when at leisure, and at half-past 10 A.M. I went into his office and found him and General Grant together. Supposing they had some special matters of business, I withdrew, with the remark that I was close at hand, and could come in at any moment. In the afternoon I went again into Mr. Stanton's office, and we had a long and most friendly conversation; but not one word was spoken about the "tenure-of-office" matter. I then crossed over Seventeenth Street to the headquarters of the army, where I found General Grant, who expressed himself as by no means pleased with the manner in which Mr. Stanton had regained his office, saying that he had sent a messenger for him that morning as of old, with word that "he wanted to see him." We then arranged to meet at his office the next morning at half-past nine, and go together to see the President.

That morning the National Intelligencer published an article accusing General Grant of acting in bad faith to the President, and of having prevaricated in making his personal explanation to the Cabinet, so that General Grant at first felt unwilling to go, but we went. The President received us promptly and kindly. Being seated, General Grant said, "Mr. President, whoever gave the facts for the article of the Intelligencer of this morning has made some serious mistakes." The President: "General Grant, let me interrupt you just there. I have not seen the Intelligencer of this morning, and have no knowledge of the contents of any article therein" General Grant then went on: "Well, the idea is given there that I have not kept faith with you. Now, Mr. President, I remember, when you spoke to me on this subject last summer, I did say that, like the case of the Baltimore police commissioners, I did suppose Mr. Stanton could not regain his office except by a process through the courts." To this the President assented, saying he "remembered the reference to the case of the Baltimore commissioners," when General Grant resumed: "I said if I changed my opinion I would give you notice, and put things as they were before my appointment as Secretary of War ad interim."

We then entered into a general friendly conversation, both parties professing to be satisfied, the President claiming that he had always been most friendly to General Grant, and the latter insisting that he had taken the office, not for honor or profit, but in the general interests of the army.

As we withdrew, at the very door, General Grant said, "Mr. President, you should make some order that we of the army are not bound to obey the orders of Mr. Stanton as Secretary of War," which the President intimated he would do.

No such "orders" were ever made; many conferences were held, and the following letters are selected out of a great mass to show the general feeling at the time:

1321 K STREET, WASHINGTON,
January 28, 1868, Saturday.

To the President:

I neglected this morning to say that I had agreed to go down to Annapolis to spend Sunday with Admiral Porter. General Grant also has to leave for Richmond on Monday morning at 6 A.M.

At a conversation with the General after our interview, wherein I offered to go with him on Monday morning to Mr. Stanton, and to say that it was our joint opinion be should resign, it was found impossible by reason of his (General Grant) going to Richmond and my going to Annapolis. The General proposed this course: He will call on you to-morrow, and offer to go to Mr. Stanton to say, for the good of the Army and of the country, he ought to resign. This on Sunday. On Monday I will again call on you, and, if you think it necessary, I will do the same, viz., go to Mr. Stanton and tell him he should resign.

If he will not, then it will be time to contrive ulterior measures. In the mean time it so happens that no necessity exists for precipitating matters.

Yours truly,
W. T. SHERMAN, Lieutenant-General.

DEAR GENERAL: On the point of starting, I have written the above, and will send a fair copy of it to the President. Please retain this, that in case of necessity I may have a copy. The President clearly stated to me that he relied on us in this category.

Think of the propriety of your putting in writing what you have to say tomorrow, even if you have to put it in the form of a letter to hand him in person, retaining a copy. I'm afraid that acting as a go-between for three persons, I may share the usual fate of meddlers, at last get kinks from all. We ought not to be involved in politics, but for the sake of the Army we are justified in trying at least to cut this Gordian knot, which they do not appear to have any practicable plan to do. In haste as usual,

W. T. SHERMAN.

HEADQUARTERS ARMIES OF THE UNITED STATES,
January 29, 1888.
DEAR SHERMAN: I called on the President and Mr. Stanton to-day, but without any effect.

I soon found that to recommend resignation to Mr. Stanton would have no effect, unless it was to incur further his displeasure; and, therefore, did not directly suggest it to him. I explained to him, however, the course I supposed he would pursue, and what I expected to do in that case, namely, to notify the President of his intentions, and thus leave him to violate the "Tenure-of-Office Bill" if he chose, instead of having me do it.

I would advise that you say nothing to Mr. Stanton on the subject unless he asks your advice. It will do no good, and may embarrass you. I did not mention your name to him, at least not in connection with his position, or what you thought upon it.

All that Mr. Johnson said was pacific and compromising. While I think he wanted the constitutionality of the "Tenure Bill" tested, I think now he would be glad either to get the vacancy of Secretary of War, or have the office just where it was during suspension. Yours truly,

U. S. GRANT.

WASHINGTON D. C., January 27, 1868.

To the President.

DEAR SIR: As I promised, I saw Mr. Ewing yesterday, and after a long conversation asked him to put down his opinion in writing, which he has done and which I now inclose.

I am now at work on these Army Regulations, and in the course of preparation have laid down the Constitution and laws now in force, clearer than I find them elsewhere; and beg leave herewith to inclose you three pages of printed matter for your perusal. My opinion is, if you will adopt these rules and make them an executive order to General Grant, they will so clearly define the duties of all concerned that no conflict can arise. I hope to get through this task in the course of this week, and want very much to go to St. Louis. For eleven years I have been tossed about so much that I really do want to rest, study, and make the acquaintance of my family. I do not think, since 1857, I have averaged thirty days out of three hundred and sixty-five at home.

Next summer also, in fulfillment of our promise to the Sioux, I must go to Fort Phil Kearney early in the spring, so that, unless I can spend the next two months at home, I might as well break up my house at St. Louis, and give up all prospect of taking care of my family.

For these reasons especially I shall soon ask leave to go to St. Louis, to resume my proper and legitimate command. With great respect,

W. T. SHERMAN, Lieutenant-General.

[Inclosure]

WASHINGTON, D. C., January 25, 1868.

MY DEAR GENERAL: I am quite clear in the opinion that it is not expedient for the President to take any action now in the case of Stanton. So far as he and his interests are concerned, things are in the best possible condition. Stanton is in the Department, got his secretary, but the secretary of the Senate, who have taken upon themselves his sins, and who place him there under a large salary to annoy and obstruct the operations of the Executive. This the people well enough understand, and he is a stench in the nostrils of their own party.

I thought the nomination of Cox at the proper juncture would have been wise as a peace-offering, but perhaps it would have let off the Senate too easily from the effect of their arbitrary act. Now the dislodging of Stanton and filling the office even temporarily without the consent of the Senate would raise a question as to the legality of the

President's acts, and he would belong to the attacked instead of the attacking party. If the war between Congress and the President is to go on, as I suppose it is, Stanton should be ignored by the President, left to perform his clerical duties which the law requires him to perform, and let the party bear the odium which is already upon them for placing him where he is. So much for the President.

As to yourself, I wish you as far as possible to keep clear of political complications. I do not think the President will require you to do an act of doubtful legality. Certainly he will not without sanction of the opinion of his Attorney-General; and you should have time, in a questionable case, to consult with me before called upon to act. The office of Secretary of War is a civil office, as completely so as that of Secretary of State; and you as a military officer cannot, I think, be required to assume or exercise it. This may, if necessary, be a subject for further consideration. Such, however, will not, I think, be the case. The appeal is to the people, and it is better for the President to persist in the course he has for some time pursued--let the aggressions all come from the other side; and I think there is no doubt he will do so.

Affectionately, T. EWING.

To--Lieutenant-General SHERMAN.
LIBRARY ROOM, WAR DEPARTMENT,
WASHINGTON, D. C., January 31, 1868.

To the President:

Since our interview of yesterday I have given the subject of our conversation all my thoughts, and I beg you will pardon my reducing the same to writing.

My personal preferences, as expressed, were to be allowed to return to St. Louis to resume my present command, because my command was important, large, suited to my rank and inclination, and because my family was well provided for there in house, facilities, schools, living, and agreeable society; while, on the other hand, Washington was for many (to me) good reasons highly objectionable, especially because it is the political capital of the country; and focus of intrigue, gossip, and slander. Your personal preferences were, as expressed, to make a new department East, adequate to my rank, with headquarters at Washington, and assign me to its command, to remove my family here, and to avail myself of its schools, etc.; to remove Mr. Stanton from his office as Secretary of War, and have me to discharge the duties.

To effect this removal two modes were indicated: to simply cause him to quit the War-Office Building, and notify the Treasury Department and the Army Staff Departments no longer to respect him as Secretary of War; or to remove him and submit my name to the Senate for confirmation.

Permit me to discuss these points a little, and I will premise by saying that I have spoken to no one on the subject, and have not even seen Mr. Ewing, Mr. Stanbery, or General Grant, since I was with you.

It has been the rule and custom of our army, since the organization of the government, that the second officer of the army should be at the second (in importance) command, and remote from general headquarters. To bring me to Washington world put three heads to an army, yourself, General Grant, and myself, and we would be more than human if we were not to differ. In my judgment it world ruin the army, and would be fatal to one or two of us.

Generals Scott and Taylor proved themselves soldiers and patriots in the field, but Washington was fatal to both. This city, and the influences that centre here, defeated every army that had its headquarters here from 1861 to 1864, and would have overwhelmed General Grant at Spottsylvania and Petersburg, had he not been fortified by a strong reputation, already hard-earned, and because no one then living coveted the place; whereas, in the West, we made progress from the start, because there was no political capital near enough to poison our minds, and kindle into life that craving, itching for fame which has killed more good men than bullets. I have been with General Grant in the midst of death and slaughter when the howls of people reached him after Shiloh; when messengers were speeding to and from his army to Washington, bearing slanders, to induce his removal before he took Vicksburg; in Chattanooga, when the soldiers were stealing the corn of the starving mules to satisfy their own hunger; at Nashville, when he was ordered to the "forlorn hope" to command the Army of the Potomac, so often defeated--and yet I never saw him more troubled than since he has been in Washington, and been compelled to read himself a "sneak and deceiver," based on reports of four of the Cabinet, and apparently with your knowledge. If this political atmosphere can disturb the equanimity of one so guarded and so prudent as he is, what will be the result with me, so careless, so outspoken as I am? Therefore, with my consent, Washington never.

As to the Secretary of War, his office is twofold. As a Cabinet officer he should not be there without your hearty, cheerful assent, and I believe that is the judgment and opinion of every fair-minded man. As the holder of a civil office, having the supervision of moneys appropriated by Congress and of contracts for army supplies, I do think Congress, or the Senate by delegation from Congress, has a lawful right to be consulted. At all events, I would not risk a suit or contest on that phase of the question. The law of Congress, of March 2, 1867, prescribing the manner in which orders and instructions relating to "military movements" shall reach the army, gives you as constitutional Commander-in-Chief the very power you want to exercise, and enables you to prevent the Secretary from making any such orders and instructions; and consequently he cannot control the army, but is limited and restricted to a duty that an Auditor of the Treasury could perform. You certainly can afford to await the result. The Executive power is not weakened, but rather strengthened. Surely he is not such an obstruction as would warrant violence, or even s show of force, which would produce the very reaction and clamor that he hopes for to save him from the absurdity of holding an empty office "for the safety of the country."

This is so much as I ought to say, and more too, but if it produces the result I will be more than satisfied, viz., that I be simply allowed to resume my proper post and duties in St. Louis. With great respect, yours truly,

W. T. SHERMAN, Lieutenant-General.

On the 1st of February, the board of which I was the president submitted to the adjutant-general our draft of the "Articles of War and Army Regulations," condensed to a small compass, the result of our war experience. But they did not suit the powers that were, and have ever since slept the sleep that knows no waking, to make room for the ponderous document now in vogue, which will not stand the strain of a week's campaign in real war.

I hurried back to St. Louis to escape the political storm I saw brewing. The President repeatedly said to me that he wanted me in Washington, and I as often answered that nothing could tempt me to live in that center of intrigue and excitement; but soon came the following:

HEADQUARTERS ARMY OF THE UNITED STATES,
WASHINGTON, February 10, 1868.
DEAR GENERAL: I have received at last the President's reply to my last, letter. He attempts to substantiate his statements by his Cabinet. In this view it is important that I should have a letter from you, if you are willing to give it, of what I said to you about the effect of the "Tenure-of-Office Bill," and my object in going to see the President on Saturday before the installment of Mr. Stanton. What occurred after the meeting of the Cabinet on the Tuesday following is not a subject under controversy now; therefore, if you choose to write down your recollection (and I would like to have it) on Wednesday, when you and I called on the President, and your conversation with him the last time you saw him, make that a separate communication.

Your order to come East was received several days ago, but the President withdrew it, I supposed to make some alteration, but it has not been returned. Yours truly,

U. S. GRANT.

[TELEGRAM.]

WASHINGTON, D. C., February 18, 1868.

Lieutenant-General W. T. SHERMAN, St. Louis.

The order is issued ordering you to Atlantic Division.

U. S. GRANT, General.

[TELEGRAM]

HEADQUARTERS MILITARY DIVISION OF THE MISSOURI,

St. Louis, February 14, 1868.

General U. S. GRANT, Washington, D. C.

Your dispatch is received informing me that the order for the Atlantic Division has been issued, and that I am assigned to its command. I was in hopes I had escaped the danger, and now were I prepared I should resign on the spot, as it requires no foresight to predict such must be the inevitable result in the end. I will make one more desperate effort by mail, which please await.

W. T. SHERMAN, Lieutenant-General.

[TELEGRAM.]

WASHINGTON, February 14, 1868.

Lieutenant-General W. T. SHERMAN, St. Louis.

I think it due to you that your letter of January 31st to the President of the United States should be published, to correct misapprehension in the public mind about your willingness to come to Washington. It will not be published against your will.

(Sent in cipher.)

[TELEGRAM.]

HEADQUARTERS MILITARY DIVISION OF THE MISSOURI,

St. Louis, MISSOURI, February 14, 1868.

General U. S. GRANT, Washington, D. C.

Dispatch of to-day received. Please await a letter I address this day through you to the President, which will in due time reach the public, covering the very point you make.

I don't want to come to Washington at all.

W. T. SHERMAN, Lieutenant-General.

[TELEGRAM.]

HEADQUARTERS MILITARY DIVISION OF THE MISSOURI,
St. Louis, MISSOURI, February 14, 1868.

Hon. John SHERMAN, United States Senate, Washington, D. C.

Oppose confirmation of myself as brevet general, on ground that it is unprecedented, and that it is better not to extend the system of brevets above major-general. If I can't avoid coming to Washington, I may have to resign.

W. T. SHERMAN, Lieutenant-General.

HEADQUARTERS OF THE ARMY,
WASHINGTON, D. C., February 12, 1868.

The following orders are published for the information and guidance of all concerned:

U. S. GRANT, General.

EXECUTIVE MANSION,
WASHINGTON, D. C., February 12, 1868.

GENERAL: You will please issue an order creating a military division to be styled the Military Division of the Atlantic, to be composed of the Department of the Lakes, the Department of the East, and the Department of Washington, to be commanded by Lieutenant-General W. T. Sherman, with his headquarters at Washington. Until further orders from the President, you will assign no officer to the permanent command of the Military Division of the Missouri.

Respectfully yours,
ANDREW JOHNSON.

GENERAL U. S. GRANT,
Commanding Armies of The United States, Washington, D. C.

Major-General P. H. Sheridan, the senior officer in the Military Division of the Missouri, will temporarily perform the duties of commander of the Military Division of the Missouri in addition to his duties of department commander. By command of General Grant:

E. D. TOWNSEND, Assistant Adjutant-General.

This order, if carried into effect, would have grouped in Washington:

1. The President, constitutional Commander-in-Chief.

2. The Secretary of War, congressional Commander-in-Chief.

3. The General of the Armies of the United States.

4. The Lieutenant-General of the Army.

5. The Commanding General of the Department of Washington.

6. The commander of the post-of Washington.

At that date the garrison of Washington was a brigade of infantry and a battery of artillery. I never doubted Mr. Johnson's sincerity in wishing to befriend me, but this was the broadest kind of a farce, or meant mischief. I therefore appealed to him by letter to allow me to remain where I was, and where I could do service, real service, and received his most satisfactory answer.

> HEADQUARTERS MILITARY DIVISION OF THE MISSOURI,
> St. Louis, MISSOURI, February 14, 1868.
> General U. S. GRANT, Washington, D. C.

DEAR GENERAL: Last evening, just before leaving my office, I received your note of the 10th, and had intended answering it according to your request; but, after I got home, I got your dispatch of yesterday, announcing that the order I dreaded so much was issued. I never felt so troubled in my life. Were it an order to go to Sitka, to the devil, to battle with rebels or Indians, I think you would not hear a whimper from me, but it comes in such a questionable form that, like Hamlet's ghost, it curdles my blood and mars my judgment. My first thoughts were of resignation, and I had almost made up my mind to ask Dodge for some place on the Pacific road, or on one of the Iowa roads, and then again various colleges ran through my memory, but hard times and an expensive family have brought me back to staring the proposition square in the face, and I have just written a letter to the President, which I herewith transmit through you, on which I will hang a hope of respite till you telegraph me its effect. The uncertainties ahead are too great to warrant my incurring the expense of breaking up my house and family here, and therefore in no event will I do this till I can be assured of some permanence elsewhere. If it were at all certain that you would accept the nomination of President in May, I would try and kill the intervening time, and then judge of the chances, but I do not want you to reveal your plans to me till you choose to do so.

I have telegraphed to John Sherman to oppose the nomination which the papers announce has been made of me for brevet general.

I have this minute received your cipher dispatch of to-day, which I have just answered and sent down to the telegraph-office, and the clerk is just engaged in copying my letter to the President to go with this. If the President or his friends pretend that I seek to go to Washington, it will be fully rebutted by letters I have written to the President, to you, to John Sherman, to Mr. Ewing, and to Mr. Stanbery. You remember that in our last talk you suggested I should write again to the President. I thought of it, and concluded my letter of January 31st, already delivered, was full and emphatic. Still, I did write again to Mr. Stanbery, asking him as a friend to interpose in my behalf. There are plenty of people who know my wishes, and I would avoid, if possible, the publication of a letter so confidential as that of January 31st, in which I notice I allude to the President's purpose of removing Mr. Stanton by force, a fact that ought not to be drawn out through me if it be possible to avoid it. In the letter herewith I confine myself to purely private matters, and will not object if it reaches the public in any proper way. My opinion is, the President thinks Mrs. Sherman would like to come to Washington by reason of her father and brothers being there. This is true, for Mrs. Sherman has an idea that St. Louis is unhealthy for our children, and because most of the Catholics here are tainted with the old secesh feeling. But I know better what is to our common interest, and prefer to judge of the proprieties myself. What I do object to is the false position I would occupy as between you and the President. Were there an actual army at or near Washington, I could be withdrawn from the most unpleasant attitude of a "go-between," but there is no army there, nor any military duties which you with a host of subordinates can not perform. Therefore I would be there with naked, informal, and sinecure duties, and utterly out of place. This you understand well enough, and the army too, but the President and the politicians, who flatter themselves they are saving the country, cannot and will not understand. My opinion is, the country is doctored to death, and if President and Congress would go to sleep like Rip Van Winkle, the country would go on under natural influences, and recover far faster than under their joint and several treatment. This doctrine would be accounted by Congress, and by the President too, as high treason, and therefore I don't care about saying so to either of them, but I know you can hear anything, and give it just what thought or action it merits.

Excuse this long letter, and telegraph me the result of my letter to the President as early as you can. If he holds my letter so long as to make it improper for me to await his answer, also telegraph me.

The order, when received, will, I suppose, direct me as to whom and how I am to turn over this command, which should, in my judgment, not be broken up, as the three departments composing the division should be under one head.

I expect my staff-officers to be making for me within the hour to learn their fate, so advise me all you can as quick as possible.

With great respect, yours truly,

W. T. SHERMAN, Lieutenant-General.

To the President.

DEAR SIR: It is hard for me to conceive you would purposely do me an unkindness unless under the pressure of a sense of public duty, or because you do not believe me sincere. I was in hopes, since my letter to you of the 31st of January, that you had concluded to pass over that purpose of yours expressed more than once in conversation--to organize a new command for me in the East, with headquarters in Washington; but a telegram from General Grant of yesterday says that "the order was issued ordering you" (me) "to Atlantic Division"; and the newspapers of this morning contain the same information, with the addition that I have been nominated as brevet general. I have telegraphed my own brother in the Senate to oppose my confirmation, on the ground that the two higher grades in the army ought not to be complicated with brevets, and I trust you will conceive my motives aright. If I could see my way clear to maintain my family, I should not hesitate a moment to resign my present commission, and seek some business wherein I would be free from these unhappy complications that seem to be closing about me, spite of my earnest efforts to avoid them; but necessity ties my hands, and I must submit with the best grace I can till I make other arrangements.

In Washington are already the headquarters of a department, and of the army itself, and it is hard for me to see wherein I can render military service there. Any staff-officer with the rank of major could surely fill any gap left between these two military officers; and, by being placed in Washington, I will be universally construed as a rival to the General-in-Chief, a position damaging to me in the highest degree. Our relations have always been most confidential and friendly, and if, unhappily, any cloud of differences should arise between us, my sense of personal dignity and duty would leave me no alternative but resignation. For this I am not yet prepared, but I shall proceed to arrange for it as rapidly as possible, so that when the time does come (as it surely will if this plan is carried into effect) I may act promptly.

Inasmuch as the order is now issued, I cannot expect a full revocation of it, but I beg the privilege of taking post at New York, or any point you may name within the new military division other than Washington. This privilege is generally granted to all military commanders, and I see no good reason why I too may not ask for it, and this simple concession, involving no public interest, will much soften the blow, which, right or wrong, I construe as one of the hardest I have sustained in a life somewhat checkered with adversity. With great respects yours truly,

W. T. SHERMAN, Lieutenant-General.

WASHINGTON, D. C., 2 p.m., February 19, 1888.
Lieutenant-General W. T. SHERMAN, St. Louis, Missouri:

I have just received, with General Grant's indorsement of reference, your letter to me of the fourteenth (14th) inst.

The order to which you refer was made in good faith, and with a view to the best interests of the country and the service; as, however, your assignment to a new military division seems so objectionable, you will retain your present command.

ANDREW JOHNSON.

On that same 19th of February he appointed Adjutant, General Lorenzo Thomas to be Secretary of War ad interim, which finally resulted in the articles of impeachment and trial of President Johnson before the Senate. I was a witness on that trial, but of course the lawyers would not allow me to express any opinion of the President's motives or intentions, and restricted me to the facts set forth in the articles of impeachment, of which I was glad to know nothing. The final test vote revealed less than two thirds, and the President was consequently acquitted. Mr. Stanton resigned. General Schofield, previously nominated, was confirmed as Secretary of War, thus putting an end to what ought never to have happened at all.

Retirement

WAR DEPARTMENT, ADJUTANT GENERAL'S OFFICE, WASHINGTON, February 8, 1984.

The following order of the President is published to the army:

EXECUTIVE MANSION, February 8, 1884.
General William T. Sherman, General of the Army, having this day reached the age of sixty-four years, is, in accordance with the law, placed upon the retired list of the army, without reduction in his current pay and allowances.

The announcement of the severance from the command of the army of one who has been for so many years its distinguished chief, can but awaken in the minds, not only of the army, but of the people of the United States, mingled emotions of regret and gratitude--regret at the withdrawal from active military service of an officer whose lofty sense of duty has been a model for all soldiers since he first entered the army in July, 1840; and gratitude, freshly awakened, for the services of incalculable value rendered by him in the war for the Union, which his great military genius and daring did so much to end.

The President deems this a fitting occasion to give expression, in this manner, to the gratitude felt toward General Sherman by his fellow-citizens, and to the hope that Providence may grant him many years of health and happiness in the relief from the active duties of his profession.

By order of the Secretary of War:
CHESTER A. ARTHUR.
R. C. DRUM, Adjutant-General.

To which I replied:

St. Louis, February 9, 1884.
His Excellency CHESTER A. ARTHUR, President of the United States.

DEAR SIR: Permit me with a soldier's frankness to thank you personally for the handsome compliment bestowed in general orders of yesterday, which are reported in the journals of the day. To me it was a surprise and a most agreeable one. I had supposed the actual date of my retirement would form a short paragraph in the common series of special orders of the War Department; but as the honored Executive of our country has made it the occasion for his own hand to pen a tribute of respect and affection to an officer passing from the active stage of life to one of ease and rest, I can only say I feel highly honored, and congratulate myself in thus rounding out my record of service in a manner most gratifying to my family and friends. Not only this, but I feel sure, when the orders of yesterday are read on parade to the regiments and garrisons of the United States, many a young hero will tighten his belt, and resolve anew to be brave and true to the starry flag, which we of our day have carried safely through one epoch of danger, but which may yet be subjected to other trials, which may demand similar sacrifices, equal fidelity and courage, and a larger measure of intelligence. Again thanking you for so marked a compliment, and reciprocating the kind wishes for the future,

I am, with profound respect, your friend and servant,
W. T. SHERMAN, General.

This I construe as the end of my military career. In looking back upon the past I can only say, with millions of others, that I have done many things I should not have done, and have left undone still more which ought to have been done; that I can see where hundreds of opportunities have been neglected, but on the whole am content; and feel sure that I can travel this broad country of ours, and be each night the welcome guest in palace or cabin; and, as "all the world's stage, and all the men and women merely players," I claim the privilege to ring down the curtain.

W. T. SHERMAN, General.

References and Resources

These resources were valuable in preparing this edition. We urge anyone in possession of letters, diaries and memoirs from the Civil War era to share these with others through these websites and libraries.

Soldier Studies. http://www.soldierstudies.org/index.php
Civil War Gazette. http://www.civilwargazette.faithsite.com/content.asp?ListSG=5976
Dakota State University. http://www.homepages.dsu.edu/jankej/civilwar/diaries.htm
Civil War Letters. http://civil.war-letters.com/
Project Gutenberg. http://www.gutenberg.org/catalog/
Library of Congress. "Civil War Photographs".
http://www.loc.gov/pictures/collection/cwp/
Library of Congress. "Prints and Photographs". http://www.loc.gov/rr/print/

Photo Credits

All images courtesy of the Library of Congress
Winter quarters of Capt. Bissell, Army of the Potomac, LC-B811-1246
Mississippi River Fleet, U.S. gunboat "Brown", LC-USZ62-62362
General Sheridan (right), General Katz (sitting) and friend, LC-DIG-cwpbh-03205
Our Peace Commissioners for 1865: Sheridan, Grant, Sherman, Porter, Lincoln, Farragut, and Thomas, LC-DIG-cwpb-07620
Five Forks, Virginia (vicinity). Confederate prisoners on the way to the rear. Captured at Five Forks, LC-B811- 3198
Louisa May Alcott, LC-USZ61-452
Wounded soldiers from the battles in the "Wilderness" at Fredericksburg, Va.,May 20, 1864, LC-USZC4-4582
Washington, D.C. Patients in Ward K of Armory Square Hospital, LC-B817- 7822
Washington, District of Columbia. Surgeons at Finlay Hospital, LC-B817- 7853
Portrait of Maj. Gen. Grenville M. Dodge, officer of the Federal Army, LC-B813- 1672
Atlanta, Georgia. Federal picket post shortly before the battle of July 22, LC-B811- 2719
Andersonville Prison, Ga., August 17, 1864--Southwest view of stockade showing the deadline, LC-USZ62-122695
Richmond, Va. Castle Thunder, Cary Street, LC-DIG-cwpb-02506
Doctors examining a Federal prisoner returned from prison, LC-USZC4-7961
Confederate prisoners for exchange, LC-USZ62-49101
The Battle of Shiloh, LC-USZ62-3579
Lincoln and his family, LC-DIG-pga-03267
Washington, D.C. President Lincoln's funeral procession on Pennsylvania Avenue, LC-DIG-cwpb-00593
Gen. William T. Sherman on horseback at Federal Fort No. 7, LC-DIG-cwpb-03628
Sherman's men tearing up railroad track, LC-DIG-cwpb-03356
Sherman portrait, LC-DIG-cwpb-07139